Tales of the Mighty Dead

Tales of the Mighty Dead

Historical Essays in the
Metaphysics of Intentionality

Robert B. Brandom

HARVARD UNIVERSITY PRESS

Cambridge, Massachusetts
London, England
2002

Library of Congress Cataloging-in-Publication Data

Brandom, Robert.
    Tales of the mighty dead : historical essays in the metaphysics of
intentionality / Robert B. Brandom.
      p.   cm.
    Includes bibliographical references and index.
    ISBN 0-674-00903-7 (alk. paper)
    1. Philosophy—History.   I. Title.

B72 .B685 2002
190—dc21   2002068618

For my sons, Eric and Russell, exemplary cartesian products of the mammalian and the discursive— dear to my heart, fierce and learned in discussion, and altogether their own special, admirable selves.

CONTENTS

      Observation to the Arguments of "Empiricism and the
      Philosophy of Mind"   348

      I. Sellars's Two-Ply Account of Observation   349

      *II. 'Looks' Talk and Sellars's Diagnosis of the Cartesian
          Hypostatization of Appearances   353*

      *III. Two Confirmations of the Analysis of 'Looks' Talk
          in Terms of the Two-Ply Account of Observation   357*

      *IV. A Rationalist Account of the Acquisition of
          Empirical Concepts   359*

      V. Giving Theoretical Concepts an Observational Use   362

      *VI. Conclusion: On the Relation between the
          Two Components   364*

      Notes   369
      Credits   409
      Index   411

Tales of the Mighty Dead

Introduction: Five Conceptions of Rationality

This is a work in the history of systematic philosophy, and it is itself animated by a systematic philosophical aspiration. In my earlier book *Making It Explicit* (and even more in the argumentative path drawn from it in *Articulating Reasons*), systematic considerations were in the foreground, with historical ones relegated to the background. This book reverses that figure-ground gestalt, bringing a reading of the philosophical tradition to the fore. Whereas the other books were heavily systematic and only lightly historical, this one is heavily historical and only lightly systematic. The interactions it seeks to establish between text and interpretation, however, between the historical and the philosophical, between points of view discerned or attributed and those adopted or endorsed, are sufficiently intricate that it is worth saying something somewhat systematic about the conception of philosophical historiography that governs it, if the sort of enterprise being undertaken is to be properly understood.

There is a familiar perspective from which neither the historical story nor its metaphilosophical rationale would appear as of the first importance. Analytic philosophy in its youth was viscerally hostile both to historical philosophical enterprises and to systematic ones. For that movement of thought initially defined itself in part by its recoil from the excesses of philosophical programs tracing their roots back to Hegel, for whom history and system jointly articulate the form of reason itself. This self-understanding was never unanimous. In the middle third of the twentieth century Wilfrid Sellars—one of my particular heroes—stood almost alone among major figures in the analytic tradition in both

1

casting his project in a systematic mold, and motivating and articulating it in terms of an original rethinking of major episodes in the history of philosophy. But institutional success often diminishes the felt need for the purity and rigoristic exclusionism characteristic of the fighting faiths of embattled innovators in the early days of their struggles. With time it has become clearer, I think, that commitment to the fundamental analytic credo—*faith* in reasoned argument, *hope* for reasoned agreement, and *clarity* of reasoned expression (and the greatest of these is clarity)—is not incompatible with a philosophical understanding of philosophical understanding as admitting, indeed, perhaps even as requiring, both historical and systematic forms.

Greater tolerance for the systematic impulse in philosophy has been encouraged, I think, by the example of such towering contemporary figures as David Lewis and Donald Davidson (both, as it happens, teachers of mine at Princeton years ago). They are both masters of the genre of philosophical writing distinctive of the analytic tradition: the gemlike self-contained essay. Yet in that medium, each has carried through philosophical projects that, in virtue of the comprehensiveness of their aim and the unity of the basic principles appealed to in explanations, deserve comparison with the great philosophical systems of old. And greater appreciation of the contribution that attention to historical antecedents can make to our understanding of contemporary philosophical problems has come in part from the concrete examples of progress of this sort in particular subdisciplines. So, for instance, it would be a rare writer on, say, practical reasoning who would not acknowledge the crucial importance of detailed work on Aristotle, Hume, and Kant both for understanding the current state of play and for finding a way forward from it.

Behind such low matters of disciplinary sociology, though, lie fundamental philosophical issues about the nature of rationality. It will be helpful in thinking about the sort of rational reconstruction of a philosophical tradition undertaken here to consider five models of rationality: logical, instrumental, translational, inferential, and historical. I do not claim that this list is exhaustive, and I do not claim that these models are mutually exclusive. But they will perhaps serve to place a kind of historical understanding in a larger philosophical space.

On one picture, to be rational is to be logical. Being sensitive to the force of reasons is a matter of practically distinguishing logically good arguments from those that are not logically good. For a set of claims to serve as a good reason for another claim is for there to be a logically valid argument relating them to that claim as premises to conclusion. Nonlogical facts and the meanings of nonlogical vocabulary contribute to reasoning only by providing premises for logically valid inferences.

The program of assimilating all good reasoning to this model has been immensely influential and productive in the philosophical tradition. It took its modern form when Frege vastly increased the expressive power of logic by giving us formal control over the inferential significance of quantificationally complex properties. The success this idiom was shown to have in codifying mathematical reasoning—by Frege himself, by Hilbert, and by Russell and Whitehead—was a major impetus for logical empiricism, whose central project was to extend the logical model of reasoning to include empirical science. Just when it looked as though the limits of this enterprise had been reached, technical advances in the logical expression of modalities gave the undertaking new life.

The logical model of reasoning is most at home close to its origins: in codifying *theoretical* inference, the way beliefs can provide reasons for other beliefs. The instrumental model of reasoning begins with *practical* inference—in particular, the way desires or preferences, together with beliefs, can provide reasons for *action*. It identifies rationality with intelligence, in the sense of a generalized capacity for getting what one wants: the reason of Odysseus, rather than of Aristotle. What one has reason to do, on this model, is what provides a means to an endorsed end. Means-end reasoning is formally codified in rational choice theory, in both its decision-theoretic and game-theoretic species. Dutch book arguments show that utility (the measure of preference) will be maximized by practical reasoners who assign probabilities to compound beliefs in ways that satisfy the axioms of classical probability theory. And the laws of classical logic can be deduced as special cases from those axioms. So the instrumental model of rationality has some claim to subsume the logical one as a special case.

One thing to notice about these two models of rationality is that they both treat (nonlogically) contentful beliefs and desires as inputs. *Given* a set of beliefs, and perhaps desires, they purport to tell us which connections among them are *rational:* which constellations of them provide genuine *reasons* for which others. They accordingly presuppose that the *contents* of those psychological states can be made intelligible independently and in advance of considering *rational* connections among them. The idea that one can first fix the meaning or content of premises and conclusions, and only then worry about inferential relations among them, is characteristic of traditional and twentieth-century empiricism. This implicit semantic commitment is questioned, however, by the rationalist tradition in semantics, which sees issues of what is a reason for what as essential to the identity and individuation of the conceptual contents that stand in those inferential relations.

The logical and instrumental models of reasons are also (and not coincidentally) alike in their formality. Each sees rationality as being a matter of the *structure* of reasoning rather than its *content*. The substantial content of the beliefs and desires that provide the premises for candidate theoretical and practical inferences are wholly irrelevant to the rationality of the conclusions drawn from them. *All* that matters for the correctness of the inference is that they have the form of deductively valid inferences or maximization of expected utility *given* those premises. The premises themselves are beyond criticism by these models of rationality, unless and insofar as they themselves were acquired as conclusions of prior inferences, which *are* assessable in virtue of *their* form—and then only relative to the prior (only similarly criticizable) commitments that provide their premises.

A model of rationality that is not in this way purely formal is the translational-interpretational model, most fully developed by Davidson. According to this view, to say that some behavior by others is rational is roughly to say that it can be mapped onto *our* linguistic behavior in ways that make it possible for us to converse with them—at least to draw inferences from their claims, to use them as premises in our own reasoning. The idea is to use our own *practical* know-how, our ability to distinguish reasons from nonreasons and to tell what follows from what, to assess the *theoretical* rationality of others. They are rational insofar as their noises (and other behavior, described in nonintentional terms) can be mapped onto ours so as to make them make sense by our standards: to exhibit them as believers in the true and seekers after the good by our own lights. Rationality, then, is by definition what *we*'ve got, and interpretability by us is its definition and measure.

Rationality is not on this view a formal matter at all. For the unintelligibility or wackiness of the substantive, nonlogical beliefs and desires we take our interpretive targets to be evincing in their behavior, both linguistic and nonlinguistic, is every bit as relevant to assessments of their rationality as the connections between them we discern or take them to espouse. We have to be able to count the others as agreeing with us in the contents of and (so) connections among enough of their beliefs and desires to form a background against which local disagreements can be made intelligible, if we are to find them interpretable, that is, rational— for what they have to show up as beliefs and desires—at all.

Rationality as interpretability can also claim to subsume or incorporate both the logical and the instrumental models of rationality. For the first, the explicit form of a Davidsonian interpretation includes a recursive truth theory for the idiom being interpreted, including novel sentential compounds that have never actually been used. So identifying expressions functioning as logical vocabulary can provide a formal framework within which the rest of the interpretive process can take place. Being *logical* creatures is on this view a necessary condition of being *rational* ones, even though there is a lot more to rationality than just that. For the second, making the behavior of the interpreted creatures intelligible requires attributing sample bits of practical reasoning. And Davidson takes it that those will have the form of what he calls "complete reasons": constellations of beliefs and desires that rationalize the behavior according to the instrumental model. Unless one can interpret the target behavior as for the most part instrumentally rational, one cannot interpret it at all.

Finally, the interpretive model does not take the *rational* connections among psychological states or the sentences that express them to be irrelevant to the *contents* they are taken to evince. On the contrary, what makes something have or express the content it does is what makes it interpretable in one way rather than another. And that is a matter of its connections to other things, the role it plays in the overall rational behavioral economy of the one being interpreted. What makes it right to map another's noise onto this sentence of mine, and so to attribute to it the content expressed by that sentence in my mouth, is just that its relations to other noises sufficiently mirror the relations my sentence stands in to other sentences of mine: what is evidence for and against it, and what it is evidence for and against, as well as what environing stimuli call forth my endorsement of it and what role it plays in practical reasoning leading to nonlinguistic action. Those consequential relations are of the essence of interpretability, and so of rationality on this model.

I have offered only the briefest of reminders about these first three conceptions of rationality, since they are established and familiar, and have been ably expounded, elaborated, and defended by others. The final two conceptions differ in these respects. But they are if anything more important for understanding the body of this work. So they call for somewhat fuller sketches.

A fourth model of rationality is the inferentialist one I elaborate in *Making It Explicit*. On this view, to be rational is to play the game of giving and asking for reasons. Utterances and states are propositionally contentful just insofar as they stand in inferential relations to one another: insofar as they can both serve as and stand in need of reasons. Conceptual contents are functional inferential roles. The inferences that articulate conceptual contents are in the first instance *material* inferences, rather than logical ones, however—inferences like that from A's being to the west of B to B's being to the east of A, or from a coin's being copper to its melting if heated to 1084° C. but not if heated only to 1083°. To be rational is to be a producer and consumer of reasons: things that can play the role of both premises and conclusions of *inferences*. So long as one can assert (put something forward as a reason) and infer (use something as a reason), one is rational. The details of the particular material inferential connections one subscribes to affect the contents of the sentences that stand in those relations, but so long as the connections are genuinely *inferential,* they are *rational*—in a global sense, which is compatible with local failures of rationality, in that one makes bad inferences or reasons incorrectly according to the content-constitutive material inferential commitments governing those particular sentences.

This inferential view of rationality develops and incorporates a broadly interpretational one. For to take or treat someone in practice as offering and deserving reasons is to attribute inferentially articulated commitments and entitlements. Such deontic scorekeeping requires keeping two sets of books, one on the consequences and antecedents of the other interlocutor's commitments when they are conjoined with other commitments one attributes to her, and the other on the consequences and antecedents of those commitments when they are conjoined with the commitments one undertakes or endorses oneself. This is a matter of being able to map another's utterances onto one's own, so as to navigate conversationally between the two doxastic perspectives:

to be able to use the other's remarks as premises for one's own reasoning, and to know what she would make of one's own. Although the details of this process are elaborated differently—in terms of the capacity to specify the contents of another's commitments both in the way that would be made explicit by *de dicto* ascriptions of propositional attitude, and in the way that would be made explicit by *de re* ascriptions of the same attitudes[1]—deontic scorekeeping is recognizably a version of the sort of interpretive process Davidson is talking about. A kind of interpretability is what rationality consists of on this inferentialist picture too.

Embedding an inferentialist semantics in a normative pragmatics offers further resources for developing that common thought, however. For my claim in *Making It Explicit* is that there is another way to understand what it is to be inferring and asserting, besides interpretability. Nothing is recognizable as a practice of giving and asking for *reasons*, I claim, unless it involves undertaking and attributing *commitments*. And those commitments must stand in *consequential* relations: making one move, undertaking one commitment, must carry with it further commitments—presystematically, commitments whose contents follow from the contents of the first commitment. Further, a practice of giving and asking for reasons must be one in which the issue of one's *entitlement* to a commitment one has undertaken (or that others attribute) can arise. And those entitlements, too, must stand in consequential relations: entitlement to one move can carry with it entitlement to others.[2]

On the basis of considerations such as these, I identify a particular structure of consequential commitment and entitlement that deserves to be called *inferential*. The two flavors of deontic status generate three sorts of consequential scorekeeping relations, and so three dimensions along which genuine material inferential relations are articulated:

- Commitment-preserving inferential relations are a generalization to the case of material inferences of deductive relations. For example, since C. S. Peirce is the one who established a universal standard for the meter based on the wavelengths of light, any who are committed to Peirce having been a great philosopher are, whether they know it or not, committed to the one who established a universal standard for the meter based on the wavelengths of light having been a great philosopher.
- Entitlement-preserving inferential relations are generalizations to

the case of material inferences of inductive relations. For example, since falling barometric readings correlate reasonably reliably (via a common cause) with the stormy weather ahead, one who is both entitled and committed to the claim that the barometric reading is falling has some reason entitling (in a weak, noncoercive sense) commitment to the claim that stormy weather is ahead.

- Incompatibility entailments are generalizations to the case of material inference of modally robust relations. Two claims are incompatible (according to a scorekeeper) if commitment to one precludes entitlement to the other. For instance, claiming that the patch is wholly red is incompatible with the claim that it is wholly blue. One claim incompatibility entails another if everything incompatible with the second is incompatible with the first (but perhaps not vice versa). For example, being a lion entails being a mammal in this sense, because everything incompatible with being a mammal (for instance, being an invertebrate, or a prime number) is incompatible with being a lion.

I call a practice of attributing commitments and entitlements *inferentially articulated* if deontic score is kept in a way that respects relations of all three of these kinds.[3]

These three flavors of inference determine the intercontent, intrapersonal inheritance of commitment and entitlement. If in addition a practice contains testimonial intracontent, interpersonal inheritance that has what I call a "default and challenge" structure, and language exits and language entries assessed interpersonally by reliability,[4] then I call the practice in question *discursive*. Part Two of *Making It Explicit* shows what further articulation, by substitution inferences and the anaphoric inheritance of substitution-inferential potential, explicable entirely in terms of these, is then involved in having locutions playing the broadly inferential functional roles of singular terms and complex predicates, of proper names, definite descriptions, and demonstratives, of semantic vocabulary, intentional vocabulary, and a variety of other sophisticated logical categories. The overall claim is that the practices exhibiting the broadly inferential social structure of inheritance of normative statuses that I call "discursive" are just those that will be interpretable with respect to our own. The claim that this formal characterization in terms of inferentially articulated normative statuses, and the material one in terms of mappings onto our own practices, are two ways of picking out the same practices is a bold and potentially falsifiable empirical claim. I do not claim to have demonstrated, in *Making It Explicit*, the truth of the conjecture that these two notions of rationality in fact coincide. But one of the guiding systematic theoretical aspirations of that book is to give a structural characterization of practices that deserve to be thought of as built around the giving of and asking for *reasons*—one that will suffice to ensure material interpretability in terms of our own linguistic practices.

I have already indicated that the normative inferentialist view of meaning-constitutive rationality should be thought of as a way of developing the basic insights of the interpretational approach to rationality. It also leads to novel understandings of what lies behind the logical and instrumental models. Seeing semantics and the understanding of rationality as two sides of one coin, and understanding both in terms of the material inferential articulation of commitments and entitlements (the normative pragmatics behind the inferential semantics), together open up the possibility of a different way of thinking about the relation between logic and rationality. Instead of seeing conformity with logical truths as what rationality consists in, one can see logical vocabulary as making possible the explicit codification of meaning-constitutive inferential relations. On such an expressive view of the function of logic, the task characteristic of logical locutions as such is to let us *say*, in the form of explicit claims, what otherwise we could only *do*—namely, endorse some material inferential relations and reject others. Prior to the introduction of the conditional, for instance, one can implicitly take or treat the material inference (in any of the three senses botanized above) from *p* to *q* as a good or bad one, endorsing or rejecting it in practice. Once a suitable conditional is available, though, one can explicitly *claim that p* entails *q*. And explicit claims are the sort of thing we can *reason* about, ask for *evidence* or *arguments* for. The expressive job of specifically *logical* locutions is to make inferential relations explicit, to bring them into the game of giving and asking for reasons as things whose own rational credentials are available for inspection and criticism. And since, according to the inferentialist approach to semantics, it is those rational relations in virtue of which ordinary nonlogical expressions *mean* what they do, by making inferential relations explicit (claimable, fit themselves to serve as premises and conclusions of other inferences), and so subject to reasoned criticism and reasoned defense, logical locutions bring essential aspects of the semantic contents of those expressions out of the darkness of implicit practical discrimination into the daylight of explicitness. Logic does not *define* rationality in the most basic sense, but by making it possible for us to express explicitly the already rational relations articulating the contents of all our thoughts, it ushers in a higher level of rationality. It is a tool for the expression and exploration of the consequences of and discordances among our rational—because inferentially articulated—commitments. In short, logic is the organ of semantic self-consciousness.[5] On this account, being *logical* creatures is an achievement subsequent to and dependent on being *rational* ones.

Practical reasoning also looks different from the inferentialist semantic perspective when it is elaborated in terms of normative statuses. Practical inferential relations can be thought of as governing transitions (commitment or entitlement inheritance) from doxastic to practical commitments, that is, from the commitments acknowledged in assertions to commitments to *do* something. Seen from this angle, expressions of preference or desire show up as codifying commitment to the propriety of patterns of practical inference. Thus S's preference or desire to stay dry is a commitment to inferences of the form:

$$\frac{\text{Only doing A will keep me dry.}}{\therefore \text{I shall do A.}}$$

in much the same way that the conditional $p \rightarrow q$ expresses a commitment to the correctness of inferences from p to q. In both cases it is a mistake to confuse the statements that make inference licenses explicit with *premises* required for the inference to be licit in the first place—for reasons Lewis Carroll has made familiar in "Achilles and the Tortoise."

Further, preferences and desires are only *one* sort of practical inference license. For in general, this is the expressive role distinctive of *normative* vocabulary as such. Thus a statement of the obligations associated with some institutional status, such as "Civil servants are obliged to treat the public with respect," licenses inferences of the form:

$$\frac{\text{Doing A would not be treating the public with respect.}}{\therefore \text{I shall not do A.}}$$

This institutional pattern of practical inference differs from the preference pattern in that the latter is binding only on those who endorse the

preference in question, while the former is binding on anyone who occupies the status in question, that is, on civil servants—regardless of
their desires. Another pattern of practical reasoning is codified by normative claims that are not conditioned on occupation of an institutional
status. Thus, "It is wrong to (one ought not) cause pain to no purpose"
licenses inferences of the form:

$$\frac{\text{Doing A would cause pain to no purpose.}}{\therefore \text{ I shall not do A.}}$$

Endorsing the unconditional normative claim is committing oneself
to the bindingness of this form of practical inference for *anyone,* regardless of preferences or institutional status.[6]

On the inferentialist picture, *all* of these 'oughts'—the instrumental,
the institutional, and the unconditional—are in the most basic sense *rational* oughts. For they codify commitments to patterns of practical *reasoning.* From this point of view, the humean, who insists on assimilating
all practical reasoning to the first or instrumental model, on pain of a
verdict of practical irrationality, and the kantian, who insists on assimilating all practical reasoning to the third or unconditional model, on
pain of a verdict of practical irrationality in the form of heteronomy, are
alike in pursuing Procrustean explanatory strategies. The real questions
concern the justification of normative commitments of these various
forms: the circumstances under which one or another should be endorsed, and what considerations speak for resolving incompatibilities
among such commitments in one way rather than another. The catholic
inferentialist conception of rationality and the expressive view of logic
it engenders suggest that a misunderstanding of the *logical* (that is, inference-codifying) expressive role of normative vocabulary lies behind
views that see *every* instance of one or another of these (and, indeed,
other) patterns of practical reasoning as in principle lacking rational credentials until and unless it can be reduced to or derived from one of the
others. I've already indicated that from the inferentialist point of view,
both the reductive logical and instrumental conceptions of rationality
alike suffer from implicit reliance on naïve, because atomistic, semantic
conceptions, which make rational connections among beliefs and desires irrelevant to their content. (The holism that inferentialism brings
in its train, and the functionalism of which it is a species, are common

topics of many of the essays that make up the body of this book.) It should now be clear that from that same point of view, both the logical and the instrumental conceptions of rationality stem from mistaken philosophies of logic—misunderstandings of the expressive role of logical vocabulary (which includes, on this view, normative vocabulary). As a result, they mistake the shadow of rationality for its substance.

The inferentialist approach to rationality, semantics, and intentionality will be much in evidence in the rest of this book. But there is another approach, due to Hegel, that informs it as well. This is a *historical* conception, which understands rationality as consisting in a certain kind of reconstruction of a tradition—one that exhibits it as having the expressively progressive form of the gradual, cumulative unfolding into explicitness of what shows up retrospectively as having been all along already implicit in that tradition. Generically, this view, like the inferentialist ones, begins with the idea that being rational is being a concept user. Rationality consists in both being subject to (assessment according to) conceptual norms and being sensitive to them—being both bound by, and able to feel the force of, the better reason. In the most basic case, being rational is saying of what is that it is—in the sense of *correctly* applying universals to particulars, classifying the particulars as they *ought* to be classified, characterizing them in judgment by the universals they *really* fall under, according to the norms that implicitly govern the application of those universals. At this point, though, a question can be raised: How should we understand the fact that determinate conceptual norms are available, determining for each universal which particulars it is correctly applied to?

The interpretivist pointed out that both the logicist and the instrumentalist about rationality implicitly presuppose that we can make sense of the contentfulness of beliefs and desires in advance of thinking about rational connections among them. The inferentialist pointed out that the interpretivist about rationality does not tell us what it is about the structure of our own practices—the practical foundation of interpretation, onto which any others must be mappable in order to count as rational or discursive—in virtue of which *they* deserve to be thought of as rational or discursive. The historicist about rationality, in turn, points out that the inferentialist takes for granted a set of inferentially articulated norms as an already up-and-running enterprise. But under what conditions are determinate conceptual norms possible? What do we have to *do* to establish or connect with, subject ourselves to, such determinate norms? That this issue requires investigation is the final demand in this series of ever more radical critical questionings of the *semantic* presuppositions of theories of rationality.

For Hegel, the question arises in the context of a constellation of pragmatist commitments. Concepts for him, as for Kant, are norms for judgment. They determine proprieties of application to particulars of terms that, because of the normative role they play in such judgments, express universals. But he also has the idea that the *only* thing available to settle *which* universal a word expresses is the way that word—and others linked to it inferentially—has *actually* been applied in *prior* judgments.[7] And now we can ask: What is it about their use that makes these terms express one determinate universal rather than a somewhat different one? How do the applications of universals to particulars that have actually been made at any point in time—both noninferentially by observation, and inferentially as a consequence of applications of other, inferentially linked, universals to particulars—manage to settle whether it would be correct to apply that term to some particular that has not yet been assessed? How does what we have *actually done* with the terms, the judgments we have actually made, settle what we *ought to do* with them in novel cases?

The model I find most helpful in understanding the sort of rationality that consists in retrospectively picking out an expressively progressive trajectory through past applications of a concept, so as to determine a norm one can understand as governing the whole process and so project into the future, is that of judges in a common law tradition. Common law differs from statutory law in that all there is to settle the boundaries of applicability of the concepts it employs is the record of actually decided cases that can serve as precedents. There is no explicit initial statement of principle governing the application of legal universals to particular sets of facts—only a practice of applying them in always novel circumstances. So whatever content those concepts have, they get from the history of their actual applications. A judge justifies her decision in a particular case by rationalizing it in the light of a reading of that tradition, by so selecting and emphasizing particular prior decisions as precedential that a norm emerges as an implicit lesson. And it is that norm that is then appealed to in deciding the present case, and is implicitly taken to be binding in future ones. In order to find such a norm, the judge must make the tradition cohere, must exhibit the decisions that have actually been made as rational and correct, given that the norm she finds is what has implicitly governed the process all along. Thus each of the prior decisions selected as precedential emerges as making explicit some aspect of that implicit norm, as revealing a bit of the boundary of the concept.

Such a process is rational in a distinctive, structured sense. The rationality of the current decision, its justifiability as a correct application of a concept, is secured by rationally reconstructing the tradition of its applications according to a certain model—by offering a selective, cumulative, expressively progressive genealogy of it. At each stage in its development, it is insofar as one *takes* the tradition to be rational, by a Whiggish rewriting of its history, that one *makes* the tradition be and have been rational. A certain sort of rationality—in its most explicit and self-conscious form, one characteristic of the self-reflection of the high culture—consists in a commitment to understanding the tradition that gives one words to speak by exhibiting it in this form. This is reason's march through history. In this way, as Hegel puts it, contingency is given the form of necessity. That is, judgments that show up first as adventitious products of accidental circumstances ("what the judge had for breakfast," or, less frivolously, contemporary confluences of intellectual, social, and political currents) are exhibited as correct applications of a conceptual norm retrospectively discerned as already implicit in previous judgments. (For Hegel, as for Kant, 'necessary' always means according to a *rule*.) Telling a story of this sort—finding a norm by making a tradition, giving it a genealogy—is a form of rationality as systematic history.

Hegel thinks that taking there to be genuine conceptual norms in play—and so taking it that there is a difference between judging and inferring correctly and incorrectly—is taking it that there is such an expressively progressive genealogical story about their development. (Compare Davidson's view that taking someone to mean or believe something *is* taking it that there is an interpretive mapping of their noises onto one's own satisfying certain constraints.) Rational reconstruction of a tradition of actual applications—making a past into a history—is a kind of reflection on it, a kind of self-consciousness. Another way he puts his point is then that *consciousness*, understood as the inferentialist does, as the application of inferentially articulated concepts in judgment, presupposes *self*-consciousness, in the sense of at least implicitly *making* norms out of actual applications, or *finding* those norms in such applications. In fact, for Hegel, the inferentialist notion of consciousness and the historical notion of self-consciousness are reciprocally sense-dependent concepts, two sides of one coin. Neither is intelligible apart from the other.

Such genealogical self-consciousness can itself be more or less explicit. At its most explicit, this sort of reflection, self-consciousness, intelligibility, or transparency is expressed in the form of the kind of narrative of maturation Hegel—theorizing as a member of the first generation really to be gripped by the possibility and potential of intellectual history—offers us in his *Phenomenology*. And the point of his *Logic*, as I understand it, is to give us a vocabulary in which to make explicit the process by which ordinary determinate concepts acquire content by being applied in experience.[8] One need not think that he succeeded—never mind that he succeeded in any final sense—in order to esteem the enterprise.

On a much smaller, less ambitious scale, this book is meant to sketch the outlines of such a systematic history. It is an exercise of this sort of genealogical, historical, expressively progressive reconstructive rationality, addressed to a particular constellation of philosophical concepts. (Indeed, on an even smaller scale, this introduction is written in the same genre.) As Hegel recognized, the process of determination that is *finding* implicit concepts by explicitly *making* a tradition does not leave everything as it was before. One of his most basic ideas is that cultural formations such as philosophical traditions, like self-conscious individual selves, exhibit the peculiar freedom that consists in having what they are *for* themselves be an essential element of what they are *in* themselves. This, for him, is what it is to be discursive, normative, *geistig* beings, rather than merely *natural* ones. The way we understand and conceive what we are doing affects what we *are*, in fact, doing. We find a way forward by reconstruing the path that brought us to our present situation.[9] The systematic historical model of rationality is a theoretical codification of the thought that a distinctively valuable sort of prospective guidance is afforded by a special kind of retrospective insight.

It is an essentially pluralistic thought. The idea I have been aiming to put on the table is that offering a systematic contemporary philosophical theory and a rational reconstruction of some strands of the history of philosophy can be two sides of one coin, two aspects of one enterprise. In one sense, of course, telling stories about how we got ourselves into the pickle we are in can be self-serving: a matter of rewriting the history of philosophy to make the present day a safe and congenial environment for views that are in any case going to be recommended. The upshot of the foregoing account of this form of rationality is that the telling of such stories is partly constitutive of the commitments (and so the self) that are in that case served. But in my view, the best philosophical response to such a narrative is not belief or endorsement but the telling of *more* such stories. It is the thinker who has only one such idiom in which to express and develop his self-understanding who is in thrall. So the sense in which such a story claims to be *correct*—the sense of *endorsement* for which it petitions—is *not* an *exclusive* one. It is not incompatible with there being other legitimate ways of telling the story, motivating other contemporary philosophical undertakings.

What I am recommending and practicing here is one among many forms of intelligibility, motivated first by producing *instances* of it, and only then an account of what *sort* of understanding (according to the expressive cumulative genealogical model of rationality) it is capable of embodying and conveying. Part One of this work offers (in Chapters 1 and 2) a historical context—a way of understanding the tradition that is the horizon of intelligibility being at once created and appealed to in what follows. And in Chapter 3 it offers a methodological rationale, a way of thinking about the sort of systematic historical enterprise that is being undertaken in the work as a whole. Part Two then presents more detailed stories, excavations into the tradition at various points, anchoring and motivating, if all goes well, a rational reconstruction of the normative trajectory of thought instituted by the figures considered and incorporated in the tradition that thereby becomes visible.

Chapters 4 through 12 offer essays on Spinoza, Leibniz, Hegel, Frege, Heidegger, and Sellars. This is an apparently motley group—but the aim is that they will seem less so after we work through this material than they would before. In each case my concern is with the *semantic* theory of the philosophers in question: their understanding of the *contents* of thoughts, beliefs, claims, and practical comportments, and with the accounts they give of their representational *aboutness*. The topic is accordingly *intentionality,* in a sense broad enough to include both what it is to have a thought *that* things are thus and so, and what it is to be thinking *of* or *about* things in a certain way. When these figures are viewed through the lens provided by this constellation of concerns, a set of overlapping themes and explanatory strategies comes into view. Generally, or for the most part, the explanations of intentionality on offer here are functionalist, inferentialist, holist, normative, and social pragmatist in character. No one of these features is shared by all the figures considered, and no figure exhibits them all. But my claim is that, taken together, those family resemblances bind these philosophers into a distinctive and recognizable retrospectively discernible tradition. The hope is that by making out a case for this claim it is possible at once to enrich our understanding of the philosophical topics being addressed, to provide a new conceptual vantage point from which to view our philosophical ancestors, and to highlight some central features of the sort of rationality that consists in discerning a philosophical tradition, by elaborating a concrete instance of such an enterprise.

Part Two can be read without Part One, at the cost of not understanding how I see the essays there as fitting together and defining a tradition, and what sort of enterprise I understand myself to be engaged in there. Part One can be read without Part Two, at the cost of not seeing any actual example of the sort of undertaking I theorize about there. My intent is that—like any proper text or tradition—the whole be more than the sum of its parts.

ONE

Talking with a Tradition

1

Contexts

I. Kant and the Shift from Epistemology to Semantics

One of Kant's master ideas is that what distinguishes thinkers and agents from merely natural creatures is our susceptibility to certain kinds of *normative* appraisal. Judgments and actions essentially involve *commitments* as to how things are or are to be. Because they can be assessed according to their *correctness* (truth/error, success/failure), we are in a distinctive sense *responsible* for what we believe and do.

Kant makes a normative turn: a shift from the sort of ontological demarcation Descartes offers of selves as thinking beings, to a deontological demarcation of selves as loci of responsibility. This move underwrites some of Kant's most characteristic claims. Thus the judgment appears for him as the minimal unit of experience, whereas the tradition he inherits had focused on the term (singular or general) because judgments are the smallest units for which we can take cognitive (justificatory) responsibility. Judgments have a subjective form, marked by the "I think" that can accompany all our representations, indicating who is responsible *for* or committed to the (correctness of the) judgment (the transcendental unity of apperception as a co-responsibility equivalence class). And judgments have an objective form, the "object = X," indicating what the judgment makes the judger responsible *to* (for its correctness). For Kant, concepts are rules determining what one has committed oneself to by applying the concept in judging or acting—and so what would count as a reason entitling one to or justifying such a commitment. The key philosophical puzzles about concepts accordingly concern their *Gültigkeit* or *Verbindlichkeit:* their validity or bindingness, a kind of authority laying obligations on those who use them. Kant wants to understand what it is for the use of concepts to make us responsible, for the norms of correctness they embody to have a grip on us, and further to make us responsible *to* something (what we are thinking *about*), on which we thereby count as having an intentional grasp.

Kant is the first thinker explicitly to take as his task the explanation of our character as *discursive* creatures in terms of our liability to various kinds of *normative* assessment. But when in "Was ist Aufklärung?" he looks back at his predecessors, he finds this theme to have been the implicit organizing principle of a tradition. He sees the Enlightenment as announcing and promoting our emergence from the tutelage of childhood to the incipient autonomy of adolescence. And that coming of age is taking person-defining *responsibility* for our *endorsement* of even inherited attitudes, claims, and goals. Descartes's meditator practices a particularly pure, radical, and rigorous version of this project. But it is no less visible in the political tradition of Hobbes, Locke, and Rousseau, who teach us to see our political institutions as our creatures, as things we are responsible for and bound by in the way we are responsible for and bound by what we do and have done.

By showing us this common thread, Kant retrospectively rationally reconstructs a tradition, exhibiting it as having an implicit, practical unity. The unity first emerges as an explicit theoretical principle in his own work—work that has the shape it does only because of the understanding it embodies of the significance of the tradition it thereby comes to epitomize and in a certain sense to complete. That broad movement of thought encompasses another, more finely grained development. The Enlightenment understands the discursive in terms of *rational* commitments. The responsibility to which it calls us is ultimately answerability to the *reasons* we have for our judgments and actions. Those reasons are the only authority acknowledged as legitimate. As it shows up in Descartes, this concern has the effect of pushing into the foreground the topic of *knowledge:* true belief justified by reasons. The threat that sets the criteria of adequacy for accounts addressing this topic is epistemological skepticism: the worry that reasons genuinely justifying our beliefs are not to be had. Even if many of our beliefs are true, we might still not be able to fulfill the responsibility to justify them with reasons, which is required for us to count as knowers.

Kant digs deeper. He sees that the epistemological issue presupposes a semantic one. The Cartesian skeptic asks what reason we have to suppose that the world is as we represent it to be in thought. An inquiry into the conditions of *successful* representation is accordingly an appropriate road to a response. Kant takes as his initial focus *intentionality* rather than *knowledge*. He asks about the conditions of even *purported* representation. What makes it that our ideas so much as *seem* to point beyond themselves, to something that they are *about?* The threat that sets the criteria of adequacy for accounts addressing this topic is *semantic* skepticism: a worry about the intelligibility of the very idea of representation. Kant thinks, further, that responding to this more radical form of skepticism, by explaining what it is for one thing to be about or purport to represent another, suffices to defuse the epistemological threat as well. The soft underbelly of epistemological skepticism is its implicit semantics. For Kant, the aboutness characteristic of representings is a normative achievement. Representings answer for their correctness to how it is with what (thereby) counts as represented. To take one thing as representing another is to accord to the latter a certain kind of *authority* over the former, to see the representing as in a distinctive way *responsible* to what is represented. (On the practical side, the normative approach can be extended to intendings and what is intended.) Understanding discursivity is understanding this sort of normativity. That is the task that stands at the very center of Kant's philosophical undertakings.

This trajectory of Enlightenment philosophizing about the discursive—from concern with knowledge to concern with intentionality, so from epistemology to semantics—like that about the normative, also culminates in Kant's distinctive problematic. But there is a temptation to take it that Kant is the *first* to address the semantic issue. That temptation is encouraged by the empiricists' relative lack of attention to the problem of understanding representational purport, as opposed to that of justifying our hopes and beliefs regarding our representational success. (Hume is a prime example.) Again, the failure to appreciate and address the normative character of knowledge involved in both justification and intentionality is what led Kant to claim that "the celebrated Mr. Locke" produced only a "physiology of the understanding." Nonetheless, there is good reason to think of the semantic concerns as in fact coeval with the epistemological ones, and of Kant here, as elsewhere, as explicitly thematizing concerns that had been all along implicit in the Enlightenment philosophical tradition. At least Kant's rationalist precursors during the early modern period were already usefully engaged in an enterprise that might be called "the metaphysics of intentionality."

II. Descartes and the Shift from Resemblance to Representation

The need philosophers such as Spinoza and Leibniz felt to tell a story of this sort developed under quite specific circumstances. Ancient and medieval hylomorphic theories understood the relation between appearance and reality—between how things seem or are taken to be and how they are—as in the favored case one of the sharing of a form. That is to say that it was understood in terms of *resemblance:* the sort of partial sharing of properties (e.g., shape, color) that is one way pictures can be related to what they are pictures of. The scientific revolution required a different, much more general model. The reality Copernicus discerned—a rotating Earth and a stationary sun—did not at all resemble the familiar appearance of a stationary Earth and a revolving sun. Galileo found that he could get the best mathematical (for him this meant geometrical) grip on the motions of ordinary objects by using lengths of lines to represent periods of time, and the areas of triangles to stand for speeds. In each case he was exploiting relations not happily thought of in terms of resemblance. And Descartes's mathematical physics represented the extended physical world (after Galileo, sensibly thought of as geometrical in its motions as well as its spatial extent) by algebraic equations. Again, the equations of circles and lines ($x^2 + y^2 = 1$, $ax + by = c$) do not at all *resemble* the geometrical figures they describe.[1]

Descartes sees that a more abstract notion is required to make sense of these relations. Something can evidently represent something else in the sense of being a sign of it without sharing the properties (even formal ones) required for resemblance. The master idea of the theory of knowledge in the period initiated by Descartes was, accordingly, to be that of *representation.* Descartes himself divided the world into two kinds of things: mental things, whose nature it is to represent, and physical things, which could only be represented. But what is it for something to be a representing in the relevant sense? (Words and pictures in books are not.) What is it to be a representation *for* or *to* someone? What makes someone's rabbit-idea so much as *seem* to be about rabbits? (I'll argue below that the form of this question that mattered for Spinoza and Leibniz was a broadly functionalist one: What is it to take, treat, or use one thing *as* a representation of another?) Descartes himself is not very explicit about how such representational purport should be understood. Indeed, he often allows himself to appeal to the very scholastic, ultimately nonexplanatory vocabulary of formal and objective existence of things that according to his basic insight needs to be overcome. In spite of such backsliding on the semantic issue, and in spite of his giving pride of place to the project of showing that things could be in reality as appearance represented them to be, that is, concern with the conditions of the *success* of representation, rather than with what representational content or purport consists in, Descartes nonetheless put on the table a wholly novel semantic idea that was to be critical for the subsequent tradition.

For the model of the relation between representing and represented— and so the model for the relation between appearance and reality, and therefore for that between mind and body—that drives and structures his philosophic thought is drawn from his discoveries in analytic geometry. Geometry, the study of the mathematical laws governing extension, could, thanks to Galileo, be seen to encompass not just shapes but their motions. Identifying the physical with what is so governed, Descartes then could see a paradigm of the discursive representation of the physical (the extended) in the relation between an algebraic equation and the geometrical figure it determines. But, as he also saw, the capacity of a string of symbols to represent a determinate extended figure is wholly a creature of its place in a *system* of such symbols, *all* the suitable expressions of which can be correlated with figures in such a way that differences in which symbols occur at various places in the algebraic expressions correspond to differences in the geometrical properties of the correlated figures. What makes it possible for an equation such as $x^2 + y^2 = 1$ to represent a circle is that there is a *global isomorphism,* a structure preserving mapping, from the system of equations to that of geometrical figures. (The development and exploitation of that mapping had, of course, been the basis of the young Descartes's epoch-making mathematical achievements.)

Two consequences of this model are of particular significance for the metaphysics of intentionality as pursued by Descartes's successors. First is a *holist* point: in order to understand representation, one must look

at the whole structured system of representings. The traditional notion of form, and so of the features underwriting a resemblance, is local
and atomistic. It concerns only the intrinsic properties of the item itself.
By contrast, the representational properties of an item, on Descartes's
model, depend on how the whole system of representings maps onto
what is representable. One cannot determine the representational purport or potential of a representing item by considering just that one
item. Second, as a result, the first step in understanding the relation between a representing and what it represents is to consider the relation
between that representing and other representings. The vertical relations
between thoughts and things depend crucially on the horizontal relations between thoughts and thoughts.

III. Rationalism and Functionalism

The development of this structural idea, which remains inchoate in Descartes's thought, is one of the ties that bind Spinoza and Leibniz to Descartes in the tradition of rationalism. Spinoza's idea that each individual thing is at once a mode of the attribute of thought and a mode of
the attribute of extension is not, I claim, supposed to define the relations
between representing ideas and represented things, since we can represent things outside our bodies. In fact, the relation between the attributes provides only the metaphysical background and raw materials for
an elaborate, multilayered account of the relations among modes that
makes some of them intelligible as representations of others.

In telling that story, Spinoza introduces a new mode of explanation—
one that, while building on the mechanical, moves decisively beyond it.
He starts atomistically, with modes that are, or correspond to, the simplest bodies (*corpora simplicissima*). He then considers larger totalities
that are formed from them, in virtue of the causal and inferential relations they stand in to one another (depending on which attribute we
consider them under). All this is available to the kind of understanding
he calls "Ratio," which permits us to discern and apply the laws of nature in empirical science and the laws of thought in logic. But he takes it
that crucial features of the universe—in particular, the intentionality by
which thoughts point beyond themselves, purporting to represent other
things—are not in principle intelligible in these terms. Grasping and explaining these features requires moving to a new, higher sort of under-

standing: *scientia intuitiva*. It is characteristic of this sort of understanding that it moves *down* from the relational wholes discerned by the
exercise of Ratio, to consider the *roles played* or *contributions made* by
smaller wholes in the context of those larger ones. Ultimately, what matters is the maximal whole that is "Deus sive Natura." But along the way,
we discover that the representational purport of an idea depends on the
boundaries of the mind we assess it with respect to. Spinoza here describes a kind of rational and causal *functionalism*. That mode of explanation is addressed in the first instance to the organic, but its ultimate
target is the intentional. It depends on an essentially *holistic,* top-down
individuational principle that works on the results of the atomistic, bottom-up accounts available at the level of Ratio. This additional functionalist step is the essential move in Spinoza's metaphysical account of the
intentionality of thought.[2]

Leibniz's mature account of what has to be true of something for it to
count as a state of conscious awareness of something is also holist, because broadly functionalist. He, too, starts with a sort of semantic primitive. For Spinoza it was the possibility of one mode showing up in
two attributes. For Leibniz, each perception has as an intrinsic property
(one it would have in every possible world) its *expressive range:* the
range of attributes (themselves ultimately compounded out of perceptions) whose occurrence can be inferred from the existence of that perception alone. This expressive relation is ubiquitous in a Leibnizian
world, applying to the inorganic, as well as the organic and intentional.
The challenge Leibniz addresses in his semantic theorizing is to account
for apperception, and eventually for distinct ideas, in terms of that primitive notion of expression, which holds even for unconscious perceptions. His answer is that perceptions acquire more than the atomistic significance of their intrinsic expressive range because perceptions joined
in a single monad can function to underwrite *multipremise* inferences.
Notoriously, all the perceptions of any single monad suffice to determine
the whole world it inhabits—though that expressive labor is divided
among individual perceptions very differently in different kinds of monads. Taking the essential role that *memory* plays in consciousness as his
leading idea, Leibniz accounts for various sorts of awareness in terms of
the role that individual perceptions play in the *developmental sequences*
generated when sets of perceptions give rise to other, subsequent such
sets. Distinctness of ideas, at the high end of the great epistemological

chain of being, is understood in terms of *recognition*, when one state of affairs outside the monad is represented by two different apperceptive chains of perceptions within the same monad. Thus Leibniz's strategy for explaining higher-order intentional capacities is to appeal to the significance that perceptions acquire in the context of other perceptions, to which they are joined either in a temporal progression or in being perceptions by a single monad. It is a functionalist, holist explanatory strategy.[3]

IV. Rationalism and Inferentialism

Another tradition-defining strand of early modern rationalism comes to explicit expression in Leibniz as well. It is a conception of conceptual content as consisting in role in reasoning. The fundamental concept of the dominant and characteristic understanding of cognitive contentfulness in the period initiated by Descartes is of course *representation*. Rationalists such as Spinoza and Leibniz accepted the central role of the concept of representation in explaining human cognitive activity. But they were much more concerned than Descartes to offer explicit, detailed metaphysical accounts of what it is for one thing to represent another. The primitives they appealed to are *inferential* relations: facts about what is a reason for what. They were explicitly concerned, in a way that Descartes was not, to be able to explain what it is for something to be understood, taken, treated, or employed *as* a representing *by* the subject: what it is for it to be a representing *to* or *for* that subject (to be *tanquam rem*, "as if of things," as Descartes puts it). Their big idea was that the way in which representings point beyond themselves to something represented is to be understood in terms of *inferential* relations among representings. States and acts acquire conceptual content by being caught up in inferences, as premises and conclusions.

Spinoza did not appreciate the normative character of the order and connection of ideas that Kant and Hegel would insist on (under the heading of 'necessity', *Notwendigkeit*, which for them means what happens according to a *rule*). But for him the inferential relations that order and connect ideas mirror the causal relations that order and connect things. And it is in terms of functional role with respect to those inferential-causal relations that he seeks to explain intentional, that is, representational phenomena. Leibniz's semantic primitive, the association with each perception (modification of a monad) of an expressive range, is a kind of inferential potential. His paradigm is the way in which one can make inferences from facts about a map ("There is a blue wavy line between the two black dots") to facts about the terrain it maps ("One must cross a river to go from Berlin to Leipzig"). In fact, this inferential story is what Leibniz makes of the structural isomorphism that underwrites Cartesian analytic geometry. Leibniz, the great gradualist, nonetheless insists against the empiricists that there is a sharp line to be drawn between percepts and concepts. Whereas the preconceptual content of mere perceptions is a matter of inferential conclusions that can be drawn from noninferential facts about them (as in the map example), the conceptual content of concepts is a matter of the inferential relations among them. For him the holistic character of conceptual content takes the form of an *inferential* holism, because the *functionalism* about the intentional that underwrites it is a *rational* functionalism. What gives a perception the significance of an apperceiving *that* things are thus and so is its role in reasoning.

Thus a big divide within Enlightenment epistemology concerns the relative explanatory priority accorded to the concepts of representation and inference. The British empiricists were more puzzled than Descartes about representational purport: the property of so much as *seeming* to be *about* something. But they were clear in seeking to derive inferential relations from the contents of representings rather than the other way around. In this regard they belong to the still-dominant tradition that reads inferential correctnesses off from representational correctnesses, which are assumed to be antecedently intelligible. That is why Hume could take for granted the contents of his individual representings but worry about how they could possibly underwrite the correctness of inductive inferences. The post-Cartesian rationalists, the claim is, give rise to a tradition based on a complementary semantically reductive order of explanation. (So Kant, picking up the thread from this tradition, will come to see their involvement in counterfactually robust inferences as essential to empirical representations having the contents that they do.) These *inferentialists* seek to define representational properties in terms of inferential ones, which must accordingly be capable of being understood antecedently. They start with a notion of content as determining what is a *reason* for what, and understand truth and representation as features of ideas that are not just manifested in, but actually *consist* in, their role in reasoning.

From this vantage point, the division of pre-Kantian philosophers into representationalists and inferentialists appears as the deepest structure underlying the traditional division of them into empiricists and rationalists. Leibniz uses the notion of inference or reasoning to draw a sharp line between conceptual representation and merely perceptual representation. This makes it possible for him to build up an *account* of what conceptual awareness consists in. Being aware of some external thing—in the sense of applying a concept to it, so as to be able to reason about it—is for the rationalists an achievement that has a distinctive sort of structure. But it requires that one *already* have a concept available to classify something under, in order to be aware of it in this sense. And that raises the question of how those conceptual capacities are acquired. The holism required by construing concepts as nodes in a network of reasons puts further constraints on a story about concept acquisition. By contrast, for the empiricist representationalists, awareness is an atomistic, primitive capacity of purported representation. Concepts are understood to be acquired by abstraction from exercises of the basic capacity for preconceptual awareness.

The problem of making intelligible the possibility of acquiring concepts was not soluble within the framework of pre-Kantian rationalism. The appeal to innateness was a desperate measure that neither stemmed from the roots of the rationalist vision nor carried conviction. It amounted to giving up the explanatory enterprise at this point. Kant's singling out of the judgment as the unit of cognitive responsibility, commitment, and authority, and hence of normatively significant *awareness*, reinforced the bright line the rationalists had drawn between conceptual and nonconceptual representations. And his understanding of theoretical (as well as practical) responsibility and authority as a matter of liability to *rational* assessment (i.e., assessment as to the *reasons* one has for making a judgment or producing an action) supported and developed their *inferential* criterion of demarcation for the conceptual. Yet Kant also did not offer a convincing account of concept acquisition: of how it is possible to come into the space of reasons and (so) concepts. He did, however, introduce the thought that—as I put the point above—what matters to begin with is the normative grip concepts have on us, not our

grip on them. (This is the move to thinking in Kantian categories of necessity rather than Cartesian categories of certainty.) That is, the key
thing is to understand how concepts let us bind or commit ourselves.
This is the idea that opened up the possibility of a resolution of the problem of concept acquisition in the rationalist tradition.

V. Hegel and Pragmatism

Such a resolution required another move as well. What is needed is
one of the most basic Hegelian emendations to Kant's normative rationalism: an understanding of normative statuses such as commitment, responsibility, and authority as *social* achievements. Hegel construes having bound oneself by applying a concept as occupying a certain sort of
social position, having a certain sort of social standing. The issue of concept acquisition then becomes transformed into the question of what
one must do in order to count as having undertaken a particular conceptually (inferentially) articulated commitment, or claimed a particular conceptually articulated authority. For each individual coming into
language, learning to engage in discursive practices, the concepts are always already available. The transition from not being able to produce a
performance with that sort of social significance to being able to do
so does not seem mysterious in the way that acquiring concepts had
seemed to be according to Leibniz's story. (Problems remained concerning how to understand the *determinateness* of the conceptual content of
such commitments, but that is a further issue.)[4] For this is a change that
can take place largely outside the individual—as scratching a signature
onto a piece of paper can either have no legal significance or be the undertaking of a contractual obligation to pay the bank a certain sum of
money every month for thirty years, depending only on whether it is
performed one day before or one day after the author's twenty-first birthday and consequent automatic achievement of legal majority.[5] Of course,
the question of how the concepts themselves develop in the linguistic
community then becomes paramount.

Hegel's idea is that understanding the normative character of intentional states as conceptually contentful requires adding another dimension to the functionalism about intentionality that was already characteristic of the rationalist tradition. Only a *social* functionalism, he
thinks, can accommodate Kant's normative insight. Leibniz had broken

the Spinozist parallelism of the inferential and the causal-developmental order, treating these as independently varying factors in his metaphysical account of conscious awareness of external bodies. Hegel adds a third dimension to his account, besides the inferential and the normative: the social. As for Leibniz, the functional significance of a perception depends not only on its inferential expressive range and what other perceptions precede and succeed it, but also on the other contemporaneous perceptions of its monad; so for Hegel the content of a commitment depends functionally not only on its inferential connections and role in an expressive developmental sequence, but also on the commitments acknowledged and attributed by other members of the same community. Understanding the intentional content of a belief or intention requires considering its role with respect to all three dimensions. This social dimension of Hegel's functionalism, and the holism that inevitably goes with it, is picked up both by the early Heidegger and the later Wittgenstein. Indeed, in all three of these figures we find functionalism about intentionality taking the form of *semantic pragmatism*: the view that the content expressed by linguistic expressions must be understood in terms of the *use* of those expressions. While retaining this bit of the rationalist tradition, Heidegger and Wittgenstein (like the classical American pragmatists) do not subscribe to the inferentialist strand. Sellars, however, reunites all of the classical elements once more.

2

Texts

In the foregoing pages I've sketched the principal structural elements of a tradition in early modern philosophy that can be seen to be picked up and developed in various ways by later figures. The emphases and filiations that articulate that story are not conventional wisdom—but I think they are defensible, and I find them both enlightening and suggestive. My painting the picture with bold colors and broad brush strokes here is animated by the conviction that the result is an illuminating context and background against which to view the detailed historical philosophical studies that form the second part of this work. It consists of nine essays: one each on Spinoza and Leibniz, two on Hegel, two on Frege, two on Heidegger, and one on Sellars. With the exception of the Leibniz piece and the first Hegel essay, they do not much address themselves to the larger currents of thought to which the figures and views they discuss belong. But I think they mean more if situated in the developing tradition I sketch in Chapter 1.

I said that I think that narrative is defensible, though my concern here has been to tell the story rather than to offer evidence for its correctness or value. The detailed readings and arguments of the substantive essays provide some of that evidence. Of course, they address only a relatively small subset of the many sweeping claims I have been making. Nonetheless, they provide some solid points of textual contact, and so some discipline to that speculative intellectual history. The essays were written over a period of twenty-five years. (The Spinoza essay was written when I was a graduate student, while the first Hegel piece is my most recent work—part of a book on Hegel that is still some years from completion.)

They were certainly not written in an attempt to fill in some antecedent picture that I had of a tradition to which they belong. On the contrary, that picture (and the tradition it retrospectively constitutes) was the cumulative product of detailed investigations of the sort epitomized here. Inferentialism began to emerge for me as a theme in pre-Kantian epistemology only on the completion of the Leibniz essay, when I was in a position to ask myself what the view I attributed to him there had in common with the view I had already worked out concerning Spinoza. Only in writing the first Hegel piece did I begin to think about the larger significance of the holistic ways of thinking that are ushered in by functionalist approaches to intentionality. In short, the more narrowly focused historical studies and the emerging grand narrative have developed together in the sort of dialectical relationship that Dilthey talks about under the heading of the hermeneutic circle—whereby an initial reading of a whole text results from initial readings of its parts, and then is available to contribute to more considered readings of parts, which lead in turn to a new appreciation of the whole, and so on.

In this chapter I describe a bit more specifically the topics, theories, and arguments on offer in the rest of the book. In Chapter 3 I then say something more about the methodological motivations, presuppositions, and aspirations that govern the enterprise. But first, it will be useful to survey these essays for the overlapping and connecting themes that tie them together as diverse perspectives on a coherent and recognizable emerging tradition.

I. Spinoza

Chapter 4 in this book, "Adequacy and the Individuation of Ideas in Spinoza's *Ethics*," is an attempt to sketch the workings of the metaphysical machinery Spinoza calls into play to explain how our thought can represent or be *about* the physical world. It is often thought that Spinoza does not have much to offer along these lines. For it can seem that he just builds in at the very ground floor of his metaphysical edifice both a mind/body dualism and the sort of parallelism between them required to make intelligible both the acquisition of knowledge through perception and the efficacy of thought in action, which offered such hurdles to the Cartesian system. After all, Spinoza associates with each idea—in his jargon, each "mode in the attribute of thought"—its "object," which is the *same* mode of substance, as exhibited in any *other* attribute, the only example of which that we have access to being the attribute of extension. (Compare Descartes's talk of the sun as existing both objectively, in being represented, and formally, in the realm of extension.) The relation between any idea and its object is then just the particularization of the fundamental relation between the different attributes of the one substance that is "Deus sive Natura." It is just a special case of *identity.*

But this cannot be right. The "one mode in two attributes" story would give a wholly unacceptable account of intentionality. For the physical object that is the expression in the attribute of extension of the finite mode of the attribute of thought that is an individual human *mind* is just the *body* of that human individual. And all of the less complex ideas that make up that mind have as their objects parts of that corresponding body. So if what one could mentally *represent* were only the *objects* of the ideas in one's mind, one could represent only states of one's own body. This may indeed be where the story must begin, but it clearly must continue by saying what it is to *take* or *treat* thoughts—or, for that matter, the bodily states they correspond to—as pointing beyond themselves, as standing for or representing or somehow being *about* things outside that individual mind and body.

This thought can be formulated as an explicit criterion of adequacy on an account of intentionality. What might be called the *Distal Constraint* requires that an account of mental or psychological intentionality[1] explain how it is possible for us to represent, think about, or be aware of anything other than what is most proximal to us in the causal chain of events that leads to our knowledge of such things. Thus we must explain how we can be aware of anything further upstream in the chain of cause-and-effect than our own brain states, retinal images, and so on.

It is worth noticing that this problem has as much bite today as it did for Spinoza (and, as we will see, Leibniz). The leading idea of some important contemporary programs in naturalized semantics is to understand the representational content of a state (say, a belief) in terms of its counterfactually reliable covariance with some sort of worldly state of affairs. That my awareness is *of* a sounding bell is in part a consequence of the state I am in being reliably elicited, even in a range of counterfactual circumstances, by the sounds made by bells. But the bell and my belief that there is a bell stand at opposite ends of a whole chain of more or less reliably covarying causes and effects, including the wavelike movement of the intervening air, the vibration of my eardrum, and a cascade of neurophysiological events. The more proximal an event kind is in this chain—the closer to its terminus in the formation of a perceptual judgment—the more reliably it covaries with that judgment. For at each stage, the intervening effect *can* be produced by causes other than the canonical ones. (The air might be being moved that way by something other than a bell, my eardrum might be being vibrated that way by a magnetic field, playful neurologists may be directly stimulating my auditory nerve, and so on.) Something other than simply the chain of reliably covarying events must be appealed to in order to single out some more or less distal region of that chain as an object of awareness or judgment, as what one of my resulting states represents or is about, if accounts along these lines are to underwrite consciousness of anything outside the body. My point is not that it is impossible to do this. Fred Dretske[2] appeals to *triangulation* within the individual: what matters is that there be at least *two* such chains of reliably covarying events, which can terminate in contentful states of the same kind, and which also overlap at some more distal point in the chain. (He offers as a simple example a thermostat that has two different information channels about the temperature of a room, either of which can result in the furnace being turned on or off.) Donald Davidson[3] appeals to *social* or *interpretive* triangulation: what matters is where the causal chains that terminate respectively in the *interpreter's* claim and the *interpreted* claim have a common element. I mention these contemporary cases only as evidence that the Distal Constraint on accounts of intentionality is not merely a historical curiosity, of interest only as showing the limitations of quaint, long-discarded metaphysical systems.

This challenge for Spinoza has, of course, been noticed before—though it has not been given the prominence I think it deserves. The treatment on which I build my account is due to Daisy Radnor. In an acute discussion, she details the reasons for thinking that Spinoza both *must* have and actually *does* have a systematic notion of what an idea *represents*, in addition and by contrast to what is its *object*. She does not, however, explain how Spinoza can be entitled to appeal to such a notion, given the metaphysical system in which he is working. In effect, she offers a Ramsified extension of his theory—that is, one produced from his explicit pronouncements by prefixing it with a second-order existential quantifier saying just that *there is* a notion of ideas representing things (including extended things outside the body associated with the mind in which the idea occurs) that has certain systematic features. What I do in this essay is show how to build such a conception out of the raw materials Spinoza has made available, and then show how this particular way of analyzing the representation relation makes sense of various dark but central features of his view.

This is above all a *semantic* question. But Spinoza's distinctive *epistemology* puts significant constraints on the answer, and thereby offers important clues. One of his basic epistemological thoughts is that ideas can be assessed as to the *adequacy* with which they represent what they are about (not necessarily their *objects,* with which they are, in an important sense, simply identical). One of the key observations is that the adequacy of one and the same idea can vary with the mind it is considered as a part of. All our inadequate ideas are also ideas in the more capacious and comprehensive mind of God (which just is nature under the attribute of thought), and considered as parts of *that* whole they are one and all adequate. And there is further reason to think that even what an idea should be understood as representing (never mind how adequately) depends on the mind of which it is considered as a part. That is, Spinoza endorses a kind of *holism* about these fundamental epistemological and semantic properties. It is only as parts of determinate wholes that items acquire properties of these sorts. The basic idea of the essay is that semantic content is conferred on a mode by the inferential/causal role that it plays in the mind/body to which it belongs. Spinoza offers a *functionalist* approach to intentionality, in terms of the *causal* and *inferential* relations in which modes of the two attributes must in any case be taken to stand, together with the metaphysical identity of ideas with their corporeal objects.

The more specific suggestion about his theory that I offer is that what an idea represents to a particular mind containing it is settled in two stages. First, in order to see what an idea represents, one must see how it is taken or treated by the mind in question. This is a matter of what other ideas it gives rise to. So we look to begin with at what follows it in a process of inference, what conclusions are actually drawn from it. Given the parallelism of attributes, this is a matter of the bodily states (modes in the attribute of extension) that are *causally* brought about in part by the *object* of the idea whose intentional content we are assessing. (More will be caused by it in God's mind than in ours, since effects outside our own bodies are included.) Then what the original idea represents can be identified with the *whole* cause (the sufficient cause, what Spinoza—not by accident—calls the "adequate" cause) of (the object of) those subsequent ideas. So an idea represents the object of the full cause of the idea to which it is a proximate or contributing cause. Where one idea gives rise to a number of others, the intersections of their several adequate causes are available for more specificity. The idea *adequately* represents that extended situation just in case the idea whose *object* is that extended state is *deducible* from the representing idea.

I present various sorts of textual evidence for this reading, relying particularly on one of Spinoza's letters. But in the main, I think the best arguments for the reading are of the Harmanian inference-to-best-explanation sort. The basic construction is uncontroversially (I think) available to Spinoza. There is some direct evidence that he endorses it. But it also makes the best sense of further doctrines he espouses that are otherwise quite difficult to understand. On the epistemological side, this account of the adequacy of ideas (in part in terms of Spinoza's notion of an adequate cause) makes sense of the three levels of knowledge in the *Ethics:* confused knowledge, Ratio, and *scientia intuitiva.* The last of these has been found particularly mysterious. Spinoza's Ratio is principled scientific knowledge, of the sort we are accustomed to expect to find thematized by a canonical Enlightenment thinker. But the final, higher, philosophical level of intuitive knowledge, which is knowledge of things through knowledge of God, is harder to get a handle on.

This difficulty is particularly significant because two very important, more specific kinds of knowledge are said to become available only at this third level. First, the *conatus*—the active individuating force that defines and determines the boundaries of the finite modes, which we are told is the way each particular thing expresses in a determinate manner the power of God (by which he is and acts)—can be grasped only by understanding at the third level, of *scientia intuitiva.* Second, the only finite mode whose *conatus* we are told anything about is the human mind, where it is identified with *self-consciousness*—which accordingly defines what a *self,* a determinate mind, is. So the determinate identity and individuation of all the most important kinds of individual modes—of self-conscious *selves,* thoughts or *ideas,* and the *objects* of those thoughts or ideas—are supposed to become intelligible only with this special sort of understanding.

Spinoza defines ideas as mental conceptions. He says that he chose this term to indicate an *activity* of the mind. Elsewhere he argues that the essence of each idea is a particular affirmation or act of will. Ideas are conceiv*ings*, then: practical *doings*. I suggest we think of *what* one is doing as passing to *other* ideas, ideas that in that sense *follow from* the earlier ones. The talk of an act of will is talk of *committing* oneself by drawing conclusions from it, using it as a premise in reasoning and a basis for planning. That is, conceiving is applying concepts in the sense of making judgments. It is *by* drawing those conclusions (via the identity-of-modes-expressed-in-different-attributes relation to the causal processes corresponding to those inferential ones) that a mind *takes* its ideas to be *about* some part of extended nature—and thereby *makes* them be about it. This is what it is for those ideas to *purport* to say how things are with that part of the world. And the account of the adequacy of ideas says what it is for that purport to be successful.

The story I tell on Spinoza's behalf starts with causal and inferential relations among finite modes, by building up networks of these parallel sorts of relations. This bit of the story corresponds to what Ratio can know. For there are general principles (articulated in terms of Spinoza's *notiones communes*) that govern these bottom-up constructions of wholes out of parts. But then, following the clue offered by what Spinoza says in the letter I mentioned above, we reverse explanatory direction and look at the properties various ideas get by playing the roles that they do in larger wholes. This is the sort of understanding Spinoza calls "intuitive." It turns out that so much as *being* a finite mode is a matter of playing a certain sort of role in a larger whole. It is for this reason that the individuating *conatus* can only be understood intuitively—that is, *functionally*. So there is an especially intimate relation between this ontological principle of individuation and the epistemological notion of the adequacy of ideas. At the unattainable limit of this form of understanding, where every finite mode is fully understood in terms of the role it plays in the whole universe, stands the mind of God, in which all ideas are adequate.

Self-consciousness for a finite mode consists in consciously representing some of one's ideas *as* ideas partly constitutive of a particular finite mind. Spinoza's doctrine of *idea ideae*, ideas of ideas, is the locus of his treatment of this topic. One traditional problem in the vicinity is that Spinoza says that ideas of ideas are related to the ideas they are ideas of as the mind is related to body. But he also says that the ideas of ideas that constitute the sort of consciousness under consideration (what in Leibniz becomes apperception) are distinct from the ideas they are ideas of. Not all ideas come with ideas of them. If one understands the first claim to be about the relation of mind to the body—that is, as saying that ideas of ideas are related to the ideas they are of in the same way that ideas are related to their natural objects in the attribute of extension, that is, by a kind of *identity*—then these seem to be incompatible claims. But the trouble evaporates once we have available the possibility that an *idea ideae represents* another idea, rather than having it as its *object*. The result is:

> The idea *A* represents idea *B* just in case the object of *B*, which is *B* it-self (of course *B* has an extended object as well), is the adequate cause of the ideas of which *A* is a proximate cause. *A* will then be an *adequate* idea of *B* just in case *B* is deducible from *A* . . . In general, *A* will be an adequate cause of *B* just in case the adequate cause of the idea of which *A* is a proximate cause (namely *B*) is deducible from *A*.[4]

In these terms it is possible to explain why it is of the essence of the mind to conceive itself adequately, and so to be free and active. For the mind functioning as the adequate cause of its own modifications is just the whole-part determination (immanent causation, mutual adaptation of parts, etc.) which is the *conatus* or individual essence of the mind. It is free and active to the extent to which it is a relative whole determining its parts, and not so far as it is a relative part superseded by other finite things whose power exceeds that of the human mind. Functionalism and (so) holism are the basic structural features of this metaphysics of the mental.

II. Leibniz

Chapter 5, "Leibniz and Degrees of Perception," offers novel readings of important Leibnizian doctrines concerning perception, apperception or awareness, and the sophisticated sort of knowledge that is articulated by distinct ideas. For Leibniz, *perceptions* constitute the most important species of *representations*. They are distinguished from other species of that genus, in particular from mathematical representations (which Leibniz seems to have thought of in cartesian terms of global isomorphisms),[5] we are told, in that they are "*expressions* of many in one." The whole set of contemporaneous perceptions of any monad expresses the whole universe. Perceptions are said to come in *degrees*, of distinctness or, equivalently, perfection. It is in terms of this fundamental metaphysical notion that we are to understand both the diversity of points of view of the monads, by which they are individuated, and the preestablished harmony among those perspectives in a single universe that is Leibniz's systematic synthesis of the principles of maximal unity and of maximal multiplicity. I offer a model of degrees of distinctness of perceptions, and use that to offer detailed readings of a number of themes central to Leibniz's account of intentional phenomena, especially his account of what is required for *consciousness* or *awareness* of one's perceptions, that is, in Leibniz's terms, for apperception.

The fundamental building block of Leibniz's metaphysics of the mental is his notion of one representation *expressing* a manifold in a unity, in the way characteristic of perception. Following his methodological maxim that we should construe those things of which we do not have distinct ideas on the model of those things of which we do have distinct ideas—a principle that lives on in Hegel's practice of understanding what is implicit in terms of its relation to what is explicit—I understand the sense of 'containment', the sense in which the many is 'in' a unity, in *inferential* terms. That is, the model is at base the way many consequences can be, as Leibniz elsewhere says, *contained in* a set of premises, in virtue of containment relations among *concepts* (rather than percepts). The expressive range of a perception may be thought of as the set of monadic attributes (perceptions by that monad and by others) whose occurrence is deducible from the occurrence of the perception in question. Degrees of perception then can be thought of as corresponding to more-or-less-in-one—that is, as a matter of the relative richness of inferential consequences. This account is based on some earlier work by Montgomery Furth, in something like the same sense in which the Spinoza piece works out an idea of Radnor's. Although the union of the expressive ranges (in this inferential sense) of all the perceptions of any monad express the entire universe, they can do so in quite different ways, depending on how the expressive labor is divided among more and less perfect or distinct perceptions.

Although one can make sense of a lot of what Leibniz says about and in terms of the relative distinctness of perceptions by appeal to this model, it does not immediately yield an account of what is distinctive of those perceptions of which we are *aware*—that is, of the *app*erception that distinguishes *conscious* monads from the rest. For our *bodies* are defined by Leibniz as whatever we have the most distinct perceptions of, and our bodies are not the exclusive, or even preeminent, objects of our awareness. So the same problem arises for Leibniz as for Spinoza: How are we to understand the boundaries of our bodies, and the possibility of being aware of anything beyond them? In this case, the metaphysical raw materials available for addressing that question about intentionality are provided by the notion of perceptions differing in the degree of distinctness they display.

The main question can be subdivided into two. First, what is the relation between a perception that is an apperceiving and the perception that is its immediate object, in virtue of which we may say that awareness is occurring at all? That is, how is apperception a perception "of" the perception that is its internal object? Second, what is the relation between this constellation of perceptions and that external object that they constitute an awareness of? The second is where the issue of how awareness can be addressed to items outside the body. I suggest that the first question can be answered by understanding awareness as the product of two characteristics: an earlier perception metaphysically produces a later one, and the expressive range of the later one stands in an appropriate relation to the expressive range of the former. These are, respectively, relations among perceptions at the level of *force* and relations at the level of *content*. Awareness is what occurs when a perception is taken as a mark of another more expressively complete perception. A perception is noticed to the extent to which it is *developed*, that is, gives rise to a perception whose expressive range is a superset of that of the original perception. Looking at what perceptions a given perception produces is Leibniz's way of working out the idea that the essence of consciousness is *memory*. Memory requires a relation at the level of content, besides one at the level of production. The requirement of *expressive development*—that one perception (or a class of them) gives rise to a more distinct (expressively powerful) perception—corresponds to an emphasis of attention. It construes apperception as a kind of *focusing* on the content of a prior perception.

The building blocks of this account are of two sorts: the ultimately inferential relation of *expression* between the perceptions of different monads, and the pseudo-causal relation of *production,* whereby a set of perceptions of one monad "metaphysically gives rise to" a further perception or perceptions of the same monad. Apperception or awareness is then an emergent property exhibited by some perceptions, in virtue of the *functional role* they play in a whole system. Although the system itself can be understood in terms of how it is built up atomistically out of such relations among perceptions, the functional roles played by various perceptions in that relational structure is intelligible only holistically, by working back down from the whole to its parts.

The holist consequences of this functionalist approach to intentionality is particularly evident when we turn to the issue of the *external* objects of apperceptive awareness. It is the expression relation that connects perceptions to objects (accidents) outside the monad of which they are modifications. But what is it for a perception to be an awareness? Leibniz's answer is a functional one; he tells us what it is to *take* or *treat* a perception *as* an awareness *of* something external. What is required is *recognition* of an object by marks. To recognize a feature of an external object is to be aware of it—to respond to one's initial perception expressing that feature *as of* that feature, namely, by developing the original content. When this is done in thought (perception inferentially articulated in that it occurs in accordance with distinct ideas and necessary truths), it takes the form of a clear idea. Recognition by marks is what corresponds to distinct ideas (though even the non-sapient brutes have enough of an associative "shadow of reasoning" to have an analogue of it). This requires being aware of some feature *as* a mark of a particular object. In the explicit case,[6] this requires what Leibniz calls "recognition judgments"—a thought and a usage that are both picked up by Frege in the *Grundlagen,* when he defines how an expression must function substitutionally and inferentially in order to be a singular term. Recognition judgments *triangulate* on an object by taking it that *two* sets of marks pick out the *same* thing. Thus, for Leibniz as for Frege, they are to be expressed explicitly in the form of identity statements. For instance, gold might be recognized by taking it that *the most malleable metal* is ($=$) *the heaviest metal.* So we should ask what recognizing is, that is, what it is according to Leibniz to *take* two sets of marks *as* marks of the *same* object (the apperceptive or recognitive status expressed discursively by reasoning beings in the form of identity statements).

The implicit analogue (below the explicit level of thought) of this sort of directedness by triangulation through recognition by marks happens when two (sets of) perceptions are expressively developed by a common successor perception, whose expressive range includes the union of theirs. So a perception expressing the accidents *heaviest metal,* and one expressing the accidents *most malleable metal,* are jointly developed by one whose content includes *both* sets of accidents. That the content of the successor may include more than is included in either of its antecedents allows a dog to take both the appearance of a certain stick and a grimace of his master's as marks of an impending beating without thereby having an awareness of the beating that extends no further than the coincidence of stick and grimace.

So Leibniz actually introduces the triangulation strategy, which (as I indicated above) has been appealed to by contemporary theorists as diverse as Davidson and Dretske to solve the problem—fundamental to *their* metaphysics of intentionality—of singling out a distal stimulus as what some internal state should be understood as a response to. On this account, whether a perception counts as an apperception, and if so *what* it counts as an apperception of—both what perception(s) should be understood as its immediate object, and what worldly state of affairs it is intentionally directed to—depend not just on the intrinsic (inferential) expressive features of the perception itself but also on its relations to other perceptions of the same monad. One must look at the whole monad as it develops its expression of its world over time in order to settle which of its perceptions count as apperceptions, and what they make the monad aware of. The similarities between Leibniz's inferential-causal functionalist metaphysics of intentionality and that of Spinoza are striking. I think these structural similarities of approach and of detail are not mere artifacts of my readings. If they are not, they define a rationalist tradition with a different and more specific unity than is often found. The two principal elements articulating the metaphysics of intentionality developed in that tradition are the *holism* consequent on its broadly functionalist approach, and the *inferentialism* that looks to *role in reasoning* to understand the intentional contents conferred on (what thereby are intelligible as) representings by the relations among items that are contentful in that sense.

The inferentialist side of Leibniz's rationalism consists in the dependence, in the order of explanation, of the concepts of awareness and representation on the concept of inference—even for monads incapable of thought. Inference is the primitive that anchors both ends of the explanatory structure presented in Chapter 5 and sketched here. First, the basic theoretical auxiliary I introduced, the notion of an individual expressive range, is explicitly explained in terms of inference. The expressive range of a perception is that set of accidents (nonrepeatable occurrences of complex property-types) which may be inferred from the occurrence of that perception alone (i.e., if nothing else were known about its universe). It is only insofar as there are primitive inferential facts of this form that this explanatory scheme gets off the ground. At the other end, the model in terms of which awareness and recognition consciously by marks (the Fregean model of recognition) are explained is that of distinct *ideas,* which as we have seen are *inferentially* articulated ideas, which can be had only by beings capable of reason. At the high end of the spectrum of intentionality is specifically *conceptual* awareness: the sort that consists in bringing something under a distinct idea or concept, whose content essentially depends on its role in reasoning. This sort of awareness requires that one *already* have concepts to classify things under before one can be conceptually aware of them. As I read him, Leibniz already had the conceptual resources to respond to the inevitable question: Where do we get these concepts, if not by abstraction from previous experiences or episodes of awareness? The appeal to innate ideas, which is often thought to be at the core of rationalism, is on this view a consequence of collateral commitments that are quite peripheral to his fundamental views. In contemporary forms of inferentialism (particularly in Sellars's "Empiricism and the Philosophy of Mind") this difficulty is responded to by combining Kant's shift of perspective from our grip on concepts to their grip on us with Hegel's idea (taken up in the twentieth century by Heidegger and Wittgenstein) that conceptual norms are *socially* instituted and administered.

III. Hegel

Traditions are lived forward but understood backward. The detailed claims and constructions presented in the Spinoza and Leibniz essays and rehearsed here are particularly important for my story because the further back one discerns a tradition whose defining themes become clear only with later developments, the more contentious the attributions are liable to be. In the discussions of the essays that follow, I build on the themes introduced already while adding some further ones.

As I hope was clear from the discussion in Chapter 1, Kant plays an absolutely pivotal role in the larger narrative to which I want to understand these essays as contributing. Unfortunately, I am not now in a position to tell a story about his metaphysics of intentionality of the sort I am aiming at with these others. I console myself with the thought that between the Leibniz work and the Hegel work, in an important sense, I've got him surrounded (even if I haven't closed in). At any rate, the more detailed story on offer in Part Two of this book skips over Kant's watershed innovations in this emerging tradition to address Hegel's. As a result of explicitly making the turn that privileges semantics over epistemology, Kant had thought harder about the notion of *conceptual content* than any of his predecessors. One of the results was an emphasis on the notion of *modality*. For he understands (to adopt the phrase Sellars used as the title of one of his less comprehensible essays) "concepts as involving laws, and inconceivable without them." To use an example that was surely crucial for him, one cannot count as understanding the concept of mass if one does not understand its lawlike relation to the concepts of force and acceleration. I think this view should be understood as a development of the *inferentialism* Kant inherited from his rationalist predecessors. He takes it that the contentfulness of concepts *essentially* involves *rational relations* with other concepts, according to which the applicability of one provides *reasons* for or against the applicability of others. Applying one concept can *oblige* one to apply another, *preclude* one from applying a different one, and *permit* one to apply still others. Concept use, then, involves a *normative* dimension. Kant understands concepts as the rules that ultimately determine the correctness of such inferential moves.

Two features of Kant's way of thinking about intentionality and conceptual content are of particular significance for the strands in Hegel's thought that are followed out and developed in the two essays presented here. First is the *holism* about conceptual content implicitly brought into play by picking up on these rationalist ideas. Second is the significance of the relation between the *content* of concepts and the *process* (which Kant calls "synthesis") of applying them, for the sense in which the concepts involved in that process ought to be thought of as *determinate*.

Taking up these themes involves a shift of emphasis in the sort of intentionality that is going to be the initial metaphysical explanatory target. Searle offers this pretheoretical delineation of the subject matter of his book *Intentionality*: "If a state S is Intentional then there must be an answer to such questions as: What is S about? What is S of? What is it an S that?"[7] Up to this point our concern has been with the first two sorts of questions: questions about representational purport and success—and with the sort of awareness that it requires or engenders. The Hegel essays consider his views about the third sort of question. The primary issue is how to understand the nature and possibility, not to begin with of ofness or aboutness, but of the sort of determinate conceptual content that Hegel takes it is exhibited both by the way the world is and by the way we *take* the world to be.[8] So the relation of the concept of <u>intentional content</u> to that of the activities of a <u>self</u> continues to be a topic.

The scope of the rationalists' *functionalism* is substantially expanded, however. For Hegel places the sort of inferential/causal *process* central to that functionalism in the larger frame of *historically* extended *social practice*. Transposed into this key, functionalism takes the form of *pragmatism*—'pragmatism' in the sense of a particular kind of *use* theory of *meaning* and *content*. Kant had seen that intentionality crucially involves a *normative* dimension. Both the horizontal relations among intentionally contentful states and the vertical relations between them and what they represent underwrite assessments of *correctness*—of reasoning and representing, respectively. Kant agrees with the rationalists that awareness is *conceptual* awareness. Experience is the application of *concepts* in judgment (and action). He accordingly faces the same question they did: If one must *already* have concepts available in order to have experience, where do the concepts come from? Normative structures are *presupposed* by the application of concepts in judgment and action—activity that counts as judging and acting only because and insofar as it is subject to assessment as correct or incorrect according to the standards set by the *content* of the commitments one has undertaken. Kant locates the origin of those normative structures in *transcendental* activity rather than *empirical* activity, in the noumenal rather than the phenomenal realm. But the relations between these are less than clear. Kant's idiom leaves a lot of options open.

Hegel brings things back to earth. Kant must have been thinking about a structure of our ordinary cognitive and practical doings. Hegel understands that transcendental structure to be *functionally* conferred on what, otherwise described, are the responses of merely natural creatures, by their role in inferentially articulated, implicitly normative social practices. The system within which something can play the role of a

determinately contentful conceptual commitment is for him deployed
along three dimensions. Normativity (Fregean *force,* as nearly as we can
map these vocabularies on one another, given the massive differences in
the collateral commitments of these philosophers) is a product of *mutual
recognition*—the structure of the social as such. On this view, "all transcendental constitution is social institution."[9] The commitments and responsibilities instituted by these reciprocal acknowledgments of authority and responsibility are contentful insofar as they have the structure of
conceptual commitments (applications of concepts)—that is, insofar as
they play distinctively *inferential* roles in reasoning, as premises and
conclusions. Finally, the *contents* of the *conceptual commitments* undertaken in judgment and action are *determinate* in virtue of the position
they occupy in a tradition of actual use, retrospectively construed as
expressively progressive, in taking the form of the gradual unfolding into
explicitness of the content of the commitments that were all along implicit in the judgments actually made and the actions actually performed. What we actually do, perform, and produce affects the contents
of the conceptual norms, and so what inferences and exclusions determine what we *ought* and ought not to do, perform, and produce. But it is
those norms that make what is done have the significance of a *doing*—
the undertaking of a determinately contentful commitment—at all.

So from the Hegelian point of view, there is no particular problem
about how we come to be able to be conceptually aware of things. By
(for instance) using certain words, we give concepts a grip on us, place
ourselves under their sway, implicitly recognize their standards as authoritative for assessments of what we are committed and entitled to.
Those norms are implicit in the applications of concepts that have actually been made (what we did actually take-true or make-true)—in the
concrete practical tradition bequeathed to us by our predecessors. They
are administered by our contemporaries and successors—by those we
recognize and so grant such authority. The social, inferential, and historical dimensions define the functional system within which, according to
Hegel's metaphysics of normativity, the activity of a natural creature can
have the spiritual *(geistig)* significance of being the undertaking of determinately contentful, inferentially articulated commitment.

The first Hegel essay, Chapter 6, "Holism and Idealism in Hegel's
Phenomenology," introduces the structure in Hegel's thought that I call
objective idealism. The second, Chapter 7, "Some Pragmatist Themes in

Hegel's Idealism," sketches central elements of the further structure I call *conceptual* idealism: the structure and unity of the *concept* is the same as the structure and unity of the self-conscious *self*. The first essay presents an account of the transition from "Consciousness" to "Self-Consciousness," in the *Phenomenology*. This is a story about the idealism according to which the objective world is intelligible as determinate only as part of a larger story that includes an account of the activity of knowing subjects. The theme of Chapter 6 is that the idea that there is a determinate way things are entails a kind of conceptual *holism*; that of Chapter 7 is that conceptual *norms* can be understood as determinate only insofar as they exhibit a structure of reciprocal authority modeled on the way social substance *(Geist)* is synthesized by mutual recognition.

The first story begins with the thought that the way things objectively are must be *definite* or *determinate*. The essence of determinateness is modally robust *exclusion*: if things are one way, there are some other ways they cannot be. Relations of *material incompatibility*—"determinate negation"—articulate a basic structure of Hegel's metaphysics. Material *incompatibility* relations induce modally robust material *consequence* relations. (*Schließen* is rooted in *ausschließen*.)[10] Hegel is with his rationalist predecessors in the centrality he gives to *inferential* relations. But he sees something *beneath* the inferential relations. They are derived from more basic relations of material exclusion or incompatibility. For Hegel, to be *conceptually* articulated is just to stand in material relations of incompatibility and (so) consequence. In this sense, not only thoughts (as thinkings) but also the objects, properties, states of affairs are conceptually articulated. This sense of "conceptual" does not in any obvious way derive from our understanding of processes of conceiving or practices of applying concepts. The discussion follows out one chain of reasoning to the conclusion that even so, one cannot understand what it is for two properties or states of affairs to *be* incompatible without understanding what it is for discursive practitioners to *take* them to be incompatible.

A number of passages suggest that Hegel is committed to *strong individuational holism* about conceptual content: Conceptual contents are identified and individuated solely by the relations of material incompatibility (and hence material inference) they stand in to one another. That is, articulation by relations of material incompatibility should be understood not just as *necessary* for determinate contentfulness (of states of affairs or properties on the objective side, and propositions and predicates on the subjective side), but also as *sufficient* to define it. But there is at least a prima facie problem in making strong individuational holism intelligible: if the relata are identified and individuated only by the relations they stand in to one another, how are the relations identified and individuated?

In understanding holism about determinate conceptual contents articulated by material incompatibility (and so consequence) relations, it is useful to keep in mind some suggestions and distinctions that Hegel does *not* explicitly make. First, Harman has argued provocatively but persuasively that there are no such things as rules of deductive inference. For if there were, they would presumably say things like "From *p* and *if p then q*, infer *q*." But that would be a bad rule. One might already have much better evidence against *q* than one had for either *p* or the conditional. In that case, one should give one of them up. What deductive logic really tells us is not to believe all of *p, if p then q,* and *~q*. But it does not tell us what to *do* inferentially. It merely specifies some deductive *relations* of entailment and incompatibility which *constrain* what we should do without *determining* it. Inference is a *process;* implication is a *relation.* What I will call "the Harman point" is that in thinking about determinateness in terms of relations of material incompatibility that are more basic than inferential ones, we should still distinguish between *relations* and *processes.* Second is a thesis about the relation between these two. *Conceptual pragmatism* says that grasp of a concept (conceptual content) is a practical capacity, mastery of a practice, or the capacity to undergo or engage in a process; it is the capacity to *do* something.

prag

Third is a distinction between two sorts of dependence. Concept P̲ is *sense dependent* on concept Q̲ just in case one cannot count as having grasped P̲ unless one counts as grasping Q̲. Concept P̲ is *reference dependent* on concept Q̲ just in case P̲ cannot apply to something unless Q̲ applies to something. The distinction between these is enforced by the observation that sense dependence does not entail reference dependence. For example, we might define something as having the property of being **pleasant**, in a regimented sense, just insofar as it *would* tend to produce a subjective state of *pleasure* in creatures like us who are sensorily exposed to it. Then one cannot understand the concept pleasant unless one understands the concept pleasure. But because of the modal, counterfactual nature of the definition relating the intensions, it still makes perfect sense to talk about there having been pleasant things before there were human beings, and in possible worlds in which there never are human beings. For a spectacular sunset might in either of these cases be such that it *would* produce pleasure *if* suitable creatures were aware of it.

In these terms, then, we can state the principal thesis of Hegel's objective idealism. One can understand the concept of a determinate *objective* world only to the extent to which one understands *subjective* processes of acknowledging error (which is treating two commitments one finds oneself with as *incompatible*). Put another way, the concepts of incompatibility$_{obj}$ (which can hold among properties, or among states of affairs) and incompatibility$_{subj}$ (which can hold among predicates, or among propositional contents of commitments), and *therefore* the concepts of an objectively determinate world, on the one hand, and of error and experience—which characterize the *process* of resolving incompatible commitments—on the other, are reciprocally sense dependent.

I suggest three more specific objective idealist claims, which both in the context of Hegel's metaphysics are consequences of the more general version, and (so I claim) are defensible in their own terms in our own day. The concepts singular term and object are reciprocally sense dependent. The concepts asserting and fact are reciprocally sense dependent. The concepts necessity and law, on the one hand, and counterfactually robust inference, on the other, are reciprocally sense dependent.

I then argue that *holism* should be understood as itself a reciprocal sense dependence claim. It follows that objective idealism is a kind of holism. The main claim of the discussion is then that, according to Hegel, the *only* way to make *holism,* and so *determinateness,* intelligible is *objective idealism.* Filling in that idea, I offer a model of how a *subjective process* can make intelligible *objective holistic relational structures.* It is *holistic role abstraction,* beginning with *signs,* and ending with *roles* played by those signs, or *contents expressed* by them, thought of in terms of higher-order relations among *sets* of those signs. In terms of this notion, it is possible to make sense of the dialectical process of "traversing the moments" that structures Hegel's philosophical methodology. It shows up as just the sort of process one must engage in to understand a holistic structure of conceptual relations.

By the end, then, I have argued that understanding the *objective* world as *determinate* for Hegel entails that it must be understood as a *holistic relational structure,* that there is a prima facie problem with the intelligibility of strongly holistic relational structures, for an understanding of *idealism* as a *sense* dependence relation of *objective determinateness* on *subjective processes of resolving incompatible commitments,* and for an understanding of holism also as a *sense* dependence relation. Disentangling issues of *sense* dependence from those of *reference* dependence shows idealism as a respectable and potentially defensible response to genuine conceptual problems. Finally, not only *objective idealism* but also Hegel's distinctively structured dialectical *process of understanding* emerge as required to understand the *holistic* relational structures that Hegel takes to be implicit in the notion of a world that is *determinately* one way rather than another.

Chapter 7, "Some Pragmatist Themes in Hegel's Idealism" considers a further species of idealist claim. *Conceptual* idealism moves beyond the reciprocal sense dependence of determinate conceptual content and the activities of a self (defined as what can be committed and authoritative) endorsed by objective idealism. Conceptual idealism is a thesis about the conceptual itself—the whole structure of objective conceptual relations of material incompatibility and consequence and subjective conceptual processes of resolving incompatible commitments and drawing inferences. According to this thesis, the whole structured constellation of subject-defining processes and object-defining relations should itself be modeled on one of its aspects: the activities of the self-conscious self. The aim of the discussion is to explain a basic *idealist* thesis: the structure and unity of the *concept* is the same as the structure and unity of the *self.* The strategy is to do that by appealing to a fundamental *pragmatist* thesis derived from a kind of functionalism that looks historically at a discursive social practice. It is the claim that the *use* of concepts determines their *content*—that concepts can have no content apart from that conferred on them by their use.

The Hegelian argument I see as running through that pragmatist thesis to culminate in conceptual idealism begins by considering the nature and origins of the *determinate contents of empirical conceptual norms.* It follows out one of the strands of thought leading from Kant to Hegel. As I understand him, Hegel thinks that Kant has not inquired deeply enough into the conditions of the possibility of the *determinateness* of the rules that specify the contents of ordinary empirical concepts. Strictly, all Kantian rational creatures can do is apply concepts. Empirical and practical activity consists in applying concepts, which set the standards of correctness for those performances, which play the functional roles of qualifying them as judgments and actions just by being subject to such concept-guided assessments. How is it that candidate knowers and agents have access to the determinate conceptual norms presupposed by their cognitive and practical experience?

Kant develops a *two-level* strategy: conceptual norms are *instituted* by transcendental activity (at the level of noumena), and only then available to be *applied* in empirical activity (at the level of phenomena). Carnap also has a two-level account: *first* one stipulates *meanings, then* experience dictates which deployments of them yield true *theories.* With respect to this issue, I think it is enlightening to understand Hegel as standing to Kant as Quine stands to Carnap. Quine's *pragmatism* consists in his development of a one-level account in contrast to Carnap's two-level account. The practice of using language must for him be intelligible not only as the *application* of concepts by using linguistic expressions, but also equally and at the same time as the *institution* of the conceptual norms that determine what would count as correct and incorrect uses of linguistic expressions. Experience is at once the application and the institution of conceptual norms. It is the process of their use in judgment and action that confers on concepts their determinate content. This pragmatist functionalism about conceptual content, I suggest, is the key to Hegel's conceptual idealism.

One of the clearest statements of that idealism is in the *Science of Logic:*

> It is one of the profoundest and truest insights to be found in the *Critique of Pure Reason* that the *unity* which constitutes the nature of the *Notion* [*Begriff*] is recognized as the *original synthetic* unity of *apperception,* as the unity of the *I think,* or of self-consciousness . . . Thus we are justified by a cardinal principle of the Kantian philosophy in referring to the nature of the *I* in order to learn what the *Notion* is. But conversely, it is necessary for this purpose to have grasped the *Notion* of the *I.*[11]

To understand this, we need to think about the fixed end of the analogy: Hegel's account of selves. The core idea structuring Hegel's social understanding of (self-conscious) selves is that they are synthesized by *mutual recognition.* That is, to be a self—a locus of conceptual commitment and responsibility—is to be taken or treated as one by those one takes or treats as one: to be recognized by those one recognizes. This is another broadly functionalist doctrine: natural beings become selves by coming to stand in certain sorts of relations to one another.

Enlightenment conceptions of the normative are distinguished by the essential role they take to be played by normative *attitudes* in instituting normative *statuses*. (Implicit social contract theories of political obligation are a case in point.) It does not make sense to talk about commitments and entitlements, responsibility and authority, apart from our practices of taking or treating one another *as* committed or entitled, responsible or authoritative. This thought should be understood as another holist, reciprocal sense dependence thesis. The more specific version of this thought that Hegel develops is what he makes of what Kant made of Rousseau's. It might be called the *autonomy thesis*: the distinction between force, coercion, or mere *constraint* on me, on the one hand, and legitimate *authority* over me, on the other, consists in the latter's dependence on my *endorsement* or *acknowledgment* of the authority *as* binding on me.

Hegel talks about authority and responsibility in terms of 'independence' and 'dependence', which for him are always *normative* independence and dependence. On his view, I have a certain *independence* in which commitments I embrace. Apart from my acknowledgment (my attitudes), they have no normative force over me. But in exercising that very independence, I am at the same time *dependent* on the attitudes of others, who attribute and hold me to the commitment, and thereby administer its content. And the others, reciprocally dependent on my recognition, display a corresponding moment of independence in their attitudes of attribution and assessment of my commitments and responsibilities. The actual *content* of the commitment one undertakes by applying a concept (paradigmatically, by using a word) is the product of a process of *negotiation* involving the reciprocal attitudes, and the reciprocal authority, of those who *attribute* the commitment and the one who *acknowledges* it. What one's claim or action is *in* itself results both from what it is *for* others and what it is *for* oneself. The reason that the process of reciprocal recognition, and so the structure and unity of selves, provides not only the *context* of but also the *model* for the institution and application of conceptual norms is that it is not just one example of how norms are constituted by reciprocal authority (mutually dependent moments). *Wherever* a *norm* can properly be discerned, there *must* be distinct centers of reciprocal authority and a process of negotiation between them. For this, Hegel thinks, in line with the autonomy thesis, is the nature of the normative as such.

We have seen that, following the rationalists, Hegel understands concepts, the contents of norms, as essentially *inferentially* articulated. His talk of "mediation" is a way of referring to relations of *material inference*, and his talk of "determinate negation" is a way of referring to relations of *material incompatibility.* How is this inferential articulation of conceptual content supposed to be understood on the model of the sort of reciprocal recognition that institutes determinately contentful norms? By two analogies between (a) *inferential* recognitive relations of reciprocal authority and (b) the fundamental and paradigmatic *social* recognitive relations:

(a1) particulars : universals : individuals as characterized by universals (presented in judgments)

::

(b1) particular desiring organisms : recognitive communities : self-conscious individual selves

and

(a2) particular individual concepts : the holistic inferentially articulated system of concepts that is the Concept : determinately contentful concepts applying to particulars (presented in judgment)

::

(b2) particular desiring organisms : recognitive communities : self-conscious individual selves

The idea is that *immediate* judgments (noninferential reports) express a dimension along which particulars exert an authority over the universals or concepts that apply to them. Mediate judgments express a dimension along which universals or concepts exert an authority over the particulars to which they apply. The process of negotiation between acknowledged authorities upon their disagreement is the process of administering the sometimes opposed authorities of particulars and universals. It is constitutive of *both* the Concept, as the holistic system of all the determinate universals (empirical concepts) related by material inference and incompatibility (mediation and determinate negation), *and* the characterized particulars presented by a set of judgments, a set of commitments that are actual applications of universals to particulars.

In addition to the *social* and the *inferential* dimensions of recognitive negotiation of reciprocal authority, there is a third: the *historical*. It arises because negotiating and adjudicating the claims of reciprocally conditioning authorities, administering conceptual norms by applying them in actual cases (to particulars that immediately present themselves), is a *process*. In that process of experience, conceptual norms *develop*. Hegel wants to insist that if one ignores the process by which concepts develop—what other concepts they develop out of, and the forces implicit in them, in concert with their fellows, that lead to their alteration (what Hegel will call their "negativity")—then the sort of content they have is bound to remain unintelligible. (Compare Leibniz's notion of the expressive development of perceptions as determining *their* content.) The authority of the past applications, which instituted the conceptual norm, is administered on its behalf by *future* applications, which include assessments of past ones. It is for later users of a concept to decide whether each earlier application was correct or not, according to the tradition constituted by still earlier uses. In doing so, the future applications exercise a reciprocal authority over past ones. The reciprocal recognitive structure within which Spirit as a whole comes to self-consciousness is *historical*. It is a relation between different time slices of Spirit, in which the present acknowledges the authority of the past, and exercises an authority over it in turn, with the negotiation of their conflicts administered by the future. This is the recognitive structure of *tradition,* which articulates the normative structure of the process of *development* by which concepts acquire their contents by being applied in experience.

In summary: Hegel's *pragmatism* consists in his commitment to understanding determinately contentful empirical conceptual norms as instituted by *experience,* the process of *using* those concepts by applying them in practice: making judgments and performing actions. Hegel's *conceptual idealism* consists in understanding this process of experience as exhibiting a constellation of reciprocal authority whose paradigm is mutual recognition: the structure and unity of the self-conscious individual self. Thus we are to use the same concepts in terms of which we understand *selves* to understand *concepts*. Reciprocal recognition is for Hegel the structure that makes the normative intelligible as such. The recognitive structure of reciprocal authority necessary to make intelligible the bindingness of determinately contentful norms has three dimensions: *social, inferential,* and *historical*. In its paradigmatic *social* form, it institutes both individual self-conscious *selves* (the subjects of commitments and responsibilities) and their communities (the selves bound together by attributing and assessing commitments to one another, holding one another responsible). In its *inferential* form, this structure characterizes the relationship between particulars and universals in the process of making *judgments* that is experience: the application of determinate concepts. It is exhibited as well in the relations of reciprocal authority by which applications of some determinate concepts condition the applicability of other, inferentially related concepts, thereby constituting the "community" of all determinate concepts, structured by relations of mediation and determinate negation, that is, the Concept. In addition to these two forms of reciprocal recognition, there is a third: the *historical*. It arises because negotiating and adjudicating the claims of reciprocally conditioning authorities, administering conceptual norms by applying them in actual cases (to particulars that immediately present themselves), is a *process*. In that process of experience, conceptual norms *develop*, along with the body of claims or judgments expressing the commitments that arise from applying those concepts. This developmental process of progressively determining the content of concepts by applying them in concert with their fellows is to be understood as the way determinately contentful conceptual norms are *instituted*. The key to understanding this is one of Hegel's most basic thoughts: his way of working out the Kant-Rousseau insight about a fundamental kind of normativity based on autonomy according to the model of reciprocal authority and responsibility whose paradigm is mutual recognition.

IV. Frege

It can seem like a long way from Hegel to Frege, but situating both in the rationalist tradition brings them closer together. At least at the beginning of his career, Frege pursues an inferentialist approach to conceptual content. His seminal first work, the *Begriffsschrift* of 1879, takes as its aim the explication of "conceptual content" (*begriffliche Inhalt*). The qualification "conceptual" is explicitly construed in inferential terms:

> There are two ways in which the content of two judgments may differ; it may, or it may not, be the case that all *inferences* that can be drawn from the first judgment when combined with certain other ones can always also be drawn from the second when combined with the same other judgments. The two propositions 'the Greeks defeated the Persians at Plataea' and 'the Persians were defeated by the Greeks at Plataea' differ in the former way; even if a slight difference of sense is discernible, the agreement in sense is preponderant. Now I call that part of the content that is the same in both the *conceptual* content. Only this has significance for our symbolic language [*Begriffsschrift*] . . . In my formalized language [*BGS*] . . . only that part of judgments which affects the possible inferences is taken into consideration. Whatever is needed for a *correct* [*richtig*, usually misleadingly translated as "valid"] *inference* is *fully expressed*; what is not needed is . . . not.[12]

Two claims have the same conceptual content if and only if they have the same inferential role: a good inference is never turned into a bad one by substituting one for the other.[13] This means that conceptual content is a theoretical concept whose defining job is the explanation of the functional roles that expressions or states exhibiting such content play in a system of inferences. It does not entail that conceptual content must be understood as functionally *conferred on* expressions and states by the role they play in inference (whether thought of as a kind of process or as a kind of relation). But there is an individuational isomorphism between conceptual contents and inferential functional roles. One consequence may be that these notions are reciprocally sense dependent, in that one cannot count as able to deploy the concept conceptual content unless one also counts as able to deploy the concept inference, and vice versa. As with the early modern rationalists and Hegel, understanding the *contents* of thoughts requires understanding the rational relations they bear to one another in a larger constellation.

Frege's *Begriffsschrift* is remarkable not just for the inferential idiom in which it specifies its topic, but equally for how it conceives its relation to that topic. The task of the work is officially an *expressive* one: not to *prove* something but to *say* something. Frege's logical notation is designed for expressing conceptual contents, making explicit the inferential involvements that are implicit in anything that possesses such content. As the passage quoted above puts it: "Whatever is needed for a correct inference is fully expressed." Talking about this project, Frege says: "Right from the start I had in mind the expression of a content . . . But the content is to be rendered more exactly than is done by verbal language . . . Speech often only indicates by inessential marks or by imagery what a concept-script should spell out in full."[14] The concept-script is a formal language for the explicit codification of conceptual contents. In the preface to the *Begriffsschrift,* Frege laments that even in science concepts are formed haphazardly, so that the ones employing them are scarcely aware of what they mean, of what their content really is. When the correctness of particular inferences is at issue, this sort of unclarity may preclude rational settlement of the issue. What is needed is a notation within which the rough-and-ready conceptual contents of the sciences, beginning with mathematics, can be reformulated so as to wear their contents on their sleeves.

Since conceptual content is understood in terms of its specifically *inferential* articulation, what is needed is a way of making inferential relations *explicit*—that is, a way of putting them into a form in which they can be *asserted*. The very first piece of logical vocabulary Frege introduces, the conditional, plays exactly this inferential role. He says: "The precisely defined hypothetical relation between contents of possible judgments has a similar significance for the foundations of my concept-script to that which identity of extensions has for Boolean logic."[15] I think it is hard to overestimate the importance of this passage in understanding what is distinctive about Frege's *Begriffsschrift* project. After all, contemporary Tarskian model-theoretic semantics depends precisely on relations among extensions. Frege is saying that his distinctive idea—in what is, after all, the founding document of modern formal logic—is to do things otherwise. Why the conditional? Prior to the introduction of such a conditional locution, one could *do* something, one could treat a judgment as having a certain content (implicitly attribute that content to it) by endorsing various inferences involving it and rejecting others. After conditional locutions have been introduced, one can *say,* as part of the content of a claim (something that can serve as a premise and conclusion in inference), *that* a certain inference is acceptable. One is able to make explicit material inferential relations between an antecedent or premise and a consequent or conclusion. Since, according to the inferentialist view of conceptual contents, it is these implicitly recognized material inferential relations that conceptual contents consist in, the conditional permits such contents to be explicitly expressed. If there is a disagreement about the goodness of an inference, it is possible to say what the dispute is about, and to offer reasons one way or the other. The conditional is the paradigm of a locution that permits one to make inferential commitments explicit as the contents of judgments.[16]

Frege follows Kant in giving explanatory pride of place to the *judgments* and judgeable contents expressed by whole declarative sentences over those expressed by subsentential expressions such as singular terms and predicates. For Frege, the reason is that declarative sentences are the unit to which the pragmatic force of *assertion* can be attached—they are the minimal unit that can be *taken true*. This is recognizably a version of Kant's seeing judgments and actions as *normative* units: units of responsibility or commitment. (And it is the same line of thought that the later Wittgenstein endorses by taking sentences to be the smallest linguistic unit whose freestanding utterance makes a move in the language game.) This notion of explicitness or conceptual awareness as propositional provides the targeted endpoint for the process of *expression*; for it determines what counts as *saying* or *thinking* something.

We can make sense of this sort of contentfulness either in terms of inference or in terms of truth. For Frege promulgates what we might call his fundamental semantic principle: that good inferences never take one from premises that are true to conclusions that are not true. The reciprocal sense dependence claim implicit in this principle can be exploited in two different explanatory directions. If one already understands truth (as Frege insists we must implicitly do for pragmatic reasons: in order to be able to produce and consume assertions or judgments, which are *takings*-true), then one can use it to sort inferences into the good and bad. If one already understands inference (as Frege insists we must implicitly do for semantic reasons: in order to be able to grasp the conceptual contents of any judgeable content), then one can use it to sort claims into the true and false.[17] Frege himself insisted that one should not make inferences from false premises. For inference is a process whereby one endorses a conclusion on the basis of endorsing some premises. The crucial inferential *relations* among judgeables, which articulate their conceptual contents, can be exhibited by endorsing *conditionals,* whose expressive job it is to make those relations (and so those contents) explicit. In this way, Frege endorses the distinction that underlies the Harman point.

I hope these few general remarks will serve to indicate how a set of rationalist themes can be discerned in Frege's initial approach to the sort of intentionality expressed by sentences and the use of 'that' clauses: propositional semantic content. The two Frege chapters presented here, "Frege's Technical Concepts," and "The Significance of Complex Numbers for Frege's Philosophy of Mathematics," however, concern intentionality in the sense of being *of* or *about* some *objects* (which are not themselves the sort of thing that can be *expressed* by using a sentence). Their common topic is Frege's views about what is required for us to secure reference to particular objects, to be talking or thinking of or about them. What must we do or have done in order to have succeeded in making ourselves in the right way responsible for the correctness of our thought to how it is with some particular object(s)? In the "Perception" chapter of the *Phenomenology,* Hegel explains how one might move from an understanding of the contents of the deliverances of sense in terms of their material exclusion of one another, to an understanding of those contents as having an object/property structure. The key point (a version of Aristotle's) is the observation that a property can have an *opposite* or complement, in the sense of another property that is had by all and only objects that do not have the first. But an *object* cannot coherently be thought of as having an opposite or complement, in the corresponding sense of an object that has all and only the properties that the first object does not have. For even the properties incompatible with a given property may be incompatible with one another. (Being a prime number and being an invertebrate are both incompatible with being a mammal.)

Frege's way into objects is not through incompatibility but through inference. He lays out this line of thought in the *Grundlagen der Arithmetik.* In that work he is concerned to argue that counting numbers are objects, and to show what we would need to do to secure reference to them by logical means alone. Numbers provide a particularly good test case for thinking about reference to or representation of objects generally, for two reasons, one general, and one more specific to numbers. First, the category of *objects* as what is in a particular way reidentifiable and individuatable just is the category of *countables.* So we can hope to learn what objects are by learning what is required for countability. Second, numbers cannot be assumed at the outset to be *physical* or even *actual* objects—ones with which we can interact causally. So we will not be distracted by the details of the sort of causal commerce we can have with physical objects, and must think much more generally about the *role* such commerce would have to play in order to count as performing the functional role of *picking out objects* in the way required for number claims to be answerable to them for their representational correctness.

The line of thought Frege pursues can be thought of as comprising three parts. First is a *triangulation* strategy. In order to count as having picked out an object, one must pick it out in *two* ways. Objects are things that can be "recognized as the same again" when given in a different way. (An object one can in principle refer to only one way is the sound of one hand clapping.) Distinguishing a mode of presentation of an object from the object presented requires appeal to some *other* mode of presentation of the *same* object.[18] Such triangulations are expressed by "recognition judgments": identity claims linking two different singular terms. Thus Frege says that for what an expression makes cognitively available for us to "have a definite character" as an object our judgments are about, it is necessary that "it can be recognized again beyond doubt as the same, and can be distinguished from every other." As a result, "for every object there is one type of proposition which must have a sense, namely the recognition-statement."[19]

Second, Frege argues that numbers are *objects* by arguing that numerals are *singular terms*. What might be called Frege's referential principle is that objects are what singular terms (purport to) refer to.[20] Like the fundamental semantic principle relating the concepts good inference and truth, this principle linking the concepts singular term and object can take the shape of a reciprocal sense dependence thesis, and so underwrite a holism. Given that this one relates the *activity, practice,* or *process* of using expressions *as* singular terms to the *objects,* with their properties and relations, that those expressions represent, this sort of holism would also be an objective idealism. Besides being construed as *reciprocal* sense dependence, Frege's referential principle can be appealed to in the service of either of two complementary asymmetric orders of explanation. One might understand the use of singular terms by understanding them as having the semantic job of picking out individual objects. Or one might understand objects as what it is that singular terms have the semantic job of picking out. Kant had already pursued a version of this second sort of strategy, by approaching the notion of the objects we know things about in terms of the role of representations of particularity via intuition in cognition in the form of judgments. In the *Grundlagen*, Frege follows the Kantian order of explanation.

The third element of Frege's approach is the sort of approach he offers to the key concept in the referential principle. Quine's version of that principle is "singular terms are expressions that purport to refer to exactly one object."[21] He goes on immediately to add that his talk of "purporting to refer" should be understood as only a colorful way of talking about a distinctive grammatical role. Frege says exactly how subsentential expressions need to be used in order to play that distinctive grammatical role. That is, he says what functional role in a system of *inferences* connecting *judgments* they must play in order to qualify as singular terms. The two Frege essays presented here as Chapters 8 and 9 both address challenging issues that arise—for Frege and for us—when one pushes out to the edges from what for the core cases is clearly a fundamental insight.

The key to Frege's strategy for giving a definite meaning to the notion of playing the semantic role of a singular term is the idea of considering the effects of *substitution* of one expression for another. His primary semantic notions are inference and truth. Both are intimately related to what we *do* in thinking and talking by the notion of *judging* or *asserting*. But subsentential expressions such as singular terms do not by themselves *say* anything that can be true or false, or (what is the same thing) can serve as and stand in need of a reason. They are not *directly* semantically significant. So Frege's task is to say how they can be *indirectly* semantically significant, by somehow contributing systematically to the meanings of the directly semantically significant expressions (sentences) in which they are used. He does this by operationalizing the notion of the *contribution* the occurrence of a subsentential expression makes to the significance of the sentences (now themselves construed as semantically compound expressions) in which it appears as a significant component. The idea is that the role in judgment characteristic of singular term usage is determined for each one by the class of other expressions intersubstitutable with it without altering the semantic role of the sentence in which it occurs. Call a one-premise inference in which the conclusion is a substitutional variant of the premise a substitution inference. Then one can think of the *indirectly* inferential role of a singular term as settled by a class of good substitution inferences. The inference from (what is expressed by) "Frege understood quantification" to (what is expressed by) "The author of the *Begriffsschrift* understood quantification" is a good substitutional inference inasmuch as Frege *is* the author of the *Begriffsschrift* (and so is its converse). Intersubstitutability manifests co-reference, and co-reference is understood as reference to the *same* object.[22] The path of explanation is from sameness of substitution-inferential role (a horizontal relation) to each expression referring (vertically) to the same object. In the first Frege essay, Chapter 8, these are distinguished as corresponding to two senses of '*Bedeutung*': as substitutional functional role, determining an equivalence class of subsentential expressions, on the one hand, and on the other as some further thing that is not an expression, and that fixes that equivalence class by standing to all and only those expressions in a further relation of aboutness. The question of how we should understand the relation between these two is obviously of the first importance for thinking about the relation between intentionality as judgeable contentfulness ('that' intentionality) and representational intentionality ('of' intentionality).

The first element of Frege's approach to this issue—objects specified by recognizability, reidentifiability, by triangulation—underwrites a concern with identity as individuation. The second element—approaching the concept <u>object</u> through its internal connections to (sense dependence on) the concept <u>singular term</u>—enjoins attention to the subjective use of expressions in understanding our talk of objective objects. The third element—tracking the goodness of substitution inferences—then provides the means for combining these two. "In universal intersubstitutability, all the laws of identity are contained," Frege says.[23] Nontrivial identity statements play the roles both of expressing recognition of an object as the same again, when given in two different ways ("recognition judgments"), and of licensing all the intersubstitution inferences linking the expressions flanking the identity sign. The force of the Kant-Frege direction of explanation is to understand licensing intersubstitutability of expressions as what recognizing an object as the same again consists in. And since recognizing an object as the same again in the way expressed explicitly in endorsing a recognition statement is not only necessary but also sufficient for referring to it, it is in terms of identities as symmetric substitution-inference licenses that we are to understand what it is to think or talk about objects at all. The form of Frege's metaphysics of representational intentionality is substitution-inferential triangulation.

The two Frege chapters that appear in Part Two ask what it is one must be able to *do,* how expressions must *function* or be *used* (inferentially and substitutionally), in order to achieve a certain semantic result: reference to objects. In its most general terms, Frege's answer seems clear: one must fix the senses of all the recognition judgments in which a term occurs. The recognition judgments are expressed by identity statements linking different singular terms. And the sense of an identity statement is its functional role as licensing symmetric substitution inferences. Both essays concern ways of introducing singular terms so as to secure reference to objects, and both raise problems about reconciling those modes of introduction with Frege's criteria of adequacy. In the first, "Frege's Technical Concepts," the particular process considered is *abstraction:* moving from a field of objects antecedently available semantically (i.e., that we can already refer to or pick out) to a field of new objects, by appealing to an equivalence relation on the old objects. This is the process by which Frege approaches the *targets* of his semantic explanations: to begin with, the counting numbers, and eventually, other general kinds of magnitudes, including rational, real, and complex numbers. But when we ask about the intelligibility and defensibility of the process of abstraction as a way of securing reference to objects, the stakes are particularly high for Frege. For *all* of his own technical concepts, from *Sinn* and *Bedeutung* to course of values, introduce the objects that fall under them by some sort of abstraction. The ultimate aim of this first Frege chapter is to argue that the process of abstraction does not in principle afford us sufficient raw materials to satisfy Frege's criteria of adequacy for introducing expressions functioning as genuine singular terms—that is, given his way of exploiting the sense dependence of object on singular term, for introducing objects—namely, settling the senses of all the recognition judgments concerning the terms introduced by that process. The second essay, Chapter 9, on the significance of complex numbers for Frege's program, considers a different set of procedures for securing reference to new objects, given that one can refer to familiar sorts of objects—in this case, moving from a semantic grip on real numbers to a corresponding grip on complex numbers. The enterprise of the Frege's *Grundgesetze* depends on the possibility of using the expressive resources available at one stage to prove the existence and uniqueness of the referents of newly introduced expressions at the next. But there are serious formal challenges facing such an enterprise.

These two chapters are the only ones in this book that are seriously *critical* of the views I attribute to the authors discussed. The other essays are wholly *constructive:* attempts to make sense of the tenor and detail of the texts by the controlled deployment of a few basic distinctions and commitments. One reason, of course, is that Frege sets out both the raw materials he allows himself and the criteria of success for his semantic enterprise much more clearly and rigorously than any thinker before him. What he is trying to do is much more specific than the very general ways of thinking about content that I was introducing on Hegel's behalf. It also matters that, by contrast at least to Spinoza and Leibniz, we are still trying to figure out how to achieve the sort of result Frege wanted, by using the specific sorts of conceptual tools he introduces. Problems can be raised for the accounts of aboutness I attribute to Spinoza and Leibniz, and we might learn something important about inferentialist, functionalist, holist approaches to semantics, or about triangulation strategies in general, from thinking about them. But the details of the relation between the order and connection of things and the order and connection of ideas in Spinoza, or the expression of many in one by perceptions of a monad, are unlikely to be found in the armamentarium we would apply to work out solutions along these lines today. In any case, the intent in the Frege pieces is not wholly critical. At the end of the second Frege essay, a suggestion is made for loosening the criteria of adequacy for introducing singular terms and expressions generically like them—on the basis of which a way out of the problems raised for Frege's approach can be envisaged.

"Frege's Technical Concepts" is also unusual here in being the most evidently an occasion piece. Its basic structure is that of a review of two books about Frege, one by David Bell and the other by Hans Sluga. I have overcome my reservations about including it here because it uses the innovations of those readings to put in place what seems to me still to be a useful overview of a number of contested issues in Frege interpretation that are of prime importance for understanding the overall structure of his views about the representation of objects. And it is in terms of that overview that I construct the particular challenge to his procedures with which the discussion ends. Bell offers a way into the crucial distinctions and connections that define the system within which Frege's technical concepts—sense, reference, truth value, and so on— play their characteristic explanatory roles. And Sluga contributes a crucial historical framing that makes visible the way Frege's thought on these issues develops from the *Grundlagen* to the *Grundgesetze*. "Frege's Technical Concepts" is in fact an exercise in reading his text, although the first parts of the essay take the form of doing so by reading other readers rather than by reading the text directly. This is the only one of the chapters that has this form, although Radnor is important as a starting point in the Spinoza discussion, as Furth is in the Leibniz one.

The second definition of number Frege considers in the *Grundlagen* attempts to introduce both numbers and the concept <u>number</u> simultaneously, by an abstractive definition. The analogy he offers is to introducing directions as objects, along with the concept of <u>direction</u>, by saying that two lines have the same direction just in case they are parallel to each other. Being parallel is an equivalence relation: it is reflexive, symmetric, and transitive. That ensures that directions, individuated by that relation on lines, will have at least the minimal formal properties necessary for statements relating them to be construed as identities. Frege famously rejects this definition because of what has come to be called the "Julius Caesar problem." The proposed definition would not fix the sense of *all* identities involving directions, but only those of the form "the direction of line l = the direction of line m." I call these "functionally *homogeneous* identities," since the expressions flanking the identity sign each have the form "$f(a)$." That is, each purports to specify an object as the result of applying a function (the direction of, or the number of) to a familiar sort of object. Abstraction, seeking as it does to introduce at once both the values of the function and the function itself, does not settle the truth values of *hetero*geneous identities, such as "the direction of line l = Julius Caesar." Frege responds by offering a third definition, in which it is specified what *kind* of thing numbers are: they are extensions of concepts. Applying this model to the case of directions would yield a definition of the direction of line l as the extension of the concept <u>parallel to l</u>. About the kind (and so the function) involved, Frege offers only a disingenuous footnote saying, "I assume it is known what extensions are." Even though the notion of extension was part of the standard pre-Fregean logical apparatus, this is nonetheless a startling remark. For in the first part of the book Frege savagely criti-

cizes other authors for appealing to primitives they cannot make clear—
paradigmatically, the notion of a unit. And he has *not* defined *this* logical
notion in his *Begriffsschrift*. In "Function and Concept" he later reme-
dies this oversight, defining extensions as the courses of values of concepts. The concept <u>course of values of a function</u> is one he introduces
there—by abstraction. That is, all we are told about them is that the
course of values of a function $f(x)$ is identical to the course of values of
a function $g(x)$ just in case for all arguments x, the values $f(x) = g(x)$.
The Julius Caesar problem with directions remains unsolved for courses
of values. In the *Grundgesetze*, Frege finally does address this issue. In
section 10 of that work, he offers a technical trick for stipulating the
truth values of functionally heterogeneous identities. The main claim
of Chapter 8 is that although this trick can be regarded as acceptable
within the narrow confines of the technical project of the *Grundgesetze*,
when thought of as Frege's final answer to the Julius Caesar problem
about abstraction first raised in the *Grundlagen*, it is fallacious.

In fact, the story is even more interesting. For, as Frege evidently
came to realize, there is a separate problem with abstractive definitions,
which arises antecedently to and independently of the Julius Caesar
problem. It has to do with the attempt to fix the truth values already of
the functionally *homo*geneous identities. It would still be a problem even
if we had a solution to the Julius Caesar problem. It is a result of what
may be called the *permutation* argument. The idea of getting to refer to
(talk or think about) a range of objects by engaging in a process of *abstraction*,[24] if it is itself thought of very generally, is this. There is a function, call it the abstraction function ABS, that takes one from a domain
of familiar objects, and an equivalence relation on those objects, to a
new domain of objects, and a many-one function that assigns elements
of the new domain to elements of the old domain. If a,b are elements of
the old domain D, and the equivalence relation on that domain is $R_\approx$,
then the function f is defined by the abstraction schema:

(A) $f(a) = f(b)$ iff $R_\approx(a,b)$,
         and $D' = \{y: \exists x \varepsilon D(y = f(x))\}$.

For example, let D be the set of lines in a Euclidean plane and $R_\approx$ be the
relation of being parallel to. Then D' is the set of *directions* of lines, and f
assigns each line its direction. Here, then, is the permutation argument.

If abstraction really were a *function,* that is, given an old domain and an equivalence relation, yielded a new domain and function from the old domain to the new one ($ABS(D, R_\approx) = <D', f>$), then it must be the case that if (A) holds for f and $R_\approx$, and if there is some function g on D such that

(i) $g(a) = g(b)$ iff $R_\approx(a,b)$,   then
(ii) $(\forall x)[f(x) = g(x)]$.

For otherwise abstraction does not yield a unique result. We suppose it does, and derive a contradiction. For any D' that has more than one member, there will be at least one function X from D' to D' that is a *minimal permutation* of D' (i.e., an automorphism that is not an identity mapping,) that just swaps two elements. That is, it satisfies:

(a) $X(d_1') = X(d_2')$ iff $d_1' = d_2'$, and
(b) $\exists d_1', d_2' \varepsilon D' [(d_1' \neq d_2') \& (X(d_1') = d_2') \& (X(d_2') = d_1')]$.

For definiteness, we can specify that for any *other* element d' of D', besides $d_1', d_2', X(d') = d'$. Now we can define another function from D to D', by

(iii) $\forall x \varepsilon D [g(x) = X(f(x))]$.

Given the way g is defined in terms of f and X, it is clear that (i) above holds for g, that is, that $g(a) = g(b)$ iff $R_\approx(a,b)$, just in case it holds for f—as it does by hypothesis. If ABS really is a function, then (ii) must hold as well. But it follows from (b) that there are elements of D for which f and g (the composition of X with f) diverge. That is, it follows that:

(iv) $\exists d_1, d_2 \varepsilon D [(f(d_1) \neq g(d_1)) \& (f(d_2) \neq g(d_2))]$.

For all we have to do is pick d_1, d_2 so that $f(d_1) = d_1'$ from (b) and $f(d_2) = d_2'$ from (b)—the two elements that X permutes. Since (iv) contradicts (iii), ABS does *not* define a function. In the example, if f assigns each line the set of lines *parallel* to it as its direction, g could assign each line the set of lines *perpendicular* to it (which are, accordingly, all parallel to one another). Such a g will satisfy (a) and (b). Nothing about the abstraction schema (A) settles *which* function from lines to directions is to be singled out, even if we assume that we know what D', in this case the set of directions, is—namely, sets of parallel lines. Thus abstraction does not suffice even to settle the senses of all of the functionally *homogeneous* identities involving the objects it purports to give us semantic access to.

I said above that Frege evidently came to see this point. It is clear because in the *Grundgesetze*, when he seeks to justify his introduction of courses of values by abstraction (using the schema $'xf(x) = 'yg(y)$ iff $\forall z[f(z) = g(z)]$), his argument explicitly appeals to the possibility of permutation. In an argument that Gregory Currie has rightly called "brilliantly imaginative," he uses the possibility of permutations of the target domain, which causes troubles with the *homo*geneous identities, as the basis for a construction that purports to settle the truth values of the *hetero*geneous identities. That is, he thinks that putting the two problems together yields a solution to both. This would indeed be remarkable if it could be done—but it cannot. The punch line of my essay is that this brilliant argument in fact fails to justify, by Frege's own lights, the claim that reference to objects—paradigmatically, now, courses of values of functions—can be secured by abstraction. As a result, a fatal flaw in the *Grundgesetze* becomes visible that is independent of the *inconsistency* that results from the unrestricted application of Axiom V, which introduces courses of values—even though both stem from that abstractive definition. This failure of Frege's brilliant but difficult argument has not been remarked on, I think, because it has not typically been thought of in the context of the trajectory of problems that runs from the second *Grundlagen* definition of number, through the subsequent introduction of extensions, their reconstrual as courses of values in "Function and Concept," to the final treatment of courses of values in the *Grundgesetze*. Nor, as "Frege's Technical Concepts" argues, is this the extent of the damage. For it also has not been sufficiently recognized that *all* of Frege's own theoretical concepts are themselves introduced by the same sort of abstractive definition. So it is not just courses of values but the intelligibility of Frege's talk of truth values, senses and referents, and even functions and objects themselves that is at risk.

Like Kant, Frege worried about what is required for objects to be given to us in such a way that our thoughts ought to be understood as being *about* them, in the sense that those thoughts were responsible to the objects for their correctness in the sense of truth (what is affirmed in judging or asserting, and conveyed in inference). This is unambiguously recognizable as a *semantic* issue, rather than an *epistemological* one (which is not to say that semantic issues cannot have epistemological consequences). His development and employment of substitutional tools for carving up judgeable contents (believables and assertibles) is an epoch-making advance in our understanding of what it is for it to be *objects* that are given to us.[25] And he set in place a basic and indispensable set of tools for thinking about what it is for objects, or anything else, to be *given* to us, to be semantically accessible. The first Frege chapter argues that Frege's procedure for introducing us semantically to objects by abstraction cannot satisfy his own rigorous criteria of adequacy for being entitled to use an expression as a singular term, that is, *as* referring to or representing an object. The second Frege chapter addresses a different way of introducing singular terms so as to secure reference to objects: constructing expressions in the old vocabulary and deploying it to form complex term expressions with respect to which one can prove the quantified identity statements expressing the existence and uniqueness of the objects they permit the recognition of. The paradigm of this is showing in logical terms that one is entitled to use natural number expressions, but the *Grundgesetze* strategy is to do it repeatedly, to rational, real, and then complex numbers. For Frege, the criteria of adequacy of this enterprise are set at each stage by the requirement that the senses of the singular terms have been fixed, by settling the truth values of all of the recognition judgments (identities) involving it and other terms. The main claim of the second chapter on Frege is that the understanding of the uniqueness aspect of the individuation of objects that is incorporated in this requirement cannot in principle be satisfied for a large range of cases that were important to Frege. Most clearly, the symmetries of behavior between elements of the complex plane and their conjugates precludes unique reference, in this sense, to any of them. The resources provided by the language of real numbers do not suffice to pick out individual complex numbers, in the strong sense of the phrase "pick out individuals" that Frege insists on. And once one has seen this for complex numbers, it becomes clear that the phenomenon arises widely for mathematical objects.

In fact, this is just the same sort of problem that besets term introduction by abstraction. In both cases, the objects supposed to be picked out by the new candidate terms admit of a certain kind of *permutation,* or equivalently they exhibit a certain kind of *symmetry.* The result is a kind of holistic *indistinguishability* of the symmetric or permutable elements—those that play the same functional role with respect to the symmetry. In fact, all that matters is what is *invariant* under permutation, and that is what the lesson of Frege's own use of noting invariance under substitution should have taught. But he demands a stronger kind of distinguishability in order to count as an object to which one has achieved reference—a kind that is incompatible with the presence of sufficiently thoroughgoing global symmetries. The question then arises of how his requirements on individuation might be relaxed so as to avoid this unpalatable consequence while staying true to as many of his other insights and commitments as possible.

The problem is created by the fact that systematically swapping each complex number for its complex conjugate leaves intact all the properties of the real numbers, all the properties of the complex numbers, and all the relations between the two sorts of numbers. It follows that those properties and relations do not provide the resources to describe or otherwise pick out complex numbers uniquely, so as to stick labels on *them* rather than their conjugates. In many ways we can tell them apart, though. We know there are two of them and not one, for instance. And you cannot substitute its conjugate for a number without turning true mathematical identities into false ones—unless you do the same for all the other numbers involved in those identities. So any number can be distinguished from its conjugate by substitutions that turn out not to be truth preserving (substitution inferences that are not good), *if* all the other numbers can be distinguished from their conjugates. We may say that the complex numbers are only *hypothetically* specifiable: specifiable *if* others introduced the same way are. But since the question is about establishing semantic contact with the whole object *kind* exhibiting the symmetries, merely hypothetical specifiability does not provide a way to introduce singular terms referring to objects so introduced. Frege, at any rate, insisted on *categorical* specifiability or distinguishability of objects, by insisting that the truth values of all identities formulable in the combined old and new vocabulary be unambiguously settlable. But if we go back to the original motivations, in the context of the *Grundlagen* project where it is introduced, uniqueness mattered originally because it was necessary for countability—where once existence has been settled, the issue of one or two or more is of the essence. But *distinguishability,* by *local* substitutions that do *not* preserve truth, is sufficient for countability. So merely hypothetical specifiability is enough for this purpose.

The idea, then, is that one might relax Frege's requirements on introducing singular terms, so as to allow genuine reference in cases where systematic permutation threatens it—specifically for complex numbers and other mathematical objects, but perhaps as an instance of a response that is sufficiently general as to apply to the case of abstraction as well. At least for these cases, we might require only hypothetical specifiability. One could think of this move in two quite different ways. One might think of it as involving a sort of *semantic axiom of choice:* once one has picked out (categorically specified) *one* element of a hypothetically specifiable kind, then all the others can be specified relative to it. So we just assume as an axiom that we are entitled to suppose that to have been done. After all, if you ask a mathematician *which* square root of −1 *i* is, she will probably say, "It doesn't matter a bit. Pick one." Alternatively, we might think that there is something wrong with the picture according to which we are entitled to be puzzled about how we would go about "picking one" if nothing about their relation to the real numbers (or, indeed, to geometry) breaks the global symmetry. (The chapter touches on the way this argument develops Kant's discussion of the right and left hands and the semantic problem they might be taken to pose.)

One might think instead that there is just a kind of expression, perhaps another species of the same genus as singular terms in the more demanding Fregean sense, which behaves in almost but not all regards just like singular terms. There are some inferences that go through for terms admitting categorically specifying introductions, but not for those that admit only hypothetically specifying introductions. In order to be entitled to use expressions of this sort, we should be able to keep control over the substitutional inferential commitments their use involves, so that we do not overstep the moves we are entitled to. The difference between merely distinguishable and genuinely isolable objects, between hypothetically and categorically specifiable ones, is the difference between two patterns of substitution-preserving-something: the first if *incomplete* or *indiscriminate* substitution fails to preserve some semantically relevant whatsis, the second if *general* or *systematic* substitution (also) fails to preserve it.[26] So long as we make only the inferences to which we are entitled by the pattern of substitutions that governs the expressions we introduce, we would seem to be as entitled to use this sort of expression as we are for Fregean singular terms. We might think of them as picking out objects of a special kind—a kind the specification of which does not preclude global symmetries. The claim would then be that we *can* establish contact with things of *this* kind, by the sorts of procedures Frege in fact appeals to in the *Grundgesetze*. This possibility would seem to be underwritten, at least in principle, by exploiting the sense dependence relation between <u>object</u> and <u>singular term</u> from the direction of the subjective use of term expressions to the grasp of what objective items they make semantically or intentionally available (the more controversial direction in which to exploit the sense dependences that objective idealism asserts).

It is striking in the present context that in these studies we see Frege's substitution-inferential way of moving from 'that'-intentional expressiveness to 'of'-intentional representation raising issues about the nature and conditions of the *determinateness* of singular term reference and objects, as Hegel raised corresponding issues about conceptual content and ways the world could be. Kant, too, began his investigation of intentionality with the judgment. In his case, that was the unit to start with because it is judgments (and actions) that one can take *responsibility* for— they are the unit of *commitment*. Frege follows Kant in distinguishing sharply between the normative and the natural. His complaint against psychologistic logicians—the empiricists and naturalists of his day— was that they did not distinguish between how people *did* think and how they *ought* to think. They studied processes rather than what provides reasons for normative assessments of them: content. Frege is concerned above all with the *proprieties* that govern inference and judgment, and seeks to understand content as what accounts for them. Frege is even more explicit and clear-headed in his pursuit of semantic issues than Kant is, and he starts by distinguishing his subject matter in terms of the kind of *normative* significance distinctive of intentional content. But Frege is not unconcerned with the activity of judging, just because his ultimate target is the notion of the content that is judged (taken-true, a distinctive sort of commitment). Truth, he tells us, is not definable in a noncircular way, since an implicit grasp of it is presupposed in every judgment. But just because it is—because judging is implicitly taking-true—in judging (and acting, which is making-true), we *do* implicitly grasp the notion of truth, just by being able practically to commit ourselves in asserting and believing. In order to understand truth, Frege says, we must look at what we are *doing* in attaching assertional force to a judgeable content. He does not himself so much as begin on a study of force. He does show us the shape of the explanatory work such a theory might be called on to perform. As Wittgenstein would later see, Frege opens the doorway to that pragmatism about content that consists in a kind of social practical functionalism or use theory of meaning—though he clearly is not tempted to pass through it himself.

V. Heidegger

In *Sein und Zeit,* Heidegger brings us through that pragmatist doorway. There he introduces two structures of intentional directedness: *Zuhandensein,* translated as "readiness-to-hand" or "availability," and *Vorhandensein,* translated as "presence-at-hand" or "occurrence." *Vorhanden* things are what they are independently of their relations to our activities. They are paradigmatically objective items that stand in lawlike causal relations to one another. But more broadly, any *fact*—indeed, any *possible* state of affairs, which can be expressed in a declarative sentence or 'that' clause, anything that is a candidate for being *asserted* or *believed,* any way things are merely *represented* to be—has this kind of being in Heidegger's classification. The broad sort of intentionality or awareness indicated by talk of things being *vorhanden* or present to us comprises all the various sorts of high-end intentionality that we have considered so far in our highly selective whirlwind retrospective tour of a tradition in the metaphysics of intentionality. For in keeping with the rationalist threads we have been tracing through that tradition, the themes that have been put forward as holding that tradition together, our focus has been on *conceptual awareness:* what one acquires by bringing something under a concept, that is, by putting one's response to it in a form that can serve both as premise and as conclusion in *reasoning.* So, for instance, everything involved in the most recently rehearsed Fregean project of using the concept of substitution inference to move from the sort of 'that' intentionality expressed by sentences to the sort of 'of' intentionality expressed by singular terms belongs to Heidegger's category of the *vorhanden.*

By contrast, the availability of *zuhanden* things is a kind of *preconceptual* intentionality. Heidegger's general term for things that show up in this way is "equipment." The readiness-to-hand of a piece of equipment consists in its having a certain practical significance. This significance in turn consists in its appropriateness for various practical roles and its inappropriateness for others. The fundamental structure of the *zuhanden* is practically taking or treating something *as* something. For example, at the most basic level, an animal takes or treats something in practice as food by—as Hegel puts it—"falling to without further ado and eating it up." Heidegger adds to this picture the distinctively *normative* significances things can get by the way they function in skillful human doings subject to social assessment as correct or incorrect, better or worse. What one treats something *as* is as suitable to play some particular role in a practice or process. Hammers are a paradigm of a kind of entity that exhibits this sort of being. To take something as a hammer in practice is to treat it as suitable for driving nails. They are *properly* used in the practice of driving nails, although it is possible to use them as ballast or weapons. The practical norms determining the correct way of using bits of equipment typically relate them to other bits of equipment—hammers to nails, nails to boards, tires to cars, cars to roads, and so on. The *holistic* totality of such practical normative equipmental involvements Heidegger calls "the world."

The practical functional significances that define things as *zuhanden* are *normative* signficances. That is, the practical roles that some item can be taken to play (accordingly as one is disposed to respond to it in specified ways) already occupy a behavioral space that admits of *assessments* along such practical dimensions as proper/improper, correct/incorrect, and successful/obstructed. Whereas what is *vorhanden* has *properties,* what is *zuhanden* has *proprieties.*[27] As Hegel does, Heidegger understands this implicit normativity as *socially* instituted. The first Heidegger essay, Chapter 10, follows out the profound significance this view has for how he understands all the ontological categories.

The classical agenda-setting Enlightenment challenge for the metaphysics of intentionality is to find room in the physical world that natural science describes for the sort of normative features characteristic of conceptual awareness: the way judgments and representations are intelligible as such only insofar as they are subject to assessments of their *correctness.* The question has been, roughly, how to understand the advent of the *zuhanden* in a world that comes only with the *vorhanden* in it. And the characteristic Enlightenment response has been to see normative significances as *our* products, as cloaks of meaning that *we* throw over the intrinsically normatively naked objects (i.e., ones that are in some sense fully specifiable in nonnormative vocabulary) revealed to us by our conceptual dealings with them, which achieve their most sophisticated form in science. Heidegger is interested rather in the sense in which it is our practical nonconceptual dealings with things that form the necessary background for understanding how it is possible for us to achieve the disinterested representational perspective from which we judge or state how things are, without appealing to any particular project we might have for which it matters. He wants to show how *Vorhandensein* is precipitated out of *Zuhandensein*—how the capacity to *say* or *think* anything depends on our practical capacities to *do* things correctly or incorrectly. This is a basic pragmatist project: to explain knowing *that* in terms of knowing *how*, what it is to entertain conceptually *explicit* contents in terms of what is *implicit* in various sorts of generically nonconceptual practices.

One of Heidegger's conceptual innovations is the thoroughly non-Cartesian (and, in that sense, non*subjective*) account he offers of the sort of implicitly normative social practices within which the most basic sort of awareness occurs. (This is a theme that is pursued further in the chapter on Sellars, as it is in both the Hegel chapters.) That fundamental sort of practical awareness is still understood as *classificatory,* in keeping with the tradition he is transforming. It involves taking or treating something *as* something, that is, *as* having a certain sort of normatively articulated practical significance. But the "awareness" which is the appropriation of some bit of equipment *as* having a certain significance is a public behavioral matter of how the thing is treated or responded to, not a mental act. Heidegger develops a kind of social practical *functionalism* about this basic, irreducible kind of intentionality. For Heidegger the confused, broadly cartesian notion of the subjective arises only after the category of the present-at-hand has been achieved, as that coordinate mental realm which must be invoked when one mistakenly takes the present-at-hand as ontologically primary, and looks for something to *add* to it to explain the everyday world of the ready-to-hand. In fact, on his view, we must rigorously *subtract* significances from the ready-to-hand to get the present-at-hand.

Heidegger undertakes two principal sorts of commitments regarding conceptual priority (sense dependence): one concerning the relation between the normative and the factual realms, the other regarding the relation between norms taking the explicit form of rules and norms taking the implicit form of proprieties of social practice. In each case he is turning the traditional order of explanation on its head. His question is how the capacity merely to *represent* things as being a certain way arises out of what we can *do*—out of the preconceptual, prepropositional, prelinguistic level of intentionality, namely, practical, skill-laden, norm-governed directedness toward equipment treated as available. Telling a story with this shape provides Heidegger's response to the challenge about the intelligibility of the possibility of *acquiring* the capacity for conceptual awareness that faced rationalism. It is rooted in the sort of preconceptual awareness we get by coming to participate in an always already up-and-running holistic network of implicitly normative practices. That is what enables us to respond to things *as* having a significance in the sense of playing a functional role in that network. So Heidegger understands the basic, implicitly normative practical sort of awareness as a *social* achievement. The kind of being that equipment has cannot be understood apart from the kind of social being we have.[28] In this respect, the early Heidegger stands firmly in the tradition of the Enlightenment understanding of the essential role the activity of those bound by norms plays in the very existence of the norms.

How is the domain of *Vorhandensein* to be understood as rooted in or precipitated out of the more basic (Heidegger says *primordial*) world of human significances? What do we have to *do* for things to show up to us as having *natures*, apart from the roles they play in our practical dealings? His thought is that what is required is a certain kind of *abstraction* from or dividing through by the particularities of practical contexts and interests. Generically, this is the same mechanism Frege pursued in detail for gaining semantic access to objects of the kinds most important in his account of meaning and representation, as discussed in the first Frege essay. The first Hegel essay describes the importance of abstracting functional roles for his account of conceptual intentionality. Heidegger construes the *vorhanden* as what is disclosed by using a special kind of equipment: *linguistic* equipment. More specifically, it is performances having the significance of *assertions*. Role abstraction is performed by in effect feeding things that show up to us in the first instance practically through an assertional (and in that sense "theoretical") filter. To treat something as merely present or occurrent is to respond to it by making claims about it. Thus for Heidegger the output of perception is assertion. Quite disparate practical contexts—using it as a hammer, using it as a doorstop—are assimilated insofar as they call for the same claim, say: It weighs 5 pounds. A property is abstracted from a set of proprieties.

Assertions are equipment for inferring. The proper way to respond to something (take it or treat it in practice) *as* a claiming is to draw conclusions from it. These moves may take the form of theoretical reasoning, if drawing the conclusion is making a further claim, or they may take the form of practical reasoning, if drawing the conclusion is acting on it by doing something that is not a saying. Heidegger offers an *inferentialist* account of what it is required for something to *count* practically as fact-stating, representational discourse. Attributing to the properties of the present-at-hand autonomy with respect to proprieties of practice is ceding proprieties of justification and inference autonomy with respect to the pursuit of practical projects. The cash value for this is that the equipment used to make claims can also be employed in *hypothetical* reasoning: reasoning of the "what if?" sort. When claims are embedded as the antecedents of conditionals, their assertional force (embodying the attitude of the speaker) is stripped off—and along with it, any other practical commitments or attitudes not explicit in the antecedent. By asserting inference-codifying conditionals, one is contemplating a *content*, something that can then be thought of as imbued with different sorts of pragmatic force and practical significance in various possible contexts. The possibility of merely surmising is thus a sophisticated, latecoming possibility, one that is built on and depends on the capacity to take responsibility for ordinary assertions, which are available, as mere surmises are not, for employment in practical inferences leading to action. The step back that is the bracketing of practical concerns and the achievement of a merely spectatorial theoretical view of things is to be understood in terms of assertion and inference.

The sort of inference-in-assertion that conditionals make possible provides the embedded contexts that generate the distinction between pragmatic force and semantic content. Frege taught us this way of understanding the relation between inferring and asserting as practices or processes, on the one hand, and the inferential relations and truth conditions that articulate conceptual semantic contents, on the other hand.[29] Heidegger uses the same idea in his way of following up the Harman point. Apart from specifically linguistic practice, *Zuhandensein* does not permit embedding of the right sort. The practical distance from things that distinctively *semantic* relations afford—the capacity merely to take in how things are, the capacity merely to entertain thoughts about how they might be—is available only through the institution of equipment with the practical significance of assertings and inferrings. Treating things as having objective properties is attributing to them a distinctive kind of authority: the kind that is claimed in an assertion and transmitted through inference. This is a very different authority structure from that exhibited by *zuhanden* things. By focusing on that difference, we can understand the difference between the sort of pragmatic significances exhibited by *zuhanden* things and the sort of semantic contents by means of which we access *vorhanden* things. As we shall see, this is an important point for understanding the "primordiality" of preconceptual intentionality, for Heidegger takes it that the notion of authority is reciprocally sense dependent on that of its acknowledgment in practice.

Heidegger's strategy for explaining how the *vorhanden* rests on the more primordial *zuhanden* is to describe a social, implicitly normative practice that is a *linguistic* practice in that some performances have the *zuhanden* significance of *assertings* and *inferrings*. (So described, this is pretty much the way I go about things in *Making It Explicit*.) This is rationalism about the conceptual or the semantic, representational intentionality, and pragmatism about the relation between practices or processes and objective representation. At this point it is tempting to see the world of equipment as *autonomous,* as something that could be in place before, or otherwise in the absence of the particular linguistic practices that permit anything to show up or be represented as merely *there,* objectively having properties and standing in relations. If that is right, then Heidegger is putting forward a "layer cake" picture of the relation between the two sorts of intentionality. Conceptual, theoretical, representational intentionality rests on and presupposes a more basic, autonomous level of preconceptual, practical intentionality. If we are sensible, we will see the relation as an asymmetric *sense* dependence relation, rather than a relation of reference dependence. We will not say that before we had the concepts there was no mass, no electrons, and so on. We will say rather that without understanding how the capacity merely to represent things as being a certain way is the result of applying an assertional-inferential filter to things available to us in the first instance as exhibiting various sorts of practical significance, we cannot properly understand what we are *doing* when we *say* or *think* that things are thus-and-so. Heidegger was less than clear on this point, as some notorious passages show.

But the layer cake picture cannot be right. Heidegger is committed to the claim that there is no Dasein (and hence no *Zuhandensein*) without language, without thematizing, without treating things as *vorhanden*. As the passage quoted in the title of the second chapter on Heidegger indicates, Dasein is the being (entity) that thematizes. Another way of putting this claim is to say that the capacity to treat things as extant or occurrent is an *Existentiale,* a permanent and constitutive possibility of Dasein, every bit as much as being worlded is. This is not to say that there cannot be norms implicit in social practices without norms explicit in the form of rules, which determine what is correct by saying or describing what is correct, and hence without linguistic practices including assertion. It is to say that such a prelinguistic community would *not* count as Dasein. In Chapter 11, "Dasein, the Being that Thematizes," I aim to establish this conclusion, which contradicts the layer cake model, by a close textual reading. The argument proceeds in four steps:

1. Dasein is unintelligible apart from Rede (discourse).
2. Rede is unintelligible apart from Gerede (idle talk).
3. Gerede is unintelligible apart from Sprache (language).
4. Sprache is unintelligible apart from Aussage (assertion).

If this is right, then Heidegger in fact is committed to the *reciprocal* sense dependence of the two kinds of intentionality he addresses. The structure of Dasein he is unpacking is a *holistic* one, in the sense given to that term in the first Hegel essay. In fact, one might take it as a lesson of natural science that *Zuhandensein* is also *reference* dependent on *Vorhandensein:* unless there were objective facts statable in assertions, there could not be any social practices at all. Since assertions, according to the story told in the first Heidegger essay, *are* a special kind of equipment, it is obvious that nothing can show up to us as *vorhanden* unless we are worlded. But *what* shows up to us like that need not be thought of as dependent on its showing up to us at all—by contrast to equipment, which can *be* such only by being *treated as* such.

If the sense dependence between these two sorts of intentionality is reciprocal, what becomes of the primordiality of the *zuhanden,* which invited the mistaken layer cake model in the first place? There *is* a sense in which the symmetry between the two is broken, a sense in which the significance conferred by social practices is privileged over representational content. (It is worth comparing this move to Hegel's move from symmetric *objective* idealism to asymmetric *conceptual* idealism.) In Heidegger's case, the key is the claim that "fundamental ontology is the regional ontology of Dasein." In the first Heidegger essay I construe the primordiality of *Zuhandensein* in terms of the *categorial primacy* of the social in Heidegger's story. *Zuhandensein* and *Vorhandensein* are different structures of *authority.* Equipment is what we practically take it to be. If we all use something *as* a hammer, it *is* a hammer. Communal authority is globally indefeasible concerning the practical significance of things (though locally individuals may find themselves making mistakes). The point of the institution of the special significance of assertions and inferences—treating some performances as offering *reasons* for and against others—is to put in place a different sort of authority structure: one according to which the correctness or incorrectness of what we say depends on how it is with the things we are talking *about.* That normative sense of "talking about" or "representing" is that *we* have made ourselves *responsible* to those things or states of affairs; in making claims, we acknowledge their *authority* with respect to the sorts of assessment (paradigmatically, assessments of objective *truth*) characteristic of *Vorhandensein.* And Heidegger is a social pragmatist about authority and responsibility, about norms generally. For the concepts of authority and responsibility are for him reciprocally sense dependent with the concept of certain kinds of social practical *doing*—of performances with the significance of *acknowledging* authority and responsibility, of practically *taking* or *treating* something *as* authoritative or responsible. In this respect, he stands firmly in the tradition of Hegel and his socialized version of what Kant made of the Enlightenment approach to normativity.

In Chapter 10 I discuss this sense in which the category of the social is *primus inter pares. All* the categories are for him at root social in nature, because normative. They are social in the sense given by the claim of reciprocal sense dependence of normative statuses on practical attitudes. The categories ("regions of Being") of *Zuhandensein, Vorhandensein,* and the *Mitdasein* or community through which we encounter others like ourselves must each be understood in terms of their relations to us and our practices.[30] This sense dependence is the reason why fundamental ontology is the regional ontology of Dasein. To understand Heidegger's *ontology,* we must trace out its reciprocal sense dependence on his *se-*

mantics, his account of the metaphysics of intentionality. We cannot understand the *kinds of beings* there are except by looking at the *processes* and *practices* we engage in. The meaning of Being is the being of meaning.

The two Heidegger essays are much more closely integrated than any of the other pairs presented in this volume. Although written a decade apart,[31] they amount to one sustained argument. (The principal mark of their temporal separation is the evolution of the terms used to translated Heidegger's technical terms: from "ready-to-hand" to "available" for *zuhanden,* and from "present-at-hand" to "occurrent" for *vorhanden.*) In manner they most resemble the Spinoza and Leibniz essays. Like them, they pursue an enterprise that requires careful and detailed engagement with the particulars of their authors' terminologies and texts. I think the readings offered there, while intended to be able to stand on their own, take on further weight and significance when viewed in the context of the other essays presented here, and by the application of the analytic apparatus developed in those essays (particularly that of the Hegel chapters).

VI. Sellars

The final chapter presented here follows out a construction central to the arguments of Wilfrid Sellars's masterpiece, "Empiricism and the Philosophy of Mind." Sellars may seem to be the odd man out among the figures considered here: he is not as dead as the rest are, and we have only begun to appreciate that his metaphysics may be as mighty. I have included this discussion of work done a mere half century ago because it picks up in more contemporary form a number of the themes brought into focus by the previous chapters. Beginning already with the discussion of Spinoza in the first essay, the issue arises how to understand the relation between the causal and conceptual aspects of intentionality: between the order and connection of things and the order and connection of ideas. Again in Leibniz we see a detailed constructive account of how apperceptive intentionality is the product of mental processes and inferential relations. The first Hegel chapter pursues this theme as transposed into a socially construed normative key, and the second one describes more fully how the social model of normative statuses in terms of reciprocal recognition brings together the historical/developmental dimen-

sion and the inferential dimension of concept use to fund a novel understanding of the determinate contentfulness of conceptual awareness.
The same problematic is in play in Frege, albeit only negatively. For
the lines of thought addressed in the two essays contained in this volume are defined by the task of moving from concepts to objects (intentionality in the sense of something expressed to intentionality in the
sense of something represented) *without* appeal to causal processes connecting the thinker to what is thought about. In Heidegger the issue
shows up in the form of questions about the relation between implicitly
normative, inferentially articulated social practices and the objective
states of affairs we count as talking and thinking *about* by engaging in
them.

The particular focus of the Sellars chapter is his understanding of observational capacities: the ability to make noninferential reports of, or
form perceptual judgments concerning, perceptible facts. Perception is
addressed in the Spinoza chapter, and becomes the central preoccupa-
tion of the discussion of Leibniz. The role of perception in empirical
knowledge is the topic of the "Consciousness" section of the *Phenomenology,* which is the bit of text I address most directly in the two Hegel essays. As just pointed out, this concern is complementary to Frege's, since
he is concerned to understand the possibility of *non*perceptual modes of
access to objects by inferential processes such as abstraction and domain
extension.

Sellars understands the process of applying concepts noninferentially
as the product of two more basic capacities. Performances can live two
lives. On the one hand, they serve as terminal elements in causal chains
of more or less reliably covarying events, elicited as responses to envi-
ronmental stimuli. On the other hand, they can have the social significance of undertaking normative statuses, paradigmatically *commitments.* What makes those commitments *conceptual* commitments is their
inferential articulation: the way they count as offering *reasons* for and
against further commitments. Observation reports and the perceptual
judgments they express function both as the final results of language entry moves and as the initial positions for inferential language-language
moves. Possession or expression of empirical conceptual content consists in playing an appropriate functional role with respect to both dimensions. The causal chains of reliably covarying events that link
nonconceptual stimulus to concept-applying response themselves get

conceptualized, that is, put in inferential form. For taking someone to be entitled (authoritative) in the noninferentially elicited applications of a concept, because that person is reliable, is endorsing an interpersonal *inference,* from S's judging (claiming) that-*p* to *p.* It is to respond to the claims one *attributes* to the one taken to be reliable by *endorsing* them oneself. So to understand conceptual contentfulness, Sellars adds to the *causal* dimension first the *normative* dimension Kant explicitly brought into play, understood *socially* as Hegel and Heidegger taught us to do, and then the *inferential* dimension that has always been at the core of rationalism.

The three central strategic moves in "Empiricism and the Philosophy of Mind" that I seek to understand in terms of that two-factor approach to observation are: first, the way Sellars dissolves a particular cartesian temptation by offering a novel account of the expressive function of 'looks' talk; second, his rationalist account of the acquisition of empirical concepts; and third, his account of how theoretical concepts can come to have observational uses. The first is his way of working out the rationalist project—brought to methodological self-consciousness in Hegel—of understanding immediacy in terms of mediation. Observation reports have *empirical* content because they are *noninferential* in a sense that has to do with the *process* by which they are *causally elicited.* What I call "basic" or "stripped-down" empiricism is the claim that knowledge of the empirical world depends essentially on the capacity of knowing organisms to respond differentially to different kinds of environing stimuli. (This is 'empiricism' in such a basic sense that no rationalist or idealist has ever denied it.) But observation reports have empirical *content* only because and insofar as they stand in material inferential (and incompatibility) *relations* to other such contents. In *this* sense (a matter of inferential *relations,* rather than *processes* of inferring), *nothing* can be both *non*inferential and *conceptual*ly contentful. Grasping a conceptual content requires taking it to stand in inferential relations. What is grasped must determine the proprieties of making inferential moves.

This is an inferential holism (reciprocal sense dependence) about the conceptual. It follows for Sellars that processually noninferential reports cannot form an autonomous stratum of the language: a language game one could play though one played no other. For *understanding* the reports requires placing them in appropriate inferential relations to other claims. Being able to make language-*entry* moves requires being able to make language-*language* inferential moves. And this is so no matter what the observations evince conceptual awareness of—even the current contents of our own minds. So we can never be in the cartesian predicament, aware only of our own thoughts, of how things look, seem, or appear to us, but unable to fund mediating inferences that would take us from that sort of immediate awareness of purported representings to awareness of some objective represented facts. Sellars deploys the tools provided by the rationalist tradition to curb both the ambitions of empiricism and the correlative dangers of skepticism.

The second application of the account of perceptual intentionality Sellars offers is to the issue of concept acquisition. Sellars's target (like that of the other figures considered here) is *conceptual* awareness. Being aware of something, in any sense that goes beyond mere responsiveness in its potential cognitive significance—paradigmatically in its capacity to serve as *evidence,* as a *reason* for or against some commitment, theoretical or practical—is bringing it under a concept. But where do the concepts "come from"? How is it that they are available for employment in acts or processes of awareness? How do knowers acquire concepts? At this point in the dialectic, as we saw, classical rationalists such as Leibniz threw up their hands and invoked innate ideas—denying that at least the most basic and general concepts *were* acquired at all. Sellars shows that this weak response is not the only one available.

The inferentialism about the conceptual, which Sellars shares with Leibniz, does not by itself address this issue. Sellars's explanatory strategy turns on two further commitments drawn from the tradition I have been surveying. The first is Kant's shift of the center of gravity of philosophical concern from our cognitive and practical dominion over concepts (cartesian certainty) to their normative dominion over us (kantian necessity). The second is Hegel's social practical construal of the norms we bind ourselves with by applying particular concepts. The move is *social,* in that it seeks the key to normative statuses in normative attitudes of *holding* responsible or *acknowledging* authority. This is in keeping with the further Kant-Rousseau idea, which comes out (in Hegel's version) as a *reciprocal sense dependence* claim concerning the concepts re-sponsibility and holding responsible, authority and treating as authoritative.

Sellars takes these two points over in a distinctively *linguistic* form:

grasping a concept is mastering the use of a word. (Sellars sees a one-way sense dependence of thought-content on talk-content.) Making a claim using that word can be thought of as playing a counter in a game. The player need not fully understand the significance in the game that playing that counter has in order genuinely to have made a move that has that broadly functional practical significance. Just so, I can genuinely apply the terms 'molybdenum' or 'aluminum' in claims and thoughts, even though I have little detailed idea of what I am thereby committing myself to. Each of us always comes into an already up-and-running set of implicitly normative linguistic social practices. As young ones, we begin by acquiring practical know-how about making moves that—were we to be held responsible and treated as authoritative for what we are practicing—would be language-entry moves in perception, language-language moves in inference, and language-exit moves in action. As we get better, we come to be *recognized* in Hegel's sense: treated in practice as capable of committing ourselves in judgment and action. In this way, the light dawns slowly over the whole. This is a social functionalism about the normative dimension of concept use. To a first approximation, the noises we make get to be claimings (and so what I am expressing gets to be judgments), in the same way the scratches with a pen on paper can be the undertaking of a commitment to pay the bank a certain sum every month for many years. The difference between making those same marks before and after one's twenty-first birthday is a difference not so much in one's practical understanding of the consequences of playing that counter and so making that move, as they are in the social conditions of being *recognized* as normatively capable.

In this structure, grasping a concept in the sense required to count as applying it in thought and talk can in principle be almost completely decoupled from one's practical mastery of the significance of such application. For to apply the concept is just to do something that makes it appropriate to assess one's conduct according to the norms the concept incorporates—the inferential connections that articulate its content. And the linguistic community need not condition such assessments on one's capacity reliably to distinguish what one is and is not committing oneself to thereby. Isn't it *unjust* to hold people responsible for consequences of their performance that they were not in a position to anticipate? Isn't realizing that one of the triumphs of modernity? The view being pursued here is that underneath the level of moral norms at which such a question is evidently in order is a more basic level of conceptual norms, for which the question does not really arise.

That the normative significance–inducing practices are practices of giving and asking for *reasons* is necessary for it to be *concepts* that are expressed by the words employed. For only in that case do they stand in *inferential* (consequential) relations. From our present vantage point we can understand this view[32] in terms of reciprocal sense dependence claims relating subjective (in a pragmatic rather than a cartesian sense) *processes* or *practices* to objective content-articulating *relations*. So construed, it is the Hegelian view I have called "objective idealism."

Sellars understands the sort of perceptual awareness of external objects that is expressed in observation reports as the product of exercising two different sorts of capacities: the capacity reliably to respond differentially to stimuli (which we share both with merely sentient creatures such as parrots and with merely irritable devices such as thermostats and land mines) and the capacity to take up positions and make moves in a game of giving and asking for reasons. His account of how the causal and the conceptual come together in perceptual judgment is the basis of his metaphysics of intentionality—here specialized to *empirically* accessible objects. We may lay it alongside Frege's complementary account of the nature of our semantic access to the purest of purely *inferentially* accessible objects. The ones Frege was after can be thought of as 'theoretical' in a broad sense. They are not theoretical in the narrower sense Sellars employs, because the specific functional modes of access Frege considered—through abstraction and domain extension—are structurally different from that of theory formation in the empirical sciences. For Sellars, a claim is *theoretical* to the extent to which the *only* way to become entitled to it is *inferentially*. This criterion of demarcation appeals to the *process* by which a commitment is actually produced. The final application of Sellars's two-component semantic approach is to justify the claim that this fact about the process by which knowers get to make claims about theoretical objects does *not* correspond to a basic difference in the objective states of affairs (paradigmatically, relations among objects) they thereby come to be able to represent. On Sellars's account, the difference between observable objects and purely theoretical objects is not an *ontological* difference but only a *methodological* one. That is, it is just a difference in how we come to know things, not a difference in the things themselves. There is no limit in principle, but only limits in practice, to what we can come to observe. For *all* that observability requires is (as always) the antecedent capacity to apply the concept in question (to commit oneself to the right constellation of consequential commitments by using a word) together with the capacity under some circumstances to respond *reliably* noninferentially to states of affairs by applying that concept. Since those circumstances may be quite specialized, including the presence of various sorts of instruments, the conditions on the latter are not usefully to be specified in general terms.

The application of this apparatus that I consider at the end of the Sellars essay is to his account of how what start off life as purely theoretical concepts can come to have an observational use—as the inferential commitments they involve get hooked up appropriately to reliable noninferential perceptual processes and reporting practices. I am particularly interested in a case that Sellars does *not* discuss: *normative* concepts. These are of particular interest in the context of the tradition I have been sketching, since that Kantian tradition treats the conceptual itself as essentially normative. So the question of how we come to know about proprieties, and not just properties, is a crucial one for any normative metaphysics of intentionality.

3

Pretexts

I. Methodology: The Challenge

In this final section of Part One, I want to say something about how I conceive the methodology that governs both the essays in Part Two and the readings of those readings presented here. From one point of view, those stories appear as exercises in bebop history: the familiar orienting melodies show up primarily as background for improvisation on the chord structures of the originals. I believe that exercises in this genre are one kind of valuable and legitimate use one can make of philosophical texts. (Of course, not everyone appreciates bop.) But to say this is not yet to say how we should understand what one is doing in offering such readings. One dimension constitutive of the space in which interpretation takes place is defined by the contrast between, at one extreme, what in jurisprudence are called "black letter" readings—which insist that each attributed claim be backed up by a sentence in the text that explicitly asserts it—and, at the other extreme, the hermeneutic ventriloquism practiced when the author's lips move, but only the reader's voice can be heard. Methodological self-consciousness consists in offering an explicit account of how to understand this dimension, and so of how to assess the distinctive virtues and vices characteristic of the practices it places.

More specifically, I am aware that the relations between the stories told here and my own philosophical views—as retailed in *Making It Explicit* and *Articulating Reasons*—may seem to some particularly problematic. Shouldn't one be suspicious that such disparate figures are all presented as pulling in the same general (congenial) direction? It is one thing for one's background commitments to make a reader sensitive to aspects of a thinker's work that might otherwise go unnoticed. It is quite another thing to foist one's own ideas on the inert and unresisting textual corpses of the helpless dead. The threat of such catachresis is ubiquitous and real. Tradition mongers need to keep firmly in mind the lesson of the scientist's cautionary Heideggerian equipmental homily: "To the man who only has a hammer, the whole world looks like a nail." We inferentialists, true to our Quinean heritage, are not permitted the solace that would be provided by invoking a language/theory distinction at this point. We cannot insist that while we are putting the claims of the author in a different *language,* we are not importing *theoretical* commitments thereby. For we understand a shift of idiom as always involving shifts in substantive commitments—both inferential and doxastic.

I have already offered one response to the charge that the essays of Part One represent a series of exercises in reading my views into a variety of authors: the views were at least as much read out of the authors as they were into them. For instance, before I finished the Leibniz essay, inferentialism had not been visible to me as a possible order of explanation, never mind as one embodied in an actual tradition. Again, the development of my understanding of various sorts of pragmatism[1] owed a lot to the work on Heidegger that became the two essays presented here. In no case were the pieces written with an eye to the metanarrative they participate in. Each was written for its own sake—for the sake of the story that could be found by assembling the texts, vocabulary, distinctions, and considerations that came to seem to me particularly significant. The story I rehearsed in the previous section emerges rather from them. But an autobiographical response is a shallow response; what matters is reasons, not causes.

A deeper response would look to the presuppositions of the challenge. The thought behind it is that the meanings of texts should be *found* and not *made* by interpreters. There is a way of thinking about meaning implicit in worrying about *imposing* a sense on a text, rather than *discovering* one, and it is part of a picture of which we should be suspicious. Enlightenment hermeneutics was thoroughly intentionalist. The author uses language as an instrument for the expression of thoughts that have the content they do independently of any such possibility of expression. Communication is successful if the ideas aroused in the reader have the same contents as those the speaker intended to elicit by those words. One's task as audience is to take out of what is said the same crystalline, self-contained meaning that the author placed there. Thus baldly put, hardly anyone would today subscribe to this picture (though contemporary Griceans come close). And it is no better to recoil, with some romantics, to the opposite extreme by seeing texts as shrinking to mere occasions for the imposition of meaning by their readers—as putting no constraints whatever on the free interpretive play of those who succeed in *making* them mean something (in the only sense in which anything ever means anything) by *taking* them to mean something. Such a view simply assigns to the audience the very same mythical meaning-constituting role the first view assigns to the author. Each is an unrecognizable version of the reciprocal relations of authority and responsibility that articulate the actual production and consumption of conceptual contents. The home language game of the *making/finding* distinction is empirical-practical discourse. There one clearly sees the two normative directions of fit Anscombe identified in her parable of the two grocery lists: the shopper's authoritative for what groceries are correctly bought, the detective's responsible for its correctness to what groceries are actually bought.[2] It is by no means obvious that the *making/finding* distinction applies in anything like the same way to hermeneutic discourse, where the task is discursive understanding of episodes of *concept application,* acknowledgings of inferentially articulated commitments.[3]

II. Hermeneutic Platitudes

Gadamer has developed a hermeneutic idiom that articulates a via media between seeing a text as simply dictating the meaning to be found there, on the one hand, and seeing it as a tabula rasa on which readers are free to inscribe whatever meaning they wish, on the other. For him, meaning is not fixed by the contents of the intentional states of either authors or readers. Such states amount, in effect, simply to more text that is up for interpretation in the same sense as the text they are associated with. They can be considered, but doing so is just addressing a somewhat more capacious text than that with which one started. They provide just one sort of context within which a text can be understood. But there are others.

Another of his guiding ideas is that there is no such thing as the meaning of a text in isolation from its context—at least the context of its reading. A text can be read only from some point of view, in some context. The interpreter's own attitudes and commitments form another such context. Meaning emerges in a *process,* which has the form of a *dialogue* in which the text is just one of the players. Meaning is a product of the words on the page and other features of the context in which it is situated—for instance, a tradition in which it features, or the concerns and questions a reader brings to the text. Understanding (practical grasp of meaning) consists in exercising a practical capacity to adjudicate the reciprocal claims of authority and responsibility on the part of the text and various contexts.

Relativizing assignments of meaning to contexts entails a *pluralism* about the meaning of texts. Texts can be assessed with respect to many different contexts and kind of context. Each provides a perspective on "the" meaning. Or perhaps it is better just to talk about the sort of understanding that consists in being able to navigate with and among these perspectives.[4] Further, the set of possible readings, contextual perspectives, is open-ended. There is no determinate totality of contexts. For each new text makes possible new contexts. This is one reason why each generation, indeed, each reader, must reread and reinterpret potentially tradition-defining texts, and rethink the assimilations and affiliations by which they are put into the context of a tradition. In the present context, philosophical traditions are to the fore. But the point is not limited to that kind of discursive inheritance. As T. S. Eliot wrote in his essay "Tradition and the Individual Talent":

> No poet, no artist of any art, has his complete meaning alone. His significance, his appreciation is the appreciation of his relation to the dead poets and artists. You cannot value him alone; you must set him, for contrast and comparison, among the dead . . .
>
> The necessity that he shall conform, that he shall cohere, is not one-sided; what happens when a new work of art is created is something that happens simultaneously to all the works of art which preceded it. The existing monuments form an ideal order among themselves, which is modified by the introduction of the new (the really new) work of art among them. The existing order is complete before the new work arrives; for order to persist after the supervention of novelty, the whole existing order must be, if ever so slightly, altered; and so the relations, proportions, values of each work of art toward the whole are readjusted; and this is conformity between the old and the new.

The denial of certain sorts of authority to the author of a text (what Foucault called "fetishizing the segmentation of discourse by signatures"), the relativization of meaning to context in a very broad sense, the model of dialogue, meaning pluralism, the open-endedness and mutability of semantic perspectives—I propose to call these by now familiar ways of talking "gadamerian platitudes." By calling them that, I mean not to impugn their originality, but rather to mark that they have, thanks to Gadamer's work, *become* platitudes expressing a select set of the framework attunements of hermeneutic theory.

Calling them "platitudes" suggests that I think we should believe them. But it is even more important to understand them. What is a context, and how does meaning emerge from putting a text into one? Talk of dialogue needs to be underwritten by an account of how each of the parties (text, context) exerts some sort of *friction* or nondetermining constraint on the reading that emerges from their interaction—so that not just anything goes. The gadamerian platitudes are just the sort of thing it seems to me we should want to be entitled to say about the interpretation of texts. But earning the entitlement to the commitments those platitudes express requires real work. In particular, it requires a theory of meaning that can provide a model validating such hermeneutic truisms. Making sense of hermeneutic practice, as codified in the gadamerian platitudes, should be seen as a basic criterion of adequacy of a theory of meaning. And conversely, being interpretable in terms of an independently motivatable theory of meaning should serve as a basic criterion of adequacy of our hermeneutic practice. The principal philosopher who explicitly aimed for this sort of reflective equilibrium between his practice of interpreting philosophical texts and his theory of conceptual content is Hegel. I close this part of the book by indicating how an inferentialist understanding of conceptual content underwrites and explains some of the axial gadamerian hermeneutic platitudes.

III. *De dicto* Specifications of Conceptual Content

The target here is just one kind of interpretation: grasping the *conceptual* content expressed by an utterance or text. Gadamer addresses a more general notion of interpretation, without the restriction to specifically conceptual understanding. My concern here, though, is with specifically *philosophical* texts, traditions, and readings. And for them, I claim, conceptual content is what matters.[5] On the inferentialist semantic conception, we have seen, to be conceptually contentful in the most basic sense is to play a role as premise and conclusion in inferences.[6] Conceptual content is understood as role in reasoning. The sort of understanding that is the aim of conceptual interpretation, then, is mastery of an inferential role: the ability to distinguish what follows from a claim, and what would be evidence for or against it, what one would be committing oneself to by asserting it, and what could entitle one to such a commitment.

The first, most important sort of context for assessing the conceptual content of an utterance or text is, accordingly, its inferential context. For the inferential significance of a claim—what follows from it—depends on what other claims one can treat as auxiliary hypotheses in extracting those consequences. Different sets of collateral premises will yield different consequences. (This is the Duhem point Quine relies on in "Two Dogmas of Empiricism" to argue in effect from the claim that meaning must at least determine inferential role, to the holist claim that the unit of meaning must be no smaller than a whole theory.) If I already know the fruit is a raspberry, then being told that it is red will entitle me to conclude that it is ripe. But if instead I knew to begin with that the fruit is a blackberry, then being told that it is red will entitle me to conclude that it is not ripe. The inferential significance of the claim that the fruit is red depends on the context of background commitments with respect to which it is assessed. The material inferences that articulate the conceptual contents expressed by ordinary, nonlogical sentences are in general *multipremise* inferences.[7] Each set of further premises with which a claim can be conjoined is a further *context* in which its inferential significance can be assessed.

Such a picture is not only consistent but also comfortable with taking it that what really follows from any given set of premises is a perfectly objective matter of fact. If the sample is copper and it is heated to 1083.4° C, then it will melt. In the same way, each text (in the minimally structured sense of a set of declarative sentences) has a definite inferential significance in each context of further claims. Abstractly, nothing privileges any of these contexts over any others; each highlights a genuine aspect of the overall inferential role played by that text, the contribution it makes to the goodness of inferences. Pragmatically, however, some contexts are privileged either by their relation to the circumstances of production of the text, or by their relation to the circumstances of its interpretation (and perhaps in other ways, too, depending on the practices governing the inferential scorekeeping).[8]

One inferential context that provides a perspective on conceptual content of obvious importance consists in other things the author of a particular remark or text believed. Looking at the other commitments an author would acknowledge tells an interpreter what the author *took* it that she was committing herself to by making a certain claim, what she would have regarded as evidence for it or against it, and so on. So it tells us something about how *she* understood what she was claiming. Drawing the auxiliary hypotheses for extracting inferential consequences from a claim from other commitments by the same author, or from the same work, is one natural way to privilege a class of inferential contexts. When such an interpretation of a conceptual content is made explicit in an ascription of propositional attitude, it takes the form of a *de dicto* specification of the content of the attributed commitment. This is the basic form of indirect discourse, in which a claim that could have been quoted in direct discourse is instead paraphrased. In the same Eliot essay from which the passage quoted above is drawn we find:

> Someone said: "The dead writers are remote from us because we know so much more than they did." Precisely, and they are that which we know.

But I can characterize his claim in terms he would presumably have found acceptable:

> Eliot claims that we know more than dead writers did, and that they are what we know.

The idea of *de dicto* specifications of conceptual content is for the ascriber to use words that in her mouth express the same content that the words the target did use or would have used express. Some rules for such paraphrases are clear. If Hegel says in German, "Die Vernunft ist die Gewißheit des Bewußtseins, alle Realität zu sein," I can ascribe that commitment in English: "Hegel says that reason is consciousness's certainty of being all reality." If you say, "I am bewildered by Hegel's claim,"[9] I can ascribe the same commitment in my words by: "You said that you are bewildered by Hegel's claim." Other standards of paraphrase are less clear-cut. If someone claims both that Kant is a great philosopher and that Kant revered Hamann, we might attribute also the belief that a great philosopher revered Hamann, even though that particular claim had not explicitly been made. For it follows, by reasoning we expect the believer in question to accept, from the two commitments that were explicitly ac-

knowledged. But what is one to do where the figure in question explicitly denies what appears to be a straightforward consequence of other
commitments she avows? On the one hand, merely saying that one is
not committed to something does not automatically mean that one is
not, if it genuinely is a consequence of other commitments one has acknowledged. On the other hand, such a disavowal may signal that the
author understands some of those claims differently (attributes to the
sentences on the page different inferential roles) than the interpreter
does. Under such circumstances the rules for *de dicto* specification of the
conceptual content of another's commitments are not clear.

Another dimension along which the notion of *de dicto* content specification is not well defined concerns the exact boundaries of the inferential context one is allowed to appeal to in matching the inferential significance of the reporting sentence (which occurs inside the 'that' clause
of the ascription) and of the reported one (the words the author did or
would use in acknowledging the ascribed commitment). The idea of this
sort of content specification is to extract the inferential consequences
(dually, what would be evidence for the claim) of a claim made in the
text by appealing only to collateral premises or auxiliary hypotheses that
are *co-acknowledged* with that claim. If the boundaries of the text containing the claim being ascribed are themselves clear, and if the text can
be considered as having no structure beyond being a set of claims, then
an interpreter has a reasonably straightforward criterion to apply. (It still
won't be wholly straightforward, for there are a lot of things that won't
be explicitly said in such a text but that are fair game to appeal to in extracting the consequences of what *is* said: truisms such as that there
have been black dogs, that freedom is better than slavery, that thorns can
puncture the skin . . . And issues can arise about the boundaries of the
class of such truisms it is licit to invoke in particular cases.) But if the
text in which the claim in question is made has further structure—for
instance, a narrative structure—then complications arise. For instance:
Is it appropriate to appeal to claims made early in the narrative to interpret those made later? In *Making It Explicit,* the notion of an inferential
role is introduced in Chapter 2 as articulated into the circumstances under which it is appropriate to apply the expression, and the appropriate
consequences of doing so. But in the next chapter this undifferentiated
notion of propriety is further subdivided, in terms of commitments and
entitlements. All the earlier statements then need to be reinterpreted

retrospectively, as one distinguishes between circumstances that would commit one to apply an expression and those that would entitle one to do so, and consequences one becomes committed to by applying it and those one becomes entitled to by doing so. Again, in Chapter 6 of that work the notion of substitution is appealed to in order to extend the inferentialist semantic approach from sentences to subsentential expressions. But we learn in Chapter 7 that the notions of inference and substitution presuppose (it is actually a reciprocal sense dependence relation) that of a token-recurrence structure. Everything said in the earlier chapter is implicitly to be reread in terms of this later notion. So it need not be a straightforward matter to say what, within a single well-defined text, counts as co-acknowledged with a given claim.

And, of course, the boundaries of the text one is reading can themselves be quite elastic. Ought we to worry about whether Hegel changed his mind about the structure and aim of the book he was writing halfway through the *Phenomenology*?[10] Are we allowed to appeal to things he says in the *Science of Logic* in reading things he says in the *Phenomenology*? What about statements of Fichte's with which he seems to agree? In reading *Sein und Zeit*, is it all right to appeal to what Heidegger says in his *Grundprobleme*, since that was written before his famous *Kehre*, but not to the *Letter on Humanism*, which was written afterwards? Different choices of context for *de dicto* ascription of conceptual content may have different virtues, provide different sorts of illumination. The beginning of responsible interpretation must be to make clear just how the boundaries of the context one is appealing to are determined—and so what the rules are for the sort of *de dicto* interpretation one is engaged in.

The motivating idea of *de dicto* specifications of the conceptual content of ascribed commitments is that the inferential context is to be supplied by the circumstances of *production* of the text. One engaged in this sort of interpretation is trying to specify the contents of commitments in a way that would be recognized and acknowledged *as* specifications of those contents *by* the one whose commitments they are. One is to take only the minimal account of the inevitable differences of doxastic perspective between the speaker/writer and the interpreter/ascriber required to deal with differences of language and of indexical situation. There is a way of writing the history of philosophy that aspires to this condition. One seeks to know so thoroughly what an author actually said, how his thought developed over his lifetime, what the rhetorical strategy of each work is and how it was understood by its author as fitting into the oeuvre, what his extraphilosophical concerns, attitudes, and experiences were that one can answer questions on his behalf in something like his own voice. One wants to be able to say what the author *would in fact have said* in response to various questions of clarification and extension. This is the point of view from which it is silly to try to interpret Hume if one knows only his distinctively *philosophical* antecedents and context—if one has not also read Gibbon and Adam Smith and so on. When I was first apprenticed in intellectual history, my mentor explained to me that one could not responsibly expect to understand what a thinker meant by a particular claim until and unless one had read everything that thinker had read. How else could one know what those words meant in his mouth—what contrasts he had in mind, what he took himself to be agreeing with, qualifying, or rejecting by saying that? *De dicto* intellectual history is a demanding discipline. Just having the requisite mastery over everything a philosopher actually wrote is a daunting undertaking for such prolific writers as Leibniz, Kant, Hegel, and Heidegger (though less so for those with more surveyable corpora, such as Spinoza and Frege), even before one has tried to master the traditions to which they owed allegiance and the milieus in which they lived and worked. I have heard specialized uses of the terms defined so that an *expert* is someone who knows a great deal about these things, but only a *scholar* is in a position responsibly to make negative existential claims about them all: "Wittgenstein nowhere says 'Meaning is use'" (though he does say things like "Don't look to the meaning, look to the use"), "No-one before Hegel ever took explaining how one ought to do intellectual history as a criterion of adequacy on his theory of determinate conceptual content," and so on. But inferences that depend on premises of this sort are among those that *de dicto* specifications of conceptual content aspire to capture.

IV. *De re* Specifications of Conceptual Content

The circumstances of production of a discursive text appealed to in justifying *de dicto* specifications of the contents of ascribed commitments provide only *one* important inferential context against the background of which to specify a claimable or believable (but not necessarily claimed or believed) conceptual content. The rules and elasticities I was worrying about above evidence the difficulty of codifying principles for specifying (from an at least somewhat different perspective) what speakers *think* they are committing themselves to by what they say, what they in some sense *intend* to be committing themselves to, what they *would take* to be consequences of the claims they made. But besides the question of what one *takes* to follow from a claim one has made, there is the issue of what *really* follows from it. If I claim that this coin is made of copper, I am, whether I realize it or not, committing myself to its melting at 1083.4° C. Unless that claim is true, what I have said is not true either. To vary the example: if Henry Adams believed that the inventor of the lightning rod did not reside in Philadelphia, and if Ben Franklin in fact is the inventor of the lightning rod, then Henry Adams believed *of* Ben Franklin (*as*, we might want to say, the inventor of the lightning rod) that *he* did not reside in Philadelphia. This sort of characterization of the actual inferential content of the claim Henry Adams made is just what is wanted when one is assessing the *truth* of that claim. For if one has discovered not only that Ben Franklin did in fact invent the lightning rod, but also that he did reside in Philadelphia, then one has found out that what Henry Adams said is not true. One must specify the content of a claim correctly in order to assess its truth. If the right thing to say is that what Henry Adams said is not true, then we must be specifying its content correctly when we say that Henry Adams claimed of Benjamin Franklin that he did not reside in Philadelphia.

That ascription employs what we might call a "denotationally *de re*" specification of the content of the ascribed claim. The rules for such ascriptions are that

T is committed to "S claims of t that ϕ(it),"

just in case there is some term t' such that

T is committed to "S claims that $\phi(t')$,"

where this expresses a *de dicto* ascription in the sense discussed above, and

T is committed to "$t = t'$."

In this weak, merely denotational, sense, if Ortcutt believes that the shortest spy is a spy, and Rosa Kleb is the shortest spy, then although he may have no way of knowing it, Ortcutt believes *of* Rosa Kleb that she is a spy. For he believes something that is true if and only if Rosa Kleb is a spy. Denotational *de re* ascriptions specify conceptual content by saying what it is one is talking *about,* in the normative sense of which object one needs to investigate the properties and relations of in order to assess the *truth* of the claim in question. Thus I can cross the chasm created by the vast differences of belief separating me from the Zoroastrian priest and extract from his extravagant remarks information that I can use as premises for my own inferences if I can specify the content of his claim not only with the *de dicto* "He believes that Zoroaster is granting us his beatitude," but also the *de re* "He believes of the sun and of shining that it is doing that."

The belief specified by a denotationally *de re* ascription and that specified by a *de dicto* ascription are the *same* belief. It is just the belief that the inventor of the lightning rod did not reside in Philadelphia that *is* the belief *of* Benjamin Franklin that he did not reside in Philadelphia. The difference is in the context of collateral premises in which the claim is situated in order to assess its inferential significance. In the *de dicto* case, one draws the auxiliary hypotheses for the multipremise inferences involving the target claim from other commitments the one acknowledging the target commitment would acknowledge. This is the perspective from which one wants to specify the content of a commitment if one is interested in what other commitments the speaker/writer in question would acknowledge, or in what he would do to try to bring about various kinds of states of affairs. In the denotational *de re* case, one draws the auxiliary hypotheses for those multipremise inferences from the *facts* that determine what *actually* follows from what. That is to say that each ascriber draws those auxiliary hypotheses from the facts *as she takes them to be;* that is the best any of us can do. The ascriber's commitments are the facts as she takes them to be. That is why when the ascriber is interested in *truth,* that is, in what she herself should be committed to, what she should rely on as premises for further inferences of her own, she assesses the inferential significance of the ascribed claim from the inferential context provided by her own commitments regarding how things actually are with what the other one is (according to the ascriber) talking *about.*

Once again, the important thing to realize (a point that is explained and argued for in much greater detail in Chapter 8 of *Making It Explicit*) is that the *de dicto* ascription of a belief that $\phi(t)$ and the *de re* ascription of a belief *of t'* that ϕ(it) are not ascriptions of *different beliefs*. They do not ascribe beliefs with different contents. Rather, they specify the single conceptual content of a single belief in two different ways, from two different perspectives, in two different contexts of auxiliary commitments. The significance of the presence of one sentence among the premises of a multipremise material inference—the difference its presence makes to what does and does not follow from the rest—depends on what the rest of the premises are. So in this sense saying what does and does not follow from a sentence must be at least implicitly relativized to a set of commitments that serves as the background against which one is going to assess the inferential significance of the claim in question. The choice of auxiliary hypotheses that distinguishes denotational *de re* specifications of the conceptual content of ascribed commitments has at least an equal claim to illuminate the commitment undertaken as does the choice of auxiliary hypotheses characteristic of *de dicto* specifications of conceptual content. If the colonel orders his soldiers to cross the river within twenty-four hours, he is, in effect, ordering them to do, within the general bounds of their authority, anything that is necessary, and something that is sufficient to bring about the ordered result. If achieving that result requires cutting down sixty trees (and doing that is within the bounds of their authority, or the colonel's) then in a real and practically important sense he has ordered them to cut down the trees, whether or not he has thought about the matter or even would accept that that is a consequence of his order.

It follows from this way of thinking about meaning that besides encompassing *de dicto* intellectual historiography, we ought also to acknowledge the legitimacy of *de re* textual interpretations. These will be specifications of the very same conceptual contents that are specified by *de dicto* ascriptions. But in the *de re* case, those contents are specified from a different point of view: from the context provided by collateral premises that are, from the point of view of the ascriber, *true*. *De re* specifications of conceptual content attempt to say what *really* follows from the claims made, what is *really* evidence for or against them, and so what the author has *really* committed herself to, regardless of her opinion about the matter. The *de re* style of intellectual historiography requires laying *facts* alongside the claims of the text, in extracting consequences, assessing evidence, and so delineating their conceptual content. Responsibility for justifying these auxiliary hypotheses rests with the ascriber, rather than with the one to whom the commitments whose contents are being specified are ascribed. So if Russell can establish that there are at least two things one can mean by "X is a part of Y"—one corresponding to set membership and the other to inclusion as a subset—he is entirely justified in querying Plato to see what can be made of various of his claims when we distinguish the two senses. (The most devastating outcome would be to find that on occasion he uses the term 'part' with the circumstances of application appropriate to one of the senses, but drawing consequences from that application that are appropriate only to the other.) If Sellars can establish that 'experience' can be used either to mean the act of experienc*ing* something or the content that is experienc*ed,* then he is justified in interrogating Berkeley's arguments to see which of them can be made out with one consistent interpretation of the term.

The essays in Part One include exercises in both *de re* and *de dicto* interpretation. The second Heidegger chapter, for instance, is pretty pure *de dicto* reading—even though it is unclear to what extent Heidegger was aware of the conclusion I insist is an immediate consequence of his avowed commitments. At the other end of the spectrum, the first Hegel chapter is basically a *de re* reading. It crucially depends on claims that *I* undertake—the Harman point, the fact that (material or formal) consequence relations can be defined in a natural way from (material or formal) incompatibility relations, and so on—without claiming that Hegel would have acknowledged them. The first Heidegger chapter depends crucially on importing a pragmatist claim about the social nature of authority, in delineating his abstract categories. In some intermediate cases, the provenance of the auxiliary hypotheses is more equivocal. The global symmetry of the complex plane is the primary *fact* in the light of which I assess Frege's logicist and semantic projects in the second Frege essay. The criticisms that result would apply whether or not Frege was aware of this fact. But he understood that fact as well as anyone— although if I am right he evidently did not think through its inferential significance as a context in which to assess some of his other central commitments. By contrast, Frege evidently had *not* appreciated the permutation argument concerning abstraction when he wrote the *Grundlagen,* and evidently did not appreciate the subtler facts about the limitations of the argument form he used to respond to that argument in the *Grundgesetze.* Again, the Distal Constraint on an account of intentionality—that it is a fundamental criterion of adequacy on such a theory that it explain how we can be aware of, or think about, things outside of our own bodies—reflects *our* acknowledgment of an obvious fact. It would be fair to assess Spinoza's and Leibniz's theories by this measure, independently of their acknowledgment of it. In fact, they surely would have acknowledged it as a constraint, even if they do not talk about it as such in their texts.

A generation ago the history of philosophy tended strongly toward *de re* readings. (One might think in this connection of the vastly influential works by which Strawson and Bennett for the first time made Kant's theoretical philosophy into respectable topics for analytic philosophers.) If I read the sociology of the current situation correctly, there has been a substantial backlash to this practice, in favor of immensely patient and textually informed *de dicto* readings. I hope it is clear that I do not think there is anything wrong with going about things this way. But it is a mistake to think that one or the other of these styles of content specification *gets things right* in a way the other does not. Both are wholly legitimate ways of specifying the contents of the very same conceptual commitments expressed by the words on the page. It is only if one masquerades as the other, or is just unclear about the rules it acknowledges in selecting auxiliary hypotheses—that is, about the inferential context it is operating in—that error or confusion results. The response counseled by recognition of the essentially perspectival character of conceptual content construed as inferential role is irenic, tolerant, and pluralist: let a hundred flowers blossom.

And notice that in each case, once the context from which collateral premises are to be drawn has been specified, there can be an equally objective matter of fact concerning what the inferential significance of a textual claim is relative to that context. That is, *de dicto* and *de re* readings can both be assessed as to their correctness in specifying conceptual content relative to a context. We can disagree and make mistakes about, investigate, and resolve disputes concerning what actually follows from what is said, once a context is specified from which to draw our auxiliary hypotheses. And the same can be said for our inclusion of various claims in such a context, once the *kind* of context (*de dicto* or *de re*) has been settled. For one must *justify* the attribution of a given claim as one the author did or would acknowledge commitment to, that is, must justify taking it to be a licit collateral premise in the *de dicto* case. And the ascriber must *justify* each claim he takes to be true, that is, must justify taking it to be a licit collateral premise in the *de re* case. The fact that one can independently and individually assess the rational warrants for attributing (in the *de dicto* case) or endorsing (in the *de re* case) the claims that make up the inferential context with respect to which conceptual content is specified means that these claims provide *friction* for and *constraint* on that process. In this respect, at least, they play a role in hermeneutic discourse analogous to that played by noninferential observation reports in empirical discourse. It should at any rate be clear that the relativity of specifications of conceptual content to inferential context as here construed in no way has as a consequence that "anything goes" or that the meaning of a particular text is wholly indeterminate or "up for grabs."

We are now in a better position to understand why the distinction between extracting what is already a fully formed inferential significance from a text, on the one hand, and foisting one on it from the outside, on the other, is unhelpful in thinking about the conceptual hermeneutic enterprise. Such applications of a making/finding distinction are inappropriate in light of the relativity of inferential significance to a context of collateral commitments. The conceptual content of a claim can in principle be specified only against the background of some such set of commitments. The interpreter has considerable choice in selecting such a context or inferential perspective. But once such a point of view has been selected—paradigmatically, once the choice has been made to offer a particular variety of *de dicto* or *de re* content specification, and so to privilege a particular inferential context—then it is not at all up to the ascriber what the significance of the claims in question is in the chosen context. The context is, if you like, made; but then the inferential significance of a text in that context is found. The perspectival character of conceptual content ensures that both moments, making and finding, will be in play in any ascription.

In this particular way, and for the special (but central) case of *conceptual* content, the inferentialist theory of meaning of *Making It Explicit* explicates and justifies the gadamerian denial that the making/finding distinction confronts the theorist of textual interpretation with a genuine dilemma. In this same sense (explication and justification for a central but special case), that theory can be seen to underwrite the other large-scale hermeneutic claims I picked out earlier as "gadamerian platitudes." Authorial intentions play a privileged role in *de dicto* specifications of conceptual content. (Though, of course, different sorts of *de dicto* ascription may assign this privilege differently: New Critical readings may restrict us to the words on the page, for some way of drawing the boundaries around the text considered. Others may allow into the context other texts or remarks of the same author, or even other things we can infer about her attitudes.) But this is because the claims the author acknowledges commitment to serve to define the contexts with respect to which a content specification counts as *de dicto*. It is *not* because those contexts are themselves privileged in that they provide specifications of conceptual content that are more correct, adequate, or true than *de re* specifications done from the point of view provided by other contexts. All contexts define in principle equally valid perspectives from which to specify the conceptual content of a claim. Authorial intentions, whether stated by the author or inferred by an interpreter, provide just *one* sort of context against the background of which inferential significance can be assessed. Any general privileging of *de dicto* over *de re* ascriptions must be rooted in pragmatic, rather than semantic, considerations—and here by 'pragmatic' I mean the vulgar sense of relativity to the purposes, interests, and plans of the interpreter.

This hermeneutic consequence of inferential semantic theory results from its perspectival character. And that is to say that the denial of certain kinds of authorial authority is a consequence of the analogue within that theory of conceptual content of the gadamerian relativization of meaning to context, in a sense broad enough to include the commitments acknowledged by the interpreter, as well as those acknowledged by the producer of a text. What I have called the "perspectival character" of inferential roles (and hence of conceptual contents) is that the inferential significance of a claim—paradigmatically, what new consequential commitments result from undertaking such a commitment— is primarily a matter of its role in *multipremise* inferences. Since we have many choices concerning those collateral premises, each of which yields a genuine inferential significance of the claim, and so a genuine perspective on its inferential role, there are many contexts with respect to which its content can be specified in ascriptions. This conceptual perspectivism accordingly underwrites the interpretive *pluralism* that is another hallmark of gadamerian hermeneutics. For the same reason, at least in the specific case of *conceptual* content, the inferentialist approach to meaning offers a justification of the claim of the *open-endedness* of the sort of semantic interpretation one undertakes in specifying the content of a commitment one ascribes to another. Every new text provides a new context, against the background of which one might assess the inferential significance of any given claim.

V. Tradition and Dialogue

One context that is of particular significance for the enterprise in which I have been engaged in Part One of this work is that of the *tradition* in which one situates a particular text. Establishing such a context—the sort of thing I was trying to do in Chapters 1 and 2—is itself no negligible accomplishment. As Eliot says in the essay quoted above: "Tradition . . . cannot be inherited. If you want it you must obtain it by great labour." Here one supplements the words on the page by further claims made by others whom the interpreter, but not necessarily the authors involved, sees retrospectively as engaged in a common enterprise, as developing common thoughts or concepts. One might treat such ascriptions *de traditione* as another species, besides ascriptions *de dicto* and *de re.* I prefer to use '*de re*' generically, to refer to *any* ascription relative to a context (from a point of view) that is *not* restricted to commitments the interpreter takes it would be acknowledged by the author of the text—that is, to use it as the complement to '*de dicto*'. The paradigmatic case, where the further commitments defining the inferential context are those acknowledged by the interpreter, can then be marked out as *immediate de re* ascriptions. If at least some of the collateral commitments appealed to in extracting inferential significances are ones the interpreter *attributes* but does not *acknowledge,* then the *de re* specification of conceptual content can be said to be *mediated* by those attributions. In the important special case of ascriptions *de traditione,* the context is a mixed one. For delimiting a tradition involves both *undertaking* commitments concerning the relations of various texts one to another, and *attributing* commitments on the basis of what is said in those tradition-defining texts. The reason for adopting this generic use of '*de re*' is that in producing a specification of conceptual content from the point of view provided by any arbitrary context of collateral commitments, the interpreter must, among other things, do what he would do if those commitments *were* his own and he were making an immediate *de re* ascription. The interpreter must, in all but the *de dicto* cases, in this sense implicitly adopt the perspective from which the content specification is being offered. As the mixed attitudes essential to ascriptions *de traditione* show, however, this is by no means all that can be going on in mediated *de re* ascriptions. Further structure of various sorts may also be significant. Because of their distinctive deontic structure, ascriptions *de traditione* are a particularly significant kind of mediated denotational *de re* ascription, and deserve their own designation.

One central and characteristic gadamerian trope presents interpreting a text as engaging in a kind of *dialogue* with it. This is a way of talking about a distinctive structure of reciprocal authority exercised by, and reciprocal responsibility incumbent on, interpreter and interpreted. Once again, for the case of specifically conceptual interpretation, thinking about a context of collateral commitments as what relates conceptual content to inferential significance and thereby supplies the necessary background for specifications or characterizations of such contents in explicit ascriptions offers a dialogical model with a further articulated structure. It is worth applying one of the basic thoughts of the first Hegel chapter in Part Two here: taking account of the difference between dialogical relations and dialogical processes, and thinking a bit about the relations between them. *De re* readings of any sort are inherently dialogical in a relational sense. First, they commingle premises from two different sources (voices, in an extended sense). In this sense, each of them has its "say." For the collaboration of the commitments of the two as it were interlocutors consists in their relation to their joint inferential consequences. The consequences they lead to are in general common in the sense that the support of each is required for the conclusion, rather than in the sense of being shared, that is, already a consequence of what is drawn from each source. They are shared in the sense in which Fred and Ginger share a dance (something intelligible only in terms of what they are both doing), though they are moving differently, rather than in the sense in which soldiers marching in step share a gait. Something emerges inferentially from the collaboration of premises that was not contained in any of them apart from its fellows—though such consequences may be thought of as *implicit* already in the premise, in the perspectival sense that it *would* follow if the premise is set in the right context.

There are dialogical processes and practices in play, too. Interpretation in the sense of interpreting is a kind of doing. Even in the case of *de dicto* readings, the consequences of a set of premises must be extracted by the interpreter. In *de re* readings, by drawing conclusions from the text in the context, the interpreter is actively mediating between two sets of commitments. Text-and-context on the one hand, and interpreter on the other, both have their distinctive roles. Still, the interpreter's activity is responsible to the actual inferential relations. Except for the important case of immediate *de re* readings, then, the interpreter's own commitments make a difference to the outcome only if she makes a mistake—if she does not know or cannot figure out what really follows from what. (Of course we are often in that position. But that fact is not germane in the present context.) This is a consequence of the inferentialist semantic externalist claim that what really follows from what is not restricted to what is envisaged by the one having the belief or making the claim (or indeed, by anyone else).

The most important notion of hermeneutic dialogue underwritten by inferentialist semantics is a different one, however. For according to the development of that view in *Making It Explicit,* practical *grasp* or *understanding* of conceptual content is the ability to *navigate* and *negotiate* between the different perspectives from which such a content can be interpreted (implicitly) or specified (explicitly). This is the kind of know-*how* that knowing, believing, or claiming *that* consists in. It is the capacity to move back and forth between the perspective-relative inferential significances made explicit in *de dicto* and *de re* specifications of one and the same conceptual content. When one can say both "S believes that a bunch of bloodthirsty fanatics occupied the village," and "S believes of a bunch of gallant freedom fighters that they occupied the village," one is calibrating claims (and concepts applied therein) according to the different doxastic perspectives of the author and the target of the ascriptions in a way that makes clear what inferential significance as premises they would have for each.[11] Mapping different inferential significances, relative to distinct contexts, onto one another in this way is what taking them to be expressions of the same conceptual content consists in. For once again, it is the *same* conceptual content that is being attributed by the two ascriptions. (This is why the stories told in Part Two can be tales of the mighty dead in both the subjective and objective genitive readings of 'of': both offering renderings of stories told *by* the mighty dead, and themselves being stories *about* the mighty dead.) Grasp of conceptual content in this sense is essentially dialogical, even in cases where one or more of the contexts in question is not associated with an interlocutor authorized to engage on its behalf in processes of expounding, expatiating, and answering for it.

This is the way mediated denotational *de re* ascriptions of the sort I have been calling *de traditione* are dialogical. The understanding they express involves "talking with a tradition" in a dual sense. One corresponds to an instrumental sense of 'with'. An interpreter employs the tradition as a means of expression, a way of specifying the contents, claims, and texts it comprises. For one uses the commitments characteristic of the tradition as tools to extract from them an inferential significance—one perspective on a conceptual content. In the species of *de traditione* reading that are concerned with virtual semantic influence of the sort provided by any sort of context, rather than with actual causal influence, one may appeal to later developments in characterizing earlier ones—as I have done liberally in the tradition-contexted readings of the readings of Part Two presented in Chapter 2. But there is also a conversational sense of 'with' in which one can talk with a tradition. The sort of understanding that is made explicit in immediate *de re* characterizations of the claims and texts a tradition comprises is a *critical* one. For it is manifested in the process of moving back and forth between the perspective provided by the tradition and what is true (according to the ascriber): the commitments the ascriber herself is prepared to undertake and defend. This is the form in which one engages a tradition in a dialogue aimed at deciding what commitments one ought oneself to undertake.

A conceptual perspective or context can be called 'phenomenological' in a hegelian sense if it is *both* a retrospective interpretation of a text *de traditione and* an immediate *de re* reading—that is, when it is one in which the ascriber herself occupies the most developed position in the tradition: the inheritance structure of phenomenal views. What I do in Chapters 1 and 2 is supposed to be a bit like this. If in addition the context is one that contains logical expressive resources sufficient to make explicit the semantic contents articulating those views—not just mapping expressions with one inferential significance onto those with another, across contexts, but *saying* what follows from what—then the perspective is of the kind Hegel classifies as "Absolute Knowing." My methodological remarks in this chapter are gestures intended to begin backing up the thought that a suitable inferentialist idiom might supply such expressive resources.

The inferentialist theory of meaning that underwrites the gadamerian platitudes is itself an episode in the tradition in which I have been situating the figures discussed in Part Two, as brought into focus by the stories told there. It provides a context for an immediate *de re* reading that is also a retrospective *de traditione* reading. For it, too, amounts to a metaphysics of intentionality. Even from the attenuated sketch offered here it is clear that a perspectival inferential semantics addresses the relation between the expressive and the representational species of intentional contentfulness: what we are saying or thinking and what we are talking or thinking *about*. The first is made explicit by using 'that' clauses, and the second by using 'of' or 'about'. But the senses of these terms that play this expressive role (by contrast, for instance, to the 'that' of demonstration, the 'of' of possession, and the 'about' of approximation) are just those employed in the regimentations of *de dicto* and *de re* ascriptions we have been employing. The difference between what is expressed by the content specifications of these two sorts of ascriptions can in turn be explained by the dependence of inferential significance on a context of auxiliary hypotheses to be conjoined with it in multipremise inferences. We understand the *relation* between what now appear as the expressive and the representational *dimensions* of intentionality in terms of the *process* of navigating between the different perspectives or contexts specified by different potential interlocutors. This is the dialogical, because perspectival, structure of the practical capacity that is inferential understanding.

VI. Reconstructive Metaphysics

Thus far, I have been talking about different ways in which one can specify one and the same conceptual content, corresponding to different perspectives from which it can be viewed or different contexts in which it can be set. Besides acknowledging and exploiting this dimension of variation, though, the particular genre of metaphysical reading practiced in both parts of this book employs another in seeking systematic illumination of the texts addressed. For the methodology pursued here is explicitly *reconstructive*. It approaches the conceptual contents of textual claims by a method of selection, supplementation, and approximation that locates those contents by means of a grid that, except in limiting cases, is always too coarse to place them exactly.

A reading of this sort addresses a particular target set of claims, concepts, and distinctions. In all the essays considered here, that target includes some philosopher's claims about intentional or semantic phenomena, and the particular conceptual apparatus that philosopher deploys to discuss those phenomena. Picking out such a target may involve selection of passages and claims within the texts being considered. Thus the Leibniz chapter, for instance, concerns itself only with a subset of the claims that he makes in his *New Essays,* and the Spinoza chapter addresses only a small fraction of the picture presented in the *Ethics.* The topic in each of these cases is specifically claims about the mechanisms underlying our capacity to think or represent various kinds of things. In the first Heidegger chapter, the categorial distinction between *Zuhandensein* and *Vorhandensein* is one of the primary explanatory targets, and in the second Hegel chapter, the analogy between concepts and self-conscious selves plays that same role. As was indicated by the discussion of *de re* readings, there is no reason why the target claims need be restricted to *de dicto* characterizations of what appears in the text. External criteria of adequacy, perhaps drawn from the interpreter's view of the phenomena (as in immediate *de re* interpretation), may be included as criteria of adequacy. Thus the Distal Constraint deserves to be in the explanatory target of a reading of Leibniz's or Spinoza's metaphysics of intentionality, independently of his acknowledgment of it. For a semantic account that could not underwrite the possibility of our thinking about things outside our own bodies would be crippled. The target of a reconstructive reading is determined by first *selecting* from the texts in question, and then possibly *supplementing* them. Each of the essays in Part Two takes as its target a topic (an aspect of intentionality) that is sufficiently central and significant in the work of the figure in question that one could hope to use an understanding of it as a base camp from which to explore other important regions. The success of each should be assessed by its usefulness as a backbone to support and orient further readings.

The next step in such a reading is further selection. Within the view that has been taken as a target, a few claims are taken by the interpreter as central, basic, or fundamental. An example would be the role played by associating inferential expressive ranges with perceptions in the Leibniz essay. Another is the introduction of new concepts by abstraction in the first Frege essay. The aim is to strip down the target claims to a core set, on the basis of which it is then possible to reconstruct all the rest. Once again, supplementation may be needed after this selection. Thus the distinctions between reference dependence and sense dependence, and again between inferential relations and inferential processes, are crucial elements in the interpretive raw materials deployed in the first Hegel chapter. An account of assertion is used to similar effect in the first Heidegger chapter.

The next stage of the reconstructive reading is then to use the selected and supplemented raw materials to define the concepts and derive, by multipremise inferences, the claims of the selected and supplemented target. The point of getting clear, crisp versions of the concepts and claims that have, by an exercise in differential emphasis, been picked out as central, is to see how many of the more specific doctrines can then be *translated* into this spare but controlled idiom. Thus, for instance, in the first Heidegger chapter, the concept of presence-at-hand or occurrence is explicated in terms of an account of readiness-to-hand or availability, together with a story about what it is for some bit of equipment to play the role of assertions or mere representations. In the second Hegel chapter, the idea of synthesizing social substance and self-conscious selves by mutual recognition is deployed to explain the sense in which concepts can be understood as determinate. And in the Sellars chapter, the two components into which his account of observation and perception has been analyzed—reliable differential responsive dispositions and inferential proprieties concerning word use—are shown to be sufficient by themselves to underwrite three of the central arguments of "Empiricism and the Philosophy of Mind." In each of these cases, elements of the explanatory raw materials are assembled in new ways, to *construct* versions of the target claims. The triangulation strategy employed in the Leibniz chapter, the set-theoretic constructions in the first Hegel chapter and the two on Frege, the social story about the categories and the way the notion of equipment is specialized to the inferential case in the first Heidegger story—all these produce from the raw materials conceptual machinery that grinds out the target textual concepts and claims. They are, as it were, elements of the inferential vector space spanned by the basis vectors that are the interpretive raw materials.

The supplementation of the selected interpretive basis is conducted with an eye to this subsequent phase of the process. Two processes belonging to the same broad genus, with which it may be useful to compare and contrast this one, are model completion in mathematics and the postulation of theoretical entities in empirical science. Adding elements to a mathematical structure can make it more regular and better behaved—as sequentially acknowledging negative, rational, real, and complex numbers brings with it the possibility of finding roots for ever larger classes of polynomials. Again, we can work with much simpler laws of nature if we fill out our ontology by recognizing objects that are not observable by us. The hermeneutic case is distinguished from these by the fact that its *objects,* and not merely the claims and concepts the theory itself deploys, are conceptual contents. This means that what one is projecting from the supplemented-selected basis is inferential roles. Some contexts in which a basis claim can be situated afford perspectives in which it is possible to derive more of the target claims than others do. That is one reason why supplementation is often wanted to improve the possibilities of modeling the inferential roles of target claims and concepts.

Finally, one assesses the adequacy of the reconstruction. Is the functionalist suggestion for what Spinoza means by *scientia intuitiva* sufficient to underwrite the various claims he makes about this form of understanding? Do the various senses of 'distinctness' reconstructed ultimately from expressive perceptual ranges do justice to the use Leibniz wants to make of them? Do the notions of objective idealism and of conceptual determinateness that result from the two Hegel chapters fit well with other things Hegel says? Are the aspirations with respect to which Frege's arguments are found wanting (because those aspirations are not satisfiable by constructions from the raw materials deemed available) recognizably central to his aims? Do the pragmatist readings of *Zuhandensein, Vorhandensein,* and *Dasein* support the distinctions and relations among them that Heidegger insists on? Can Sellars's arguments really be understood in terms of the simple account of observation that provides the raw materials for their reconstruction?

This sort of stripping down and building back up—a process whose motto is "reculer pour mieux sauter"—is a form of understanding. When I was a graduate student, my teacher David Lewis advocated a picture of philosophy like this. The way to understand some region of philosophical terrain is for each investigator to state a set of principles as clearly as she could, and then rigorously to determine what follows from them, what they rule out, and how one might argue for or against them. The more disparate the starting points, the better sense the crisscrossing derivational paths from them would give us of the topography of the landscape they were embedded in. What is recommended is *hermeneutic triangulation:* achieving a kind of understanding of or grip on an object (a conceptually articulated content) by having many inferential and constructional routes to and through it. The more paths one knows through the wood, the better one knows one's way around in it. Commitment to this sort of methodology made Lewis exhilaratingly willing to think through the wildest possible premises. (I remember extensive discussions on a thought of Pavel Tichy's: that perhaps there is some number *n* such that it is a necessary truth that each world contains exactly *n* objects.[12] The fact that one cannot come up with the slightest reason to think this claim might be true does not mean one would not learn anything from thinking through what would follow if it were.) In its most extreme form, this sort of pluralism is prepared to be completely indiscriminate about the conceptual raw materials that provide its premises. But one need not go that far in order to appreciate the sort of illumination such exercises can bring. (Nonetheless, if the raw materials selected for the reconstructions on offer in Part Two seem merely idiosyncratically or even perversely chosen, one can still hope on Lewisian grounds that they can even so contribute to our generally knowing our way around in the vicinity of the texts they deal with.)

The method of reconstructive metaphysics can be applied to particular texts, as we see in Part Two. It can be applied to a contemporary literature, as I do, in effect, in *Making It Explicit*. The attempt to achieve a reflective equilibrium between a theory of meaning and hermeneutic practice, as codified in the gadamerian platitudes, has been pursued here by treating the latter as an interpretive target and the former as providing the interpretive raw materials. Tacking the metaphysics of intentionality provided by the reconstructions of *Making It Explicit* onto the tradition in the metaphysics of intentionality ostensively defined in Part Two and explicitly sketched in Chapters 1 and 2 does indeed, as Eliot indicates in the passage cited above, alter ("if ever so slightly") the previous order, and so readjust the "relations, proportions, and values" of each in relation to the whole tradition they make up (a central part of what Derrida called "the white mythology"). One retrospectively acquires thereby a different sense both of the tradition defined by the figures dealt with here, and of what one is doing in using basic ideas such as that of <u>inference</u> to situate them in such a tradition. The process and practice of <u>talking</u> with a tradition achieves a certain kind of *self-consciousness*, when to the implicit skill of engaging in such a dialogue is added explicit theoretical understanding of what one is doing.

The aim and aspiration of the systematic metaphysicians of old—for present purposes, paradigmatically Spinoza, Leibniz, and Hegel—was to craft a restricted and controlled idiom in which everything could be said, the apparent paucity of expressive resources appealed to at the outset notwithstanding. I think this sort of conceptual engineering remains in principle a viable enterprise today—however nervous-making some may find the prospect of seeking to rebuild Neurath's boat at sea by testing how many planks can be thrown overboard before it sinks. One objectionable, but separable and optional, concomitant of the systematic metaphysical project has historically been a tendency to denigrate those aspects of the target that are not smoothly reconstructable out of the favored conceptual raw materials. Thus the sensible world, relations, time, and so on are judged "unreal," relegated to the realm of mere appearance. Lewis's perspective suggests that the right lesson is that we can learn a lot from seeing which phenomena are, and which are not, reconstructable from specified raw materials. But any invidious assessments that are made as consequences of the incapacity of those raw materials to underwrite some bit of the target should be directed at least as much at the choice of basic conceptual tools as at the missed targets. One need not pursue metaphysics in its exclusionary form.

And so it is when the target phenomena we aim to understand better by stripping down to some elements that thereby are privileged over others—the distinctions of attention and emphasis on which any reconstructive reading is based—are *de dicto* specifications of conceptual contents ascribed to a historical philosophical text. What does not fit—that is, claims that either cannot be underwritten by the interpretive raw materials one has assembled or that have bad consequences when read in the context provided by those raw materials—need not for that reason be dismissed as somehow not genuinely expressive of the views put forward in the text. Rather, we should learn what we can from the distinction between what is brought out into the light by the selected and supplemented context and what is in this sense relegated by it to the shadows. Each perspective has something to teach us about the text on which it is a perspective. The pluralism we saw to be a consequence of the perspectival character of conceptual contents begins at home: the accounts presented in both parts of this book are just some among many possible ones, to be esteemed insofar as they are enlightening, but invested with no other sort of authority. In particular, the genre of historiography practiced in Part Two and theorized about in Part One—metaphysically reconstructive denotational *de re* readings (including both immediate *de re* and *de traditione* elements) of conceptual contents—is not put forward here as *better* than other possible ones, say, New Critical *de dicto* ones, which restrict themselves to inferences fundable by the words on the page, or authorial *de dicto* readings, which appeal to the context provided by what the author read, the historical circumstances of composition, and so on. So long as one is explicit about which sort of methodology one is pursuing, what rules determine the admissibility of various elements into the context that provides the conceptual perspective from which one reads a text, assessments of the *legitimacy* of one approach or another should give way to assessments of their hermeneutic *fruitfulness:* the sort of understanding they yield.

I opened the discussion of methodology in this section with a musical trope: the image of bebop historiography, in which a melody is treated as an occasion for improvisation on its chord structure. I can close by being a little more precise about the point the image is supposed to be making. The familiar melody, which can seem to go missing in bebop versions, corresponds to *de dicto* specifications of the conceptual content of a text. But it turns out that one can learn as much or more musically about that very same melody by exploring variations—that is, reading the image— by the sort of recontextualization of a conceptual content effected by *de re* specifications of it (including radically reconstructive ones). In each case, a distinctive and valuable kind of understanding is achieved when one can perceive them as providing different perspectives on one and the same item.

I have been concerned here to say something about the hermeneutic process that leads from a text to a kind of understanding: the essentially dialogical capacity to navigate among different inferential perspectives on the conceptual contents deployed in the text. This, I claim, is the basic task of reading. But it should not be forgotten that there is a complementary hermeneutic process, which leads from that sort of implicit practical conceptual understanding to its explicit expression or codification in a text. This is the basic task of writing. One can think of these phases of discursive practice as complementary and mutually irreducible—as hermeneutic exhaling and inhaling, in a cycle in which explicit sayings give rise to implicit practical capacities and vice versa—rather than reductively, by thinking of readings just as the way texts give rise to further texts, or of texts just as the way understandings give rise to further understandings. My hope is that the conceptual apparatus put in play here can provide a framework within which one can better assess the success with which the essays in the second part of this work convey the conceptual contents specified by their reconstructive *de re* readings of some of the works of the mighty dead metaphysicians of intentionality.

TWO

Historical Essays

4

Adequacy and the Individuation of Ideas in Spinoza's *Ethics*

In this chapter I argue that Spinoza's theory of knowledge is best understood as based on a reduction of intentional relations to causal relations. It follows from two of Spinoza's basic theses that some detailed account of intentionality is necessary to his project: that the order and connection of ideas is the same as the order and connection of extended things, and that universal causal determinism governs the relations of extended things. We shall see that the concept of <u>adequate ideas</u> on which Spinoza bases his theory of knowledge requires intentional notions such as that some mind has an idea *of* (or representing) some thing. Spinoza must accordingly give an account of such relations which allows them to be translated into assertions of necessary causal relations between extended things. I explicate this reduction of intentionality using two guiding ideas: a novel interpretation of the individuation of extended modes (carried over to the attribute of thought by the psycho-physical parallelism) and an expanded version of the definition of the adequacy of ideas given by Radnor.[1] Providing such a framework enables me to interpret coherently the *conatus* (Spinoza's mysterious individuating principle), the three levels of knowledge, and the relation between this ontological principle of individuation and the epistemological notion of the adequacy of ideas. Elaborating this relation culminates, in the final section, in an explication of Spinoza's doctrine of intuitive self-consciousness.

I. Ideas Do Not Represent Their Correlated Bodily Objects

The central notion around which Spinoza weaves his theory of knowledge is that of the adequacy of an idea to the thing of which it is the idea.

121

The definition of an adequate idea is an idea "which, insofar as it is considered in itself, without relation to the object, has all the properties or intrinsic marks of a true idea."[2] An interpretation of this concept must account for the fact that it is vital to Spinoza's purpose that all ideas be adequate in the divine mind, while many are inadequate in the human mind.[3] The notions of error and evil, and the coherence of Spinoza's treatment of finitude, depend on distinguishing adequate from inadequate ideas and explicating the relativity of that distinction to context (the mind of which the idea is a part). Considered as a problem of individuation, the adequacy of ideas will require interpretation by means of two principles. First, Spinoza must offer some principle that will tell us when we are confronted with two ideas and when we are confronted with only one (a use of "same idea" which disregards context). Second, he must offer some principle whereby we can distinguish the various contexts of a single idea in which it is adequate or inadequate. This principle would individuate more finely than the first, making distinctions ignored by that principle (distinguishing ideas-in-a-context, rather than ideas *simpliciter*). Nevertheless, it is clear that we cannot determine the circumstances under which an idea is adequate unless we can distinguish one idea from a group of related ones.

Ideas are modes of substance conceived under the attribute of thought,[4] and are hence identical with their objects, which are those same modes, conceived under the attribute of extension. Spinoza individuates substance into modes, which may then be conceived under any of an infinite number of attributes (though only thought and extension are available to human beings). Each extended thing is thus the object of an idea. It is clear that this line of thought offers no convenient handle by which we may grasp the stricter individuation according to adequacy (describing the conditions under which one and the same idea can be adequate or inadequate to that thing "of" which it is the idea).[5] Knowing the object of an idea does not tell us anything about its adequacy. Spinoza does say that

> we clearly understand what is the difference between the idea, say, of Peter, which constitutes the essence of Peter's mind, and the idea of the said Peter, which is in another man, say, Paul. The former directly answers to the essence of Peter's own body . . . ; the latter indicates rather

the disposition of Paul's body than the nature of Peter . . . The modifications of the human body, of which the ideas represent external bodies as present to us, we call the images of things.[6]

Radnor argues persuasively that only according to such a distinction between the object of an idea and the thing represented by that idea can we make sense of Spinoza's epistemology, since humans can have ideas "of," for example, the sun, but never have an idea whose object is the sun.[7]

Presupposing such a notion of representation, Radnor further suggests that an "adequate idea of X" (representing X) be glossed as "an idea which represents X" and "whose object includes X."[8] I will develop this suggestion, adopting provisionally the following definition of adequacy: An idea I which represents an extended thing X is an adequate idea of X just in case the idea whose object is X is deducible from the idea I. The relation of adequacy so defined is "intrinsic" in Spinoza's sense, concerning only what ideas are deducible from an idea, and not whether the idea "conforms" to the thing it represents. Thus an idea which represents the sun will be adequate only if the idea whose object is the sun is deducible from the initial idea. We may notice both that this is a plausible thing to mean by "an adequate idea of the sun" (one from which could be deduced that complete idea which is identical to the sun, though conceived in the attribute of thought) and that we would not expect Spinoza to claim that humans can have such an idea of the sun. Spinoza does tell us that we have adequate ideas of "those things which are common to all bodies,"[9] such as motion, presumably because we can infer an idea whose object is one of those common things from any idea whose object has motion, be it part of the human body or not. Since one and the same idea can be adequate in the mind of God and inadequate in a human mind, according to our interpretation of adequacy that idea must be able to represent one thing to God and another thing to a human being (the other prima facie possibility, that deductive relations themselves are context relative, will turn out to be either inconsistent with God's infinite inclusiveness, or equivalent to the relativity of the representation relation according to the definition offered below). We must be able to determine the conditions of this relativity of the representation relation to the context of a mind in order to settle specific questions concerning adequacy.

II. The Individuation of Objects

The suggestion concerning the notion of the adequacy of ideas enlightens us only to the extent to which we can determine the principles of individuation of the objects of ideas, the things represented by ideas, the minds containing various ideas, and the relations of deducibility and causation between ideas and bodies, respectively. Spinoza has given us a much more detailed discussion of extended individuals than he ever does of thought or thinking ones, so we will approach the issue of individuation from that direction. Spinoza begins with the *corpora simplicissima*. Only states of motion-and-rest distinguish these simplest bodies, which move sometimes more quickly and sometimes more slowly.[10] "A body in motion or at rest must be determined to motion or rest by another body," which was similarly determined, and "a body in motion will continue in motion until it be determined to a state of rest by another body."[11] Spinoza thus sets out to exhibit a world of ideally elastic[12] "billiard balls" of microscopic size. This world is layered, consisting of individuals of many degrees of complexity, all ultimately constructed out of the *corpora simplicissima*. The following definition elaborates:

> When a number of bodies of the same or of different magnitudes are pressed together by others, so that they lie one upon the other, or if they are in motion with the same or with different degrees of speed, so that they communicate their motion to one another in a certain fixed proportion [*ratione*]—these bodies are said to be mutually united, and taken together they are said to compose one body or individual, which is distinguished from other bodies by this union of bodies.[13]

If a number of *corpora simplicissima* are kept in contact with one another, they are treated as a single composite individual. This definition clearly holds good even if the composite individual so formed is in motion relative to its surroundings, so long as the relative motions of the constituents are slight enough that they maintain mutual contact. In the second clause of the definition, Spinoza allows a more complicated sort of relative motion as well. The parts of an individual must communicate their motions to one another according to some fixed ratio or proportion definitional of the complex individual. In a series of explanatory lemmas,[14] Spinoza indicates that other parts "of the same nature" may replace the parts of such a composite individual without damage to the identity of the whole. Similarly, all the parts may "become greater or less proportionately" within a single individual. More important, any number of constituents may be forced to change the direction of their motion so long as they continue to communicate those motions in the same proportion as before, without destroying the individual. It is difficult to see what all of this comes to in detail, though the outlines are clear. Spinoza calls a system of the simplest bodies an individual just in case it exhibits a certain sort of stability. One instance of that stability is the maintenance of a fixed set of spatial relations. A system whose components are in relative motion may also be stable, however, provided that a change of motion in one part is communicated to the others according to a fixed rule. The parts of such a composite individual thus adjust themselves to changes within certain limits. An uncomplicated composite individual like a stone may react to a collision of one of its parts by a coherent change in the motion of all of its parts, that is, by moving as a whole. If it does not, it breaks up into noncommunicating pieces and is destroyed.

We can define more complicated individuals made up of first-order individuals. Again we require only that changes in the motions of the parts be communicated to the other parts by a fixed rule. In continuing the hierarchy so as to include the whole universe, Spinoza emphasizes again his conception of stability through change:

> If we now imagine a third kind of individual composed of those of the second kind, we shall discover that it can be affected in many other ways without any change of form. Thus, if we advance *ad infinitum,* we may easily conceive the whole of nature to be one individual, whose parts, that is to say, all bodies, differ in infinite ways without any change of the whole individual.[15]

The *corpora simplicissima* maintain their state of motion and rest until disturbed, but any collision alters them. We distinguish composite individuals from one another by the proportion which must be maintained in the communication of motions of the parts. Higher-order individuals can remain identical through much greater changes than can the lower ones. The infinite individual preserves the communication of its parts under all circumstances (there is no external motive for change of any sort) and is thus immutable, while its parts change constantly.

This vision of an infinite sequence of ever more inclusive individuals with ever greater ability to resist destructive change offers some help in the interpretation of the "proportion of communicated motion" criterion of identity and individuation for the middle-sized individuals we are directly acquainted with. We may take the immutability of the infinite extended individual—an individual we can hardly help identifying with the "face of the whole universe, which, although it varies in infinite modes, yet remains always the same"[16]—as an expression of the conservation of momentum. A particle colliding with another "communicates its motion" with the final velocities being related according to a fixed proportion, namely, the inverse ratio of the masses of the colliding particles. Spinoza has not mentioned the masses, merely the fixed ratio which results, but in this he is a good Cartesian. Since this result is due to a law of nature, as we would have it, the communication of motion according to fixed proportions cannot fail in the universe as a whole. It can fail in any finite individual simply because momentum need not be conserved in finite systems.[17]

III. The Individuation of Ideas

In order to appreciate the difficulties of this layered scheme of individuals, we must examine the parallel attribute of thought, and consider how, according to the account of adequacy sketched in section I of this chapter, we might come to know individuals constructed as suggested by this scheme. We do not yet have a good enough grasp of individuation in the *Ethics* to redeem our promissory note concerning the notion of representation. Spinoza's initial use of the term and his general theory of perception give us enough information to show that perception must lead to inadequate ideas, however. According to the definition I gave earlier, confused cognition (inadequate ideas) will arise just in case an idea representing something is such that its object is not an adequate cause of the thing represented (or, equivalently, the idea of the thing represented is not deducible from the representing idea). It might seem that no perception could lead to adequate knowledge for Spinoza. For perception is a cognition corresponding to a bodily state which is caused at least in part by the impingement of an external body on the soft sensory surfaces of the human body.[18] In the passage introducing representation cited above, Spinoza talks of the bodily objects of the ideas representing things as "images." When I catch a ball, the ball is a proximate cause of an impression which its round shape makes on my hand. Such perception representing the ball would be adequate just in case the idea whose object is the ball could be validly inferred from the representing idea, namely, the idea whose object is the image of the ball. This is not the case, since at most the outline of the ball is impressed on my body. Thus something other than that particular ball could have caused the bodily image, and consequently the idea whose object is the ball cannot be deducible from the idea whose object is the image we have taken as representing the ball.

This argument does not imply that no adequate ideas are to be had about the bodies which impinge in perception. Spinoza points out[19] that external bodies and those which constitute the human body have many properties in common. All such common notions must be conceived adequately, for they are deducible alike from the bodily correlate of an idea and any external body.[20] All bodies have in common their attribute of extension, their common timeless generation from the immediate infinite mode of extension, that is, motion and rest, and the mediate infinite mode—the face of the whole universe, the infinite immutable extended individual.[21] Since these *notiones communes* must be conceived adequately, rational mechanics, an adequate notion of motion and rest, is possible. This is the "second kind of knowledge," called 'Ratio'.[22] (The "first kind of knowledge" is confused or inadequate knowledge. Only the second and third kinds are adequate.)

Spinoza says that this kind of knowledge treats particular things as mere instances of general properties (e.g., of motion and rest) so that we cannot know individuals by it.[23] I discussed the various orders of extended individuals in section II from the universal point of view of Ratio, following Spinoza's own treatment. I did not, then, touch on the essence of any individuals in that discussion, but offered merely a general characterization of the property of *individuality* insofar as it is common to all bodies. I defined a system of bodies as an individual just in case a certain sort of stability of contact and the ordered communication of motions among the parts is maintained. That earlier discussion did not offer reasons for the achievement and maintenance of a particular configuration. Yet surely accidentally stable systems cannot constitute all the particular enduring things we see around us. Some account must be given of the amount of stability we find around us, for it is far in excess of what is plausible if the account of Ratio is the whole story. When I catch a ball, why do I not fly apart at the contact like the set at the beginning of a game of pool? There is nothing in Spinoza's billiard parlor world resembling friction among the parts of the solid which are in contact, nor are there circular motions or fields of force. Spinoza has an appropriate rule for changes of direction in collisions,[24] which should make my bodily parts respond the way the massed billiard balls do to an impact. We can say what sort of imperviousness to disintegration by external influence is required for individuality using the mechanics of Ratio. We cannot explain why there should be any. Spinoza's solution of this difficulty is the doctrine of the *conatus*, the effort an individual expends to maintain itself. This doctrine cannot be approached on the level of Ratio, but only by the third kind of knowledge, *scientia intuitiva*, which is founded on the knowledge achieved by Ratio.

From the point of view of Spinoza's total project, the prime positive result of the investigation of common properties by Ratio is an adequate idea of God. We have seen how an adequate idea of the immediate infinite mode of extension is possible in the second kind of knowledge. But by the definition of a mode, any mode can only be conceived through substance,[25] which must accordingly be conceived adequately if any mode, infinite or not, is so conceived. We can restate this argument: since motion-and- rest are caused immediately by God, and knowledge of an effect depends on and involves knowledge of the cause, the adequate knowledge of motion-and-rest Ratio assures us of involves adequate knowledge of God.[26] This is essentially the argument of *Ethics* ii, 45–47. Ratio provides an adequate idea of God's essence, and hence sets the stage for intuition to reverse the direction of inquiry, beginning with God and proceeding down to finite individual essences.

Spinoza introduces the principle of individuation we are to achieve by intuitive knowledge in this way: "The effort [*conatus*] by which each thing, insofar as it is in itself, endeavors to persevere in its own being is nothing but the actual essence of the thing itself."[27] The mind has such a *conatus*, of which it is conscious.[28] Spinoza calls the *conatus* of that mode which is both the human mind and its body "appetite." This statement only gives notice that there is some principle other than chance to account for the observed stability of things. An *effort* which they expend to persevere timelessly individuates particular things; the effort helps them maintain a stable configuration. The only help Spinoza gives us with this difficult concept is in the proof of Proposition 6, where he deduces the existence of the *conatus* from the fact that each particular thing expresses in a determinate manner the power of God, by which he is and acts.[29] Our adequate idea of God thus entails in some fashion an adequate idea of the various individuating "efforts," but it is unclear in what fashion.

IV. *Scientia intuitiva*

Epistle 32, where Spinoza elucidates his use of the terms 'whole' and 'part', is the key to understanding the progression by *scientia intuitiva* from an adequate idea of God's essence to an adequate idea of the essences of individual things:

> I consider things as parts of some whole, insofar as their natures are mutually adapted so that they are in accord among themselves as much as possible; but insofar as things differ among themselves each . . . is considered to be a whole, not a part.

Spinoza's example is blood, composed of different particles of lymph and chyle. We say that to the extent to which they are mutually adapted to form a single fluid, they are parts of a whole, while to the extent to which they differ, opposing one another, each is a whole itself. The relative nature of the notions of whole and part is obvious. Spinoza imagines a tiny worm living in the blood, discerning and understanding the collisions and rebounds of the particles:

> That worm would live in this blood as we live in this part of the universe, and he would consider each particle of blood to be a whole, and not a part. And *he could not know how all the parts are controlled by the universal nature of the blood, and are forced, as the universal nature of the blood demands, to adapt themselves to one another, so as to harmonize with one another in a certain way.* (emphasis added)

There are three premises here: first, that there is a conditioning of parts by the whole they are included in. That this determination is active in some sense (an effort) seems an unavoidable conclusion from the terms 'forced' and 'controlled by'. Second, he asserts that the worm, who is in full possession of a history of collisions and communications of motion, could never discern the action of the whole on its parts. Third, Spinoza claims that we are in the same situation in our part of the universe as the worm is in the blood: we also observe motions of bodies, but cannot discover the control of these bodies by the wholes they compose.

The comparison of this situation with the one confronting us when we consider the individuation of extended bodies according to the second kind of knowledge is obvious. Like the worm, we can in principle know everything about the laws governing motion and rest. That knowledge is sufficient to allow us to recognize individuals, but not sufficient to account for their existence. The universal knowledge of Ratio cannot comprehend why there should be such stable systems. The principles of rational mechanics thus underdetermine individuation. In this letter Spinoza asserts that there is a whole-part determination which "mutually adapts" the parts of a whole, and which cannot be determined by a consideration of the motions involved. Such a holistic determination is just what we need to occupy the place of the *conatus*, which Spinoza has described elsewhere as the individuating principle available only to the third kind of knowledge.

Spinoza justifies his assertion of the merely rational worm's inability to discern the whole-part determination with two claims. First:

> For if we imagine that there are no causes outside the blood and no other bodies to which the particles of blood could transfer their motion, it is certain that the blood would remain always in its state . . . and so blood would always have to be considered a whole and not a part.

Spinoza thus believes that individuals, if unperturbed by external influences, will be perfectly stable, as the face of the whole universe is, since motion would always be transferred to another part of the whole. He makes this same claim more opaquely in the *Ethics:* "A thing cannot be destroyed except by an external cause."[30] The rest of Spinoza's justification takes us beyond the idealized situation of isolated individuals, qualifying the first statement:

> But, since there are very many other causes which in a certain way control the laws of the nature of blood, and are in turn controlled by the blood, hence it comes about that other motions and other changes take place in the blood, which result not only from the mere relation of its parts to one another, but from the relation of the motion of the blood and also of the external causes to one another; in this way blood has the character of a part and not a whole.

Spinoza thus makes the fact that the blood is only a relative whole crucial to justifying the inability of the rational worm to distinguish the
force which the blood's universal nature exerts on its parts. The reason
why the worm cannot (and we, living in our portion of the universe,
cannot) distinguish the controlling operation of a relative whole on its
parts is that that determination can always be attributed to the external
causes impinging on the relative whole. If the blood were an absolute
whole, we would be forced to recognize the unity which an individual
imposes on its parts, as we were in fact led to do in the case of the conservation of momentum (motion-and-rest) in the maximal extended individual. Spinoza goes on to say that all finite wholes are only relative
wholes.

Consider the emerging picture of rational mechanical inquiry. Beginning with whatever level of bodies we can observe most easily, we may
chart the mutual communications of motions. Upon analyzing these
data according to the mechanical principles sketched in Part Two of the
Ethics, we would discover that we cannot fully account for the motions
of the observed bodies on the basis of those physical principles applied
just to the system under observation. The stage is set for the discovery of
the whole-part determination, and indeed Spinoza claims that that discovery would be made by Physics—if only the system under observation
were an absolute, and not merely a relative whole. But since the system
we observe shares with all other finite systems its function as a part of a
more inclusive whole, it is a whole only relatively. Consequently the
possibilities for the application of our physical principles have not been
exhausted. The system under observation was not isolated, and was per-
turbed by collisions from the outside, as we see when we widen the
scope of our observation to include a larger whole whose parts interact
with our initial system. We should thus not have expected our principles to have accounted for the motions of the initial system solely on the
basis of the observations of that system, for external causes were involved. We must extend the observations and attempted explanations to
the next most inclusive whole, and then to the next after that, with no
complete account of any of the motions along the way (because no
awareness of the control by wholes of their parts) until we reach an absolute whole. Of course, since Spinoza has shown in the opening arguments of the *Ethics* that there is only one absolute whole in this (or any)
attribute, and that this whole is infinite, it will never be reached by such

a progression. Consequently the worm, functioning merely at the level of Ratio, will never know the determination of blood particles by blood's universal nature, and we cannot know about a similar determination in our part of the universe by our rational mechanics.

These failures, however, are failures of Ratio, which, while it cannot reach God by analyzing the motions of finite extended systems directly, can, as I have shown, achieve adequate knowledge of his essence by another means. Spinoza tells us that this opens the way for *scientia intuitiva,* the third kind of knowledge, to reverse the vicious ascent in search of *conatus* by Ratio, and "proceed" down from an adequate knowledge of the infinite modes to an adequate knowledge of some finite, relative wholes. Ratio could not discover these essences, because the effects of the whole-part determination (the mutual adaptation of parts which is the *conatus* and hence the essence of individual things) cannot be separated from the effects of membership in a more inclusive whole without prior knowledge of the essence of that larger whole. Only intuitive knowledge, proceeding from the essences of the more inclusive to the less inclusive wholes can make the required distinction and discern the essence which individuates. Spinoza refers to the whole-part determination which intuition follows as the expression of God's power by finite things.[31] He also refers to the conditioning of finite parts by infinite wholes as "immanent causation," thereby contrasting it with the mutual causal conditioning of two bodies which interact as (relative) wholes.[32] Intuitive knowledge is said to follow the course of atemporal emanation of essences.

The descent of intuition from the essence of God to the essences of particular things must be different in kind from the step-by-step analysis by which Ratio proceeds, for there is no next smaller whole after the "face of the whole universe." There would thus be an infinite number of "steps" for reason to go through to get to any particular individual. But Spinoza's sole nonmetaphysical example of the different kinds of knowledge contrasts the step-by-step figuring of a proportion by Ratio to "just seeing it" by immediate intuition,[33] so this is an expected difference. It also suggests that we must not expect a discursive explication of intuition, and Spinoza's own efforts at presentation of the notion reinforce this. Since Spinoza specifically denies that all particular extended modes can be deduced from an adequate idea of extension, yet affirms that we can have adequate ideas of the essences of particular things,[34] it must be either that the essence of any particular thing (but not all together) can be intuited by a finite mind, or that there is a distinguished class of particular things any one of which may be intuited, while others cannot. My interpretation of intuition will entail the second alternative, but Spinoza offers no direct pronouncement on this issue. He does say that we can have intuitive knowledge of our own minds and their modifications.[35] We shall concentrate on this example and not consider intuitive knowledge in other cases. I have sketched the rational mechanics which is the object of the second kind of knowledge, and we have seen that the essences which individuate things are not approached on that level of knowledge. I have characterized those essences as principles of stability exhibited in the mutual adaptation of parts according to the whole they constitute. We have remaining to us the problem of individuating ideas in a human mind, in order to complete the characterization of the representation relation, and hence the notion of adequacy. Accordingly, we move to the parallel attribute of thought, and apply the insights gleaned during our sojourn in the realm of extension, with the goal of describing a framework within which we may discover what an adequate idea of a particular thing, namely, the human mind, consists in.

V. A Proposal about Representation

The analysis of the individuation of extended things began with the *notio communis* of motion-and-rest, the immediate infinite mode of extension. The corresponding immediate infinite mode of thought is understanding.[36] We must assume that we can conceive ideas as layered, stable systems of simpler ideas corresponding to the scheme for extended individuals, for the "order and connection" of the two systems is identical. But Spinoza has not offered us a rational psychology relating the "states of understanding" associated with ideas in the way in which he sketched a rational mechanics relating the states of motion-and-rest of extended things. The parallelism of ideas and bodies, however, allows us to draw some inferences, as we will see below. In particular, there must be some causal analogue of the intentionality of ideas—the fact that ideas can represent things, be ideas *of* things. All ideas in the human mind have as their objects affections of the human body (states of motion-and-rest of constituent systems of the body). Yet some of these ideas are "taken as images" of external bodies by a particular mind. Further, I argued in section I that what a particular mind takes an idea to represent depends on what mind is considered, as well as what idea is considered. Let us then take the context of an idea in a particular mind as the criterion for determining what that mind takes the idea to represent. In particular, consider the mind as the correlate in the attribute of thought of a chain of causal influences whose links are the complex extended individual corresponding to the human body in different states of motion-and-rest. We will consider the idea(s) immediately following the idea we are interested in as determining what that idea is "taken" to represent.[37] Thus, each idea I is a proximate cause[38] of some effect E in the mind in question.[39] E in turn has an adequate cause C (which includes I). We say that I represents the object C' of C and, derivatively, any part of C'. The strategy and motivation of such a functional definition should be clear. The only relation available to reconstruct the intentionality of representation by relating something inside the mind to something outside it is the relation of causation. If we wish to retain a Radnor-type analysis of adequacy, we may not take what a thing represents as determined by the causal *antecedents* of I. For the conjunction of these two moves would entail that the object of and thing represented by an adequate idea are mutually deducible from each other, which is clearly false to Spinoza's usage.

The justification of the definition must come from its plausibility for interpreting the ways in which Spinoza uses representation. Consider first ordinary perception, which Spinoza tells us will present only a confused idea "of" an external individual.[40] We suppose that I have a bodily state which the incidence of sunlight on my eye causes. According to our definition, what, if anything, the idea whose object is that state represents (is an idea "of") depends on what ideas follow it in my mind. Suppose further, then, that the idea whose object is a state of my eye is a proximate cause of an idea whose object is the bodily state of my larynx forming the word 'sun'. Spinoza's discussion of a similar case of ideas related according to idiosyncratic associations rather than universal logical relations within a given mind[41] indicates what relations he conceives as relevant. My speech depends on the fact that "if the human body has once been affected by two or more bodies at the same time, when the mind afterwards imagines any of them, it will straightway remember the others also."[42] The adequate cause of my pronunciation of the word 'sun' thus includes the past impingement of sunlight and my verbalization elicited somehow in the process of learning English, as well as the immediate impingement of sunlight which initiates the associative pattern on this occasion. The idea whose object is the state of my eye as sunlight affects it represents both the sun and an incident in my past, according to our definition. This idea will be an adequate idea of the sun just in case the idea whose object is the sun is deducible from it. Since an arc lamp could have induced the same bodily state of my eye, no such deduction is valid. Similarly, the idea will be an adequate idea of the origin of my association just in case that association is deducible from the idea in question (that is, if from the idea whose object is the state of my eye one could validly deduce that that state had in the past been contemporaneous with another, corresponding to a movement of my larynx). That no such deduction is permissible is just the meaning of the idiosyncratic nature of such associations, depending as they do not simply on universal logical relations, but also on the arbitrary (from a logical point of view) boundaries of finite individuals.

The only examples we have so far of adequate ideas are ideas which represent *notiones communes,* such as extension or motion-and-rest. Let us suppose that I have an idea whose object is a state of my arm muscles resulting from the impact of a ball I have just caught. There are many ideas which might follow such a one according to various associations of mine. Spinoza assures us nonetheless that *notiones communes* "will be represented by an adequate idea in the mind" and "cannot be conceived except adequately."[43] It must be that some idea which in fact follows the one in question follows in virtue of universal logical relations. This would be the case if the next idea has as its object the bodily state of my muscles slightly farther along my arm, where the momentum of the catch is "communicated" according to physical necessity. In that case the adequate cause of the idea of which the representing idea is the proximate cause would include both the representing idea and the universal properties of motion-and-rest corresponding to the conservation of momentum. By our definition the original idea would thus be "of" this *notio communis.* It would be an adequate idea, since from the initial bodily state one may validly deduce the appropriate general properties "common to all bodies."[44]

We next proceed to consider the *conatus* in the attribute of thought, and then to the only example Spinoza ever offers of a particular thing which may be known adequately (by the third kind of knowledge): the human mind in its self-awareness.

VI. *Conatus*

The principle or "effort" of *conatus,* which timelessly individuates modes under the attribute of extension, manifests itself as a control or force exerted on parts by the whole comprising them. Since the order and connection of ideas is the same as the order and connection of extended things, a similar control must constitute the *conatus* in the attribute of thought. Spinoza's analysis of the *conatus* for ideas is more complicated than that for extended things, however, as the notion of the *activity* of a complex idea (mind) links the adequacy of ideas to the individuative *conatus.* Spinoza says that the *conatus* when applied to the mind alone is called will *(voluntas).*[45] He also says that "there is in the mind no volition or affirmation and negation save that which an idea, inasmuch as it is an idea, involves."[46] In proving this proposition, Spinoza argues that a particular affirmation (or will) is the essence of each idea. He claims that this demonstration justifies his comment after the definition of an idea as a mental conception that he chose the term 'conception' to indicate the *activity* of the mind.[47] It is not clear why the claim that a particular affirmation *(conatus)* is the essence of each idea should entail that the mind is active. Considering the definition of activity in this context, we find a further notion linked to the individuation of ideas:

> I say that we *act* when anything takes place either within us or external to us, whereof we are the adequate cause, that is, when through our nature something takes place within us or externally to us, which can through our nature alone be clearly and distinctly understood.[48]

Reading this definition into the claim above, we find that Spinoza is claiming that ideas are activities of the mind containing them (inasmuch as it is a mind, that is, a whole, that is, relatively), which by his definition means that the mind is the adequate cause of its own modifications, since the essences of ideas are particular affirmations.

On the model of my previous discussion of whole-part determination in extended individuals, there are three sorts of relations of importance for the notion of activity: that of part to part within the relative whole being considered, that of a whole to its parts, and that of the parts of a more inclusive whole to the parts of the included whole (we will ignore higher-order effects). The mirroring of extended connections demands that a mind counterfactually isolated from external forces (that is, an absolute whole, in which relations of the third sort were missing) would be the adequate cause of all its own modifications (the states of "understanding" of its ideas, paralleling the states of motion-and-rest of their objects). A mind is thus active just insofar as it is a relative whole and not a relative part of some more inclusive whole. Since every finite complex is a whole only relatively, however, a human mind will never be the adequate cause of all its modifications. In view of the definition of activity, we can restate this result by saying that the power (*conatus*, activity) of external things surpasses that of the human mind: "It is impossible that man should not be a part of nature or that he should be capable of undergoing no changes save such as can be understood through his nature alone."[49] If some state of ideas in a mind is the effect of the action of the whole mind and the states of the other parts, then the mind is an adequate cause of that modification of the mind, and is active with respect to it. The essence of the mind in question then "affirms" that modification.

Spinoza establishes the connection of the individuation of ideas (via the *conatus*, the determination of parts by the wholes containing them, which is activity) to the theory of knowledge and the notion of adequate ideas as follows: "The activities of the mind arise solely from adequate ideas; the passive states of the mind depend solely on inadequate ideas."[50] This proposition follows from the interpretations I have offered of the adequacy of ideas and the activity of minds. Thinking of the mind as a system of ideas with logical relations among them corresponding to the causal relations among the bodies of an extended system, we find three cases exemplifying the causes of a modification of a mind. First, a single idea, constituting a part of the mind and itself modified by its presence in that whole, may be the adequate cause of some internal modification in the mind. Second, several such parts could together constitute the adequate cause of a modification. Finally, the adequate cause of such a modification could include things external to the mind. In the third case the mind is not active but passive, since the mind in question does not include the adequate cause of the modification. In this case none of the ideas inside the mind (which are partial causes of the modification) are adequate, for each is a proximate cause of the modification whose adequate cause includes the external thing, and could not be adequate unless the external thing were deducible from their objects. If that were the case, however, we could consider the situation as an example of the second case, since we could comprehend the modification in terms of the internal causes, which are accordingly adequate by the definition. In the first case the situation is as clear, for the mind is active just in virtue of one idea's being an adequate cause of its changes of state, and in that case the idea is adequate—that is, it represents only what follows from its object.

But what of the second case? In this situation the mind is active; no external causes figure in its internal modification. Yet it seems that no individual idea is adequate, for only the conjunction is an adequate cause of the modification, so that each one represents things not deducible from *its* object, although deducible from the conjoined objects. In this one case, Spinoza seems to rest the mind's activity on inadequate ideas, contrary to his assertion above. Spinoza holds, however, that "if several individual things concur in one action, so as all to be simultaneously the cause of one effect, I consider them all, so far, as one particular thing."[51] The second case thus reduces to the first, and Spinoza establishes the correlation of the mind's activity with its possession of adequate ideas, according to the interpretations I have offered for those terms. Of course, by the same principle we ought to restate the third case, for it is not accurate to speak of the collaboration of internal and external causes. There is one individual which causes any given modification. From the perspective of the infinite mind of God, all such ideas are adequate, representing only what follows from their objects.[52] They can be inadequate only with respect to a finite mind, just in case the individual which is an adequate cause of a modification is not a part of (an idea in) that mind. The individuation of minds by their activity is thus dependent on the epistemological categorization of adequate ideas. Individuation of complex ideas of all levels according to their *conatus* (whole-part determination), called "affirmation" for simpler ideas and "activity" for those complex enough to be considered minds, depends on separating the effects of inclusion in a larger whole from the effects of parts external to such a whole, just as in extended systems.

VII. Ideas of Ideas

We now know something about the individuation of modes of either attribute by the *conatus* which mutually adapts the parts so as to form a whole recognizable by the general principles of Ratio. We have yet to account for the adequate knowledge of particular essences which Spinoza claims a third kind of knowledge, *scientia intuitiva,* achieves. My final consideration of the doctrine of "ideas of ideas" or *idea ideae* in the *Ethics,* will bring together three more or less separate issues left by the previous discussion. First, the doctrine of *idea ideae* includes the statement that these ideas are "of" other ideas in the sense in which the mind is "of" the body, namely, identity. This doctrine as it stands explicitly contradicts the reading of "idea of *X*" as "idea representing *X*" which I borrowed from Radnor in section I.[53] Second, the human mind (and its modifications) is the only finite individual Spinoza ever instances as an object of intuitive knowledge (by an *idea ideae* "of" the mind), so it offers the only opportunity to interpret the possibility of adequate knowledge of the individuating *conatus.* Finally, there is Spinoza's contention that the human mind is self-conscious in knowing its own *conatus.*[54]

The difficulty with respect to the first issue is not just that the interpretation I have suggested demands that ideas be "of" the things they represent if we are to make sense of the notion of adequate ideas (although this is certainly true). On Spinoza's own terms, we cannot in general read "an idea of *X*" as "an idea whose object is *X*." When we have our adequate idea of God, surely God is not the *object* of the idea (else that idea would simply be the divine mind). Similarly for the adequate ideas of "common notions": How could motion-and-rest be the object of an idea in the human mind? Yet Spinoza introduces his discussion of the *idea ideae* with an argument from Proposition 21: "The idea of the mind is united to the mind in the same way as the mind is united to the body."[55] This claims that ideas of ideas are identical with their object ideas since, like mind and body, they characterize a single mode and lack even the distinction of attributes existing in the mind-body case. The apparent inconsistency of this doctrine with our interpretation of representation derives from that reading's faithful rendering of Spinoza's own principles rather than from a failure to do so. Indeed, since the point of this series of propositions is to show that in the absence of intuition we have only an inadequate idea of the human mind, what sense could Spinoza attribute to this claim if that idea is in fact *identical* with the mind? My analysis resolves this difficulty for the representation interpretation, and hence for Spinoza. In doing so it tries to make sense of the possibility of both adequate and confused ideas of the human mind. The adequate idea involves activity on the part of the mind, as my discussion of individuation and intuition requires. My discussion points to a plausible doctrine of self-consciousness by viewing the *idea ideae* as instances of representing ideas as previously discussed.

The most desirable state of affairs would be that in which we were allowed to interpret ideas as representing other ideas. In that case consciousness of self would be assimilated as an instance to the general scheme of consciousness "of" X, namely, an idea representing X. Further, it would be clear how there could be inadequate ideas of the mind, namely, in any case in which the represented idea (the mind) is not deducible from the object of the representing idea (e.g., if the representing idea is a proper part of the whole mind, excluding parts relatively independent of itself). Again, by our definition of representation, an idea adequately representing the human mind would have two characteristics: it would be a proximate cause of a state of "understanding" whose adequate cause is the whole mind, and the whole mind thus represented would be deducible from the representing idea. The adequacy of the idea of the mind would be equivalent to the activity or freedom of the mind, just as in Spinoza's view, for it is only when the mind is an adequate cause of its own states that those states represent that mind in the sense already explicated. Finally, the mind functioning as the adequate cause of its own modifications is just the whole-part determination (immanent causation, mutual adaptation of parts, etc.) which I have identified with the *conatus* or individual essence of the mind. Consciousness of the self (having an adequate idea of the mind) is thus consciousness of the activity of the mind, and hence of its individuating essence. Subject to the condition of being able to justify allowing one idea to represent another, then, a plausible doctrine of self-consciousness as adequate knowledge of the individual essence or activity of the human mind is an immediate result of the interpretation I have offered of adequacy and individuation.

This happy conclusion is still only hypothetical. My definition of the thing an idea represents is "the object of the adequate cause of the subsequent ideas" (those ideas of which the representing idea is a proximate cause). The thing represented is the *object* of some idea, and hence not itself an idea. The possibility of knowing extended modes requires the passage to objects in framing this definition. We could take ideas as representing other ideas on the basis of the definition of representation only if it is possible for one idea to be the object of another. But this is just the doctrine which Spinoza put forth in *Ethics* ii, 21–29, and which I found so mysterious and unmotivated: the point of the scholium to Proposition 21 is the reminder that the definition of an object of X for Spinoza would be "the mode exhibited in one attribute by X, as exhibited in any attribute." Of course, Spinoza never gives the definition of 'object' explicitly in these terms (we were led to believe that the object was always the mode exhibited in the other[56] attribute) but the latter rendering is quite consistent with what went before, and is even given some justification in the letters.[57] The notion that an idea can be related to an idea in the same way in which the mind is related to the body, which seemed to be an unintelligible basis for a doctrine of self-consciousness, is precisely what the most natural doctrine requires according to the interpretations I have offered here. Idea A represents idea B just in case the object of B, which is B itself (of course, B has an extended object as well), is the adequate cause of the ideas of which A is a proximate cause. A will then be an *adequate* idea of B just in case B is deducible from A.[58] Thus if A is an adequate cause of the idea in a mind of which it is a proximate cause (if the ideas follow logically from A), then A will be an adequate idea of itself. In general, A will be an adequate cause of B just in case the adequate cause of the idea of which A is a proximate cause (namely, B) is deducible from A, that is, just in case A is itself such an adequate cause, which is just in case the mind is active. The more inclusive idea, the human mind, can adequately represent itself and its parts in the same fashion. It is then aware of itself in just the same way in which it can be aware of the sun, or of motion—namely, by representation. Further, just insofar as an idea in the mind adequately represents that mind (the mind is active and free), the whole mind is an adequate cause of the states of its parts, which is the correlate in the attribute of thought of the whole-part determination constituting the essence of that particular mind.

Since this immanent causation of the states of the parts by the state of the whole constitutes the essence of the human mind, it is our essence to be free and active (insofar as our mind is "in itself," i.e., is a relative whole and not a relative part). So it is of the essence of the human mind to conceive things, in particular itself, adequately. It succeeds to the extent to which it is a relative whole determining its parts, and fails so far as it is a relative part superseded by other finite things whose power exceeds that of the human mind.

The way in which we know our own minds adequately differs from that in which we know the *notiones communes*, for the particular essence individuating the object of our knowledge, the activity of the mind, constitutes both the thing known and the knowing of it. Intuitive knowledge is thus immediate and simple. The complexity of the other kinds of knowledge is the result of a finite limitation, and we can discard them when we know as God knows, intuitively. Intuitive knowledge proceeds according to the descending order of whole-part determination. It is knowledge of that adequate causation of the states of the idea-parts by the mind-whole (so far as the individual is determined by its own essence; that is, so far as it is a relative whole), which is the *conatus* and essence of the individual.

In this chapter I have offered interpretations of some of the central notions of Spinoza's *Ethics*. Spinoza uses the concepts of activity, freedom, and intuitive adequate knowledge of the individual essence of the human mind as the basic tools with which his ethical project is to be carried out in the final portions of his great work. It is to be hoped that the elucidation of these notions which is offered here can be of help in our attempts to understand those further doctrines which give Spinoza's project its name.

5

Leibniz and Degrees of Perception

The concept of representation is at the center not only of seventeenth-century theories of knowledge but of their corresponding ontologies as well. Descartes was impressed and inspired by mathematical innovations that enabled, on the one hand, a precise geometrical account of the optical transformations of figures and images in vision and, on the other, the formally adequate representation of such geometrical situations by nonspatial, discursive expressions in coordinate algebras. God aside, the real was for him accordingly divided into the purely geometrical realm of extension and the realm of thought (taking algebra as its model), which represents what is extended. Leibniz, with a reservation of profound consequence for subsequent German idealism, would deny metaphysical reality to what is representable but not itself a representing. Defining perception as the representation or expression of the many in the one,[1] Leibniz adumbrates a metaphysical system whose primary features follow from the doctrine that to be is to perceive. Put in his inherited terminology, monads alone are true substances, and perception is their fundamental attribute. Perceivings, the modifications of substances in that attribute,[2] are monadic properties. Relations, for example, spatial ones, cannot *be* perceivings, but are rather merely perceivable, as features of the multiplicity that is unified in a single perception. As nonperceiving creatures of perception, space, time, and matter—no less than color and odor—are relegated to the second-class metaphysical status of "true phenomena."[3]

To understand Leibniz's version of reality as a privileged class of representings,[4] we must understand four features of his account of perception. First, the genus of which perception is a species is that of *expression* or representation. Leibniz says generally, "One thing expresses another . . . when there is a constant and regulated relation between what can be said of the one and of the other."[5] Favorite examples are the relations between a map and the corresponding geographical region and between a minature model of a machine and the machine itself. Second, as noted above, the specific difference defining *perceptual* representations is that in perception a multiplicity is expressed in a unity. Third, each monad (indeed, each set of contemporaneous perceptions of any monad) expresses its whole world[6]—the "flower in the crannied wall" doctrine occasionally glossed by the claim that a perfect intelligence could deduce every feature of the universe from the consideration of the perceptions of a single monad. Fourth, perception comes in *degrees,* variously referred to as degrees of perfection or distinctness.

The last of these features is of cardinal metaphysical importance, since it is explanatorily responsible both for the diversity of points of view of the monads and for the preestablished harmony between them that is Leibniz's systematic synthesis of the principles of unity and of maximal multiplicity. Leibniz explains the relation between the diversity of monadic perspectives and the expression by each of its whole world in the *Monadology:*

> [A] The nature of the monad being to represent, nothing can limit it to representing only a part of things, though it is true that its representation is merely confused as to the details of the whole universe, and can be distinct for a small part of things only, that is, for those which are the nearest or the greatest in relation to each individual monad. Otherwise each monad would be a divinity. It is not in the object but in the modification of their knowledge of the object that the monads are limited. They all move confusedly toward the infinite, toward the whole, but they are limited and distinguished from each other by the degrees of their distinct perceptions.[7]

In this passage, the metaphysical differentiation of the monads is displayed as rooted in *epistemic* differences between perceptions, ranged along a dimension from "distinct" to "confused." The same doctrine is put in slightly different terminology in the *Discourse,* twenty-eight years earlier:

[B] Thus a substance, which is of an infinite extension insofar as it expresses all, becomes limited in proportion to its more or less perfect manner of expression.[8]

In Leibniz's discussion of causal action and passion, we meet a more specific application of the principle that monads are distinguished from one another not by what they express or perceive but by how perfectly or distinctly they do so. In strict metaphysical terms, monads cannot affect one another. Rather, each derives its current perceptions from those immediately past according to its own internal principle or individual concept. So a special account must be offered of the *appearance* of interaction between disparate substances, which is their mutual harmony in all forming a *world* together. In the *Discourse,* Leibniz explains:

[C] The action of one finite substance upon another consists only in the increase in the degrees of expression of the first, combined with a decrease in that of the second . . . When . . . a change occurs by which several substances are affected (in fact every change affects them all) I think we may say that those substances which by this change pass immediately to a greater degree of perfection or to a more perfect expression, exert power and act, while those which pass to a lesser degree disclose their weakness and suffer.[9]

In the *Monadology,* the point is put like this, identifying the idiom of perfection with that of distinctness of perception:

[D] The created being is said to act outwardly insofar as it has perfection and to *suffer* from another insofar as it is imperfect. Thus *action* is attributed to a monad insofar as it has distinct perceptions, and passion insofar as it has confused ones.[10]

The crucial explanatory role played in Leibniz's metaphysics by the various degrees of perception thus lends urgency to the question of how we are to understand the dimension along which quantitative comparisons of "perfection" or "distinctness" can be made. In section II, below, an account of perception is developed which seeks to answer this question, presenting an integrated treatment of the four primary features of Leibniz's notion of perception, as indicated above. Section I is devoted to formulating criteria of adequacy for such an account by delineating difficulties that any explication of the doctrine of degrees of perception must face and assembling the basic textual claims that must be reconciled and adjudicated. In particular, the concept of awareness (Leibniz's "apperception") will emerge as what we must get clear about in order to appreciate the order of perfection of perceptions. The conclusion of the analysis of section II is a reading in terms of which Leibniz's rationalism is seen to consist in the dependence, in the order of explanation, of the concepts of awareness and representation on the concept of inference (even for monads incapable of thought).

I. Distinctness of Perception and Distinctness of Ideas

The best account we have of degrees of perception is due to Montgomery Furth. The *awareness* substances have of their perceptions comes in degrees, according to Leibniz, ranging from the conscious, inferentially articulated recognition of a sample of gold by an assayer, down through the "minute perception" of each ocean wave breaking against the shore, which, though individually indiscriminable, nevertheless contributes to the sound a soul with the proper organs is aware of the surf as producing. In an important essay, Furth has shown how sense can be made of the occupation of a perspective or point of view by primordially non-spatial monads, provided that the grades of distinctness of perception (or degrees of perfection of expression) that individuate those monads are identified with different distributions of the intensity of consciousness attending each monad's expressively complete set of perceptions of its world. Furth concludes:

> [E] It seems that the numerical diversity of harmonious monads can reside only in differences in the clearness [sic] or degree of consciousness with which they experience various portions of their universe(s); if Leibniz's talk of "perspective" comes to anything, it must come to this.[11]

According to this view, degrees of perception are really degrees of apperception. Furth supports this reading by showing how differences in visual perspective and phenomena such as the occlusion of our view of a distant object by a nearer one can be analyzed in terms of differences in degree of awareness of different regions of space. Although the textual basis he presents is thin (passage [A] above is the only ground he offers), evidence for the thesis that distinctness or perfection of perception is consciousness of it can be found:

[F] But a soul can read within itself only what it represents distinctly; it cannot all at once develop all that is enfolded within it, for this reaches to infinity.[12]

[G] The soul itself does not know the things which it perceives until it has perceptions which are distinct and heightened. And it has perfection in proportion to the distinctness of its perceptions.[13]

[H] We are never without *perceptions,* but we are necessarily often without *apperceptions,* viz.: when there are no distinct perceptions.[14]

(Only the first of these passages is from the work Furth was considering.) We can certainly conclude that distinctness of perception is a *necessary* condition for apperception. Nowhere does Leibniz identify apperception with the occurrence of distinct perceptions, but the burden of proof should rest with those who would deny the sufficiency of distinctness to say what else is required for awareness.

Yet there are some difficulties attendant on the identification. Since for Furth monads are distinguished from one another by the degrees of their perceptions rather than by the objects of those perceptions (which would be the same for all the monads in a world), it follows that there can be at most one monad so "bare" that it is without even the dullest consciousness of its perceptions. Leibniz is clearly committed to the compossibility of a multiplicity of bare monads—those lowest on the scale of perfection of perception. But these are defined as endowed with perception but not *sensation* or sentience,[15] which is reserved to animal souls. These terms in turn occur in different texts both in a wide sense— sensation defined as perception accompanied by memory, which as we shall see is equivalent to apperception for Leibniz—and in a narrow sense, in which sensation is enabled by association with a particular kind of organic body possessing sense organs. In the narrow sense, which is how I will use the term 'sensation,' there is no reason to suppose that all apperception is comprised and hence that mere entelechies are excluded from some form of indistinct consciousness (= apperception). Yet in the *Monadology* we read that "if we had nothing distinctive [*rien de distingué*] in our perceptions, and nothing heightened [*relevé*] so to speak, and of a higher flavor, we should always be in a state of stupor. This is the state of the naked monads. We see too that nature has given heightened perceptions to animals by the care she has taken to provide them with organs which gather numerous light rays."[16] If we may take *distingué* to be synonymous with *distincte,* which Leibniz used in the passages quoted above, then it seems that we cannot distinguish between stuporous monads by their distinguished perceptions. It is in keeping with the general strategies of Leibniz's thought that consciousness be seen as occurring in even the least of substances—if perception goes all the way down, why not apperception? Yet if this is his doctrine, one would expect Leibniz to say so. He tells us that all monads perceive, but never that they all apperceive.[17] In section II we will see how Furth's main insight can be rescued from the consequence that all monads are conscious to some degree.

More serious difficulties arise when we consider the consequences of Furth's account of degrees of perception for monads advanced enough to be associated with animal bodies, however. The trouble is that Leibniz holds that "although each created monad represents the whole universe, it represents more distinctly the body which is particularly affected by it and of which it is the entelechy."[18] Or, in the terminology of the *Discourse,* all the soul's perceptions "correspond of themselves to that which happens in the universe at large, but more particularly and more perfectly to that which happens in the body associated with it, because it is in a particular way and only for a certain time according to the relation of other bodies to its own body that the soul expresses the state of the universe."[19] If degrees of distinctness of perception (perfection of expression) are interpreted as degrees of awareness, it follows that we must be more intensely aware of anything that is happening in our bodies than of anything external to them. On this view, if on a certain occasion I am more aware of the moon I gaze at than of the eye employed, then the moon has become part of my body, or the eye has ceased to be such a part, or both. We should treat this unwelcome implication not as simply one among many difficulties or incoherences in Leibniz's account of mind-body relations, but also as evidence against the outright identification of degrees of awareness and degrees of perception. For Leibniz himself often uses examples[20] concerning bodily processes such as digestion of which we are less aware than of external happenings such as the burning of a neighbor's barn. Leibniz simply does not hold that our bodies are that portion of the world of which we are most *aware,* as the "clearest is nearest" doctrine endorsed by Furth must claim. Nor could it be argued that what I am *really* aware of when my neighbor's barn burns is the state of my sense organs produced (in the vulgar, not the metaphysical, sense) by the conflagration.[21] For even if such a confining restriction of possible objects of awareness could be included in a plausible reinterpretation of the rest of Leibniz's thought, a distinction would still be required between the sense in which I am aware of my retina *as* expressing or representing flames and the sense in which I am *not* aware of the lining of my stomach as representing the digestive processes it partakes in. And this distinction will still not coincide, either on the side of representing or of represented, with the distinction between my body and the rest of the world. Furth's detailed reconstruction of spatial perspective in terms of differential awareness involves only objects *external* to our bodies and cannot be extended to those bodies themselves.

These specific difficulties with Furth's suggestion will be reexamined in section II below, as an interpretive strategy which avoids them is developed. First, however, we must look a little more closely at Leibniz's terminology. When introduced in the *Discourse,* perceptual degrees are referred to as arrayed along a dimension of greater and lesser *perfection*. This usage is not surrendered, persisting in later works in such passages as [D] above. In later works, though, the preferred and official portrayal of perceptual degrees is in terms of a range from *distinct* to *confused* perceptual expression (which are terms used only occasionally in this sense in the *Discourse*).[22] A common mistake among commentators on the doctrine of degrees of perception, which seems to stem historically from Russell's loose paraphrases in his classic work, is to talk instead about degrees of *clarity* of perception. Leibniz is, uncharacteristically, careful not to do so himself. (Furth falls victim to this error in passage [D], already quoted, as does Martha Kneale in her article cited in the discussion of action below. Popular histories such as Frederick Copleston's repeat this mistaken diction.)[23] There is good reason for his care on this point since the centerpiece of Leibniz's epistemology is a set of technical definitions of what it is in virtue of which an idea may be called *clear,* rather than obscure, and *distinct,* rather than confused. These definitions (intended to improve what Leibniz saw as uncritical Cartesian usage) were formulated in Leibniz's first mature work[24] and endorsed by him until the end of his life, being either repeated or cited in every major work. That the same terms should be chosen (sometimes in Latin, sometimes in French) for the polar opposites, allowing us to speak both of distinct and confused *perceptions* and of distinct and confused *ideas,* is clearly a datum of the first importance for understanding degrees of perception—a datum obscured by mistaking degrees of distinctness for degrees of clarity. The significance for our interpretive task of Leibniz's choice of identical technical terms in discussing perceptions and ideas is enhanced by the fact that Leibniz *defines* 'distinct' and 'confused' as they apply to ideas, as he does *not* in their application to perceptions.

Ideas for Leibniz are dispositions, habits, or capacities to have certain kinds of perceptions, including in some cases thoughts. When concerned with discussions of innateness, Leibniz distinguished further between ideas and concepts or notions, the latter being actually formed dispositions, the former being higher-order capacities to have concepts.[25] But elsewhere he is not careful about this distinction, as I shall not be. Ideas are sorted into clear or obscure depending on whether or not they enable *recognition* of the object of the idea, as my idea of sweetness does but my idea of this morning's substitute bus driver does not.

> Clear knowledge, in turn, is either confused or distinct. It is confused when I cannot enumerate one by one the marks which are sufficient to distinguish the thing from others, even though the thing may in truth have such marks and constituents into which its concept can be resolved. Thus we know colors, odors, flavors, and other particular objects of the senses clearly enough and discern them from each other but only by the simple evidence of the senses and not by marks that can be expressed.[26]

The corresponding passage in the *Discourse*—"*When* I am able to recognize a thing among others, without being able to say in what its differences or characteristics consist, the knowledge is confused"[27]—makes it clear that it is *discursiveness* that is the essential difference between distinct and confused (*clair-confus*) concepts. The passage continues:

> It is when I am able to explain the peculiarities which a thing has that the knowledge is called distinct. Such is the knowledge of an assayer who discerns the true gold from the false by means of certain proofs or marks which make up the definition of gold. But distinct knowledge has degrees, because ordinarily the conceptions which enter into the definitions will themselves have need of definition, and are only known confusedly.

Talk of distinctness of knowledge, ideas, and concepts is all explicitly made subject to these definitions. As we shall see, it is not uncommon for Leibniz to invoke the degrees of distinctness of ideas and the degrees of distinctness of perceptions in a single passage, and references of both sorts occur in all the major works (e.g., *Discourse* 23). It is therefore tempting to identify these uses, taking distinct perceptions as the acts which realize the dispositions that are distinct ideas (and similarly for confused ones), particularly in the light of the following remark: "Just as being is revealed through a distinct concept, however, so existence is revealed through a distinct perception"[28] (where being is the order of possibility, and existence that of actuality). I take it that this identification has been implicitly endorsed by most commentators, insofar as they recognize the two uses of *distincte* at all.[29] But we have seen that awareness or apperception presupposes distinct perceptions, and we know that not only rational spirits like humans, but all animal souls as well have apperception. Yet the beasts of the field, though they have sensation and hence awareness, cannot formulate definitions, enumerate marks, or in general *explain* their recognitive capacities as required for the possession of distinct ideas. The doctrine of degrees of perception requires that *all* monads have perceptions that are distinct to some degree. But possession of an idea distinct to *any* degree requires reason, which only those monads that are spirits possess. Nonrational animals cannot have distinct ideas, but must have distinct perceptions. It follows that we must give different accounts of these two notions and cannot take them to be related as potency to act. For the division of substances into bare monads with perception only, souls adding apperception, and spirits adding thought, is fundamental to Leibniz's metaphysics.

The claim that we must distinguish the distinctness of ideas from the distinctness of perceptions is clearly an important one, so let us examine it a little more closely. Leibniz's most complete and systematic treatment of epistemological issues is in the *New Essays,* which discusses both distinct perceptions and distinct ideas extensively. We find there fairly direct statements to the effect that the capacity to reason is presupposed by the possession of distinct ideas of knowledge: "The true mark of a clear and distinct notion of an object is the means we have of knowing therein many truths by a priori proofs."[30] So it is sufficient for the distinctness of an idea that it be inferentially developable ("a priori" being for Leibniz a mark of what pertains to reason, inference, and thought). Distinctness of an idea is also a necessary condition for intellectual analysis, as we see in a discussion of empirical recognitive capacities: "But this *clear image* or this feeling which we may have of a regular decagon or of a weight of ninety-nine pounds consists only in a *confused idea,* since it is of no avail in discovering the nature and properties of this weight or of this regular decagon, which demands a distinct idea."[31] Again we read that "ideas, when reason cannot judge of their compatibility or connection, are confused."[32] The same conclusion concerning the difference between distinctness of perceptions and of ideas can be reached by three lines of argument from less directly relevant texts.

First, one doctrine concerning distinct ideas is that "the soul is a little world, in which distinct ideas are a representation of God, and in which confused ideas are a representation of the universe."[33] This thesis is an obvious reflection of the earlier *Discourse* claim that "the spirits express God rather than the world, while other simple substances express the world rather than God," where spirits have just been defined as intelligent or reasoning souls.[34] This difference is explained as stemming from the fact that spirits can understand necessary truths, and hence are like God, as cannot those natures which are either "brutish and incapable of recognizing truths [animals], or are wholly destitute of sensation and knowledge," bare monads without the capacity to recognize and hence to have clear ideas, the lowest grade of knowledge. Together, these passages limit distinct ideas to intelligent souls, excluding the merely sentient beasts.

Second, notice that the difference between distinct and confused *ideas* is a qualitative one, whereas that between distinct and confused *perceptions* must be a quantitative one. Distinct ideas do come in degrees (of adequacy), but the basic notion is all-or-none, according to whether recognition actualizing some clear idea is performed *by* recognizing certain enumerable *marks* or not.

> I have sometimes defined an adequate idea as that which is so distinct that all of its ingredients are distinct, and such is nearly the idea of number. But when an idea is distinct and contains the definition or the reciprocal marks of the object it may be inadequate, viz.: when these marks or these ingredients are not also all distinctly known; for example, gold is a metal which resists the cupel and aqua fortis; it is a distinct idea, for it gives the marks or the definition of gold; but it is not perfect, for the nature of cupellation and the working of aqua fortis is not sufficiently known to us.[35]

Here, as elsewhere,[36] we can ask of each component mark whether it is distinct or not. A distinct idea all of whose marks are also distinct is *more* distinct than one whose marks are merely clear ideas. Confused ideas are thus *not* a limiting case of distinct ones. A sharp boundary exists between these two kinds of ideas, depending on whether or not the idea is a *definition* of the object, expressed as a set of "reciprocal marks" (necessary and sufficient conditions). Definition is of course a function of reason. But even if the sharp distinction were not made in this way, its very existence undercuts the identification of the sense of "distinct-confused" which applies to ideas with that which applies to perceptions, since the latter requires confused perceptions to be limiting cases of distinct ones. This point is important insofar as it is widely believed that Leibniz envisages a continuum of representation, of which the conceptual is the distinct pole and the sensual the confused pole. Such a view results from running together the doctrine of degrees of perception, which do form such a continuum but do not correlate directly with intelligibility and sensibility, and the distinctness and confusion of *ideas,* which, while not forming such a continuum, do capture the differences between ideas of reason and those of sense. Thought is perception inferentially articulated in that it occurs in accordance with distinct ideas and necessary truths. Sensation is subject not to inference but only to imaginative association. Between these there are no intermediate degrees.

A third consideration is that *clear* ideas that are merely confused require the capacity to recognize objects and thus require apperception. For if recognition did not require consciousness, then any unconscious perception that expressed a certain object would be a recognition of it and would demonstrate the existence of a clear idea. So every monad would have clear ideas of everything in its universe. But Leibniz certainly held that even spirits have many obscure ideas. So only souls, which have apperception, can have clear ideas. Recognition is the basic act of awareness, and so a soul which had *only* clear ideas would be aware. But we saw earlier that awareness presupposes the possession of *distinct* perceptions (see passage [F] above). It follows that clear ideas presuppose distinct perceptions. Thus distinct perceptions cannot be the actualizations of distinct ideas, for the actualizations of clear ideas (what would correspond, were the identification in question correct, to "clear perceptions") are recognitions—that is, perceptions that are noticed or apperceived, that require distinct perceptions although no distinct ideas are involved. Put another way, we can pair each element of the three metaphysical levels of being (bare monad, sentient soul, sapient spirit) with a corresponding element of the epistemological levels of knowledge (obscure ideas, clear but confused ideas, distinct ideas), but we *cannot* match this latter hierarchy of potencies to one of acts, of the form: perception, apperception, distinct perception. It is *thought* which belongs in the final place as actualizing distinct ideas. But then how are we to understand the doctrine of degrees of perception?

Perhaps we are reading the definition of distinct ideas too literally and hence are putting too much emphasis on the discursiveness of distinct ideas. The basic difference between clear-but-confused ideas and distinct ones is that between mere recognition and recognition by marks. It may be possible for an animal to have the capacity to recognize something by its marks, while being incapable of expressing that idea in the form of a nominal definition. It will not suffice for this that an animal which reliably recognizes a particular kind of berry as edible do so as a matter of causal perceptual fact because of some feature such as its shape. For perception of that feature may be causally necessary and sufficient for recognition of the kind of berry in question without the organism's being aware of the shape, without his having a clear idea of the mark he is in some sense using. And the component marks constituting a distinct idea must at least be clear. So to follow out this line of thought will be to fill in the notion of being aware of a mark as a mark. Each distinct idea codifies an *inference,* for example, from attribution of *resistance to a cupel and to aqua fortis* to characterization as *gold.* Perceptions which play inferential roles are *thoughts,* and only spirits have them. But beasts have what Leibniz calls "consecutions," which he says are "a shadow of reasoning." For habit may induce in beasts (or, as he says in more than one place, empiricists) sequences of perceptions based merely on association of ideas or even images connected by the imagination guided solely by particular instances, and with no idea of the reasons involved, as when a dog fears a stick he has been beaten with. Perhaps we can construct a "shadow" of distinct ideas, which is to them as the consecutions of the beasts are to thought, and which will justify attributing distinct *perceptions* to the brutes in some sense as the actualization of those ideas.

These various lines of thought about distinct ideas and distinct perceptions cannot be reconciled without some strains. But in section II, I put forward an account according to which the beasts' shadow of reasoning gives them also a shadow of distinct ideas, which in the weak sense will not require understanding (though modeled on it), while in the full sense being joined with the power of reflection. It is at any rate clear that we may not assume that we understand the use of 'distinct' and 'confused' as they apply to perceptions just because we understand them as they apply to ideas, although the use of the same paired opposites strongly argues for a connection. Although distinct perceptions are somehow related to apperception, we do not know how. And yet until we understand the notion of distinct perceptions we cannot interpret the most basic features of Leibniz's metaphysics: the levels of being, monadic perspectives, and action and passion, or indeed perception itself. The task of section II is the construction of a detailed interpretation of these matters that does justice to the difficult notion of distinctness of perception.

Leibniz sometimes seems to suggest that such interpretative effort is unnecessary, for "there is much that is innate in our mind, since we are innate, so to speak, in ourselves. There is in us: being, unity, substance, duration, change, action, perception, pleasure, and a thousand other intellectual ideas . . . immediate to our understanding."[37] Thus Descartes is chided for failing to add to the immediacy of my knowledge that I think, my knowledge that I have different thoughts, can will, and so on. At most it is claimed that these are *clear* ideas, which make us capable of recognizing their objects when they occur in us. But adequate or complete chains of explications according to distinct ideas must resolve ultimately into clear primitive concepts which we are told are identical with God's attributes. Being, unity, substance, and so on, are prime candidates for this status. Two things are strange about the inclusion of perception in this list of innate clear ideas. First, the idea of perception is described as an *intellectual* idea, although perception occurs in the beasts who have clear sensible ideas but no intellectual ones at all. Second, our introspective, clear idea of perception is an idea of perceptions which we are aware of, which are apperceived. Strictly, what we have is a clear idea of apperception. We cannot say, "Minute perceptions are just like the ones we are conscious of, only unconscious," and claim thereby to have expressed an idea (clear or distinct) as one might say, "Unobserved elephants are just like observed ones"; for, as Wittgenstein has pointed out, when mental states are at issue, awareness is the only feature that matters (cf. "It's five o'clock on the sun"). Leibniz is aware of this problem with his extension of the Cartesian notions of thought and perception to the unapperceived. He expended great efforts in the development of a theory of unconscious or "symbolic" thought (in which ideas are manipulated by marks of marks, corresponding to distinct ideas but never clearly conceived),[38] in the guise of a theory of notation. We want a similar explication of the *intellectual* idea of perception,[39] which the brutes who cannot reason according to necessary truths do *not* have, although they are aware of some of their perceptions. The innateness doctrine does not discharge this explanatory responsibility, and it is clear that we cannot make the polar notion of unconscious perception distinct merely by invoking a plenum of degrees of perception intermediate between those of which we are aware and those of which we are not.[40]

II. A Theory: Expression and Inference

I wish to make a suggestion: the expressive or representative nature of perception consists in the fact that from the existence of the modification of some monad which is a perceiving can be *inferred* the existence of various *accidents* or facts pertaining to its own monad or to others. An accident is any property of a subject which is not a maximal property, in the sense that it does not contain or entail all of the properties of that subject that are comprised by its individual concept. It is one of Leibniz's principles that "every true predication has some basis in the nature of things."[41] The basis in reality for our ordinary predications is called an accident, officially defined as "a being the notion of which does not include all that can be attributed to the subject to which this notion is attributed."[42] The subjects of ordinary predications are typically multimonadic aggregates. When we attribute sphericality to such an aggregate, for example, a billiard ball, the metaphysical basis in virtue of which this predication is true is a set of modifications of the monads which constitute the billiard ball. The impenetrability of the billiard ball will consist of a different selection of the modifications of those aggregated monads. One of the key features of the interpretation that follows is the claim that what is expressed by perceptions is a set of such accidents. This will allow an intensional reading of expression.

That the relation between expression and expressed is an inferential one is suggested by several of Leibniz's formulations, for instance, his earliest definition of mathematical expression: "What is common to all these expressions is that we can pass from a consideration of the relations in the expression to a knowledge of the corresponding properties of the thing expressed."[43] It is natural to take such "passage" from one consideration to knowledge of something else as inference. What is important about a map or a model is that we can make appropriate inferences concerning features of the mapped or modeled thing from observations concerning the features of the map and model. This reading is confirmed later in the same passage as we are told, "Similarly every entire effect represents the whole cause, for I can always pass from the knowledge of such an effect to a knowledge of its cause . . . It may also happen that the effects which arise from the same cause express each other mutually in gesture and speech," since for Leibniz the cause of a phenomenon is its sufficient reason. Expression is here clearly a generally nonsymmetric relation (as cause to effect or premise to conclusion), though capable of symmetry in particular cases. Further evidence is supplied by the use of the notion of *perfection* throughout Leibniz's mature period (a notion that supplies a crucial link to distinctness of perception). Immediately after passage [D] quoted above, the *Monadology* continues: "One created being is more perfect than another if one finds in it that which will supply a reason a priori for what happens in the other. And it is because of this that it is said to act upon the other." A similar definition is to be found in the *Discourse*,[44] where we recall that, as elsewhere, "degrees of expression" is used interchangeably with "degrees of perfection" (e.g., in passages [C], [D], and [G] above, and in *Discourse* 15).

Mathematical expression corresponds to a particularly simple case of inferrability, namely, where expressing features and expressed features stand in a one-to-one correspondence: "It suffices to the expression of one in another that there is a certain constant law of relations, by which the singulars in one can be referred to corresponding singulars in another,"[45] as each point of an ellipse can be projected onto a corresponding point of a circle. Notice that at this mathematical level expression is symmetric since one-to-one correspondences are. There seems no room for talk of "degrees of perfection" of correspondence. These facts become explicable if we read Leibniz's differentia for perceptual expression as expression of the many in the one, as appealing to his conceptual containment account of inference. One clear sense borne by the many-in-one formula[46] is that many perceptual modifications are nonspatially included in each simple substance. That this inclusion is inferential is argued by Leibniz's claim that the individual concept of the substance includes every one of its modifications, or put another way, that everything that will happen to the substance can be deduced from that concept. The present suggestion is that the many-in-one formula bears a second, less obvious but equally important sense, according to which *each* perception itself enfolds a multitude (of accidents), its expressive *range*. On this view, the mathematical expression of a circle as an ellipse differs from perceptual expression *both* in that ellipses and circles are mere aggregates and not true unities (corresponding to the first sense of the formula) *and* in that each point of the circle expresses only a single point of the ellipse. Evidence for this double reading can be found in such pronouncements as that "we can" define our essence or idea as that which includes everything which we express.[47] Given an individual concept, we can deduce not only all of its modifications but also everything expressed by them. Of course this will follow at once from the transitivity of deducibility if the expressive range of each perception is a set of accidents deducible from it, as I have suggested.

The claim then is that percepts have content in the same way in which concepts do, with each perception expressing a variety of facts about its universe. On this account, expressive content is an intrinsic feature of perceptions, each of which has its own content or set of attributes deducible from its occurrence. By contrast, the projected points of an ellipse that expresses a circle have their contents as extrinsic properties, acquired in virtue of their relations to other points on the ellipse. Deductive relationships in Leibniz's universe are always an expression of its fundamental lawfulness. Whenever an inference can be made, it is according to an underlying rule or regularity. For conic sections, laws of geometrical projection underwrite the inferences in virtue of which one expresses another. For perceptions, the preestablished harmony of the modifications of one monad with the modifications of others makes possible the inferences that give perceptions their expressive contents.

A perception provides its monad with information about the rest of the world only insofar as the preestablished harmony provides principles (laws of nature) which permit inferences from the occurrence of this particular perception, rather than any other possible one, to conclusions about facts outside that monad. We are assured of the existence of such principles only by metaphysical reasoning. The form in which that harmony manifests itself in the experience of particular monads is the physical or phenomenal world. It is accordingly facts couched in the phenomenal terms of *this* world that are the informational contents of perceptions as experienced by the monads those perceptions modify. For the monad, its world is the world of physical, perceptible attributes. Leibniz's phenomenalism entails that the deductive relations between perceptions implied by the preestablished harmony are reflected by deductive relations between those perceptions and features of the phenomenal things which appear to the perceiving monad as their objects.

In what follows, the prime argument to be offered for this sense of "many-in-one" as inferential containment of many attributes in one perception is the explanatory power the hypothesis possesses regarding Leibniz's many doctrines about degrees of perception. Besides accounting for the asymmetry of expression involving modifications of true substances evident in the application to cause-effect relations above, this interpretation gives a natural sense to talk of degrees of expression. For if many accidents are expressed in one perception, it is possible for more or fewer of them to be expressed by another perception. We may say that two perceptions differ in perceptual or expressive degree just in case the expressive range or content of one of them properly includes the range or content of the other.[48] Leibniz's standard definition of perfection is that that is most perfect which is "simplest in hypotheses and richest in phenomena."[49]

That is, one substance is more perfect than another if from fewer premises about it, more about its world can be deduced than is the case for the other. The "hypotheses" will be statements reporting the occurrence of a perception in some monad, and the "phenomena" deducible from them will be statements reporting on the inherence of an accident in some subject. Thus higher degrees of perfection of expression correspond to more inclusive sets of expressed (inferable) accidents. Consider three perceptions of a physical object. The first, p_1 represents it as red (its expressive range consists of a single accident), p_2 represents it as cubical, and p_3 represents it as red and cubical. Then p_3 will be a more perfect expression of the object than p_1 or p_2. Indeed, we can see why one might say that p_3 is more *distinct* than p_1 or p_2, and they more confused than it. For p_1 cannot distinguish the object from a red sphere, while p_2 cannot distinguish it from a green cube. Perception p_3 is both more distinguishing and more specific than the others.

On this account, the degrees of perception are a consequence of the character of perceptions as representing many in one. A cardinal virtue of this approach is that it explains how two numerically distinct monads, individuated *only* by their perceptions, can nonetheless both express the whole world. For a monad to express the whole world is for the union of the expressive ranges of all of its component perceptions to include the complete set of accidents of that world, that is, those accidents whose joint occurrence determines every particular substantial modification in that world. Different monads simply divide up that complete set of accidents among the expressive ranges of contemporaneous perceptions in different ways. In a mini-world in which no modifications exist save those in virtue of which a particular cube is red, one substance (by hypothesis "part" of the cube, since the world contains nothing else) might express its whole world by having the single perception p_3 while another has p_1 and p_2 instead. These perceptions are distinguishable, since no two of them have the same expressive range. The monads these perceptions modify are accordingly distinguishable as well, since they are qualified by distinguishable modifications. Yet each monad expresses *every* feature of its world, since for each monad there is no accident not expressed by some one of its perceptions. Each complete set of a monad's contemporary perceptions has the whole set of its world's real accidents as the union of the expressive ranges of its perceptions. But the distribution of more and less inclusive expressive ranges over that set of perceptions differs from monad to monad, and from time to time within a single monad (see passages [A] and [B] above). It is these differences in the distinctness (inferential potential) of the individual perceptions that jointly express the whole world which distinguish the various monads.

In order to follow out this suggestion for interpreting perceptual expression and its degrees as regards the notions of action and awareness explicated in terms of them, we must take note of one important respect in which Leibniz sharpened his views between 1687 and 1706. If we compare passages [C] and [D] above, we may notice that the first defines action in terms of an *increase* in the degrees of expression of a substance, while the second defines it in terms of having perceptions of a high degree, with changes in degree not mentioned. A prominent commentator[50] has argued that the earlier view is an "aberration" and that Leibniz himself did not believe its paradoxical consequences—the conclusion drawn in the *Discourse* after passage [C] that "every activity of substance which has perception implies some pleasure, and every passion some pain." The *Discourse* definition cannot be seen as merely aberrant, however, for throughout his career Leibniz held a doctrine of *development* of perception, enunciated in the same terms in the late (1714) "Principles of Nature and Grace" as in the epistemologically authoritative *New Essays,* as well as in the early *Discourse* and correspondence with Arnauld.[51]

A perception is said to "develop" or be "heightened" when it becomes more perfect or distinct, increasing its expressive degree. What happens is that where in the *Discourse* development is associated primarily with activity, and secondarily with awareness (since pleasure and pain are both apperceptive states for Leibniz), afterwards development is offered as part of the account of awareness alone (see passages [F] and [G], for instance). In the later view, awareness is a kind of activity, but not all activity is awareness. I will present detailed reconstructions of each of these notions. First I show how *differences* in degrees of expression can be seen as underwriting the attribution of cause-effect interaction between monads, without requiring the sort of active *change* of degree I will associate with awareness.

Kneale[52] is right to doubt the cogency of the claim that a pair of billiard balls engaged in a collision affect each other by causing apperceptive states of pain and pleasure, as the earlier view seemed to require. But it is not at all obvious that sense can be made of the later view either. For we know that monads are ranked by the degrees of their perceptions, with spirits ranked higher than brutes or bare monads. But then it seems we must deny that it is possible for a lower being, a stone, say, to cause pain to a brute, or for a chemical substance to put a rational being to sleep. Each of these would be action by a less perfectly expressive being upon one more so. Any view about Leibniz's account of activity must face this difficulty. The paradoxical conclusion can be avoided, however, by focusing on the differences in the degrees of perfection with which two apparently interacting substances express not their whole world, but some particular occurrence. We can be a little more precise about how the partial ordering of perceptions into degrees by the inclusion relations among their expressive ranges can be extended to partially order the time-slices of monads in which those perceptions occur, as required by the theory of causation. Let a be any set of accidents (perhaps a temporal sequence of them forming the "change" of passage [C] above), and let m and m' be two different sets of co-monadic, contemporaneous sets of perceptions. We can say that m expresses a more perfectly than m' does if it is possible to select a non-empty subset $k(m)$ of the perceptions in m such that (i) $k(m)$ is a complete expression of a, that is, every accident in a is in the union of the expressive ranges of the elements of $k(m)$; and (ii) for any subset $k(m')$ which completely expresses a, $k(m)$ is inferentially stronger than $k(m')$, in the sense that given any perception $p' \in m'$, there is some perception $p \in m$ such that the expressive range of p' is a proper subset of the expressive range of p. This condition merely generalizes the example discussed making more perfect expression (higher degrees of perception) depend on having perceptions which are richer and more specific in content.

I will justify this definition further when I discuss the development of perception and awareness. Even at this point I can remark on a cardinal explanatory virtue of the definition, however. We saw above that Leibniz believes that a cause or activity provides a reason a priori for its effects.[53] Yet his *definition* of causation in its general form as action and passion (as presented in passages [C] and [D], for instance) is in terms of differences of degree of expression. What is the relation between the definition and the claim that effects are deducible from their causes? Given our inferential reading of expression and the account above, the deducibility claim *follows* from the definition of action and passion. For it follows directly from the account of more perfect expression above that everything deducible from the occurrence of m' is also deducible from the occurrence of m; the content of the relevant passive monadic substate $k(m')$ is part of the content of the relevant active monadic substate $k(m)$. If m' is involved in the change in question, that is, if the modifications in virtue of which the accidents in a characterize the world in question, then those modifications themselves will be part of the content of $k(m)$, that is, will be deducible from it. So insofar as we can justify reading high relative degrees of expressive perfection of monadic states as corresponding to having perceptions with richer and more specific expressive ranges as above, we can explain how the active state gives a reason for or allows us to deduce the corresponding passive one.

This much results from the three interpretive suggestions offered so far: taking the expression of many-in-one which is perception to apply each to perception (as well as to the monad as a whole); taking the relevant sense of "in" to be explicated inferentially following the idiom of Leibniz's account of deducibility in terms of the containment relations of concepts; and taking degrees of perception to correspond to more-or-less-in-one, where again, according to Leibniz's intensional logic, increasing the number of accidents attributed to a subject amounts to specifying one's claim. My account also explains why mathematical expression, which is not a matter of many-in-one, does not come in degrees and seems to have nothing to do with activity and passivity. As section I argues, however, the real test of any account of degrees of perception is its treatment of the problem of *distinctness* of perception. An acceptable account must explain both directions in which the use of this term pulls: one way toward awareness, the other toward distinct ideas. The existence of these two uses of 'distinct' must be explained in the light of the sharp distinction in levels of being between those who have sensation but no more, and those who can think also and hence can have distinct ideas.[54] Even without this complication introduced by considering distinct ideas, the association between distinct perceptions and awareness causes trouble, as we have seen, since our bodies are defined as whatever we have the most distinct perceptions of (passage [H] above), and our bodies are not the exclusive or even the preeminent objects of our awareness. So let us consider awareness.

One of Leibniz's important doctrines about awareness is that apperception occurs when we not only *have* perceptions but also *perceive* those perceptions. Three basic elements must accordingly be distinguished. First, there is an apperceiving, which is a perception of an earlier perception. Second, the perception thus perceived is the immediate object of apperception—that in us to which we attend, as distinguished from the myriad of perceptions we ignore. Finally, there is that in the world, a table, perhaps, of which we are mediately aware in virtue of attending to or perceiving the immediate object of attention. There are two questions we should ask about awareness according to this structure: First, what is the relation between a perception that is an apperceiving and the perception that is its immediate object, in virtue of which we may say that awareness is occurring at all? (How is it "of" its internal object?) Second, what is the relation between this constellation of perceptions and that external object which they constitute an awareness of? In addressing this second question, I will need to explain (in accordance with the discussion of section I) how it is possible to be aware of anything except one's own body. Each of these queries must be distinguished from the related question of what it is about a perception or a feature of the world which makes it liable or likely to become an object of apperception in either of these two senses. "Novelty" is a good response to the second kind of worry, but not to the first. Unfortunately Leibniz does not carefully separate these issues in the *New Essays* (our basic source on such matters), which has obscured what he has to say about the more basic questions (what the trick of awareness consists in or how it is brought off, rather than when it is likely to be performed).

Consider the first question. I referred above to the various pronouncements establishing that the expressive development of perception is a necessary condition for awareness. Insofar as the development of perceptions involves only the expressive or representative contents of the developed and developing perceptions, development as increasing distinctness or perfection of expression has been glossed as specification of that content, understood in turn by inclusion relations holding between the sets of accidents which are their expressive ranges. In order to arrive at necessary and sufficient conditions for the occurrence of apperception, we must consider also purely material features of perceivings as vehicles for expression, features arising out of the particular representings of expressive content as they occur in the career of individual monads. For illumination of this aspect we may look to the third class of definitional remarks about apperception (the first two being those talking about perception "of" perceptions, and development), namely, those concerning *memory*. In the same texts which make so much of development, "sentiment," or feeling (the generic prereflexive apperceptive state), is defined as "perception accompanied by memory."[55] We are also told that "all attention requires memory,"[56] with the acknowledged implication that strictly all we can be directly aware of is our immediately past perceptions.[57] My claim is that appeals to memory, development, and perception of earlier perceptions determine a single account of awareness, involving both material and expressive features, though each emphasizes one or the other sort.

Mere repetition of representative content is notoriously insufficient for memory. My awareness of the table today may have the same content as yours of yesterday, but it is not a memory of your experience. To be such requires beyond the repetition of content also that the memory be *produced* in the right way. For Leibniz this "production in the right way" is a matter not of causation of phenomenal interaction between monads, but of that genuine metaphysical activity whereby the perceptions modifying a monad at any given time produce their successors according to the law which is the concept of that individual, as expressed by a contemporaneous set of appetitions codifying particular tendencies of one set of perceptions to give rise to another. For p_2 to be a memory of p_1 requires not only a relation of their contents but also that p_2 have been produced by p_1.

In general, perceptions will give rise to other perceptions whose expressive ranges bear little relation to those of their progenitors. But if p_1 both gives rise to p_2 and has its expressive content repeated or specified by p_2, then p_2 is a perception, memory, development, that is to say, an awareness *of p_1*. Awareness of or attention to a perception thus should be understood as the product of the two characteristics of metaphysical *production*[58] of the later perception by the earlier one and the expressive *specification* of the content of the first by the second, in that the expressive range of the first is a subset (proper or improper) of the expressive range of the latter. In this way, memory as requiring only repetition of content is assimilated as a limiting case to development of that content. Put another way, awareness occurs when one perception is "of" another in the dual sense of being produced *by* the first and expressing (at least) the content of the first. Thus in the representative sense of what a perception is "of," discussed above, the second perception must be of the same content as the first, in that every fact (the occurrence of an accident) deducible from the first must likewise be deducible from the second.

I have assumed that the representative content of a perception is an intrinsic feature of that perception—that a perception could not be just the modification it is without having just the content that it does—since appetitions are the differentials or tendencies on the part of perceptions to give rise to other perceptions. That is to say that awareness resides as a potential in special appetitions or developmental tendencies, which may or may not be realized by the succeeding crop of perceptions. (In fact, Lebiniz's account of intentional action is couched in terms of *distinct appetition* which reason develops so that we are aware of the inclinations which impel us.[59] The present analysis may be applied to the degrees and development of such appetitions at a higher level—with degrees of appetitions corresponding to the development which would result in the perceptions involved, and the development of appetitions corresponding to tendencies to increase development codified in higher-order appetitions governing the tendency of one appetition to give rise to another. The details of such an extension, involving as they do the perception of good and evil, lie beyond the scope of this work, however.)

So a straightforward answer to the first of our questions about apperception (about the relation between an apperceiving and the perception that is its immediate content) is available which draws together the three sorts of locutions Leibniz uses to explain awareness. This account reflects, furthermore, the primary empirical datum that, to judge from the frequency with which examples are cited and the variety of theoretical insights he thinks can be gleaned therefrom, Leibniz took as the basic object of explanation and major confirmation of his account of awareness and unconscious perception—namely, that one may remember after the event an occurrence one did not notice at the time, but must in some sense have seen in order now to recall. On my account, all perceptions are intrinsically unconscious. But though a perception might have remained undeveloped and hence unnoticed for several generations of its perceptual progeny, this is consistent with eventual development (since "to produce" is transitive). Indeed, Leibniz holds that "nothing is for nothing," that all perceptions will eventually be developed, that all monads will eventually be conscious of all that they have ever perceived. (Holding this doctrine does not, of course, defuse the objection made earlier concerning what is required to make intelligible what is meant by the notion of "unconscious" perceptions, as we still need to know what these are like *before* they are developed.)

I have already considered the sense of "distinct perception" as perception of high expressive degree that is relevant for the explanation of physical interaction. The current claim is that another sense of "distinct perception" occurs in passages such as [I] below, where awareness is at issue. In such passages, the question is how a particular set of perceptions becomes distinct in the sense of distinguished from the rest as the immediate objects of attention and are themselves perceived. My answer is that they are distinctive or remarkable in the measure of their development, that is, the *increase* in their expressive degrees. This second sense is thus defined in terms of the first. Given these two senses of 'distinct' as applied to perceptions, we can easily resolve the issue raised earlier concerning bodily awareness. The body of a dominant monad is that which it perceives most distinctly in the first sense, that is, has the richest, most detailed and inferentially powerful perceptions of. This does not mean that those perceptions are the most developing, however. There need be no special correlation between those perceptions of highest expressive degree and those which give rise to *more* expressive specifications of themselves. It is these latter that matter for awareness. So we need not be more aware of our bodies than of anything in the rest of the world. Even if each bodily perception, with its inclusive expressive range, gives rise to a perception with an expressive range of similar size, if the content of the first is not included in that of the second, there is no awareness, regardless of the expressive degrees involved (see the discussion of sensations below). It is for this reason that we can say that perceptions of our own bodies are confused.

My second question about apperception concerned the determination of the ultimate external objects of awareness. Clearly these are determined in some way by the expressive ranges of the "heightened" perceptions of which one is immediately aware. That some care is required in dealing with this issue, however, is indicated by Leibniz's account of sensation. Two major features of that account yield interpretive puzzles. First, from 1684 on it is claimed that sensations are made of a myriad of "smaller" perceptions that are its "parts":

> When we perceive colors or odors we are having nothing but a perception of figures and motions, but of figures and motions so complex and minute that our mind in its present state is incapable of observing each distinctly and therefore fails to notice that its perception is compounded of single perceptions of exceedingly small figures and motions.[60]

How is one perception "compounded" out of others? How can those parts result in the apperception that is sensation without themselves being apperceived? Second, Leibniz holds that the phenomenal qualities that are the contents of states of sensory awareness are *phantasms* or phenomenal qualities that, while grounded in some sense in the figures and motions of the bodies they express, are not qualities to be found in the world represented but rather are artifacts of our representing those motions in apperception. Thus if we were able to distinguish further the perceptual parts comprised by our sensation of green, we would discover it to be a compound of blue and yellow. These sensory phantasms would in turn disappear on further analysis; but as a result of the infinite divisibility (indeed infinite division) of matter, new phantoms will arise no matter how finely we divide our sensation.[61] Both doctrines are combined in Leibniz's likening of sensory phantasms to the artificial transparency of a toothed wheel or spoked cart wheel as it rotates, in which the individual parts move too fast for us to distinguish.

The doctrine of phantasms is puzzling because of its ambiguous status with respect to the metaphysical foundations of the possibility of *error*. For Leibniz's official view is that perception never errs, that it is only with judgment, at the level of reason, that error is possible.[62] Sensation as apperceptive is intermediate on the scale of being between mere perception and rational judgment. The phenomenal qualities of sense are somehow intermediate between the infallible representation of mere perception and the possibility of genuine error of discursive judgment. The difficulty of explicating this doctrine parallels and reproduces on the epistemological side the metaphysical embarrassment similarly arising concerning the status of space and time as "true phenomena" grounded in but in some ways misrepresenting the nature of individual substance. Sensations represent neither quite correctly nor quite incorrectly, but what sort of middle ground is envisaged here?

We need not address the question of how perceptions can be composed of or have as parts other perceptions in terms of a *spatial* notion of part-whole. Leibniz tells us that this is not the primary signification of talk of parts and wholes,[63] and it seems that he has in mind the logical relations of containment of *concepts* in one another as primitive. Following this line of thought suggests that it is the *expressive ranges* of petite perceptions which are included as parts in the expressive range of some perception which is a sensation. Suppose P to be an infinite set of perceptions which jointly give rise to p_1, whose expressive range is just the union of the ranges of the elements of P. Then p_1 will count for us as developing those perceptions, and hence will be an apperceiving, as sensations are. If none of the elements of P is individually developed, that is, gives rise to a perception more distinct of it though not of its fellows, then on our account we would have no separate awareness of that perception and hence would be ignorant of its exact contribution to the corporate awareness of the infinite set P.

Why on Leibniz's account should we have such wholesale development in preference to development of individual perceptions? This can be seen as a consequence of two general precepts. First, Leibniz holds a principle of *finiteness of apperception*, that our awareness at any given time comprises only a finite number of elements.[64] (Indeed, it is to this finiteness of apperception that the appearance of "leaps" in a continuous universe is due, according to Leibniz.)[65] Thus in the *New Essays* our ignorance of the minute perceptions making up sensations is attributed to their "infinite multitude, which keeps us from distinguishing them."[66] Next, as a result of the principle of sufficient reason, if there were a multitude of petite perceptions which differed little from one another, there would need to be some *sufficient reason,* grounded in those perceptions themselves, why one and not another of them was developed. That the little perceptions differ only insensibly from one another is frequently invoked as a reason for our failure to distinguish them. If we take the finiteness of apperception to restrict a single field of awareness to a finite number of apperceivings (i.e., perceptions which are developings of others), and if we assume as a result of the constitution of bodies the presence of infinite sets of expressively similar perceptions ripe for development, the principle of sufficient reason *requires* that perceptions developing infinite sets of their ancestors arise. Since sensation, as perception of something external,[67] must involve perceptions expressing the infinitely intricate relations of material bodies actually divided to infinity, in virtue of the association of sensation with the material impressions of bodies on the organs of sense, we can be sure that infinite sets of insensibly different perceptions will occur.

But what of the content of these joint-stock developments of infinite sets of lookalike perceptions? Whence the phantasms? The key here may be taken to be the paired notions of artificiality and abstraction as they arise in the model of the disappearance of the spokes of a spinning wheel. Such transparency is an artifact of its means of production, arising only under specifiable circumstances. In such a way we could describe the expressive range of a perception which developed an infinite number of similar minute perceptions as "artificial" just in case no perception which does not arise in that way ever has that expressive range. That is, the expressive ranges of percepts which are sensations may be artifacts of the expressive combination of an infinite number of similar precursors. It would make a neater story if the status of the contents of sensations as phantasms could be accounted for just as expressive ranges artificially inclusive in this sense, but phantasms in this sense would not be "false" enough as expressions for what Leibniz says of them. Often it is suggested that what is appercievable is what is *common* to the infinite number of petite perceptions which conspire to produce an effect (this seems to be a lesson of the discussions of how individually insensible increments in the intensity of a sound can awaken one from a sound sleep, for instance). Our failure to perceive the individuals is the failure to distinguish the unique contribution of each to the resulting awareness. To take this strand of thought seriously, a set P of petite perceptions is taken as consisting of perceptions whose expressive ranges largely overlap, though each may contain a few distinguishing accidents. A perception metaphysically produced by all of them might be said to develop (in an attenuated sense) the *set P* if it expressed a superset of what is *common* to the expressive ranges of elements of P, even though no element of P is developed in the strict sense. The common content thus apperceived is artificial in the above sense, and is false as representation in just the sense in which abstractions may be called "false" as overlooking distinguishing detail. The infinite descending hierarchy of phantasms is easily explained in these terms. If I become capable of greater discrimination concerning my sensation of green, more attentive to its origins and details—in short, more aware of the distinctions in expressive range in the collaborating petite perceptions—I may divide P into two subsets P' and P^*, each of which boasts a larger common expressive core than P did, and which separately give rise to the sensations of blue and yellow. The resegregation of P into P' and P^* occurs only because more distinguishing accidents of its elements are taken account of, and the same process can in principle occur in P' or P^* since an infinite number of differentiating features of expression are abstracted from at each stage.

On this account, then, sensation occurs when what is developed is the common core of an infinite set of perceptions so similar to one another that there is not sufficient reason for individual elements or proper subsets to be picked out as distinguished and to be individually developed. All the minute perceptions which are in this sense included in a sensation contribute to a single undifferentiated episode of sensory awareness. "These sense-ideas are simple appearance, because, being confused, they do not give the mind the means of distinguishing their contents; . . . we treat these ideas as simple ideas because at least our apperception does not divide them,"[68] Leibniz says of the recognitive dispositions (clear but confused ideas) corresponding to sensations.

The final question we must consider is what sort of perceptual act, or form of apperception, if any, corresponds to distinct *ideas* as their realization. The trouble with the ideas of sense is that "they are not distinct, because they are not distinguished by what they include. Thus we cannot give a definition of them."[69]

> Thus although in our view distinct ideas distinguish one object from another, nevertheless, as the ideas clear but confused in themselves do so also, we call *distinct* not all those which are very discriminating or which distinguish objects, but those which are well distinguished, i.e., which are distinct in themselves and distinguish in the object the marks which make it known, which an analysis or definition gives.[70]

"Distinct in itself" here may refer either to inclusiveness of expressive range or to development. The element in this account that goes beyond sensation is distinguishing within the object the marks by which it can be known. The simple recognition which actualizes clear ideas has been modeled by development of the content of a perception expressing some feature of the world. To recognize a feature is to be aware of it, to respond to one's initial perception expressing that feature *as of* that feature, namely, by developing the original content. What is wanted now is a similar account of recognition by marks, which can apply to ideas more complicated than red. What is it to be aware of some feature *as a* mark of a particular object?

Leibniz recognizes that nonreasoning animals are capable of apperceptive association, as when noticing a stick he was once beaten with makes a dog fear another beating. This is not reasoning, since it depends not on conformity to necessary principles but on adventitious facts about one's actual sensory career. But it is a "shadow of reasoning" that the brutes exhibit and that marks the limit of aspiration of empiricists.[71] Let us look more closely at what is required for such associative links to allow recognition by marks analogous to that enabled by distinct ideas. In the *New Essays*, Leibniz offers an extended and surprisingly modern discussion of the recognition of natural kinds by their marks. In his early work, Leibniz took as the expression of a distinct idea in a nominal definition statements such as "gold is the most fixed metal." This view was refined, however, as Leibniz sought to deal with a puzzle Locke raises. Locke had objected (section 50 of "On the Names of Substances" in the *Essay*) that with such a definition one could not without triviality assert that gold is fixed, whereas if we take the definition as shorthand merely for the assertion that gold is some internal essence and that being fixed is a consequence of that essence, then we are speaking of a wholly unknown essence. Leibniz's reply is that "the body given by this internal constitution is designated by other external marks in which fixedness is not comprised, as if one said: the heaviest of all bodies is also one of the most fixed."[72] Here and elsewhere in this work (see especially pp. 394 and following), Leibniz requires *two* sets of marks for recognition of an object according to a distinct idea. The problem is explicitly presented as arising from the necessity of explaining the informativeness of identity statements codifying such recognition. Thus malleability is indeed included in our complex idea of gold:

> But in order to express its malleability without identity and without the defect of *coccysm* or repetition, we must recognize this thing by other qualities, as color and weight. And it is as if we said that a certain fusible body, yellow and very heavy, called gold, has a nature which gives it besides the quality of being very soft to the hammer and capable of being made very thin.[73]

Taking Leibniz's "it is as if we said" in these passages as indicating an analysis of the sense of what is said, this dual-marks requirement exactly coincides with Frege's demand that the expressions flanking an identity sign (what in the *Grundlagen* he called "recognition statements"—for him as for Leibniz all cognitive activity consists either of recognition or of inference) express different senses, if the identity is to count as expressing a recognition at all. Our problem is thus to say what it is according to Leibniz to *take* two sets of marks *as* marks of the *same* object (the apperceptive or recognitive status expressed discursively by reasoning beings in the form of identity statements).

The marks involved in distinct ideas may themselves be merely clear, so we may take the marks to be sensory complexes in the simplest cases. But we may not then identify recognition by marks simply with passage from one such complex to another, even if some repeatable kind of passage becomes habitual. For such passage may be no more than a shift of attention, as one might have the habit of conjuring up the smell of fresh cinnamon upon seeing a white picket fence (as the result of an early experience) without in any way confounding the objects. Not every reminder is a recognition. What is required is that two separate sets of marks be distinguished both *from* each other (as the minute perceptions which are in some sense "marks" for the awareness that is recognition of sensory qualia are not) and *as* characterizing a common object which exhibits all of the accidents expressed by either set of marks. For the significance of the recognition that $a = b$ is that every accident of a is an accident of b and vice versa. Thus we are led to the following scenario for the advent of a perception which will be "distinct" in the third and strongest of our senses, namely, as the recognition by marks enabled by distinct ideas—the sense in which distinct perceptions alone furnish "matter for reason."[74] Let the first of our marks be the combination of accidents a_1 and a_2 that we suppose to be expressed by perception p_a occurring at time t_a, and let the second of our distinguishing marks be the combination of accidents a_3 and a_4 expressed by p_b occurring at a later time t_b. We may think of these as corresponding to the perception of an instance of the heaviest metal and of the most malleable yellow one, respectively. The individual in question must be aware of each of these, and as distinct (i.e., discrete). So we presume that p_a is developed by a succeeding perception p_a' and p_b is developed by p_b'. To be aware of these properties as marks of one thing, then, will be for p_a' and p_b' to be jointly developed by a further perception p_c, produced by both and whose expressive range is a superset of the union of the expressive ranges of p_a' and p_b'. P_c is then a distinct recognition of gold. It is the occurrence of a common development of the contents of p_a' and p_b' that sets off awareness of them as marks of one thing from the mere associational passage from p_a' to p_b' (considered for the moment as repeatable types) which includes habitual shifts of attention. That the content of p_c may include more than is included in p_a' or p_b' allows a dog to take both the appearance of a certain stick and an expression of his master's as marks of an impending beating (and hence of each other) without being aware of the beating as consisting entirely in that association.

The difference between the way p_c develops the content of p_a and p_b and the way a sensation develops the contents of the multitude of minute perceptions it springs from is the difference between distinguishing component marks and confusing them. In distinct recognition the perceptions developed need have no overlap of expressive range. Even if they do have some accident as common content (e.g., *metallic)*, it is the *differences* between those contents which makes distinct recognition possible. In sensation, only the *common* content is developed. Individual perceptions are not distinguished from one another, nor developed. P_a and p_b may themselves be sensations, of course, or more generally, their places may be taken by *sets* of sensations—the set associated with a heavy yellow metal sphere and that associated with a sphere of a malleable, fixed metal, for instance. In either case it seems clear that the beasts of the field could possess distinct recognitions ultimately based on their senses that differ from the inferential realization of distinct ideas *only* in that the development of expressive content essential to them is not underwritten by the necessary and general truths of reason, stemming rather from happy historical accident with regard to the acquisition of developmental appetitions. Furthermore, some account along these lines will be required if we are willing (as Leibniz seems to be) to attribute to brutes some differentiation of the field of awareness, not with regard to intensity of attention (which we model by degree of development), but as awareness of a variety of objects. Only a mechanism like that suggested will allow the segregation of features in the world of which we are separately aware into co-objectual classes. Thus a brute aware of the smells of an apple and an orange, and of a red sphere and an orange one, can in virtue of the co-development of the perception of the red sphere and the apple smell on the one hand, and the orange sphere and the orange's smell on the other, be aware of two fruits as well as four features. Such partitioning of features into objects is also needed for association to work well, so that the apple smell will in future be associated only with apples, and not with oranges.

I have discerned three different but closely related senses in which Leibniz uses the concept of <u>distinctness</u>. The first and earliest use, in terms of which the hierarchy of perfection of monads and physical interaction are to be understood, corresponds to being of high *expressive* degree, that is, having a relatively inclusive expressive range. The next use, in terms of which awareness or apperception is to be explained, is one in which a perception is distinct (and hence noticed) to the extent to which it is *developed,* that is, gives rise to a perception whose expressive range is a superset of that of the original perception. The concept of <u>development</u> accordingly presupposes and builds on the notion of <u>expressive degree</u>. The doctrine of finiteness of apperception, that only a finite number of the most developed perceptions are apperceived, together with considerations concerning the bodily origin of sensations and the principle of sufficient reason, enabled me to explain the occurrence of sensory phantasms in terms of development as well. Finally, I described a use which occurs only very late, which indeed appears to be developed in the *New Essays* in response to Locke's doctrines concerning the articulation of ideas, in which a perception is distinct just in case it constitutes recognition of some object by marks. This usage is explained by a two-stage sequence of development and is that intended when Leibniz talks of distinct perceptions as realizing distinct ideas, although strictly reason is not required for such recognition by marks.

> [I] We apperceive many things within and without us which we do not understand, and we *understand* them when we have distinct [*distinctes*] ideas of them, together with the power of reflection and of drawing from them necessary truths. Animals therefore have no understanding, at least in this sense, although they have the faculty of apperceiving impressions more remarkable and more distinguished [*plus distinguées*], as the boar is aware of a person who shouts at him, and goes straight for this person, of whom he had had before only a cloudy perception, but confused, as of all other objects which fell under his eyes, and whose rays struck his crystalline humor. Thus in my view the *understanding* [when exercised] is called *intellection,* which is a [*distincte*] perception united with the faculty of reflection, which is not in animals. Every perception united with this faculty is thought, which I do not accord to animals any more than understanding, so that we may say there is intellection when thought is distinct [*distincte*].[75]

These three senses arrayed in roughly increasing order of strength and maturity of period of development enable one to explicate all of Leibniz's pronouncements concerning distinctness of perceptions—or indeed appetitions.[76] One could hardly avoid discriminating the first two senses, since the tension between them appears even in the earliest work. The third might be discarded as unduly speculative, if one is willing to ignore various of Leibniz's late pronouncements.

The theoretical postulate which permits the detailed explication of these various phenomena of perception and apperception is the association with each perception of an *expressive range* consisting of those accidents or features of the world which are represented by that perception, that is, are deducible from its occurrence. This association of intensional content with each perception is motivated by consideration of the nature of perception and of expression according to Leibniz, in particular the need to differentiate perceptual from merely mathematical or symbolic expression in such a way as to permit the gradation into *degrees* of perceptual expression so crucial to the metaphysical role Leibniz assigns that notion. By using that hypothesis about the content of perceivings, it was possible to offer necessary and sufficient conditions for both the *occurrence* and the delimitation of *content* of *apperceivings,* including sensations.

It is important to notice that although the recognition by marks corresponding to distinct ideas is explicitly the model for the third sense of *'distinct'* as applied to perceptions, it is implicitly the model for the second sense as well. Development of a perception corresponds to passage from a mark or feature to a more inclusive delineation of an object. On the level of concepts, moving from the mark *heaviest metal* to the concept gold is moving to a concept that along with much else includes the designation *heaviest metal.* So my notion of awareness can be restated as what occurs when a perception is taken as a mark of another more expressively complete perception. When the mark is in addition apperceived *as* a mark, the third sense of distinctness arises.

This observation is important for evaluating the theoretical role assigned to the notion of *inference* in the portions of Leibniz's epistemology and philosophy of mind which I have taken to be metaphysically fundamental. Inference is the primitive which anchors both ends of the foregoing explanatory structure. First, the basic theoretical auxiliary I introduced, the notion of an individual expressive range, is explicitly explained in terms of inference. The expressive range of a perception is that set of accidents (nonrepeatable occurrences of complex property-types) which may be inferred from the occurrence of that perception alone (i.e., if nothing else were known about its universe). It is only insofar as there are primitive inferential facts of this form that this explanatory scheme gets off the ground. At the other end, the model in terms of which awareness and recognition consciously by marks (the Fregean model of recognition) are explained is that of distinct *ideas,* which as we have seen are *inferentially* articulated ideas, which can be had only by beings capable of reason. These again I take for granted.

One of Leibniz's primary methodological principles is that we should conceive those things of which we do *not* have distinct ideas on the model of those things of which we *do* have distinct ideas. I have suggested, in effect, that at least with regard to perception and representation, he also conceives those things which are not distinct ideas (inferentially articulated) on the model of those things which are. Inference is the root notion in terms of which representation and its varieties are explained. It is this in which Leibniz's *rationalism* consists: that where empiricists begin with a primitive notion of *representation* and seek to ground in it whatever inferences are to be recognized (as Hume attempts to ground causal and inductive inference), he as rationalist begins with inference and then explains the notion of representation in terms of it. It is in this sense that percepts are assimilated to concepts (efficacious ideas), as modeled on them, though we have seen that in no way can the difference between them be described as merely one of "degree."

6

Holism and Idealism in Hegel's *Phenomenology*

I. Introduction

The opening "Consciousness" section of Hegel's *Phenomenology* addresses our understanding of the physical world around us. The next section, "Self-Consciousness," begins to consider our understanding of ourselves and one another. This order of discussion is neither arbitrary nor merely convenient. Rather, one of the principal lessons we are to have learned by the end of the development of "Consciousness" is that our best conception of the world that is the *object* of our cognitive activities is intelligible only as part of a story that also considers the nature of the *subject* engaging in those activities. The rationale for this expository transition is an important strand in Hegel's *idealism.* In this chapter I offer a rational reconstruction of an argument that I see as supporting this transition and the kind of idealism it embodies.[1]

II. The Problem: Understanding the *Determinateness* of the Objective World

Hegel starts the line of thought I will be rehearsing with the everyday idea of how things are—the idea that there is some way the world is. Understanding how things are or might be is grasping a certain sort of *content.* And his first observation is that that content—the way things are or could be taken to be—must be *determinate.* That is to say at a minimum that there must be a distinction between things being that way and their being some other way.

(1) The way things objectively are must be *definite* or *determinate.*

Determinateness is a matter of identity and individuation. It concerns how one thing is distinguished from others.

   In thinking about the sort of difference implicit in the notion of determinateness, it is important for us to distinguish between two different kinds of difference. Properties (for instance) can be *different* but compatible, as **square** and **red** are. We might call this "mere" difference. But properties can also be different in the stronger sense of material incompatibility—of the impossibility of one and the same thing simultaneously exhibiting both—as **square** and **triangular** are. We might call this "exclusive" difference. Although I cannot discuss here how the point is made, in "Sense Certainty," Hegel argues that the idea of a world exhibiting definiteness or determinateness as *mere (gleichgültige,* translated by A. V. Miller as "indifferent") difference, without *exclusive (auschliessende)* difference, is incoherent. This is why compatibly different properties always come as members of families of exclusively different ones.[2]

   Hegel embraces the medieval (and Spinozist) principle *omnis determinatio est negatio.* But mere difference is not yet the *negation* that determinateness requires according to this principle. For an essential, defining property of negation is the exclusiveness codified in the principle of noncontradiction: *p* rules out *not-p;* they are *incompatible.* For Hegel, it is this exclusiveness that is the essence of negation. He abstracts this feature from the case of formal negation, and generalizes it to include the sort of material incompatibility that obtains between the properties **square** and **triangular.** (Formal negation can then reappear as the shadow of material incompatibility: *not-p* is the *minimal* incompatible of *p.* It is what is entailed by everything materially incompatible with *p.*) In a conceptually deep sense, far from rejecting the law of noncontradiction, I want to claim that Hegel radicalizes it, and places it at the very center of his thought.[3]

   So his idea is that

(2) The essence of determinateness is modally robust *exclusion.*

One understands items (for instance, propositions or properties) as determinate just insofar as one understands them as standing to one another in relations of material incompatibility.

> The many determinate properties . . . are only determinate in so far as
> they *differentiate* themselves from one another, and *relate* themselves *to
> others* as to their opposites.[4]

> It is through its *determinateness* that the thing excludes others. Things
> are therefore in and for themselves determinate; they have properties
> by which they distinguish themselves from others . . . They are deter-
> minate properties in it only because they are a plurality of reciprocally
> self-differentiating elements.[5]

The idea Hegel is working with here is a common feature of both contemporary information-theoretic and possible-worlds approaches to semantics. The concept of the information conveyed by a signal is defined
in terms of the way its reception serves to restrict, for the receiver, some
antecedent set of possibilities. Before receiving the message, I knew only
that the number lay between 0 and 100. Afterwards I know that it is an
even number in that range. (This fundamental idea must not be confused
with the much more specific strategy for working it out that assigns
numbers as *measures* of information in that sense.) The defining function of information is to rule out possibilities. Again, possible-worlds semantics sees a proposition as significant just insofar as it effects a *partition* of the space of possible worlds. Its correctness *excludes* the actual
world from one element of the partition (although rhetorically the focus
is usually put on its being *included* in the other).

The concept of material incompatibility, or as Hegel calls it "determinate negation," is his most fundamental conceptual tool. Here are two
uses of it that are particularly important for articulating the sort of idealism that is my topic.

First, relations of determinate negation allow the definition of *consequence relations* that are modally robust in the sense of supporting
counterfactual inferences—what show up at the end of "Consciousness"
in the form of *laws*. The proposition or property p entails q just in case
everything incompatible with (ruled out or excluded by) q is incompatible with (ruled out or excluded by) p. For instance, having the property
square entails having the property **polygonal**, because and in the sense
that everything materially incompatible with **square** (for instance, **circular**) is incompatible with **polygonal**. In this sense, it is *impossible* for
something to be square without also being polygonal. So we can see
(though Hegel never makes the point explicitly) that:

(3) Material *incompatibility* relations induce modally robust material
    consequence relations.

Taking his cue from the role played by the middle term in a classical syllogism, Hegel uses the term "mediation" *(Vermittlung)* in discussing the
inferential articulation of contents induced by relations of determinate
negation. Thus mediation can be understood in terms of determinate negation.[6] This is to say that for Hegel, *schließen* is rooted in *ausschließen*
(conclusion in exclusion). Together, these two sorts of relation define
what Hegel means by "conceptual" *(begrifflich)*:

(4) To be *conceptually* articulated is just to stand in material relations
    of incompatibility and (so) consequence (inference).

In this sense, conceptual articulation is a perfectly objective affair. It has
nothing obviously or explicitly to do with any *subjective* or *psychological*
process. Showing that it nonetheless does have an *implicit* connection to
such processes, and what that connection is, is the task of motivating objective idealism (that is, idealism about the objective conceptual
structure of the world).

   Given this definition, Hegel's *conceptual* realism can be seen as just the
form taken by a *modal* realism. There really are modally qualified states
of affairs: possibilities and necessities (necessitations being the inferential version of this categorical notion, and conditional possibility being
the corresponding weaker conditional modality). Further, without acknowledging them, we cannot make intelligible ordinary descriptive
predicates and properties. Again, Hegel will claim that modal realism requires objective idealism.

   Second, I started this story with the idea of how things are—the idea
that there is some way the world is. Understanding how things are is
grasping a certain sort of *content.* In talking about objectivity and subjectivity in terms of 'truth' and 'certainty', Hegel wants us to start by focusing on this notion of *content* rather than on the *objects* of (claims to)
knowledge. One reason to do this, of which Hegel's "Introduction" reminds us, is so that our philosophical idiom will not rule out from the
beginning as incoherent the possibility that how things are in themselves might also be how they are for some consciousness—that there is
a sense of 'content' in which, at least in some cases, truth and certainty
may be two different forms taken by the same content. If we start by ter-

minologically committing ourselves to a picture of consciousness as a *re-lation* between two sorts of *thing*, subjects and objects, we cut ourselves off from the shift in theoretical perspective that Hegel wants to recommend under the heading of 'idealism', which is my topic here. Talk of subjects and objects comes late in the story, not at the beginning. And when they do officially become a topic, in "Perception,"

> (5) The concepts subject and object can be defined in terms of determinate negation or material incompatibility.

Both are to be understood as loci or units of account that in a generic sense "repel" or "exclude" incompatibilities. Objects repel objectively incompatible properties (such as **square** and **triangular**), in that one and the same object *cannot* at the same time exhibit both—though they can be exhibited by different objects. And subjects repel subjectively incompatible commitments (for instance, commitment to something's being square and commitment to its being circular) in that one and the same subject *ought* not at the same time endorse both (though the same prohibition does not apply to the commitments of different subjects). The different ways in which objects and subjects "repel" or "exclude" them make it clear that incompatibility$_{obj}$ and incompatibility$_{subj}$ are *different* concepts. (Since, while one object *cannot* simultaneously exhibit objectively incompatible properties, one subject merely *ought* not simultaneously undertake subjectively incompatible commitments.) The intimate relation between these concepts—the way in which incompatibility$_{obj}$ and incompatibility$_{subj}$ turn out to be two sides of one coin, each intelligible in principle only in relation to the other—is the essence of Hegel's *objective idealism* concerning the relation between the subjective and the objective poles of consciousness.[7]

III. Holism

The notion of immediacy presupposes determinateness of content but cannot by itself underwrite it. Determinate content must be articulated by relations of material incompatibility. That realization entails rejecting the semantic atomism that lies at the core of what Wilfrid Sellars would later call the "Myth of the Given," in a work that opens by invoking "Hegel, that great foe of immediacy." The concept of immediacy can itself be made intelligible only against a background of mediating relations of exclusion. This is the conclusion of Hegel's discussion "Sense Certainty."[8]

Understanding determinate conceptual content in terms of relations of exclusion among such contents commits one, then, to some kind of *semantic holism*. Although earlier thinkers outside the empiricist tradition (especially Kant) had dipped their toes in the water, Hegel is the first thinker explicitly to take the plunge and try to think through rigorously the consequences of semantic holism. But what exactly is he committed to? To begin with,

(6) We can distinguish two grades of holistic commitment:

> *Weak* individuational holism: Articulation by relations of material incompatibility is *necessary* for determinate contentfulness (for instance, of states of affairs and properties on the objective side, and propositions and predicates on the subjective side).
>
> *Strong* individuational holism: Articulation by relations of material incompatibility is *sufficient*—all there is available to define it— for determinate contentfulness (for instance, of states of affairs and properties on the objective side, and propositions and predicates on the subjective side).

Hegel is clearly committed to the weaker claim. So, for instance, in a characteristic expression introducing it in the discussion titled "Perception," Hegel says of "differentiated, determinate properties" that "*many* such properties are established [*gesetzt*] simultaneously, one being the negative of another."[9] *One* property can be understood as determinate only by understanding *many other* properties—those incompatible with it—as similarly determinate. But is he also committed to the stronger form?

There are reasons to think that he is. Standard contemporary ways of thinking of conceptual content in terms of the exclusion of possibilities—paradigmatically information-theoretic and possible-worlds accounts—treat the space of possibilities partitioned by such a content as fixed and given in advance of any such partition. By contrast to both, the line of thought Hegel develops here does *not* take it that the possibilities are available conceptually antecedently to the possible (indeed, actual)[10] contents of messages or claims, or that the properties are already sitting there intelligibly determinate *before* the relations of exclusion among them have been considered. For what would that determinateness consist in? If immediacy *as* immediacy is *in*determinate, it seems that the relations of exclusion must be what their determinateness consists in. What might be called "asymmetric relative individuation" of one sort of item with respect to another is a relatively straightforward matter. Thus if I understand the property **red** as selecting out of the set of objects a privileged subset, namely, those that exhibit that property, I can identify and individuate another property, **not-red**, entirely in terms of its contrast with the original property. I understand it also as selecting out of the set of objects a privileged subset, defined in terms of the other, namely, the complement of the first. But this is not what Hegel offers us. He is committed to *symmetric* relative individuation, in which a whole *set* or *system* of determinate contents—comprising **red, blue, yellow,** and so on—is "posited" at once, each individuated by its relations to (its strong differences from) the others.[11] If such a view does not entail strong individuational holism, a story will have to be told about why not.

The second reason to attribute to Hegel commitment to strong individuational semantic holism is the nature of the transition from "Perception" to "Force and Understanding" that is driven by making explicit the holism that turns out to be implicit in understanding properties as identified and individuated by the relations of determinate negation and mediation in which they stand to one another (and, at a higher level, to the objects ultimately defined as centers of exclusion of them). Thus even in its first appearance, where the concept of <u>force</u> is understood as dividing into forces playing the roles of soliciting and solicited, we are told:

> These moments are not divided into two independent extremes offering each other only an opposite extreme: their essence rather consists simply and solely in this, that each *is* solely through the other, and what each thus is it immediately no longer is, since it *is* the other. They have thus, in fact, no substance of their own, which might support and maintain them.[12]

At this point, relations to other items of the same category are not merely *one* necessary element in the individuation of the items being considered. It seems that they are all there is. The whole discussion in "Consciousness" leads up to putting on the table the final holistic conception of the conceptual that Hegel calls "infinity." At the very end of that part of the *Phenomenology,* Hegel says:

> Infinity . . . in which whatever is determined in one way or another . . . is rather the opposite of this determinateness, this no doubt has been from the start the soul of all that has gone before.[13]

The conception of the conceptual as "infinite" is the axis around which Hegel's systematic thought revolves. Grasping it is the primary goal toward which the exposition of the whole *Logic* is directed. In the discussion at the end of "Force and Understanding," the "notion of inner difference,"[14] contrasting with the inadequate atomistic conception of "absolute" difference, is repeatedly equated with <u>infinity</u>. In fact, the term is introduced for the first time as characterizing what

> is itself and its opposite in one unity. Only thus is it difference as *inner* difference, or difference as *its own self,* or difference as an *infinity.*[15]

Inner difference is material incompatibility among items understood to be the items they are solely in virtue of standing in those relations of necessary mutual exclusion. Inner difference is

> a *difference* which is no *difference,* or only a difference of what is *self-same,* and its essence is unity. The two distinguished moments both subsist [*bestehen*]; they are *implicit* and are *opposites in themselves,* i.e. each is the opposite of itself; each has its 'other' within it and they are only one unity.[16]

Understanding such a holistic unity requires "the distinguishing of what is *not* to be distinguished, or the *unity* of what is distinguished."[17]

The holistic successor conception to a world of *facts*—namely, the world as having the structure of *infinity*—emerges as the lesson of the discussion of the constitutive holistic interrelations of laws.

> That the simple character of law is infinity means, according to what we have found, (a) that it is self-*identical,* but is also in itself *different;* or it is the selfsame which repels itself from itself or sunders itself into two . . . (b) What is thus dirempted [*Entzweite*], which constitutes the parts . . . exhibits itself as a stable existence . . . but (c) through the Notion of inner difference, these unlike and indifferent moments . . . are a *difference* which is no *difference* or only a difference of what is *self-same,*

and its essence is unity . . . The two distinguished moments both sub-
sist; they are *implicit* and are *opposites in themselves,* i.e. each is the opposite of itself; each has its 'other' within it and they are only one
unity.[18]

We are now to think of the whole as having its differences within it, as
an articulating structure essential both to the constitution of the whole
and to the constitution of its "self-differentiating" components.

Those components can be thought of as particular facts, particular
laws, and general laws, provided we do not forget that these cannot be
understood as atomistic elements intelligible independently of and antecedently to consideration of the modal relations of exclusion and inclusion in which they stand to one another. If we keep firmly in mind that
the topic is a holistically understood system of determinately contentful
elements that are determinately contentful, *conceptually* contentful, just
because and insofar as they are articulated by relations of material incompatibility, and hence material inferential relations, we can at least
begin to see what Hegel is trying to get across in passages such as this
one:

This simple infinity, or the absolute Notion . . . whose omnipresence is
neither disturbed nor interrupted by any difference, but rather is itself
every difference, as also their supersession; it pulsates within itself but
does not move, inwardly vibrates, yet is at rest. It is self-*identical,* for its
differences are tautological; they are differences that are none . . . that
very self-identicalness is an inner difference. These *sundered moments*
are thus *in and for themselves* each an opposite—*of an other;* thus in
each moment the 'other' is at the same time expressed; or each is not
the opposite of an 'other' but only a *pure opposite;* and so each is therefore in its own self the opposite of itself. In other words, it is not an opposite at all, but is purely for itself, a pure, self-identical essence that
has no difference in it . . . But in saying that the unity is an abstraction,
that is, is only one of the opposed moments it is already implied that it
is the dividing of itself; for if the unity is a *negative,* is *opposed* to something, then it is *eo ipso* posited as that which has an antithesis within it.
The different moments of *self-sundering* and of *becoming self-identical*
are therefore likewise only this movement of *self-supersession;* for since
the self-identical, which is supposed first to sunder itself or become its
opposite, is an abstraction, or is *already itself* a sundered moment, its
self-sundering is therefore a supersession of what it is, and therefore

the supersession of its dividedness. Its *becoming self-identical* is equally a self-sundering; what becomes identical with itself thereby opposes itself to its self-sundering; i.e., it thereby puts itself on one side, or rather *becomes* a *sundered moment*.[19]

The concept of infinity in play here is clearly a holistic one. But should we understand it as holist in the *strong* sense? It turns out that there is a real question as to whether we even *can* so understand it.

IV. Conceptual Difficulties of Strong Holism

For Hegel also realizes what the difficulty of his language perhaps makes manifest: it remains far from evident just how to understand such holistic claims in detail. We will see that one of the primary tasks driving Hegel's exposition—in particular, the crucial transition from "Consciousness" to "Self-Consciousness"—is unpacking the commitments implicit in holist conceptions of content, and assembling the conceptual raw materials needed to explain them.

Strong individuational semantic holism asks us to think of conceptual contents—that is, for Hegel, whatever is in any coherent sense *determinate*—as forming a *holistic relational structure*. Such a structure would consist of a domain and set of relations of material exclusion defined on that domain. But, further, it asks us to understand the domain elements themselves as constituted by the relations of material exclusion it stands in to other domain elements. The relata are in a sense dissolved into the relations between them. And at this point we have a chicken-and-egg problem: the relations are individuated by their relata, and the relata by the relations they stand in. But relations between *what*, exactly? The intelligibility of the relations themselves is threatened. Can we really understand relations of incompatibility without any prior grip on what is incompatible? How does the whole thing get off the ground? Once we have eschewed *a*symmetric relative individuation in favor of the symmetric variety, the strong version of holism threatens to dissolve into unintelligibility. What is supposed to be the very structure of determinateness itself seems wholly *in*determinate and unconstrained. The strongly distinguished items are defined in terms of their strong differences. There is an evident danger of circularity involved in trying to individuate some items in terms of others when the situation is symmetric. For in that case those others to which one appeals are themselves only individuated in terms of their relations to the so-far-unindividuated items with which one began. The sort of structure being described threatens to be *unendlich* in the sense that we chase our tails endlessly in search of some firm distinctions and distinguished items to appeal to in getting the process of identification and individuation started.

I think there is not just a prima facie problem in making strong individuational semantic holism intelligible, but one that is unsolvable in principle.

(7) Strong individuational semantic holism is not a coherent position.

If we are to make good sense of Hegel, we must come to see that, in spite of the ways in which his language repeatedly invites us to attribute this view to him, he is in fact *not* committed to this sort of strong holism. But we must also, then, see what it is about the view he *does* endorse that makes these forms of expression tempting. Hegel's understanding of *determinateness*—whether thought of objectively, as a matter of how things really are, or subjectively, in terms of our grasp of how things might really be—in terms of modally robust *exclusion* entails a certain kind of holism. And I have indicated that I think Hegel's *idealism* should be understood as motivated in the *Phenomenology* by being revealed as an implicit presupposition of the intelligibility of that holism. In evaluating the philosophical credentials and significance of Hegel's idealism, the argument for this claim is of the utmost importance. So it is worth some care to get it right.

V. A Bad Argument

Unfortunately, the texts that discuss this move—basically, those that describe the rationale for the transition from the consideration of the objects of consciousness, in "Consciousness," to the subjects of consciousness, in "Self-Consciousness"—invite a reading in which only a very weak argument is visible. For Hegel emphasizes from the beginning that consciousness itself must be thought of as having a certain kind of holistic structure: it is a unity that essentially consists in the relation between its distinct subjective and objective poles (what appear, for instance, as "the immediately self-differentiating moments within perception").[20] And it can *look* as though what he is saying is that once we discover the holistic character of the *objects* of consciousness, we see that they resemble consciousness itself in this respect, so that consciousness of everything should be understood on the model of consciousness of objects that themselves have the holistic structure characteristic of consciousness—that is, that we should understand consciousness generally on the model of *self*-consciousness. I will call this the "analogical argument from holism" for the sort of idealism that models consciousness on self-consciousness, thereby underwriting the expository transition from "Consciousness" to "Self-Consciousness." Thus in the penultimate paragraph of "Consciousness," after the discussion of "infinity" we find this summary of what appears to be the rationale for moving at this point to concern with *self*-consciousness:

> Since this Notion of infinity is an object for consciousness, the latter is consciousness of a difference that is no less *immediately* canceled; consciousness is for its own self, it is a distinguishing of that which contains no difference (*Unterscheiden des Ununterschiedenen*), or *self-consciousness*. I distinguish myself from myself, and in doing so I am directly aware that what is distinguished from myself is not different. I, the selfsame being, repel [*abstoßen*] myself from myself; but what is posited as distinct from me, or as unlike me, is immediately in being so distinguished not a distinction for me. It is true that consciousness of an 'other', of an object in general, is itself necessarily *self-consciousness* . . . consciousness of itself in its otherness . . . [N]ot only is consciousness of a thing possible only for a self-consciousness, but that self-consciousness alone is the truth of those shapes.[21]

The object of consciousness has the holistic relational structure Hegel calls "infinity." This is a structure of differences (exclusions) that are canceled or superseded (*aufgehoben*) in that the identity or unity of the differentiated items is understood as consisting in those relations of reciprocal exclusion. But consciousness itself is such a structure. So consciousness of objects is consciousness of something that has the same structure as consciousness. It is therefore structurally like consciousness of *selves* rather than objects. Generically, then, it is to be understood as self-consciousness.

This is a dreadful argument. If it were intended to show the *identity* of consciousness and self-consciousness (if that were the intent of the 'is' in the claim "consciousness of an 'other', of an object in general, is itself necessarily *self-consciousness*"), it would have the same form as what has been called the "schizophrenic syllogism":

$$\frac{\text{Men die.}}{\text{Grass dies.}}$$
$$\therefore \text{ Men are grass.}$$

That is, it would illegitimately infer identity from mere similarity. If, however, it is intended merely to show a structural analogy, the situation seems entirely symmetrical. Why should self-consciousness be privileged because of its holistic character as the fixed end of analogy on the basis of which to understand the holistic character of the objects of ordinary consciousness rather than the other way around? In any case, the analogy does not seem very strong. On the face of it, the relation between subjects and objects in consciousness is asymmetric: there cannot be subjects of consciousness without objects, but the very same things that can be the objects of consciousness (e.g., the physical forces theoretically postulated by natural science) can be there without subjects to be conscious of them. Of course they are not there *qua* objects of consciousness, but so what? The asymmetry would still seem to be real. Hegel *might* mean to deny that there is any asymmetry of this sort between the status of subjects and objects of consciousness, but if so he would hardly be entitled to *assume* such a view in arguing for an idealist conclusion. And there does not seem to be any corresponding asymmetry in the holistic relational structure he has discerned as implicit in the determinateness of the objective world. (One could try to work one up from the asymmetry underlined by the discussion of the inverted world—the asymmetry, namely, between the actual facts about what objects have what properties, on the one hand, and the merely possible instantiations of properties by those same objects that they, as determinate, exclude, on the other. But this seems importantly different from the subject-object asymmetry.) If this is right, then the analogy between the underlying holistic structure of the objective world arrived at by the end of "Consciousness" and the holistic structure consciousness is supposed to have would depend on a very thin and abstract respect of similarity—a slender reed on which to build an idealist edifice.

Things would look, if anything, worse if Hegel is relying on his terminology to shore up the comparison. Thus one might seek to appeal to the formula that determinate objective content (say, of a property) is a kind of "identity in difference," and then use the same words to describe consciousness. But the mere fact that the same phrase could be used about both surely counts for very little here, especially given the differences just pointed to. Again, the fact that Hegel can say that "in general, to be for itself and to be in relation to an other constitutes the essence of the content,"[22] and that one could also say that consciousness was both "for itself and in relation to an other" (i.e., essentially involved consciousness of itself and of its object) may just show the flexibility of this somewhat figurative way of speaking, rather than evidencing any very illuminating similarity. Calling the relations something stands in its "being for others" would be a pretty cheap way to buy the right to model the objects of consciousness on the subjects of consciousness, especially in the context of a social theory of self-consciousness, which explains being-for-self in terms of being-for-others. The point is not that using the same terminology for both cases cannot be earned, or that it cannot be illuminating. The point is that it must be earned in order to be illuminating. At the *end* of the story, we may see why it is useful to talk this way. But it is hard to see how these tropes by themselves can move that story along. The mere fact that it is possible to talk about the objects of consciousness and consciousness itself in terms that are so generic that we say some of the same things about both is a very weak rationale for the expository transition to "Self-Consciousness." The most it would provide is an excuse for a shift of topic, along the lines of saying, "Now, let's look at self-consciousness, since it has come up in the story." But it would provide no argument at all for any sort of interesting or controversial idealism, and no clarification of such a thesis. If this sort of argument—really a verbal slide that conflates two quite different points, one wholly on the side of objective content (facts, objects, properties), the other about the relation between such contents and knowers—were the best we could find Hegel presenting at this crucial juncture in his account, there would be no reason to take his idealism seriously.

VI. Objective Relations and Subjective Processes

A good place to start is with a distinction between inferential *processes* and inferential *relations* that emerges first in thinking about logic. Gilbert Harman has argued provocatively that there are no such things as rules of deductive inference.[23] For if there were, they would presumably say things like "From *p* and *if p then q,* infer *q.*" But that would be a bad rule. One might already have much better evidence against *q* than one had for either *p* or the conditional. In that case, one should give one of them up. What deductive logic really tells us is not to believe all of *p, if p then q,* and *~q.* But it does not tell us what to *do* inferentially. It merely specifies some deductive *relations* of entailment and incompatibility, which *constrain* what we should do without *determining* it. Inference is a *process;* implication is a *relation.* Nothing but confusion can result from running together the quite different concepts of inferential processes and inferential relations. What I will call "the Harman point" is

(8) One must distinguish, and consider the relations between, inferential *relations* (and hence relational structures)[24] and inferential *processes.*

He makes the point in connection with formal deductive logic, but it has broader applicability.

In particular, Hegel's term '*Schluß*' exhibits just this relation/process ambiguity. It is usually translated "syllogism," on the perfectly reasonable grounds that '*Schluß*' is the term historically used in Germany to discuss Aristotelean syllogistic inferences. And there are places, particularly in the *Science of Logic* discussion of the forms of syllogism, where this is the only proper translation. But the term means *inference* more generally. And while it is clear that sometimes he is talking about the relations between the different elements of a classical syllogism—for instance, about having the status or playing the role of a middle term—as we shall see, it is also clear that sometimes he is talking about the *movement* from the premises to the conclusion.[25] (Related terms, such as 'mediation' [*Vermittlung*] take similar double senses.) Indeed, one of his major concerns, I shall argue, is with the *relation* between inferential relations and inferential practices or processes.

As we have seen, Hegel has a deeper notion than that of material inference, namely, material *incompatibility.* The only sorts of inference Hegel considers as contributing to determinate conceptual content are the modally robust ones that derive from relations of exclusion. Taking material *inferential* relations (mediation, *schließen*) to be grounded in material *incompatibility* relations (determinate negation, *ausschließen*) suggests a generalization of the Harman point, to relational structures defined by *exclusion,* and (so) by *necessitation.* Hegel's version of the Harman point accordingly is something like

(9) In thinking about determinateness in terms of material incompatibility, and so in terms of inference, we should also distinguish between *relations* and *processes.*

I think it is helpful to construe the distinction between the *objective* incompatibility of situations, properties, states of affairs, or the determinate elements of an "infinite" holistic conceptual relational structure, on the one hand, and the *subjective* incompatibility of commitments, on the other hand, on the Harmanian model of *relations* and *processes* (or practices). The *process* on the *subjective* side of *certainty* that corresponds to the *relation* of incompatibility of facts or properties on the *objective* side of *truth* is *resolving* incompatible *commitments* by revising or relinquishing one of them. As a version of the point was put above, *objectively* incompatible properties *cannot* characterize the same object (objectively incompatible facts cannot characterize the same world), while *subjectively* incompatible commitments merely *ought not* to characterize the same subject. Any case where they do is a case of *error,* the acknowledgment of which (as Hegel has argued in the "Introduction") is what taking one's commitments to be answerable to an objective world (in the sense constitutive of treating them *as* representations *of* such a world) consists in. But to acknowledge an error, that is, to acknowledge the incompatibility of two of one's commitments, is to acknowledge an obligation to *do* something, to *alter* one's commitments so as to remove or repair the incompatibility.

I think that the idealism that emerges from the expository transition from "Consciousness" to "Self-Consciousness" claims, broadly, that one cannot understand the relations of *objective* incompatibility that articulate the conceptual relational structure in virtue of which the objective world is *determinate,* unless one understands the *processes* and *practices* constituting the acknowledgment of the *subjective* incompatibility of *commitments* that are thereby treated as representations *of* such a world—in the sense of being answerable to it for their correctness. Such a view about the relation between subjective cognitive *processes* and the *relations* that articulate potential objects of knowledge involves extending the Harman point along another dimension. It requires not just that there be a *distinction* between conceptual relations (paradigmatically, material inferential and incompatibility relations) and conceptual processes (of belief and concept revision), but further, that grasp of the relations *consists* in engaging in the corresponding processes. This view is a more specific version of

> (10) Conceptual pragmatism: grasp of a concept (conceptual content) is a *practical* capacity, mastery of a practice, or the capacity to undergo or engage in a process; it is the capacity to *do* something.

(Sellars propounds a linguistic version of conceptual pragmatism in claiming that grasp of a concept is always mastery of the use of a word.) Applied to the case in hand, understanding the objective relation of determinate negation or material incompatibility, which provides the most basic structure of the conceptual, is acknowledging in practice a subjective obligation to engage in the process of resolving incompatible commitments.[26]

Read back into the very simple Harman case with which we began, endorsement of conceptual pragmatism supports a stronger claim than Harman makes: the claim that one does not understand the concept of deductive implication *relations* unless one understands them *as* constraints on inferential *processes* of rationally altering one's beliefs. This is the idea that what it is for the relations in question to be *implication* relations just is for them to play a certain role in constraining rational belief change. Endorsing this thought is moving beyond the original point. For Harman does not say that what it *is* for one proposition to stand in a relation of implying or entailing another just *is* for certain inferential moves and not others to be correct or appropriate (and vice versa). He does not take the process of grasping inferential relations to be an essential defining element of what those relations are.[27]

VII. Sense Dependence, Reference Dependence, and Objective Idealism

It will be helpful here to introduce some definitions.

> (11) Concept P is *sense dependent* on concept Q just in case one cannot count as having grasped P unless one counts as grasping Q.

(12) Concept P is *reference dependent* on concept Q just in case P can-
    not apply to something unless Q applies to something.[28]

A paradigmatic sense dependence claim is Sellars's classic argument in
"Empiricism and the Philosophy of Mind" that one cannot master the
use of 'looks' talk without having mastered the use of 'is' talk. The concepts nail and hammer may be related like this: one cannot understand
what a nail is—something meant to be driven by a hammer—without
understanding what a hammer is.[29]
    One important point to keep in mind is

(13) Sense dependence does not entail reference dependence.

That is, even if the concept nail is sense dependent on the concept hammer, it would not follow that it was impossible for there to *be* nails without there being hammers to drive them. (Maybe the nails were invented
first, or all the hammers were destroyed.)[30] The point is clearest if we
look at *intensions* and *extensions* in a possible-worlds framework. Consider a property or intension defined by a *de re* comparison: **being more
massive than the Earth's sun (in fact) is.** (Calling it a *de re* comparison
just marks the familiar distinction of scope: in evaluating its application,
one *first* determines the mass of the Earth's sun in *this* world, and *then*
compares it to the mass of bodies in other possible worlds.) Now, I take
it that this intension is intelligible only in the context of another: the
mass of the Earth's sun. No one who did not understand the latter could
count as understanding the former. (Of course, understanding the concept does not require knowing what the mass of the Earth's sun is in the
sense of being able to specify a number of kilograms or pounds.) And
this is not just a point about understanding. It is a point about the
intensions themselves: one is defined in terms of (as a function of) the
other. But it is clear that there could be stars that have the property **being more massive than the Earth's sun** even though they are in possible
worlds in which the Earth and its sun never formed. That is, the dependent intension can be instantiated even though the intension it depends
on is not.
    Another example: the property **being produced by a reliable belief-
forming mechanism** is conceptually dependent on that of **being a true**   = Sense dep.
belief, because to be a reliable belief-forming mechanism is to produce
beliefs that are likely to be true. But a belief can exhibit the dependent

property without exhibiting the property it is conceptually dependent on—it can be produced by a reliable mechanism without being true.

From the fact that P_2 is defined as an intension that is a function of the intension of P_1, it simply does not follow that wherever P_2 is instantiated, so is P_1. Definitional dependence of *intensions* does not entail de facto dependence of *extensions*.

If one first extends the Harman point from formal logic, and applies it also to material inferential and incompatibility relations and then strengthens it into commitment to a kind of conceptual pragmatism, what one gets is a characteristic kind of *reciprocal sense dependence claim:*

> (14) One can understand the concept of a determinate *objective* world only to the extent to which one understands *subjective* process of acknowledging error—what Hegel calls "experience"—which is treating two commitments one finds oneself with as *incompatible.*

I think one should understand the strand in Hegel's idealism we might call "objective idealism" as codifying this genus of reciprocal sense dependence between the realm of truth and that of certainty. Given Hegel's most basic concept, a slightly more articulated version is:

> (15) Objective Idealism: The concepts of incompatibility$_{obj}$ and incompatibility$_{subj}$, and *therefore* the concepts of an objectively determinate world, on the one hand, and of error, and experience—which characterize the process of resolving incompatible commitments—on the other, are reciprocally sense dependent.

For Hegel, the conceptually fundamental reciprocal sense dependence is that between incompatibility$_{obj}$ and incompatibility$_{subj}$, epitomized in the different senses in which objects and subjects "repel" incompatibilities, respectively, of properties and of commitments.[31] But the force of the claim is probably clearer for us if we consider its applicability to what Hegel takes pains in "Consciousness" to show are phenomena definable in terms of those incompatibilities: object and property, fact, and law (or necessity).

In fact, these are three examples of objective idealist theses that I think can and should be defended on their own merits by contemporary conceptual pragmatists.[32]

First, the concepts singular term and object are reciprocally sense dependent. One cannot understand either without at least implicitly understanding the other and the basic relations between them. Only people who know how to use singular terms can pick out objects and distinguish them from properties, situations, or states of affairs. And one cannot master the use of singular terms without understanding that they stand for objects. Kant's version of idealism depends in part on his understanding of the relation between our judgments being about objects and their containing (directly or indirectly) singular representations. Frege (who would be no less horrified by the appellation "idealist" than any of our contemporaries—but who also had perhaps no less flat-footed an understanding of what the German idealists were after) argues vigorously and cogently for at least one direction of sense dependence, of object on singular term (that is, the direction that is most important for idealists), in the *Grundlagen*.

Second, the concepts asserting and fact are reciprocally sense dependent. That facts can be the contents of assertions, judgments, beliefs—that they are claimable, thinkable, believable—is an essential feature of them. One does not know what a fact is unless one understands that they can be stated. This line of thought is opposed to an explanatory strategy that would start with objects, and try to construe facts as arrangements of objects—what might be called the "Tinkertoy" picture of facts. One would then go on to understand sentences as a special kind of complex representation, one that represented not objects, but objects as characterized by properties and standing in relations. (The *Tractatus* is often misread as promulgating a view of this sort.) I think such an approach is doomed to failure at making propositional contents as such intelligible. The evident difficulties this strategy has with modal facts, probabilistic facts, and normative facts, for instance, are merely the surface manifestations of the deeper difficulties in making the notion of proposition or fact intelligible in a context in which one is not also taking into account what it is to use an expression as a declarative sentence. My aim here, however, is not to argue for this sense dependence claim, but merely to place it relative to a contrary approach to things, and to suggest that it is not a view that ought to be dismissed out of hand.

Third, the concepts necessity and law, on the one hand, and

counterfactually robust inference, on the other, are reciprocally
sense dependent. Sellars has argued for the more controversial direction of sense dependence, on the basis of his conceptual pragmatism: one has not grasped the difference between lawlike regularities and mere regularities unless one understands that the
former, but not the latter, support counterfactual reasoning.
(Hegel's version is the connection between <u>law</u> and <u>explanation</u>,
which stand to each other roughly as do the concepts <u>perceptible
property</u> and <u>acknowledging error</u>.)

In assessing these claims about the sense dependence of concepts that
articulate our understanding of the structure of the objective world on
concepts pertaining to our cognitive and practical activities, we must,
keep firmly in mind that sense dependence does not entail reference dependence (claim [13] above). The claim is *not* that if there were no cognitive activity—no resolving of subjectively incompatible commitments,
no use of singular terms, no asserting, no counterfactual reasoning—
then there would be no determinate way the world is, no objects, facts,
or laws. There is not the slightest reason to believe that Hegel thought
any such thing. Certainly making the sense dependence claims that I
take to constitute objective idealism does not commit him to such an
idea.

It may be helpful in clarifying this crucial feature of idealism to focus
on a less controversial case that is somewhat analogous to objective idealism, in that it involves the sense dependence of properties of objective
things on subjective activities. Consider *response dependent* properties.
By this I mean properties defined by their relation to the responses of
something else. The general form of such a definition might be this:

An object has property *P* just in case a creature of kind *K would* (in circumstances of kind *C*) respond to it with a response of kind *R*.

To say that *P* is a response dependent property in this sense entails that it
is sense dependent (by definition) on other concepts, notably *R*, the response (as well as *K* and *C*). One could not understand what property *P*
is unless one also understood what the response *R* is. It does not matter
for our purposes here just what properties are properly thought of as being response dependent in this sense. It is plausible that the property **hu-
morous** or **funny** is a property of this sort; a remark or event is humor-

ous or funny just in case the right people (those with a sense of humor) are disposed in appropriate circumstances to *take* it to be funny, that is, to laugh at it. Some have thought that **beautiful** is a response dependent property. The notion of response dependence has also been forwarded as an analysis of secondary quality concepts picking out properties such as **red**: to be red just is to be such that properly sighted creatures respond to it in a certain way, by having a certain kind of experience, by its *looking* red to them.[33] Regardless of whether any of these particular potentially philosophically puzzling sorts of properties are best thought of as response dependent, the concept of response dependent properties is clearly a coherent one. And it should be equally clear that it does *not* follow from a response dependent definition of the form above that in a world that lacks creatures of kind *K*, responses of kind *R*, or circumstances of kind *C*, nothing has the property *P*. For things might still have the dispositional property (counterfactually, in the cases imagined) that if they *were* placed in circumstances *C*, and there *were* creatures of kind *K*, those creatures *would* produce responses of kind *R*. Even if response dependent analyses of the sort gestured at above were correct for concepts such as beautiful and red, it would not follow that there were no beautiful sunsets or red things before there were creatures to respond to them as such, or that there are not such things in worlds that are never shared with such creatures. In the same way, and for the same reason, the objective idealist subjective-objective sense dependence claim does *not* entail that there would be no objects, facts, laws, or (to sum these all up in Hegel's master concept) objective incompatibilities (and hence a determinate objective world) unless and until there were singular term uses, assertions, practices of drawing conclusions from counterfactual situations, or activities of attempting to resolve incompatible commitments. Such a claim *would* be crazy (or, at least, both obviously and demonstrably false). But no claim of that sort is a consequence of objective idealism as here adumbrated.

[margin note: weak sense of 'is red'.]

VIII. Beyond Strong Holism: A Model

With these conceptual raw materials in hand, we are in a position to be somewhat clearer about individuational holism. Earlier I distinguished two grades of holistic commitment: according to the weaker one, relations among holistically individuated items are *necessary* for them to be determinate, and according to the stronger one, they are *sufficient*. But now we can ask: Should Hegel's holism—whether understood as strong or as weak—be understood as a *sense* dependence claim or a *reference* dependence claim? Hegel's answer is clear:

(16) Individuational holism is a reciprocal sense dependence claim.

Understanding it as a reciprocal *reference* dependence claim would be making the mistake of the First Inverted World[34]: thinking that because an object's being determinate is intelligible only in terms of its exhibiting properties that are each themselves determinate in virtue of their modally robust exclusion of other, strongly contrasting properties, that therefore where one property is possessed by an object, the contrasting ones must also be possessed by that or other objects.

   The conception of the Inverted World is what results if one mistakenly thinks that because the exclusive contrast between being positively charged and being negatively charged is essential to each being the determinate electrical property that it is, therefore in saying that one thing is actually positively charged one must implicitly be claiming that some other, corresponding thing is actually negatively charged. Hegel invokes this flat-footed way of misconstruing the significance of the holism that follows from his understanding of what determinateness consists in—in a portion of his text that many have found puzzling—in order to mark the necessity for a more nuanced construal of just what that holism does involve.

   Notice that on this account,

(17) Objective idealism is itself the assertion of a reciprocal sense dependence relation, and hence a kind of *holism*.

The looming problem I have identified concerns *strong* individuational holism: the case where *all* there is to appeal to in individuating elements of a holistic relational system is the relations they stand in to one another. The examples I offered of clearly intelligible sense dependence without reference dependence, where one intension is a function of another (paradigmatically as in response dependent properties), involved not *reciprocal* but only *asymmetric* sense dependence. One intension is taken as already specified, apart from its relations to others. Strong holism asks us to do without such antecedent, independent individuation of the items that stand in sense dependent relations of modally robust exclusion. And my claim was: without antecedent relata, we cannot really understand the relations (and so the relata). As we will see, immediacy plays a crucial role in Hegel's distinctive kind of holism. So in the end, it is a distinctive kind of *weak*, not *strong*, holism that characterizes the "infinite" relational structures within which alone anything can be understood as having determinate conceptual content—which is accordingly a version of the weak, not strong sort. The passages that seem to commit him to strong holism should be understood rather as corresponding to one (ultimately inadequate) phase in the process of grasping or understanding a holistic relational structure.

For, as conceptual pragmatism would lead us to expect, making holistic relational structures intelligible requires engaging in a fairly specific sort of *process*. The relations between the holistic relational structure and that process can then be seen both to instantiate and to support the objective idealism that results from extending and supplementing the Harman point. This, I think, is the ultimate shape of Hegel's argument for objective idealism in the first part of the *Phenomenology: determinateness* requires a kind of *holism*, and that holism is intelligible only on the hypothesis of objective *idealism*.

Here is one way to think systematically about holistically individuated *roles* that items play with respect to a set of relations: Start with some already identified and individuated *signs*, say, proposition letters. These are things we can immediately *distinguish*, that is, noninferentially discriminate or tell apart. But initially, we assume nothing about their content. That they are discriminably different is enough.[35] Next, we look at relations among them. As an example, consider the relation two sign kinds p and q stand in if, in some community, tokening both of them is subjected to a distinctive sanction.[36]

One can then define the *roles* played by signs with respect to that relation—for instance, by associating with each sentence letter the set of sentence letters that stand in the first, practical incompatibility, relation to it. We can think of such a set of incompatible sentence letters as a kind of incompatibility *content* that is *expressed by* the sentence letter it is associated with. And then we can define *new* relations on these roles or contents that are induced naturally by the relations on the signs they comprise. For instance, content incompatibility relations among the roles will shadow practical incompatibility among the underlying signs. But we can also define *entailment* relations among the contents, by p (the content expressed by 'p') entails q just in case q is a subset of p.

Roles defined this way are *abstracted* from the underlying signs in a way somewhat analogous to orthodox mathematical abstraction by the formation of equivalence classes.[37] Such abstract roles are identified and individuated entirely by relations. If we squint just enough not to distinguish the two levels of relations (the latter definable entirely in terms of the former), then the roles would appear to be identified and individuated wholly by the relations *they themselves* stand in to *each other.* That is the paradoxical formulation of strong holism. But if we do keep track of the (somewhat subtle) distinction of levels, we see that there need be nothing paradoxical about defining an abstract relational structure of roles by such a three-phase process. The *only* way to pick out the roles and their relations, however, is by engaging in the process that proceeds through the recognition of the signs and their relations at the lower level. This is a sense dependence relation: what it is to be an incompatibility role (at the second level) is defined in terms of relations on signs (at the first level). The symmetric sense dependence at the second level depends on the asymmetric sense dependence of the second level on the first.

IX. Traversing the Moments: Dialectical Understanding

Here is where I think the two-level model of holistic role formation can help in understanding Hegel:

(18) The process of grasping or understanding holistically identified and individuated items is what Hegel calls *"traversing the moments."*[38]

Because of the holistic character of the conceptually articulated objective determinate contents it must grasp in order to know the world as it is, consciousness must be

> posited in a two-fold manner: once as the restless movement [*Bewegung*] to and fro through all its moments [*welches alle seine Momente durchläuft*], aware in them of an otherness which is superseded in its own act of grasping it; and again, rather as the *tranquil unity* certain of its truth.[39]

Understanding objective idealism requires understanding the relation between the "restless *movement* to and fro through all the moments" on the subjective side, and the *content* on the objective side that is grasped thereby.

> In essence, the object is the same as the movement: the movement is the unfolding and differentiation of the two moments, and the object is the apprehended togetherness of the moments.[40]

What, then, are the "moments" of the holistic structure, articulated by objective, modally robust relations of exclusion and (so) inclusion, which Hegel thinks we must "traverse" in order to grasp the world as determinate? And what sort of "movement" is it that we are to perform? What do we need to *do* in order to count as "traversing the moments"? Almost everything Hegel wrote is structured by some version of this conceptual progression. In his hands the basic thought is a flexible one, which he adapts to many disparate topics and circumstances. So it is not easy to come up with a formula that will do justice to them all. But the basic outlines of the thought are not hard to discern. We start with two "moments" or aspects that can be abstracted from a determinately contentful thought or way the world could be. These are variously characterized: identity and difference, immediacy and mediation, being-for-self and being-for-others.[41]

Traversing the moments is how one understands the relations between these concepts and that of determinateness according to the meta-concept of *Vernunft*. Thinking that one can *first* understand the logical notions of, say, identity and difference, and *then* somehow put them together to get an adequate conception of determinateness is how one understands the relations between these concepts and that of determinateness according to the ultimately unsatisfactory and unworkable metaconcept of *Verstand*. "Running through" the two moments yields three stages, one corresponding to each moment, and the third to the distinctive way of understanding their combination and relation that is the goal and result of the process. What one does at each of those stages is, in Hegel's terminology, to "posit" [*setzen*] something determinate *as,* for instance, simply immediate being. Doing that is understanding it according to the conception of simple identity or being-for-self. "Positing *X* as *Y*" means taking or treating *X* as *Y*, understanding or representing *X* as *Y*, applying the concept *Y* to *X*, characterizing a referent *X* as picked out by a sense *Y*, specifying an extension *X* by means of an intension *Y*.[42]

Hegel envisages an expressively progressive transition from one construal to another of the objects of knowledge, each of which presupposes those that come before it. It can be illustrated to begin with by the course of thought we go through in understanding *properties* as holistically identified and individuated—the first category in which this point comes up. We can see our understanding of properties as comprising three stages:

(A) First, one grasps the property as *immediately contentful*. It is just the thing it is, brutely there. To say that one initially understands it as objectively *immediate* is to say on the objective side that one has an *atomistic* conception of it. One takes it to be possible for that property to be what it is apart from its relations to other properties. Thus, on the subjective side, one need not *consider* those relations or those other properties in order to *judge* that something has the property. The properties in play are restricted to *sense* universals, that is, to observable properties—those about which one can make judgments that are subjectively *immediate* in the sense of being *noninferentially* elicited in observation. These play the role of the primitively individuated *signs* at the first stage of holistic role abstraction. Thinking about these apart from the subjective incompatibility relations among those commitments is thinking about the objective world they present as itself consisting in observable states of affairs that are objectively immediate in the sense that the things presented in sensation are taken as being what they are apart from any relations among them.

This is a position that is unstable, however. For it does not include a coherent conception of what one grasps as *determinately contentful*. Beginning to make explicit what is implicit in such a conception requires moving to the next stage, by considering the next "moment." That is:

(B) Next, one sees that the property is determinate only insofar as it *strongly differs* from other properties, excluding them in the sense that it is impossible for one object (at one time) to have two properties that are incompatible in this sense. At this point, one has moved away from considering the property in terms of its *immediate identity* or *unity,* to considering its *relations to, mediation by, difference* or *disparity from* other properties. At this stage, relations of subjective incompatibility among the commitments are considered. They present relations of objective incompatibility among the states of affairs represented by the original commitments. Doing this, Hegel says, is moving out (in thought) from the thing (here, property) into its other. Being-for-self has dissolved into being-for-others. The property is now understood exclusively in terms of its relations to, in particular (given the relations of material incompatibility Hegel has argued articulate determinateness) its determinate strong *differences from* other properties.

This is the dissolution of the original conception of the identity of properties as immediate, without yet putting in place any stable successor conception of identity. It, too, is unstable, because positing the property as—understanding it just in terms of—mediation, exclusion, relation to others puts the relations in place without yet providing the conceptual resources to make sense of the relata. This is essentially the position I gestured at above, as threatening to leave us with no ultimately intelligible conception of properties (facts, "forces," etc.) as elements in a holistic relational structure articulated by relations of determinate exclusion. Put slightly differently, the first stage asks us to understand properties as contentful independently of the relations among them: as each picked out by senses *independent* of one another. The second stage is then a strong construal of them as *reciprocally sense dependent*. But how are we to make sense of this? If none of the senses, as it were, start off as determinate, how can distinctions among them (among what?) make them determinate? The conception of reciprocal sense dependence threatens to send us around in (infinite!) circles, without making progress on determining the content of any of the senses we run through. How are we to understand the whole thing as getting off the ground? The model of holistic role abstraction tells us exactly how we must combine the first two conceptions (content as immediate and content as strongly holistic) to yield a third. We must reconceive the things we are talking about—here properties—in such a way that the immediacies that became first available are construed as *signs*, expressing a reality articulated by the relations that we first understood at the second stage. It is relations among these *roles* that can be played by what is immediate that should ultimately be understood as standing in holistic relations one to another.

(C) In the final stage, then, one returns to the determinate content of the property, but now understands its *identity* as essentially *consisting* in its relations of exclusion of or difference from those it contrasts with (as well as its relations of inclusion to those it entails or that entail it). Whereas before one treated the determinate content as something merely *immediate*, and then as something merely *mediated*, one now grasps it as fully *mediated immediacy*.[43] One sees its being-for-self as consisting in its being-for-others. Thus at this stage we construct the roles and the new relations among them, which are taken to be *expressed by* the immediacies considered in the first stage. The underlying only *theoretically* (that is *inferentially,* i.e., by mediation) accessible *reality* is *expressed by* the observationally (noninferentially, i.e., immediately) accessible *appearance,* which serves as a *sign* of it. These determinately contentful roles are constituted entirely by their relations to one another—but these are the higher-order relations induced by the lower-level relations on the signs (immediacies).

The final stage is a conception of the property as "infinite," as a holistic role with respect to relations of material incompatibility or exclusion, but one to which the immediacy of the sense universals makes an essential contribution. The subjectively immediate commitments acquired noninferentially through sense perception are now understood as presenting an objective world whose immediacy (brute thereness) is merely a *sign,* an appearance *expressing* a richly mediated determinate, and therefore holistic, structure.

This is not a picture which has the immediacy as a mere sign for something *else,* a content. That would be a representational, not an expressive, model. An immediacy-as-sign is imbued with the content it expresses; it shows up as itself, an immediacy *as* mediated—as it must be to be determinately contentful. The inferential and incompatibility relations that make such immediacies revelatory of *only* inferentially accessible, theoretical features of reality is a passage not *beyond* itself to something else, but only to something *implicit* (in a straightforward inferential sense) in it, in the content it has. This third stage, the holistic "infinite" conception we are ultimately aiming at, is *made* intelligible *only* by the process of arriving at it. For one must *build* the holistic roles in stages, starting with something construed as immediate, and then investigating the mediation implicit in taking it to be determinate.

Here is another of the many passages in which Hegel describes this fundamental process (and I hope by this point in our story he can be heard struggling here to say something that we can now put in somewhat clearer terms):

> The movement of a being that immediately is, consists partly in becoming an other than itself, and thus becoming its own immanent con-

tent; partly in taking back into itself this unfolding [of its content] or this existence of it, i.e. in making *itself* into a moment, and simplifying itself into something determinate. In the former movement, *negativity* is the differentiating and positing of *existence;* in this return into self, it is the becoming of the *determinate simplicity.*[44]

This "movement" is what we must rehearse in order to trace the relations that articulate the sort of determinate content Hegel calls "individuality." "Negativity" appears here in its characteristic double guise: on the *objective* side, in the form of *relations* of modally robust material exclusion, and on the *subjective* side as *movement,* as the *doing* of something, the *alteration* of commitments that is the grasping and acknowledging of the significance of those relations.[45]

Looking back from the perspective achieved in "Absolute Knowledge," Hegel sums up in this way the conception we are supposed to have:

> Thus the object is in part *immediate* being, or, in general, a Thing-corresponding [*entspricht*] to immediate consciousness; in part, an othering of itself, its relationship or *being-for-another,* and *being-for-itself,* i.e. determinateness—corresponding to perception; and in part *essence,* or in the form of a universal—corresponding to the Understanding. It is, as a totality, a syllogism [*Schluß*] or the movement [*Bewegung*] of the universal through determination to individuality, as also the reverse movement from individuality through superseded individuality, or through determination, to the universal. *It is, therefore, in accordance with these three determinations that consciousness must know the object as itself.*[46]

This, then, is the framework of Hegel's idealism, providing the context in which are situated both more specific idealist claims I have suggested (concerning the relations between the concepts of <u>singular term</u> and <u>object</u>, of <u>assertion</u> and <u>fact</u>, and <u>counterfactual reasoning</u> and <u>law</u>) and the generic Hegelian reading of objective incompatibility in terms of *experience:* the process of resolving incompatible commitments. The objective world is a holistic relational structure, determinate just insofar as it is articulated by modally robust relations of material incompatibility. Such a conceptual structure is in principle intelligible only by means of a process of traversing the moments: holistic role abstraction ascending from immediacy through mediation to immediacy as expressive of purely mediated contents. The determinateness of the objective world and the structured process of grasping it are reciprocally sense dependent concepts, each intelligible only in terms of the other. So understood, objective idealism does *not* entail or involve any claims of *reference* dependence—as though our concept using activity were required to *produce,* as opposed to being required to *make intelligible,* the conceptually structured world. The thought that that world is always already there anyway, regardless of the activities, if any, of knowing and acting subjects, has always stood as the most fundamental objection to any sort of idealism. It is a true and important thought; but it is not an objection to Hegel's objective idealism, as here construed.

X. Conclusion

I have argued:

> that understanding the *objective* world as *determinate* for Hegel entails that it must be understood as a *holistic relational structure;*
> that there is a prima facie problem with the intelligibility of strongly holistic relational structures;
> for the strengthened Harman point, a specific kind of conceptual pragmatism, about construing the relation between objective *relations* and subjective *processes;*
> for an understanding of *idealism* as a *sense* dependence relation of objective determinateness on subjective processes of resolving incompatible commitments; and
> for an understanding of holism also as a *sense* dependence relation.

Hegel's claim is then that the *only* way to make holism, and so determinateness, intelligible is objective idealism.

It then remained only to say what *subjective process* can make intelligible *objective weakly holistic semantic relational structures.* For that I offer a model: *holistic role abstraction,* beginning with *signs,* and ending with *roles* played by those signs, or *contents expressed* by them, thought of in terms of higher-order relations among *sets* of those signs.

So objective idealism—a sense dependence thesis relating the concept of objective holistic relational structures to the concept of a certain kind of subjective process—emerges as a response to conceptual difficulties attendant on the conception of strongly holistic relational structures.

Disentangling issues of *sense* dependence from those of *reference* dependence shows idealism as a respectable and potentially defensible response to genuine conceptual problems. An unforeseen bonus of this way of approaching things is the provision of a novel (though admittedly telegraphic)[47] account of the *dialectical method* that structures all Hegel's philosophical accounts. That method responds to the need to understand holistic structures by traversing the moments, by starting with conceptions of what things are immediately or in themselves, then moving to grasp them as what they are mediately or for others, and then to understand what they are *in themselves* as constituted by what they are *for others,* as *mediated immediacy.* Not only *objective idealism,* but Hegel's distinctively structured dialectical *process of understanding* as well, emerges as required to understand the (weakly) *holistic* relational structures that Hegel takes to be implicit in the notion of a world that is *determinately* one way rather than another. Situating a central strand of Hegel's idealism[48] in this structure, it seems to me, sheds light both on his thought and on the issues he thought about.

7

Some Pragmatist Themes in
Hegel's Idealism

This chapter could equally well have been titled "Some Idealist Themes in Hegel's Pragmatism." Both idealism and pragmatism are capacious concepts, encompassing many distinguishable theses. Here I focus on one pragmatist thesis and one idealist thesis (though we will come within sight of some others). The pragmatist thesis (what I will call "the *semantic* pragmatist thesis") is that the *use* of concepts determines their *content*, that is, that concepts can have no content apart from that conferred on them by their use. The idealist thesis is that the structure and unity of the *concept* is the same as the structure and unity of the *self*. The semantic pragmatist thesis is a commonplace of our Wittgensteinean philosophical world. The idealist thesis is, to say the least, *not*. I do not believe that there is any serious contemporary semantic thinker who is pursuing the thought that *concepts* might best be understood by modeling them on *selves*. Indeed, from the point of view of contemporary semantics, it is hard to know even what one could *mean* by such a thought. What relatively unproblematic features of selves are supposed to illuminate what relatively problematic features of concepts? Why should we think that understanding something about, say, personal identity would help us understand issues concerning the identity and individuation of concepts? From a contemporary point of view, the idealist semantic thesis is bound to appear initially as something between unpromising and crazy.

My *interpretive* claim here will be that the idealist thesis is Hegel's way of making the pragmatist thesis workable, in the context of several other commitments and insights. My *philosophical* claim here will be that we actually have a lot to learn from this strategy about contemporary se-

210

mantic issues that we by no means see our way to the bottom of otherwise. In the space of this discussion, I cannot properly justify the first claim textually, nor the second argumentatively. I confine myself of necessity to sketching the outlines and motivations for the complex, sophisticated, and interesting view on the topic I find Hegel putting forward.

I. Instituting and Applying Determinate Conceptual Norms

The topic to which that view is addressed is the nature and origins of the *determinate contents of empirical conceptual norms.* Of course Hegel talks about *lots* of other things. This is merely the strand in his thought that I am going to pursue here. But it may seem perverse to identify this as so much as *one* of Hegel's concerns. After all, what he spends most of his pages talking about (in both of the books he published during his lifetime, the *Phenomenology* and the *Science of Logic*) is the *pure, logical,* or *formal* concepts (the pure form-determinations of the Concept) that are the successors in his scheme to Kant's categories: concepts such as par-ticularity, universality, and individuality and the distinction between what things are *in* themselves and what they are *for* consciousness or for another. But one of the overarching methodological commitments that guides my reading of Hegel is that the *point* of developing an adequate understanding of these categorical concepts is so that they can then be used to make explicit how ordinary empirical concepts work. I would say the same thing about Kant. And I think that one of the things that makes these philosophers hard to understand is that they devote relatively too much time to developing and motivating their (in the transcendental sense) logical apparatus, and relatively too little time to applying it to the use of ground-level concepts. In both cases I think one does well to keep one's eye at all times on the significance of what is being said about pure concepts for our understanding of the use of ordinary empirical concepts. Again, Hegel's idealist thesis is directed in the first instance toward what he calls *the* Concept: the holistic inferential system of determinate concepts and commitments articulated by means of those concepts. But we will see that the abstract structural claim embodied in the idealist thesis holds of both the system and its elements— and holds of the elements in part *because* it holds of the system, and vice versa.

As I read him, Hegel thinks that Kant has been insufficiently critical

regarding two important, intimately related issues. First, he has not inquired deeply enough into the conditions of the possibility of the *determinateness* of the rules that specify the contents of ordinary empirical
concepts. Second, Kant is virtually silent on the issue of their *origins*. He
has not presented a developed account of how those determinate empirical concepts become available to knowers and agents in the first place.
Kant takes over from Leibniz the rationalist understanding of knowledge and action as consisting in the application of concepts. Awareness,
Leibniz's "apperception," whether theoretical or practical, consists in
classifying particulars by universals—that is, for Kant, bringing them
under *rules*.

Hegel inherits from Kant a fundamental philosophical commitment (I
am prepared to say "insight"): a commitment to the *normative* character
of concepts. One of Kant's most basic and important ideas is that what
distinguishes judgments and actions from the responses of merely natural creatures is that they are things we are in a distinctive way *responsible*
for. They are undertakings of *commitments* that are subject to a certain
kind of normative assessment, as correct or incorrect. The norms[1] that
determine what counts as correct or incorrect he calls "concepts." So the
genus of which both judgment and action are species is understood as
the activity of *applying concepts*: producing acts the correctness or incorrectness of which is determined by the rule or norm by which one has
implicitly bound oneself in performing that act. By taking this line, Kant
initiates a shift in attention from *ontological* questions (understanding
the difference between two sorts of fact: physical facts and mental facts)
to *deontological* ones (understanding the difference between facts and
norms, or between description and prescription). This move entailed a
corresponding shift from Cartesian certainty to Kantian necessity. This
is the shift from concern with our grip on a concept (is it clear? is it distinct?) to concern with its grip on us (is it valid? is it binding?). ("Necessary" for Kant just means "according to a rule.") The urgent task becomes understanding how it is possible for us to *commit* ourselves, to
make ourselves *responsible* to a norm that settles the correctness of what
we do.[2] The problem of understanding the nature and conditions of
the possibility (in the sense of intelligibility) of *conceptual normativity*
moves to center stage. (This view about the nature of the practice of using concepts might be called "*normative* pragmatism.")

Kant tells us rather a lot about the process of applying concepts in ordinary judgments and actions. And I take it that his account of the origin, nature, and functioning of the pure concepts of the understanding, whose applicability is implicit in the use of any empirical concept, is intended to serve as a transcendental explanation of the background conditions with respect to which alone normativity in general is intelligible. But he says very little about how knowers and agents should be understood as getting access to the determinate empirical concepts they deploy. What he does say is largely programmatic and architectonic. It is clear, however, that one important structural dimension distinguishing Kant's from Hegel's account of conceptual norms concerns the relation between their production and their consumption, that is, between the process by which they become available to a knower and agent, on the one hand, and the practice of using them, on the other. For Kant tells a *two-phase* story, according to which one sort of activity *institutes* conceptual norms, and then another sort of activity *applies* those concepts.[3] First, a reflective judgment (somehow) makes or finds[4] the determinate rule that articulates an empirical concept. Then, and only then, can that concept be applied in the determinate judgments and maxims that are the ultimate subjects of the first two Critiques.[5]

Very roughly, Kant sees experience, the application of concepts, as beginning with the *selection* of concepts. The potential knower has available a myriad of different possible determinate rules of synthesis of representations. Experience requires picking one, and trying it out as a rule for combining the manifold of presented intuitions. If it does not quite "fit," or permits the synthesis only of some of the intuitions that present themselves, then a mistake has been made, and a related, overlapping, but different determinate concept is tried in its place. Thus, although it is up to the knower what concept to try out, the *success* of the attempted synthesis according to that rule is not up to the knower. The exercise of spontaneity is constrained by the deliverances of receptivity.[6]

The workability of a story along these lines depends on its being settled somehow, for each rule of synthesis and each possible manifold of representations, whether that manifold can be synthesized successfully according to that rule. This might be called the condition of *complete* or *maximal determinateness* of concepts. Only if this condition obtains— only if the empirical concepts made available by judgments of reflection are *fully* and *finally* determinate—does the Kantian account make intelligible the application of concepts as being *constrained* by the deliverances of sense, the correctness of judgments as constrained by the particulars to which we try to apply the universals that are our determinate empirical concepts. Hegel wants us to investigate critically the transcendental conditions of the possibility of such determinateness of concepts. He does not find in Kant a satisfactory account of *this* crucial condition of the possibility of experience.[7] The question is how we can understand the possibility of applying, endorsing, committing ourselves to, or binding ourselves by one completely determinate rule rather than a slightly different one. This problem is related to the one Kripke attributes to Wittgenstein.[8] It is the issue of understanding the conditions of the possibility of the *determinateness* of our conceptual commitments, responsibilities, and obligations. I do not want to dwell on what I take Hegel to see as the shortcomings of Kant's answer. For my purposes it suffices to say that Hegel takes a different approach to understanding the relation between the institution and the application of conceptual norms. In fact I think Hegel's idealism is the core of his response to just this issue, and it is here that I think we have the most to learn from him.[9]

A good way of understanding the general outlines of Hegel's account of the relation between the activity of instituting conceptual norms and the activity of applying them is to compare it with a later movement of thought that is structurally similar in important ways. Carnap and the other logical positivists affirmed their neo-Kantian roots by taking over Kant's two-phase structure: *first* one stipulates *meanings, then* experience dictates which deployments of them yield true *theories*.[10] The first activity is prior to and independent of experience; the second is constrained by and dependent on it. Choosing one's meanings is not empirically constrained in the way that deciding what sentences with those meanings to endorse or believe is. Quine rejects Carnap's sharp separation of the process of deciding what concepts (meanings, language) to use from the process of deciding what judgments (beliefs, theory) to endorse. For him, it is a fantasy to see meanings as freely fixed independently and in advance of our applying those meanings in forming fallible beliefs that answer for their correctness to how things are. Changing our beliefs can change our meanings. There is only one practice—the practice of actually making determinate judgments. Engaging in that practice involves settling at once both what we mean and what we believe. Quine's *pragmatism* consists in his development of this *monistic* account in contrast to Carnap's two-phase account. The practice of using language must be intelligible as not only the *application* of concepts by using linguistic expressions, but equally and at the same time as the *institution* of the conceptual norms that determine what would count as correct and incorrect uses of linguistic expressions. The actual *use* of the language settles—and is all that *could* settle—the *meanings* of the expressions used.[11]

Hegel is a pragmatist also in this monistic sense. He aims at a conception of experience that does not distinguish two different kinds of activity, one of which is the application of concepts in (determinate) judgment and action, and the other of which is the institution or discovery of those concepts (by "judgments of reflection"). For Hegel, empirical judgment and action is not (as for Kant and Carnap) just the *selection* of concepts to apply, or the replacement of one fully formed concept by another. It is equally the *alteration* and *development* of the content of those concepts. Conceptual content arises out of the process of applying concepts—the *determinate* content of concepts is unintelligible apart from the *determination* of that content, the process of determining it. Concepts are not fixed or static items. Their content is altered by every particular case in which they are applied or not applied in experience. At every stage, experience does presuppose the prior availability of concepts to be applied in judgment, and at every stage the content of those concepts derives from their role in experience.[12]

Hegel often couches this point in terms of a distinction between two metaconcepts of the conceptual: <u>Reason</u> (his good, dynamic, active, living conception), and <u>Understanding</u> (Kant's, and everyone else's, bad, static, inert, dead conception). Understanding concepts in terms of the categories of the Understanding is treating them as fixed and static. It allows progress only in the sorting of *judgments* into true and false, that is, in the *selection* from a repertoire fixed in advance of the correct concepts to apply in a particular instance. But Hegel wants to insist that if one ignores the process by which concepts *develop*—what other concepts they develop out of, and the forces implicit in them, in concert with their fellows, that lead to their alteration (what Hegel calls their "negativity")—then the sort of content they have is bound to remain unintelligible.[13]

II. Self-Conscious Selves

My principal aim in this chapter is to show how the idealist thesis that I put on the table at the outset contributes to the working out of Hegel's pragmatist strategy for understanding the nature and origins of the determinateness of the content of empirical concepts. That idealist thesis, recall, is the claim that the structure and unity of the concept is the same as the structure and unity of the self-conscious self. Some of the clearest statements of this central Hegelian thought are in the *Science of Logic:*

> It is one of the profoundest and truest insights to be found in the *Critique of Pure Reason* that the *unity* which constitutes the nature of the *Notion [Begriff]* is recognized as the *original synthetic* unity of *apperception,* as unity of the *I think,* or of self-consciousness.[14]

> Thus we are justified by a cardinal principle of the Kantian philosophy in referring to the nature of the I in order to learn what the *Notion* is. But conversely, it is necessary for this purpose to have grasped the *Notion* of the *I.*[15]

What I want to do next is to sketch Hegel's notion of the structure and unity characteristic of self-conscious selves—the fixed end of the idealist analogy by means of which we are to come to understand the structure and unity of concepts, including the Concept (which is what this passage officially addresses).

Hegel takes over Kant's fundamental idea that to call something a self, to treat it as an "I," is to take up an essentially *normative* attitude toward it. It is to treat it as the subject of *commitments,* as something that can be *responsible*—hence as a potential knower and agent. The question then is how to understand the nature of the normative attitudes and statuses that distinguish being a *who* from being a *what.* One of Hegel's most basic ideas is that normative statuses such as being committed and being responsible—and so knowledge and agency—must be understood as *social* achievements. Normative statuses are a kind of social status. Kant thought normativity could be made intelligible only by appeal to something beyond or behind our empirical activity. For Hegel all transcendental constitution is social institution.[16]

The practical attitude of taking or treating something as able to undertake commitments and be responsible for its doings—in the sense articulated by *concepts,* that is, the sense in which at least part of what one is committed to or responsible for is being able to give *reasons*—Hegel calls "recognition" *[Anerkennung].* The core idea structuring Hegel's social understanding of selves is that they are synthesized by *mutual recognition.* That is, to be a self—a locus of conceptual commitment and responsibility—is to be taken or treated as one by those one takes or treats as one: to be recognized by those one recognizes. Merely *biological* beings, subjects and objects of desires, become *spiritual* beings, undertakers (and attributors) of commitments, by being at once the subjects and the objects of recognitive attitudes. At the same time and by the same means that *selves*, in this normative sense, are synthesized, so are *communities*, as structured wholes of selves all of whom recognize and are recognized by one another.[17] Both selves and communities are normative structures instituted by reciprocal recognition.

This is a *social* theory of selves in the sense that selves and communities are products of the same process, aspects of the same structure. But it is a social theory in a stronger sense as well. For being a self in this sense is not something one can achieve all on one's own. Only part of what is needed is within the power of the candidate self. It is up to the individual whom to recognize. But it is not up to the individual whether those individuals then in turn recognize the original recognizer. Only when this "movement" is completed is a self constituted. I think the structure is clearest when one considers *specific* recognition—that is, attribution of some specific normative status, not just treating someone as having some normative status or other (as the subject of some responsibilities, or entitlements, commitments, or authority, which is recognition in general). For instance, it is up to me whom I recognize as a good chess player. I can settle for recognizing any old wood pusher who can play a legal game, or I can set my standards so high that only Grand Masters qualify. But it is not then up to me (certainly not up to me in the same sense) whether those I recognize as good players recognize me as a good player. If I have set my sights low enough, it will be easy to qualify. But if my aspirations for the sort of self I want to be, and so to be recognized as, are higher, it will be correspondingly more difficult for me to earn the recognition of those I recognize. This account of what it is to be a good chess player, in the various senses that term can take—and more generally, what it is to have some specific normative status—gives the candidate a certain sort of *authority*: the authority to constitute a community by recognizing individuals as members of it. But doing that is also ceding another sort of authority to those one recognizes: the authority to determine whether or not the candidate qualifies as a member of the community so constituted by the standards to which I have subjected myself. Having a normative status in this sense is an essentially social achievement, in which both the individual self and the community must participate. And both the self and the community achieve their status as such only as the result of successful reciprocal recognition.

So when we talk about the structure and unity of the "I" or of self-conscious *selves* according to Hegel, we are talking about the structure and unity produced by this process of reciprocal recognition, by which normative communities and community members are simultaneously instituted. This is what the idealist thesis proposes to use as a model for understanding the structure and unity of *concepts*. Here is a hint, to be followed up below. In recognizing others, I in effect institute a community—a kind of *universal* common to those others, and if all goes well, to me too. If they recognize me in turn, they constitute me as something more than just the particular I started out as—a kind of *individual* (self), which is that *particular* (organism) *as* a member of the community, *as* characterized by that universal. The (recognizing) particular accordingly exercises a certain sort of authority over the universal, and the universal then exercises a certain sort of authority over the individual. It is at something like this level of abstraction that we find a common structure between the social institution of selves and communities by reciprocal recognition and the relation between concepts, as universals, and the particulars that fall under them, yielding the characterized individuals (particulars *as* falling under universals) that are presented by judgments.

I think we can understand the force of this idealist line of thought by situating it in the tradition of thought about the nature of normativity out of which it grew. Enlightenment conceptions of the normative are distinguished by the essential role they take to be played by normative *attitudes* in instituting normative *statuses*. Commitments and responsibilities are seen as coming into a disenchanted natural world hitherto void of them, as products of human attitudes of acknowledging, endorsing, undertaking, or attributing them. (Hobbes's and Locke's social contract theories of the basis of legitimate political authority are cases in point.) The version of this idea that Kant develops from his reading of Rousseau has it that the distinction between force, coercion, or mere *constraint* on me, on the one hand, and legitimate *authority* over me, on the other, consists in the latter's dependence on my *endorsement* or *acknowledgment* of the authority *as* binding on me. This way of demarcating a kind of normativity might be called the *autonomy thesis*. It is the basis for Kant's distinction between the realm of nature, whose denizens are bound by rules in the form of laws of nature, and the realm of freedom, whose denizens are bound rather by their *conceptions* of rules—that is, by rules that bind them only in virtue of their own *acknowledgment* of them *as* binding.

In this distinctive sense, rules get their normative force, come to govern our doings, only in virtue of our own attitudes. One is genuinely responsible only for that for which one *takes* responsibility; one is genuinely committed only to that to which one has committed oneself.

To be a *self,* a knower and agent, is, according to Kant's original normative insight, to be able to take responsibility for what one does, to be able to undertake or acknowledge commitments. It is to be bound by norms. According to the autonomy thesis, one is in a strict sense bound only by rules or laws one has laid down for oneself, norms one has oneself endorsed. What *makes* them binding is that one *takes* them to be binding. Maintaining such a view is a delicate matter. For a question can arise about how, if I myself am doing the binding *of* myself, what I am doing can count as *binding* myself. If whatever I acknowledge *as* correct—as fulfilling the obligation I have undertaken—*is* correct, then in what sense is what I did in the first place intelligible as *binding* myself? (Compare Wittgenstein's claim that where whatever *seems* right to me therefore *is* right, there can be no question of right or wrong.) The autonomy thesis says that one only *is* committed to that to which one *has* committed oneself. But this must not be allowed to collapse into the claim that one is committed to exactly whatever one then takes oneself to be committed to, on pain of so emptying the concept of commitment of content as to make it unrecognizable as such. The authority of the self-binder governs the *force* that attaches to a certain rule: it is endorsement by the individual that makes the rule a rule for or binding on that individual. But that authority must not be taken to extend also to the *content* of the rule: to what is and is not correct according to the rule one has endorsed. For if it does, then one has not by one's endorsement really *bound* oneself by a rule or norm at all. What is chosen—the rule or law I bind myself to by applying a concept—must have a certain independence of the choosing of it. Only so can we make sense of both sides of the idea of autonomy: of *making* oneself subject to a law by *taking* oneself to be so.[18] Maintaining sufficient distinction between what one *does,* in binding oneself by applying a concept, and the *content* of the commitment so instituted is particularly challenging for any theorist committed to what I have called "semantic pragmatism." For that is just the view that it is what one does in applying concepts—undertaking commitments—that determines their content.[19]

I hope it is clear that this problem is a version of the question I earlier pictured Hegel as raising about the *determinateness* of the contents of the concepts I apply. If I have available a rule (one of many) with a content that is determinate, in the sense that it is already settled for any particular whether or not the particular falls under it (whether or not applying the concept to it would be *correct*), then I can bind myself by applying the concept. For the concept will then settle what I have obliged myself to do. But Hegel thinks Kant leaves it mysterious how I could have access to concepts, rules, or norms that are determinate in this sense. In effect, Kant just assumes that there can be such things. Hegel thinks that a rigorously critical thinker should inquire into the conditions of the possibility of such determinateness.

Hegel's idea is that the determinacy of the content of what you have committed yourself to—the part that is *not* up to you in the way that *whether* you commit yourself to it is up to you—is secured by the attitudes of *others,* to whom one has at least implicitly granted that authority.[20] His thought is that the only way to get the requisite distance from my acknowledgments (my attitudes, which make the norm binding on me in the first place), while retaining the sort of authority over my commitments that the Rousseau-Kant tradition insists on, is to have the norms *administered* by someone else. I commit myself, but then *they* hold me to it. For me to *be* committed, I have to have *acknowledged* a commitment, and others must *attribute* it to me. Only so is a real, contentful commitment instituted. Only so can I really be understood to have *bound* myself. This is, at base, why the possibility of *my* freedom (in the normative sense of the autonomy thesis: my capacity to commit myself, to bind myself by norms) depends on *others.* Thus Hegel maintains the apparently paradoxical view that the possibility of my autonomy depends on others adopting attitudes toward me. But the paradox is merely apparent: autonomy does not on this conception collapse into heteronomy.

Having a commitment with a definite content is intelligible, Hegel thinks, only in the context of a division of labor between the one who undertakes the commitment and those who attribute it and hold the undertaker to it. I get to decide which piece in the game I will play—say, the one labeled "That metal is molybdenum," or "I promise to drive you to the airport tomorrow morning"—but I do not then get to decide *what* I have committed myself to thereby, what further moves are appropriate or obligatory for one who has played that piece. My authority is real, but it is partial. And the same can be said of the others who play the game with me and simultaneously referee it. For they have no authority over my acknowledging of commitments. Their authority is operative only in the administration of those commitments—holding me to a commitment with a determinate content to which they are responsible no less than I. (Compare: the legislative and judicial functions of government.) As Hegel puts it, I have a certain *independence* in which commitments I embrace. Apart from my acknowledgment, they have no normative force over me. But in exercising that very independence, I am at the same time *dependent* on the attitudes of others, who attribute and hold me to the commitment, and thereby administer its content. And the others, reciprocally dependent on my recognition, display a corresponding moment of independence in their attitudes of attribution and assessment of my commitments and responsibilities. "Independence" and "dependence" are for Hegel always *normative* independence and dependence. In fact, these are ways of talking about *authority* and *responsibility*.[21]

The actual *content* of the commitment one undertakes by applying a concept (paradigmatically, by using a word) is the product of a process of *negotiation* involving the reciprocal attitudes, and the reciprocal authority, of those who *attribute* the commitment and the one who *acknowledges* it.[22] What the content of one's claim or action is *in* itself results both from what it is *for* others and what it is *for* oneself. I see the account Hegel offers of this process of normative negotiation of reciprocally constraining authority by which determinate conceptual contents are instituted and applied as his main philosophical contribution, at least as assessed from the frame of reference of our contemporary concerns. This process of negotiation of competing normative claims is what Hegel calls "experience" *[Erfahrung]*. Making explicit what is implicit in this process is saying how the *institution* of conceptual norms is related to their *actual application* in acknowledging, attributing, and assessing specific conceptually articulated commitments in judgment and action. It is this relationship that fills in Hegel's single-leveled, unified monistic notion of experience, the aspiration for which I have taken him to share with Quine, in contrast to the two-phase, bifurcated approach common to Kant and Carnap. It is also what the notion of reciprocal recognition is offered as a model of. The idealist claim we are considering is that concepts are instituted in the same way, and hence have the same structure and unity, as self-conscious selves.

III. Modeling Concepts on Selves: The Social and Inferential Dimensions

Hegel thinks of Spirit—the realm of the normative—as produced and sustained by the processes of mutual recognition, which simultaneously institute self-conscious selves and their communities. I have presented this picture as motivated by the problem of how to construe *autonomy* in a way compatible with the determinateness of conceptual contents, while seeing those conceptual contents as *instituted* in the same process of experience in which they are *applied* (the pragmatist's fundamental commitment). I have suggested that Hegel thinks that the boundaries around what one has and has not committed oneself to by using a particular concept (and what is and is not a correct application of it) are determined by a process of *negotiation* among actual attitudes of application and assessments of applications.[23]

This motivation for understanding *selves*—the subjects of determinately contentful commitments and responsibilities, concept users, and hence subjects of experience, knowers, and agents—in terms of mutual recognition explains why the process of reciprocal specific recognition should be taken to provide the *context* within which concepts are applied and their contents instituted and determined. But it does not yet evidently explain why the structure and unity imparted to selves and communities by their institution by reciprocal recognition should be taken to provide a *model* for concepts—to explain *their* structure and unity. The reason why the process of reciprocal recognition, and so the structure and unity of selves, provides not only the *context* of but also the *model* for the institution and application of conceptual norms is that it is not just one example of how norms are constituted by reciprocal authority (mutually dependent moments). *Wherever* a norm can properly be discerned, there *must* be distinct centers of reciprocal authority and a process of negotiation between them. For this, Hegel thinks, is the nature of the normative as such: the *only* way in which determinate contents can be associated with norms according to the conception of the normative embodied in the autonomy thesis. The commitment one undertakes by applying a concept in judgment or action can be construed as determinately contentful only if it is to be *administered* by others distinct from the one whose commitment it is. So in acknowledging such a commitment, one is at least implicitly recognizing the authority of others over the content to which one has committed oneself.[24]

But how, exactly, are we to understand the structure and unity of concepts on the model of reciprocal recognition among selves? For Hegel, as for Kant, *all* norms are *conceptual* norms: talk of norms and talk of concepts are alternatives for addressing one fundamental common phenomenon. The first thing to realize is that Hegel understands concepts, the contents of norms, as essentially *inferentially* articulated.[25] Hegel discusses this inferential articulation (in the *Phenomenology* beginning in the section called "Perception") under the headings of "mediation" *[Vermittlung]* and "determinate negation." The paradigm of mediation, the case responsible for this choice of terminology, is the role played by the middle term in a syllogism. The application of the mediating concept serves as the *conclusion* of one inference and the *premise* of another.[26] The claim that *mediation,* the capacity to play this role, is essential to concepts is the claim that being able to figure both in the premises and in the conclusions of *inferences* is essential to concepts. This is what I mean by talking about their "essential inferential articulation."[27]

In a similar way, when Hegel talks about "determinate negation," he means material incompatibility relations among concepts: the way the applicability of one concept normatively precludes the applicability of another. An example would be the way calling a patch of paint "red" precludes calling it "green."[28] Formal or logical negation (what Hegel calls "abstract" negation) is definable from the determinate or material version. The abstract negation of *p* is its minimum incompatible: what follows from everything materially incompatible with *p*. It abstracts from the determinate content of those incompatibles, and so is *merely* incompatible.[29] Together the material inferential and material incompatibility relations (relations of mediation and determinate negation) articulate the contents of conceptual norms.[30]

We are now in a position to approach the central question. The model of the sort of reciprocal recognition that institutes *selves* and their *com-*

munities applies to the institution and application of concepts in experience at two levels. First, it describes the relations of reciprocal authority that relate *particulars* to the *universals* or determinate concepts that they fall under: the way in which determinate concepts are instituted and the judgments that present characterized individuals are made. Individuals, which are particulars characterized by concepts, and determinate concepts are simultaneously instituted or synthesized—just as in the model, individual self-conscious selves, *as* members of a community (as characterized by a universal), and their communities (universals) are simultaneously instituted or synthesized. Second, it describes the relations of reciprocal authority that relate determinate concepts to one another. At this level, determinate concepts and what Hegel calls "the Concept," the great holistic, inferentially articulated *system* of determinate concepts and judgments articulated by those concepts—a sort of universal or community comprising them all—are simultaneously instituted or synthesized.

Judgments, acts of judging, come in two flavors: *mediate* and *immediate*. The mediate ones are the results of *inferences* from other judgments—that is, from the application of *other* concepts one has already made. The immediate ones are noninferentially elicited, paradigmatically *perceptual* judgments or observations.[31] Desiring animals already sort their world by responding differentially to it—treating something as food, for instance, by "falling to without further ado and eating it up."[32] Immediate judgments are ones that a properly trained and tuned animal who has mastered the responsive use of the relevant concepts will make automatically when confronted with the perceptible presence of a reportable or observable state of affairs. These noninferential applications of concepts (= immediate judgments) are wrung from or elicited by the *particulars* to which the concepts are on that occasion applied. By contrast, responsibility for (= authority over) *inferentially* elicited applications of concepts (= mediate judgments) is vested in the concepts or *universals,* whose inferential relations underwrite the judgment that is the conclusion.

Immediate judgments express a dimension along which particulars exert an authority over the universals or concepts that apply to them. *Mediate* judgments express a dimension along which universals or concepts exert an authority over the particulars to which they apply. The characterized individuals—particulars *as* falling under universals—that are presented by judgments (= applications of concepts) emerge as the product of *negotiation* between the two reciprocal dimensions of authority (each with its own dual, correlative sort of responsibility). This is the feature of concept use and development—the process of experience that is for this reason intelligible at once as the application and as the institution of conceptual norms—that is modeled by reciprocal recognition. Hegel's *Logic* aims to be the completed story of how this works.

Evidently the two sorts of authority may collide. One may find oneself immediately with commitments incompatible with those to which one is inferentially committed. Then one must *alter* some of one's commitments—either those that are authorized by the particulars (immediately) or those that are authorized by the universals (mediately). This necessity is *normative:* one is *obliged* by the incompatibility of one's judgments, by the commitments one has oneself undertaken, to adjust the authority either of the particulars or of the universal. Making an adjustment of one's conceptual commitments in the light of such a collision is what is meant by *negotiating* between the two dimensions of authority.[33] The process of adjusting one's dispositions to make immediate and mediate judgments in response to actual conflicts arising from exercising them is the process Hegel calls "experience." It drives the *development* of concepts. It is the process of *determining* their content. It is how *applying* conceptual norms is at the same time the process of *instituting* them. Conceptual contents are *determinate* only because and insofar as they are the products of such a process of *determining* them *by* applying them in inferential concert with their fellows.[34]

This process of *negotiation* between acknowledged authorities upon their disagreement is the process of *administering* the sometimes opposed authorities of particulars and universals. It is constitutive of *both* the Concept, as the holistic system of all the determinate universals (empirical concepts) related by material inference and incompatibility (mediation and determinate negation), *and* the characterized particulars presented by a set of judgments, a set of commitments that are actual applications of universals to particulars. Concepts and judgments, meanings and beliefs, languages and theories, are two sides of one coin, intelligible only together, as elements of the process of experience. This view should sound familiar: it is Quine's in "Two Dogmas of Empiricism." Seeing change of meaning and change of belief as aspects of a single process of experience, of adjusting our beliefs (including those we find ourselves with perceptually) to one another, is Quine's way of working out his pragmatist commitment. We are now in a position to see it also as Hegel's way of working out his idealist commitment.[35]

IV. Modeling Concepts on Selves: The Historical Dimension

Hegel often discusses the relation between selves and concepts in the language of *identity*. For instance:

> The Notion [*Begriff*], when it has developed into a *concrete existence* that is itself free, is none other than the *I* or pure self-consciousness. True, I *have* notions, that is to say determinate notions; but the I is the pure Notion itself which, as Notion, has come into *existence*.[36]

We have seen how the *I*, self-conscious selves in general, as the normative subjects of conceptually articulated commitments—judgments (and actions)—are synthesized as essential aspects (Hegel says "moments") of the process of experience whose other essential elements include both those judgments and the concepts that are applied in them. And we have seen that the structure and unity of this process in all its aspects should be understood in terms of the kind of reciprocal authority relations Hegel calls "recognitive." Still, the different aspects of this process and of recognitive structures generally remain distinct and distinguishable. They are not *identical* to one another in a strict or logical sense. Hegel acknowledges this. The passage above continues with a characterization of recognitive structures that is abstract in the way characteristic of the *Logic,* concluding:

> This [structure] constitutes the nature of the *I* as well as of the Notion; neither the one nor the other can be truly comprehended unless the two indicated moments are grasped at the same time both in their abstraction and also in their perfect unity.[37]

The unity of the recognitive structure leads Hegel to talk (in my view, unfortunately) of the essentially related moments of that structure as *identical.* They are not identical in the ordinary sense, since they are also essentially distinct. But he wants us to recognize them nonetheless as identical in a speculative sense. In this speculative sense, elements of a recognitive structure of reciprocal authority that are intelligible only *as* elements related to one another in such a structure are described as "identical" with one another. It is in this sense that Hegel talks about selves as being identical with their communities, about particulars as identical with the universals that characterize them, about determinate concepts as identical with the holistic Concept that comprises them as a system of inferentially related elements, and so on. Only confusion results if this speculative sense of "identical" is confused with the ordinary notion of identity. For then the specific structure of recognition by which these different elements are at once distinguished and related is in danger of collapsing. Collapsing them renders unintelligible determinately contentful normative statuses: the judgments (and actions) that make up experience, the selves that undertake, attribute, and are responsible for them, their recognitive communities, the determinate concepts that articulate those responsibilities by the relations of material inference and incompatibility that make up the greater universal that is the Concept, the particulars to which judgments have a responsibility mediated by immediate judgments, and so on.

It remains to consider one final dimension of the recognitive structure within which the relation between selves and concepts must be understood. This is a dimension Hegel also discusses in the language of identity, but in a way that should be understood, I think, neither in the strict nor in the speculative sense. I have in mind here the considerations that are raised by Hegel's claim—which looms large, for instance, in the preface to the *Phenomenology*—that Spirit as a whole should be understood as a *self*. I understand the *geistig* as the realm of conceptually articulated norms, of authority and responsibility, commitment and entitlement. Spirit as a whole is the recognitive community of all those who have such normative statuses, and all their normatively significant activities. It is, in other words, the topic of the pragmatist's enquiry: the whole system of social practices of the most inclusive possible community. Claiming that Spirit has the structure and unity of the self is another idealist thesis, and it, too, should be understood in terms of Hegel's pragmatism.

In making this second idealist claim, Hegel obviously does not mean for us to think that Spirit as a whole is just one more of us ordinary selves, an element of some community of which we are also members. But neither, I think, does he just mean that Spirit is an element of the recognitive structure of which we individual selves are elements—so that we could talk about us and the great community that comprises us recognitively as identical in the speculative sense. He means that Spirit as a whole—the whole recognitive community of which we individual selves are members, and all of its activities and institutions—has the structure and unity characteristic of the self-conscious self. In that technical sense, it is an individual, though not one associated with a particular organism, as we human selves are.

I think that there is all sorts of evidence that Hegel means his remarks about Spirit as Self to have something like this import. Certainly that is the way he is usually read. It is much less often remarked that attributing such a view to Hegel in the *Phenomenology* raises a substantial interpretive problem. For Hegel clearly subscribes there to the following three claims:

1. Spirit is a self-conscious self.
2. Self-conscious selfhood is an essentially *social* achievement, requiring actual recognition *of* and *by* an *other,* to whom the individual self achieving self-consciousness in this way is then bound in a recognitive *community.*
3. Spirit has no other; there is nothing "outside" it.

The trouble is of course that these claims are jointly incompatible. But Hegel commits himself to them all—not just casually or in a way that could represent a slip, but as essential elements of his view. Now, much of what I have said in this chapter does not represent conventional wisdom about Hegel's views. But attributing *these* three claims is not an idiosyncratic feature of my reading: it *is* conventional wisdom. Yet discussion of the conceptual problems these theses present does not loom large in the secondary literature. (The claim one sometimes hears that Hegel is in the end a kind of *subjectivist* is, I take it, at least an indirect acknowledgment of these difficulties.) It seems to me that the extent to which a reading acknowledges and provides a convincing response to this issue should serve as a fundamental criterion of adequacy for assessing it.

The account I have been sketching of the nature and significance of reciprocal recognition for understanding the nature of normative statuses provides the raw materials for such a response. Further, in doing so it fills in an important piece of the story about how *applying* conceptual norms by making judgments can be understood as a process of *determining* their content, and so as *instituting* those norms. Insofar as it does, it offers a final respect in which Hegel's *idealism* and his *pragmatism* (in the senses I have been discussing) illuminate each other.

Reciprocal recognition, I have claimed, is for Hegel the structure that makes the normative intelligible as such. In its paradigmatic *social* form, it institutes both individual self-conscious *selves* (the subjects of commitments and responsibilities) and their communities (the selves bound together by attributing and assessing commitments to one another, holding one another responsible). In its *inferential* form, this structure characterizes the relationship between particulars and universals in the process of making *judgments* that is experience: the application of determinate concepts. It is exhibited as well in the relations of reciprocal authority by which applications of some determinate concepts condition the applicability of other, inferentially related concepts, thereby constituting the "community" of all determinate concepts, structured by relations of mediation and determinate negation, that is, the Concept. In addition to these two forms of reciprocal recognition, we should recognize a third: the *historical*. It arises because negotiating and adjudicating the claims of reciprocally conditioning authorities, administering conceptual norms by applying them in actual cases (to particulars that immediately present themselves), is a *process*. In that process of experience, conceptual norms *develop*, along with the body of claims or judgments expressing the commitments that arise from applying those concepts. This developmental process of progressively determining the content of concepts by applying them in concert with their fellows is to be understood as the way determinately contentful conceptual norms are *instituted*.

Experience—at once the application and the institution of conceptual norms—is not merely a *temporal* process but a *historical* one. By this I mean that it exhibits a distinctive *recognitive* structure that is the product of the reciprocal authority exercised, on the one hand, by past applications of concepts over future ones and, on the other hand, by future applications of concepts over past ones. All there is to institute conceptual norms, to determine *what* we have committed ourselves to by applying a concept, is *other* applications of the concept in question, together with applications of concepts inferentially related to it. Thus the applications of the concept (and its relatives) that have actually been made already have a certain sort of *authority* over candidate future applications of that concept (and so of its relatives). The prior applications are authoritative regarding the meaning or content of the concept. This is the authority of the past (applications of concepts) over the future (applications of concepts)—providing a sense in which future applications are responsible for their correctness to the past ones.

But authority needs to be administered. Applications of norms instituted by prior applications need to be assessed for their correctness, according to the norms they answer to. For current applications of a concept to *be* responsible to prior applications of that concept (and its relatives), they must be *held* responsible, taken or treated *as* responsible. That is the lesson of Hegel's analysis of the conditions under which the *bindingness* of norms is intelligible, according to what he made of the Kant-Rousseau insistence on autonomy as a condition of genuine normativity—the lesson that is the basis for the model of reciprocal recognition. For we can ask in the present context: How is it possible for an application of a concept to count as *incorrect* according to the commitments implicit in prior applications? If there is nothing to the content of the concept except what has been put into it by actual applications of it (and its relatives), how can any actual application be understood as incorrect according to that content? If it cannot, then no norm has been instituted.

Here, I think, is Hegel's answer: The authority of the past applications, which instituted the conceptual norm, is administered on its behalf by *future* applications, which include assessments of past ones. It is for later users of a concept to decide whether each earlier application was correct or not, according to the tradition constituted by still earlier uses. In doing so, the future applications exercise a reciprocal authority over past ones. The model of this process that I find it most useful to keep in mind (though it is not one Hegel ever suggests) is the development of concepts of common law by precedent. Common law differs from statute law in consisting entirely of *case* law. It is not the interpretation of explicit founding laws, rules, or principles. *All* there is to it is a sequence of applications of concepts to actual sets of facts. It is for this reason often thought of as judge-made law.

Consider an idealized version of this process. Each judge inherits a tradition of cases, which can be thought of as a set of particulars (the facts of the case, described in non-legal vocabulary) to which legal universals such as "tort," "strictly liable," and so on have been applied (or withheld). The judge is in turn confronted with a novel particular case (set of facts), and must decide whether to apply or withhold application of one of those universals—classifying the actions in question as constituting a specific tort, or as involving the assumption of strict liability. The authority of the tradition consists in the fact that the *only reasons* the judge can appeal to in justifying his decision are precedential: the fact that the universal in question was actually applied or withheld in previous cases that resemble the one in question in respects the judge specifies (while of course differing in other respects). The concepts the judge is charged with applying have their content entirely constituted by the history of their actual application (along with the history of actual application of any other legal concepts that have in the tradition actually been taken to be inferentially related to them). It is this tradition to which the judge is *responsible*. The contents of those concepts have been instituted entirely by their being applied. The reciprocal authority of the judge includes[38] the authority to sort the previous cases into those that are and those that are not *precedential*. These are the previous applications that, according to the judge, demarcate the content of the concept. A prior decided case can be treated as not precedential, as not potentially authoritative with respect to the case in question, because the judge sees it as *mistaken,* given the decisions that articulate the content of the concept, that is, in light of the qualitative or quantitative preponderance of precedent. (Here the inferential connections to other concepts the judge takes to have been established by prior decisions, together with the precedents for applying those concepts, can weigh in as well.) This sort of assessment must itself be justified by a sort of rational reconstruction of the tradition of applying the legal concept in question, along with the precedents selected as most relevant, in framing the rationale for deciding the case one way rather than the other. It is because *every* decision of a case has this shape, involves the exercise of this sort of discretion or authority, and there is *nothing more* to the content of the legal concepts being applied than the content they acquire through a tradition of such decisions, that the principles that emerge from this process are appropriately thought of as "judge-made law."[39] But the contents the judges in this sense *make* is also constrained by what they *find*, the precedential applications of concepts (both immediate and inferential) whose authority the judges are subject to, at the same time that they inherit it and administer it.

Sensitized as I hope we are by now to the structure of reciprocal authority (and so of responsibility) Hegel calls "mutual recognition," we should be able to discern it in the idealized judicial process I have sketched. Past applications of concepts (decisions of cases) exercise an authority over future ones. For they supply the precedents that constitute the only rationales available to justify future decisions. They are the source of the content of the concepts later judges are charged with applying. This is the moment of independence, of recognition, of constitutive authority of the past over the future, and so the future's dependence on its past. But reciprocally, later applications of concepts by the judges who inherit the tradition exercise an authority over the earlier ones. For the significance of the authority of the tradition, what conceptual content exactly it is taken to have instituted, is decided by the judges currently making decisions. They *administer* the norms, *make* them determinately binding. This is the moment of independence, of recognition, of constitutive authority of the future over the past, and so of the past's dependence on its future. For except insofar as the current judge *recognizes* or acknowledges the authority of some prior decision, it has none. What the norm *really* is (what it is *in* itself) is the product of recognitive *negotiation* between these two poles of reciprocal authority (what the content is *for* the past judges and what it is *for* the present one).

Now, it may seem that the situation here is not symmetric. For the present judge may seem to have the last word. After all, the judge deciding a case now can ignore or at least dismiss inconvenient prior decisions, treating them as misapplications of the concepts in question—as wrongly decided cases—or as irrelevant because dissimilar to the case at issue in the respects the present judge has decided to treat as most important. So it seems that the current judge owes to the past only the debts she herself decides to acknowledge. And if and insofar as that is true, the authority of the past decisions, the content they have conferred on the legal concepts, is empty and indeterminate. The fact that the judge must justify her present decision by appealing to prior decisions then would impose a merely *formal* constraint. Her discretion in choosing and applying precedents—in effect, retrospectively reconstructing the tradition by selective omission and selective emphasis—would render that constraint contentless. The voice of the past cannot be thought of as having authority over the present, if the present can decide both which bits to listen to and how to interpret them.

This is an intelligible description of the situation, and the worries it engenders have properly engaged jurisprudential theorists. But in fact symmetry of authority, genuinely reciprocal recognition, is achieved in this process. Genuine authority, I have claimed on Hegel's behalf, must be *administered*. Talk of my being responsible to something is appropriate only where there is someone to *hold* me responsible to it. The current judge administers the norms instituted and determined by past applications. But who is there to hold the current judge responsible to the tradition of prior applications, to assess the fidelity of her decision to the content actually conferred on the legal concepts by the tradition she inherits? The appearance of asymmetry of authority between past and present is the result of not considering the answer to this question. But it is clear what the answer is. The current judge is held accountable to the tradition she inherits by the judges yet to come. For her decision matters for the content of the concept in question only insofar as its precedential authority is acknowledged or recognized in turn by future judges. If they take her case to have been misdecided, given *their* reading of the tradition she inherited, then the current judge's decision has no authority at all. The authority of the past over the present is administered on its behalf by the future. Since this process has no endpoint in principle, no finally authoritative authority not dependent in turn on its acknowledgment or recognition, the normative situation is entirely symmetrical. And to say that is to say, according to Hegel's way of working out the Kant-Rousseau autonomy thought in terms of reciprocal recognition, that genuine, determinately contentful conceptual norms *are* instituted by a process of applying them that has this historical structure.[40] Determinate conceptual norms are intelligible only as features of an actual tradition that is structured recognitively, having reciprocal authorities negotiating and administering along all three recognitive dimensions: social, inferential, and historical.

Hegel's pragmatism, I have claimed, consists in his commitment to understanding determinately contentful empirical conceptual norms as instituted by *experience,* the process of *using* those concepts by applying them in practice: making judgments and performing actions. His idealism consists in understanding this process of experience as exhibiting a constellation of reciprocal authority whose paradigm is mutual recognition: the structure and unity of the self-conscious individual self. Thus we are to use the same concepts in terms of which we understand *selves* to understand *concepts.* The recognitive structure of reciprocal authority necessary to make intelligible the bindingness of determinately contentful norms has three dimensions: social, inferential, and historical. In this chapter I have not been able to pursue the intricate interactions among these dimensions that Hegel delineates for us. But I have tried to sketch what I take to be Hegel's most basic thought: his way of working out the Kant-Rousseau insight about a fundamental kind of normativity based on autonomy according to the model of reciprocal authority and responsibility whose paradigm is mutual recognition. I think this is the master idea that animates and structures Hegel's metaphysics and logic.[41]

And as a sort of a bonus, we have also, I hope, seen enough to know how to respond to the puzzle I raised about how to understand Hegel's talk of Spirit as a whole as a self-conscious individual *self,* in the context of his insistence on the irreducibly *social* character of the achievement of self-consciousness. The reciprocal recognitive structure within which Spirit as a whole comes to self-consciousness is *historical.* It is a relation between different time slices of Spirit, in which the present acknowledges the authority of the past, and exercises an authority over it in turn, with the negotiation of their conflicts administered by the future. This is the recognitive structure of *tradition,* which articulates the normative structure of the process of *development* by which concepts acquire their contents by being applied in experience. This process is what Hegel's pragmatism and his idealism aim ultimately to illuminate. Making that structure explicit is achieving the form of self-consciousness Hegel calls "Absolute Knowledge," some of the outlines of which I have tried to convey here.

8

Frege's Technical Concepts

Today we find ourselves at the outset of a golden age in the interpretation of Frege's philosophical writings. Judged by the number of articles, books, and seminars addressing his thought, interest in Frege is at an all-time high. More important, as Frege has come out of the shadow of Russell and Wittgenstein into the full light of critical attention, the degree of sophistication of discussion has achieved a quantum improvement. Many factors conspired to bring about this result, but two events may be singled out as having made special contributions both to the resurgence of interest in and to our greater understanding of Frege's work

First is the publication, more than sixty years after his death, of that part of his *Nachgelassene Schriften* which survived the vicissitudes of the intervening years. These papers appeared in German in 1969 and in English in 1979.[1] Some of the contents are rough in form, though not without value. We are offered, for example, tables of contents and partial drafts of a textbook on logic and its philosophy which Frege made starts on at various crucial periods of his life. Even draft fragments of this sort permit important inferences from the order of presentation and different emphases given various topics to conclusions about the explanatory priorities Frege associated with his central technical concepts. But not all of the selections represent rough cuts or abandoned projects. Included are some fully polished articles, dealing with Frege's most central technical concepts—fine examples of his concise, sometimes lapidary mathematician's prose—which he had tried unsuccessfully to publish. In a number of cases, these additional texts permit the resolution of exegetical disputes occasioned by what can now be seen to be accidental lacunae and merely apparent emphases in the canonical published corpus.

The other landmark event is the publication in 1973 of Michael Dummett's monumental and long-awaited full-length treatment of Frege's philosophy of language.[2] It would be difficult to overestimate the significance of this classic work. Anyone interested in the interpretation of Frege must give it the same close attention owed to the primary texts. Its clarity of thought, patient rehearsal of considerations, and exercise of the best critical judgment in final appraisal will not be soon equaled. This chapter will not offer a systematic account of Dummett's views, since the most important of these are so intimately tied up with the development of powerful novel approaches to contemporary philosophy of language as to defy brief characterization, even by their author. The original volume has now been supplemented with another containing many valuable amplifications and clarifications.[3] The result is a 1,300-page corpus which, Dummett's complaints[4] to the contrary notwithstanding, by now deserves to be considered as setting out the canonical reading of Frege. It is so considered by the authors discussed below, and forms the background against which their own accounts are set out.

Two examples will serve to indicate the sort of interpretive advance signaled by these events. First, it was widely believed in the 1950s and 1960s that Frege intended the distinction between sense and reference to apply not to functional expressions such as predicates but only to complete expressions such as terms and sentences.[5] Although the famous essay on sense and reference does not discuss such an application of that distinction, the *Nachlass* makes clear that this is only because that discussion was reserved for a further article which is quite explicit in its endorsement of that application, but which was repeatedly rejected for publication until Frege abandoned the attempt. Several other passages reprinted in *Frege: Posthumous Writings* (see note 1) decisively refute the interpretation which would restrict the distinction to complete expressions. A somewhat less important mistake may also be mentioned as indicative, which was done in as much by Dummett's arguments as by the unearthing of further evidence. In "On Sense and Reference" Frege says, "One might also say that judgements are distinctions of parts within truth-values," and that "the reference of the word is part of the reference of the sentence."[6] These remarks have sparked the attribution of a variety of bizarre ontological views to Frege, centering on the notion of the True as representing the whole world, sometimes conceived as a Tractarian world of facts, sometimes as composed of objects (and what about the False?). The remarks stem from a hasty assimilation, soon explicitly rejected, of the relation between the argument of a function and the value it determines to the relation of part and whole. For although the function 'capital of . . .' takes the value Stockholm when Sweden is taken as argument, Sweden is not part of Stockholm. Dummett's discussion of this issue has permanently disposed of the temptation to take these remarks seriously as interpretive constraints. We shall see below, however, that there remain genuine controversies which are not so easily disposed of (concerning the senses and referents of functional expressions) which may be regarded as successors to these two mistaken lines of thought.

Dummett has shown that Frege should be treated as a modern thinker in the sense that one can think about contemporary philosophical issues of considerable significance by thinking about his concepts and their explanatory deployment, and that one cannot think about those concepts and their principles of deployment without thinking about such contemporary issues. In what follows, those concepts are approached from three different directions. First, an attempt to interpret and develop Frege's technical scheme in light of contemporary discussions of the issues he was addressing is considered. Then attention is turned to an argument to the effect that ignoring the historical context in which Frege developed his theories, treating him we might say *merely* as a contemporary, leads to substantive misinterpretation of those theories. Finally, following one strand of the account of the path by which Frege developed and defended some of his central concepts leads to a novel diagnosis of the status of those concepts.

I. Bell on Sense and Reference

One important offering is David Bell's book *Frege's Theory of Judgement.*[7] This is a clear and well-written work. The issues it raises and the form in which they are addressed merit the attention of anyone interested in the significance for current inquiry of Frege's strategic deployment of a battery of technical concepts to explain various aspects of linguistic practice. Its title is worthy of some consideration. It is a measure of the degree of sophistication of contemporary Frege commentary that a controversy exists even over how one should describe the topic which his philosophical work addresses. Of course no one disputes his concern with the foundations of mathematical reasoning and knowledge, expressed above all in his three books, the *Begriffsschrift,* the *Grundlagen der Arithmetik,* and the *Grundgesetze der Arithmetik.* But the more general conceptual framework he found it necessary to elaborate in order to express clearly and precisely his claims about the nature of mathematics and its objects cannot easily be characterized without prejudging substantial issues of interpretation. It may seem obvious that Frege was pursuing a project in the philosophy of language.[8] But such a description is misleading in the context of Frege's own insistence on the priority of thoughts (though not of thinkings) to their linguistic expression. For he was interested in natural languages only insofar as they permitted rough formulation of objective and language-independent thoughts, and he crafted artificial languages only as more adequate means for their expression. It would be inappropriate to build into the description of the subject matter at the outset a post-Wittgensteinian conviction of the wrongheadedness of such an approach by assimilating his concerns to contemporary investigations under the rubric "philosophy of language." One of the major theses of Hans Sluga's book, discussed below, is that such Whiggish presuppositions of continuity of concern have consistently led Frege's readers to overlook important strands of his thought. Dummett has also suggested "theory of meaning" as a general characterization, but this seems to apply better to his own enterprise than to Frege's. For 'meaning' is correlative to 'understanding', and Frege's concern lay at least equally with reference, which is not in general grasped when one understands a claim, as with the sense which must be grasped in that case.

In his discussion of the book,[9] Dummett objects that Bell has misdescribed his topic, in that Frege's treatment of the act of asserting is the topic of only one chapter, while the rest of the book talks about the notions of sense and reference. This seems unfair, for the heading "theory of judgment" ought to entitle Bell to offer an account of the contents which are judg*ed* as well as of the acts which are the judg*ings* of those contents. It has the advantage of placing Frege's concerns in appropriate historical and philosophical context. Bell's denomination of Frege's topic as judgment displays his recognition of the importance Frege, in company with Kant and Wittgenstein, placed on inverting the traditional order of explanation which took concepts as primary and sought to account for judgments in terms of them. At least until 1891, Frege clearly regarded the claim that concepts can only be understood as the products of analysis of judgments as one of his most central insights. Although Bell does not say so, it is equally clear in the *Begriffsschrift* (*BGS*) that Frege completes the inversion of the classical priority of concepts to judgments and judgments to syllogisms by taking the contents of sentences (judgment in the sense of what is judged rather than the judging of it) to be defined in terms of the inferences they are involved in.[10] Concepts are to be abstracted from such judgments by considering invariance of inferential role (which pertains only to judgments) under various substitutions for discriminable (possibly nonjudgmental) components of the judgment. Both in the introduction to *BGS* and in his essay "Boole's Logical Calculus and the *BGS*,"[11] the virtue of the purely formal perspicuous language of inference in nonformal contexts is described as its permitting for the first time the scientific formation and expression of concepts. Although it is for this reason that Frege called his first work a "concept script," he later came to believe this phrase misleading precisely because it obscured his doctrine of the primacy of judgments. It would be equally misleading, however, to describe Frege simply as a theorist of inference, in spite of the explanatory priority he accorded to it. For his primary theoretical focus always lay on the sentential and thence subsentential contents attributable to different expressions in virtue of the roles they played in inference, as revealed by their behavior under substitution. So "judgment," which is (a translation of) an expression Frege himself used pretheoretically to describe the object of his theorizing, seems a good choice to delimit his subject matter.

Like any other choice, however, it does prejudge some controversial issues of interpretation, for instance, that concerning the persistence in Frege's thought of the so-called "context principle." It is often unclear exactly what this principle means, but the canonical statement of it is the *Grundlagen* claim that "only in the context of a sentence does a word have any significance." (I use 'significance' here for Frege's '*Bedeutung*' because in 1884 he had not yet distinguished *Sinn* from *Bedeutung,* and the undifferentiated term should be marked.) It is often claimed,[12] even by those such as Dummett who take the putative change in view to be a serious mistake, that when Frege achieved his mature views in 1891 with the formulation of that crucial distinction he discarded the context principle. If that is so, then Bell's choice of "theory of judgment" to describe the topic of the mature semantic views he discusses would be misleading or simply incorrect. As we shall see below, Sluga argues that Frege never relinquishes the context principle. Bell does not argue this, however, nor does he even claim it. He is simply silent on this issue, as on others concerning detailed questions about the attribution of various views to Frege based on textual evidence.

Bell's enterprise lies in a different direction entirely. He is concerned to look closely at the explanatory roles played by Frege's various concepts and at the ways in which Frege takes them to be related, in order to refine and reconstruct a broadly Fregean account of the nature of judgment. In keeping with this aim, he is not engaged in the exegesis of Fregean texts, and freely discards from his reconstruction a number of doctrines which Frege clearly held, in favor of incompatible principles (for instance, in Bell's reconstruction functional expressions are assigned senses but not referents). His project is to salvage from Frege's account those insights which can be put together to form a workable theory of judgment. The result is broadly Fregean in endorsing the following "major strands" of Frege's theory:

1. There is the methodological principle that 'we can distinguish parts in the thought corresponding to the parts of a sentence, so that the structure of the sentence serves as a model of the structure of the thought'.
2. A thought is (a) objective, (b) the sense of an indicative sentence . . .
3. A thought must have at least one 'unsaturated' or functional element, otherwise its elements would fail to coalesce and would remain merely disparate atoms.
4. In a thought the complete elements refer (if at all) to objects.[13]

The nature of this enterprise makes it hard to evaluate its success. There are many issues one would think to be central to any attempt to offer a theory of judgment which Bell nevertheless does not address. For instance, although he argues that it would be wrong to require an account of judgment to restrict itself to the form of an account of the propositional attitude constructions used to attribute judgments to others, he does not justify the book's failure to present any such account as a proper part of such a theory. Again, although it has been suggested above that Bell was not obliged to restrict his attention to the notion of assertoric force (the analysis of the act of judging), one would certainly like a fuller and more satisfactory account of that notion than the cursory sketch we are offered.[14] The book does its work in a sort of methodological no-man's land between textual exegesis and theory construction owing allegiance only to the phenomena it seeks to theorize about.

This is not to say that the analysis is not enlightening, however. Bell is at his best when dissecting the explanatory role assigned by Frege to his technical concepts. When he succeeds, we learn both about Frege and about the phenomena. Consider for instance the notion of *Bedeutung*. Bell tells us that

> Frege had not one, but two notions of reference. These notions hang together so well in the case of singular terms that they are hard to distinguish in this context. In the case of predicates, however, they are not only distinguishable, they are difficult to reconcile. One notion is this: the reference of an expression is that extra-linguistic entity with which the expression has been correlated or which it picks out. The other notion of reference is that it is a property which an expression must possess if that expression is to be *truth-valuable* (to coin a phrase). By truth-valuable I mean such that it either possesses a truth-value, or is capable of being used (and not just mentioned) in a sentence which possesses a truth-value.[15]

Bell claims that although in the case of singular terms one notion can play both of these roles, since for them to be truth-valuable just *is* to be correlated with an object, in the case of sentences and functions the two notions diverge. All that Frege ever offers in the way of evidence for the application of the notion of reference to expressions in these categories is considerations showing them to be truth-valuable. Since he does not distinguish the two different notions of reference which he has in play, he feels entitled to conclude that they possess reference in the first sense as well. But this is a non sequitur, or at any rate a transition which must be justified and not simply assumed on the basis of the conflation of the two different senses of *Bedeutung*. Thus Bell rejects the notion of truth values as objects, and of functions as the references of functional expressions, as excess conceptual baggage mistakenly mixed in with the second notion of reference, which is the only one doing any explanatory work for these categories.

This analysis is clearheaded and valuable but can be faulted on two grounds, each of which amounts to a request for further analysis. First, as Dummett points out,[16] the characterization of the second notion of reference does not seem right. For as Bell has described it, reference is a property which an expression either has or lacks, depending on whether sentences containing it can have or always lack truth values. But Frege's notion is that in addition to having or lacking reference, expressions which have reference can have *different* references, accordingly as they make different contributions to the truth values of sentences containing them. The test is always substitutional: two expressions which have reference have different references if and only if in some context the substitution of one for the other changes a true sentence into one which is not true. Others who have noticed the distinction Bell is after have put things better. For instance, Ernst Tugendhat[17] (who seems to have introduced this line of thought) calls this nonrelational sense of reference "truth-value potential" and in effect identifies the truth value potential of a subsentential expression with the equivalence class of expressions intersubstitutable *salva veritate.*

The sharpening of Bell's distinction (which makes it similar to that between 'referent' and 'reference' which Dummett uses throughout *Frege: Philosophy of Language* [see note 2]) does not affect his criticism of the inference from possession of reference in this nonrelational sense to possession of reference in the relational sense, of course. But it does affect a further use he wants to make of the distinction to argue that it is incorrect to think of predicate expressions as having a reference at all, even in the nonrelational sense. For here Bell argues that Frege incorrectly takes as a necessary and sufficient condition for the truth-valuability (in Bell's sense) of predicates that they have sharp boundaries. He accordingly takes it that the assignment of reference to predicates is motivated only by this requirement, and so showing the untenability of such a requirement is sufficient to show the inappropriateness of assigning reference to predicate expression at all. This line of argument is undercut by seeing that there is more to the second notion of reference than truth-valuability. Since the denial of the cogency of the application of the notion of reference to predicates (or function expressions generally) is one of the main innovations of Bell's analysis, his failure adequately to characterize that part of Frege's notion of reference which remains when one takes away correlation with an extralinguistic object has serious consequences for the subsequent course of his argument.

Dummett, however, rejects not only Bell's characterization of the second notion of reference but also the claim that there are *two* notions of reference. He claims that the relational and the nonrelational senses represent "two ingredients of *one* notion." The second "tells us what Frege wanted the notion of reference *for,* and the other tells us how he thought that it applied to the various categories of expression."[18] It may be granted that the explanatory work Frege wanted the notion of reference for is its truth value potential or contribution to the truth conditions of sentences, and that he thought that the intersubstitutability equivalence class of equipollent expressions was determined by the correlation of all and only its members with the *same* extralinguistic entity. But it would still remain to be asked, for instance, whether the identity of the correlated object and the nature of the correlation can be inferred from the semantic equivalence class of expressions they determine, as Frege's arguments concerning the reference of sentences and functional expressions would seem to require. Such a question is in no way made less urgent or easier to answer by rephrasing it in terms of two ingredients of one notion rather than in terms of the relations of two notions. In the final section of this chapter I will argue that this difficulty is one instance of a quite general definitional failure of Frege's part, one which in another context he tried unsuccessfully to resolve in a purely technical way.

Putting the issue in these terms raises the second source of dissatisfaction with Bell's argument. For the sort of question just raised seems no less important or difficult for the paradigmatic case of singular terms than for the parts of speech Bell finds problematic. The basic substitutional/inferential methodology which yields the nonrelational sense of reference as an equivalence class of expressions vastly underdetermines the correlated objects and mode of correlation invoked by the relational sense even for proper names. Tugendhat, having formulated the nonrelational notion of reference, takes it to be *the* notion of reference, discarding correlation with an object as a realistic confusion best extruded from Frege's thought. Sluga follows Tugendhat in this regard. The reason in each case is that all that Frege's analysis of the use of expressions seems to require is the sorting of expressions according to the nonrelational sense of substitutional role. The semantic analysis he developed is a method for the perspicuous codification of inferences. Truth is what is preserved by good inferences, and subsentential expressions can be grouped into co-reference classes accordingly as intersubstitution within the classes preserves such good-inference potentials. Such an approach can give rise to specification of the conditions under which two expressions have the *same* reference, but how can it warrant a claim that the shared reference is to be identified with some object (among all those which in one way or another could be taken to determine the same co-reference classes) specified otherwise than as the reference of an expression? The answer seems to be that Frege's arguments for this identification are straightforwardly substitutional ones, in particular, that for any singular term *t* we can always substitute (saving the inferential potentials) the term *the object referred to by the singular term 't'*. The expressions which license intersubstitution of expressions are identity locutions (as Frege had argued in the *Grundlagen*), and so we are correct to say that the object referred to by the singular term 'Julius Caesar' *is* Julius Caesar. Whether this fact has the significance Frege thought it had is another matter.[19]

One of the most important discoveries of the early 1970s, from the point of view both of the interpretation of Frege and of the philosophy of language generally (for once, made independently of Dummett), concerns the need to distinguish two different explanatory roles which are conflated in Frege's technical concepts of sense. Saul Kripke and Hilary Putnam independently argued[20] that the *cognitive* notion of the sense of an expression, what one who has mastered the use of that expression may thereby be taken to understand and the *semantic* notion of the sense of that expression, what determines the reference of the expression, cannot in general be taken to coincide. In particular, in the case of proper names, no knowledge or practical capacity which can plausibly be attributed to an ordinary competent user of the name will suffice to determine the object of which it is a proper name. A similar point can be made about the use of natural kind sortals. Since Frege had required that his notion of the sense of an expression play both the cognitive and the semantic role, and since for an essential range of expressions no single notion can do so, it is apparent that his concept must be refined by dividing it into two distinct sense-concepts, whose interrelations it then becomes urgent to investigate.

A further distinction within the semantic notion of sense has been urged by a number of writers on the basis of the consideration of the behavior of indexical or token-reflexive expressions.[21] In Kaplan's idiom, we must distinguish for such expressions between their *character,* which is associated with the expression type, and the *content* associated with each contextually situated token(ing) of that type. The distinction in question is evident in the following dialogue:

A: I am anxious to get started.
B: No, it is possible that you are eager, but I am the anxious one.

We are concerned with the semantic notion of the sense of an expression, that is, with the way in which its reference is determined. In one sense both tokens of "I" have their reference determined in the same way, for in each case it is the speaker responsible for the tokening who is referred to. These expressions share a character. But in another sense A's token of "I" and B's token of "you" have their reference determined in different ways (e.g., for the purpose of tracking the referent through the other possible worlds which must be considered to evaluate the modal qualifications in B's remark). The referents of these tokenings will coincide in every possible world relevant to the evaluation of these utterances, in virtue of the identity of their contents. The characters of these expressions, together with the context in which they are uttered, determine a content which in turn determines a referent in every possible world. It is this latter task with which the semantic notion of sense is charged for nonindexical expressions. Such expressions may accordingly be thought of as those whose character determines a content without needing to be supplemented by a context. The point is that as we ask about what would be true in other worlds of the individual picked out by B's indexical utterance, there is a *double* relativity to possible worlds, accordingly as those worlds can be relevant to the two different stages in the determination of a referent. First, since B's remark could have been addressed to someone other than A, we must consult the world-context in order to determine what content is fixed by the character of the expression when uttered in that context. The individual concept so determined as a content can then be tracked through various possible worlds and assigned referents in each, so that modal claims can be evaluated.

Without referring to either of these antecedents, Bell distinguishes two notions of expression sense in a way which partakes of some of the features of each of the other distinctions. He calls his two notions "input sense" and "output sense," and introduces them by reference to two Fregean principles:

PS1: The sense of a sentence is determined by the senses of its component parts,

and

PR1: The truth-value of a sentence is determined by its sense. (And, of course, how things stand.)[22]

His claim is that although the "two principles depend for their plausibility and usefulness on there being a sense of 'sense' which remains constant throughout," in fact they demand different ones. Input sense is that notion of which principle PS1 holds, and output sense is that notion of sense of which PR1 holds. Input sense is that which is preserved by correct translations and that for which synonymy claims assert identities of sense. Subsentential expressions have input senses ("meanings"), and these combine to determine the input senses of sentences containing them. Output senses are defined as what is common to claims such as "Today I ate plum pudding," and "Yesterday you ate plum pudding." The input senses of sentences together with a context of utterance determine such output senses. The output senses of sentences are what can meaningfully be described as true or false, as per principle PR2.

As described so far, Bell's distinction amounts to the claim that the cognitive/semantic and character/content partitions of the notion of sense ought to be seen as coinciding. For the compositionality of 'sense' is a postulate required for the explanation of the possibility of understanding complex expressions, so that it must be input senses which are in the first instance grasped cognitively. Semantic senses, determining truth values of sentences, are in turn identified with output senses. But since the latter are determined by the former together with a context of utterance and the distinction is enforced by attention to indexical expressions, the character/content distinction is likewise subsumed by the difference between input and output senses.

Such an identification is clearly subject to a number of objections, as consideration of the quite different motives and functions of the conflated distinctions indicates. But these difficulties may not be insurmountable. Perhaps a useful view could be elaborated based on the assimilation of the sense in which the referent of a proper name token is determined not by what its utterer understands by it, but only by this together with a causal, historical, and social context in which the token is embedded, on the one hand, and the sense in which the reference-deter-mining sense of a token of "yesterday" is given not just by what one can understand as the meaning associated with the expression type, but only by this together with a concrete context of use. But Bell does not attempt to develop such an account. In part this is because he has nothing what-ever to say about what "contexts" are, or how these together with input senses determine output senses. And it is just here that all the detailed work is involved in making out either half of such an assimilation, and hence in justifying their conflation. But Bell is precluded from address-ing such a task by other, less defensible features of his view.

For Bell denies that subsentential expressions have output senses at all, claiming that "output sense is essentially sentential."[23] No argument or even motivation for this position is presented. It is suggested that for sentences the distinction between input senses and output senses corre-sponds to that between sentences and the statements they can be used to make, and that it is better to think of the former not as possessing truth values which change, by contrast to statements whose truth values do not, but rather to think of the former as not the kind of thing which can have truth values at all. But no reason is given for not extending this dis-tinction to subsentential expressions. The distinction between the two varieties of sense is introduced, as indicated above, in terms of two Fregean principles. PR2, the 'sense determines reference' principle, is quoted at this portion of the argument as restricted to sentences and truth values. But of course the principle Frege uses is not so restricted. Indeed, when Bell first introduces it some sixty pages earlier, it is in un-restricted form. He has just been discussing the principle he calls PR1, that the reference of complex expressions is determined by the refer-ences of their components (which Bell discards because as we have seen he does not attribute reference of any kind to functions). He says:

> Elsewhere in his writings, however, he seems to invoke a quite differ-ent principle which we can call PR2. It is this: (a) the reference of any expression is determined by its sense, (b) the sense of a complex ex-pression is determined by the senses of its component parts.[24]

Two features of *this* definition deserve comment. First, part (b) of princi-ple PR2 as here stated is what he later calls PS1 and is concerned pre-cisely to distinguish from PR2. Second, part (a) of *this* original state-ment differs from the later version in not being restricted to sentences.

Neither of these substantial changes in the significance of his expression "PR2" is announced, acknowledged, or motivated in the intervening text. Such carelessness in specifying a central interpretive principle which one has taken the trouble to name for clarity of reference is bad enough under any circumstances. It is unforgivable when essential features of one's own claims and their justifications depend precisely on the matters obscured by the sloppiness. As things stand, the reader is left with no idea why in using the two principles PR2 and PS1 (= PR2(b) in the earlier statement) to distinguish two notions of sense one should employ the later version of PR2 rather than PR2(a) from the earlier version, which is the principle Frege endorsed. Apart from the invocation of PR2, output senses are specified as what is common to the two "plum pudding" sentences quoted above. As my sketch of the character/content distinction shows, it is not at all obvious why this characterization should not extend to what is common to 'today' and 'yesterday', on the one hand, and 'I' and 'you', on the other.

Bell does, however, employ the restriction of output senses to sentences to argue for a further point. For he claims that the "context principle" of the *Grundlagen* may be understood in terms of the fact that terms only have input senses, which together with the input senses of other expressions determine sentential input senses, which in context determine a truth value. Since the reference of terms matters only in determining truth values, it is "only in the context of a sentence that a term have a reference." Clearly nothing can be made of this line of thought in the absence of a rationale for its basic premises.

These difficulties with the distinction between input senses and output senses also make it difficult to evaluate another novel interpretive suggestion which Bell offers. He concludes his discussion of the senses of proper names with the claim "The sense of a proper name, then, is that it purports to refer to a determinate object of a given sort with which it has been conventionally correlated."[25] The sense of a proper name is here taken as "that which one understands when one is able to use it correctly."[26] As indicated above in the discussion of the relation of the cognitive notion of sense to Bell's notions, this must be the input sense, for subsentential expressions are not supposed to have output senses. It is accordingly obscure what the connection is supposed to be between the senses Bell is offering a theory of here and the determination of referents for the proper names they are senses of. What then are the criteria of adequacy for an account of what a name user must be taken to understand? Bell examines the conditions under which we would want to deny that someone had mastered the use of a name, and concludes that in addition to using it as a singular term, one must at least know some sortal under which the referent is taken to fall in order to be judged a competent user. This is useful as a necessary condition, but much less plausible as a sufficient condition to be taken to be using an expression as a proper name. For a sufficient condition would seem to require that one be appropriately connected to a community of users of the name, perhaps a historically extended one, whose joint use *does* determine a referent, though no individual's use need do so. It is not obvious that merely believing that some conventional correlation has been established with an object of the right sort is sufficient to be appropriately connected with the community of users of that name. In any case, to argue for such a principle would require looking at how input senses and various specific sorts of context can together determine output senses and eventually referents for the names in question, and this Bell does not undertake.

Bell wants his notion of proper name sense in order to develop an appropriate account of the senses of functional expressions. This latter task is made especially urgent by the confrontation between his denial that the referents of functions have any explanatory value, on the one hand, with the undeniable importance in Frege's scheme of functions and concepts understood as functions, on the other. Bell's reconstruction reconciles these ideas by interpreting concepts and functions as the *senses* rather than the references of functional expressions. A concept, accordingly, is to be understood as a function which can take as arguments proper name senses of the sort he has described, and yield thoughts, the senses of sentences. While this identification of concepts must be seen as a revision rather than an interpretation of Frege's thought, it might seem that, setting that identification aside, at least the account of the senses of functional expressions as functions from the senses of argument expressions to the senses of value expressions ought to be uncontroversial. It is not, and it is instructive to see why not.

As Bell has pointed out in his discussion of senses generally, the concept of sense is required to play two distinguishable roles. First, the sense of a component of a complex expression must contribute to the determination of the sense of that complex. But also, the sense of the component must determine a reference for that component. This gives us two different ways to think about the senses of functional expressions such as predicates. On the one hand, they must combine with the senses of terms to yield the senses of sentences. On the other hand, they must be the way in which a function from objects to truth values is determined or given. It is not obvious that these two jobs can be done by one notion. In particular, Dummett has argued that "once the proper name has specified the way in which the object is given, then it has made its contribution to the sense of the sentence; if it had not, then it would be impossible to see how its sense could *both* contribute to the sense of the sentence *and* consist in the way in which the object is given."[27] That is, maintaining the coincidence of the two roles of sense in the case of proper names (presumably where our grasp is firmest) commits us not only to their divergence for functional expressions, but also to which half we give up, namely, the identification of their senses with sense functions. Peter Geach has objected to this doctrine of Dummett's,[28] and it is instructive to examine Dummett's response.

It is not disputed that once a sense has been assigned to a predicate, a function from the senses of proper names to thoughts is determined. For according to Dummett, the predicate sense is the way in which a function from objects to truth values is given. Hence, when that function is supplemented by an object, it determines a way in which a truth value is given, that is, a thought. But since a term sense will determine such a supplementing object (according to the second role of senses mentioned above), the predicate sense will induce indirectly a function from term senses to sentence senses. As Dummett says, "The question is whether the sense of the predicate just *is* that function."[29]

To argue that it is not, Dummett appeals to a further thesis of Frege's about senses, namely, that the senses of component expressions are *parts* of the senses of the complex expressions in which they occur. We have seen that it is a mistake to think of functions or their arguments as parts of the values they generate, as Frege's retraction of his careless claim that objects are parts of truth values shows. But since Frege did hold that predicate senses are parts of thoughts, we would be committing precisely this howler if we identified those senses with functions taking term senses into thoughts. This is an ingenious counterargument, but it cannot be considered decisive. For while it would be a howler to treat functions and their arguments generally as parts of the values they determine (as in the combination of Sweden and the function *the capital of . . .* to yield Stockholm), this consideration does not show that particular functions and kinds of function cannot have values which contain the functions or their arguments as parts. Stockholm is part of the value of the function *the country of which . . . is the capital.* And mathematical examples of function-values which contain functions as parts in the set-theoretic sense are easy to come by. (One thinks of the story of the oracle who offered to answer a single question, and upon being asked "What is the ordered pair whose first element is the best question I could ask you, and whose second element is its answer?" replied—falsely, I suppose— "The ordered pair whose first element is your question and whose second element is this answer.")

Insulated from this dispute about sense functions by his distinction between input senses and output senses, Bell backs up his commitment to treating the senses of functional expressions as functions by citing a number of passages, both published and from the posthumous works, in which Frege unequivocally describes such senses as "unsaturated," "incomplete," and "in need of supplementation," going so far in fact as to say that "the words 'unsaturated' and 'predicative' seem more suited to the sense than to the reference."[30] To motivate his identification of concepts with sense functions, Bell argues as follows.[31] The only reason Frege had for believing in concepts as predicate referents was the need to deal with a situation in which predicates have a sense and so determine a thought, but lack a reference, and so determine a thought which has no truth value. The only case where this can happen which does not reduce to the failure of a term to have a reference is where the predicate is not defined for the sort of argument to which it is applied. But this sort of case can be much more plausibly excluded by considerations concerning predicate *senses.* For such cross-categorial predications (such as "Julius Caesar *is* the sum of two prime numbers") ought properly to be seen as not succeeding in expressing thoughts at all. Bell's solution accordingly is to see predicates as having sortal restrictions associated with their argument places, which together with the 'sortal physiognomy' he has already assigned to proper name senses yields the result he desires. One of the benefits which might be derived from such a radical reconstruction should be made manifest by the discussion to be given below of the difficulties ensuing from Frege's insistence that functions be defined for all arguments whatsoever. As before, however, the evaluation of this thesis about senses must await some resolution of the general questions Bell has left open concerning his distinction between input and output senses.

II. Sluga on the Development of Frege's Thought

Hans Sluga's book on Frege in the "Arguments of the Philosophers" series[32] represents an approach complementary to Bell's in almost every regard. Its central aim is to reread Frege's work in the light of that of his precursors and contemporaries, rather than by reference to his successors in the analytic tradition, as has been traditional. Although Frege's unprecedented innovations in symbolic logic have made it natural to think of him exclusively in the role of the founder of a tradition—as a man without a past—Sluga argues that we ignore at our peril his intellectual climate and the influences which conditioned various aspects of his technical concepts and of the explanatory tasks he set for them. Sluga's task is not purely historical, however. For he is also concerned to set out and justify novel readings of some of Frege's purely philosophical doctrines, readings which are suggested and motivated by the historical recontextualization he recommends. The result is a stimulating new picture of Frege's thought which will be of interest even to those who are not in the end persuaded in detail by it. Furthermore, since the narrative strategy employed is to trace the development of Frege's ideas chronologically (starting, as it were, before he was born) and surveying all of his important writings *seriatim,* this book is excellently constructed to serve as an introduction to these ideas (as Bell's or Dummett's books, for instance, could not) as well as to challenge specialists.

The book's historical orientation, then, is adopted not only for its own sake, but also in order to guard against blinding ourselves to interpretively significant features of Frege's work by the importation of anachronistic prejudices. Accordingly, it is primarily in terms of the philosophical illumination they provide for our appreciation of Frege's concepts and claims that we must evaluate the success of Sluga's various invocations of historical influence. The claimed influences may be considered under four headings. First, a view is presented about who Frege took to be his philosophical opponents. Next, Leibniz is identified as a precursor. Third, claims are made about the influence of two logicians of the generation preceding Frege's, Lotze and Trendelenburg. Finally and most significantly, it is claimed that overlooking the intellectual debt which Frege owes to Kant has most seriously distorted our understanding. I will consider these claims in this order.

In his first chapter, Sluga is concerned to refute the claim that "in a history of philosophy Frege would have to be classified as a member of the realist revolt against Hegelian idealism, a revolt which occurred some three decades earlier in Germany than in Britain."[33] In this aim he succeeds unequivocally. Hegelianism had ceased to be dominant or even popular in German philosophical circles some years before Frege was born. The view against which Frege was reacting is the scientific naturalism which Sluga claims was held by the physiologists-turned-philosophers Vogt, Moleschott, Buchner, and Czolbe, popularized during Frege's lifetime by Haeckel, and shared with some reservations by Gruppe. Ontologically this view is a reductive materialism, and epistemologically it is an empiricist psychologism. Sensations are viewed as material processes of the brain. Concepts, and hence the thoughts constructed from them, are taken to be reflections of such sensations. Logic is seen as the study of the laws of thought, that is, as an empirical investigation seeking to establish the natural laws governing the association of concepts in judgment and of judgments in inference. It is this psychologism which Frege so vigorously opposed, and on those relatively few occasions when he describes his opponents as 'idealists' it is clearly this school which he has in mind.

This is a point of no small moment, especially in the context of an evaluation of Frege's role as progenitor of the analytic tradition. For his overarching objection to the naturalists is their failure appropriately to distinguish between the normative and ideal order of correct inference and justification on the one hand, and the descriptive and actual order of causation and empirical processes on the other. Their concomitant confusion of features of cognitive acts with features of the contents of those acts is merely the expression of this original sin. And in his insistence on the centrality of this basic distinction, Frege is at one with Kant and the post-Kantian idealists, and at odds with the primarily physicalist and empiricist tradition in Anglo-American philosophy which he fathered, and in the context of which it has been natural for us to read him.[34]

Throughout his book Sluga talks about Leibniz's influence on Frege, but when he specifies the details of this influence, his claims turn out to be quite weak. Like Leibniz (and Kant), "Frege is interested in the study of logic and the foundations of mathematics because they allow one to ask in a precise form what can be known through reason alone."[35] Aside from this general rationalist commitment to the possibility of a priori formal knowledge, the only Leibnizian doctrine which is attributed to Frege is the endorsement of the project of the universal characteristic. Frege explicitly describes the motivation for his *Begriffsschrift* in this way. That at this level of generality Frege owes a debt to Leibniz is hardly a novel or surprising claim, however. Sluga also discusses the influence of Trendelenburg, but in the end the claims seem to come to little more than that he was the conduit through which Frege became familiar with Leibniz's ideas.

It is otherwise with the connection discerned between Frege and the logician Hermann Lotze. The suggestion of influence here has specifically been denied as "a remarkable piece of misapplied history."[36] Yet in this case Sluga shows sufficiently striking similiarities to make the hypothesis of influence persuasive. It is known that Frege read Lotze. Indeed it has been argued that the theory of judgment in opposition to which he presents his innovation in the *Begriffsschrift* just is Lotze's formulation.[37] The essay immediately preceding "The Thought" in the journal in which it was originally published, which Sluga takes to have been intended by the editors as an introduction to Frege's essay, mentions Frege in the context of an exposition of Lotze which highlights several Fregean doctrines.[38] From Sluga's account of Lotze's views (as presented in the *Logik* of 1874 and an earlier work of 1843), one can extract eight points of similarity with Frege.

First, Lotze inveighs against psychologism and indeed is the figure Frege's contemporaries would probably have identified as leading the battle against the dominant naturalism of the day and in favor of a more Kantian position. Second, Lotze was a logicist about mathematics, although there is no hint in his works that he took the detailed working out of such a reduction to logic as part of what would be required to justify this view. Third, Lotze insists, against empiricistic sensationalism, on the distinction between the objects of our knowledge and our recognition of such objects, in much the same terms that Frege did. Fourth, Lotze emphasized and developed the Kantian strategy of explaining concepts as functions (though of course he does not have the notion of functions as unsaturated which Frege derived from his own substitutional method of assigning contents to subsentential expressions). Fifth, Lotze attacks the empiricists with a distinction between the causal conditions of the acquisition of concepts and the capacity to use such concepts in correct reasoning which mastery of the concepts consists in (see note 34). Next, Lotze offers a theory of identity statements according to which the two terms share a content, but differ in form. This is the *Begriffsschrift* view, and the language survives into the opening paragraphs of "Über Sinn und Bedeutung." Seventh, Lotze endorses the Kantian principle of the priority in the order of explanation of judgments to concepts which Frege endorses in the *Grundlagen*. Lotze does not succeed in being entirely consistent on this point, since he also is committed to atomistic principles which are not obviously compatible with the view on the priority of judgments. Although Sluga does not say so, those who take Frege not to have discarded the context principle in the post-1890 writings must find a similar tension in some of the procedures of the *Grundgesetze*. Finally, Lotze is committed to the objectivity of sentential contents, and treats them as neither mental nor physical just as Frege does. Lotze, however, specifically denies that this objectivity is grounded in the correlation of sentences with objects such as Frege's thoughts appear to be, taking a more Kantian position. Sluga, as we shall see below, argues that despite apparent statements to the contrary, we should understand this to be Frege's view as well.

This is a suggestive set of similarities to find in a prominent near contemporary logician with whose work Frege was familiar. Recognizing them as important need not commit one to minimizing the significant, perhaps dominant, differences in outlook which remain between Lotze's revived Kantianism and Frege's philosophical elaboration of his semantic methodology (although Sluga does on occasion succumb to the temptation to treat Frege's agreement with Lotze on one point as evidence that he probably agreed with him on others). Only according to the crudest notion of what philosophical originality consists in is there any incompatibility between finding enlightenment in the demonstration that these general principles were in the air and so came complete with a history and a tradition on the one hand, and the appreciation of the genius shown in the use such adopted and adapted raw materials were put to in the service of quite a different explanatory project on the other.

Sluga's most important and sustained argument, however, concerns the influence of Kant on Frege. He claims that Frege should not be thought of as a dogmatic realist about physical objects nor as a Platonist about abstract objects, as he almost universally has been thought of. He should be seen rather as a Kantian whose realistic remarks are to be interpreted as expressing that merely empirical realism which is one feature of transcendental idealism. This is certainly a radical reinterpretation. What evidence can be adduced for it? Sluga's considerations may be assembled as five distinct arguments.

First, it is pointed out that Frege joined a philosophical society whose manifesto is explicitly idealist and Kantian, and that he published in its journal. By itself, this shows little, for Frege had so much trouble getting his work into print and finding others willing to discuss it that we cannot be sure how much he would have put up with to secure such opportunities. The rationale Sluga suggests[39] is that "what tied him to the idealists was primarily his opposition to the various forms of naturalism." Specifically, Frege and the idealists (a) were anti-psychologistic, (b) endorsed an objectivist epistemology (taking the contents of judgments to be independent of their entertainment by thinkers), and (c) endorsed a rationalistic a priorism about mathematics. These points are well taken, but the views involved are all consistent with Platonism and realism generally as well as with transcendental idealism. Indeed Sluga admits that "one can read much of Frege and not raise the question of transcendentalism." So we must look elsewhere for a warrant for such an attribution.

The second argument concerns Frege's attitude toward the truths of geometry.[40] It is remarked to begin with that in his *Habilitationsschrift* Frege held a Kantian view on this topic, saying that geometry rests "on axioms that derive their validity from the nature of our capacity for intuition *(Anschauungsvermögen)*." Furthermore, throughout his career Frege describes geometrical knowledge as synthetic a priori, and on this basis rejects non-Euclidean geometry as *false*. From this fact Sluga concludes: "Frege held a Kantian view of space and hence a transcendentally subjective view of the objects that occupy it." The only elucidation offered of this crucial "hence" is the later statement that "Frege's view must be close to Kant's: Empirical objects are in space and time, but space and time are a priori forms of sensibility. That seems to imply that for Frege empirical objects can only be empirically real, but must be transcendentally ideal." That Kant believed the two views to be linked in this way falls far short of showing that Frege did so. Certainly such an argument cannot be taken to undermine an interpretation which takes Frege's realistic remarks about physical objects at face value, and admits that his views are inconsistent to the extent that he never confronted these latter with his views about geometry with an eye to reconciling them. Nevertheless, some interpretive cost is clearly associated with attributing such an inconsistency to Frege.

The next two arguments must be judged less satisfactory.[41] First, Sluga argues that in the context of Kantian transcendentalism (as just discussed), Platonic realism looks like dogmatic metaphysics. So Frege should have been expected to argue that views (a) through (c) above, on which he argues with the idealists, cannot in fact be warranted transcendentally. But Frege nowhere argues this. The trouble with this argument is that there is no evidence that Frege did not, as most of his contemporaries did, read Kant's transcendentalism as a form of psychologism. If he had done so, he would have dismissed it and so not felt the force of the demand in question. Sluga next argues that every claim of Frege's that can be taken as evidence of Frege's realism can be matched by a passage in Lotze, who had a Kantian idealistic theory of validity. This argument seems to do no more than restate the point that views (a) through (c) are consistent with either position. For it is a criterion of adequacy of anyone's transcendentally idealistic position that it have room for all of the claims the realist wants to make, suitably reinterpreted. Further, Frege does insist that thoughts are independent, not just of this thinker or that, but of the very existence or even possibility of thinkers at all. This seems to contradict Lotze's account of objectivity as rule-governed intersubjectivity.

Sluga's final argument is weightier and involves more interpretive work, in both construction and evaluation. The basic claim is that "there are strewn through Frege's writings statements that appear irreconcilable with Platonic realism. In particular the central role of the Fregean belief in the primacy of judgements over concepts would seem to be explicable only in the context of a Kantian point of view."[42] Arguing in this way obviously commits Sluga to showing that Frege does not discard the context principle when he arrives at the distinction between sense and reference. We will see below that he contributes significant new considerations to that debate in furtherance of this aim. But the incompatibility of realism with the recognition of the primacy of judgments must also be shown. The latter view is "Kantian," but it does not obviously entail transcendental idealism, which is the view in question. Sluga takes the principle of the primacy of judgments to serve the purpose for Kant[43] of refuting any atomistic attempt to construct concepts and judgments out of simple components, and in particular to resist the empiricist sensationalist atomism of Hume. Such a view is indeed incompatible with the reism of Tadeusz Kotarbinski (to which Alfred Tarski's recursive semantics owes so much), which sees the world as an arrangement of objects out of which concepts and judgments must be constructed set-theoretically.[44] But the Kantian principle need not be taken to be incompatible with Platonic realism about abstract entities such as *thoughts* which are the contents of judgments. Given that the context principle does not show that Frege was a transcendental idealist about thoughts, it seems also open to him to hold some form of realism about other objects, provided thoughts retain an appropriate primacy (as, given the very special status of truth in the late works, even those who see the context principle as discarded are committed to granting) even if he has not discarded that principle. So if the case for the persistence of the context principle can be made out, it should be taken as showing that. Frege was a Kantian in the sense of holding the context principle, not in the sense of being a transcendental idealist.

Still, this point is worth establishing for its own sake. Sluga correctly sees the *Begriffsschrift* as the confluence of three lines of thought: (1) that judgments, as involved in inference, are the original bearers of semantic significance, so that it is only by analyzing such judgments according to the procedure of "noting invariance under substitution" that such significance can be attributed to subsentential expressions ('the primacy of judgments'), (2) the Leibnizian idea of a perfect language, and (3) the idea of reducing mathematics to logic. Assuming the context principle was thus "anchored deeply in Frege's thought, it is implausible to conclude with Dummett that in his later years Frege simply let it slip from his mind."[45] Sluga advances five arguments for the persistence of the principle, and along the way addresses two commitments of Frege that have been taken to be incompatible with such persistence.

First, Sluga offers an important consideration which has not previously been put forward in the extensive literature discussing this question. The first of the 1891–92 essays that Frege wrote is a seldom read review of Ludwig Lange's *Historical Development of the Concept of Motion and Its Foreseeable End Result* titled "The Principle of Inertia." In it Frege argues at some length that the concepts of a theory are not given prior to and independent of that theory. Rather those concepts can be arrived at only by analyzing the contents which the judgments constituting the theory are given by the inferences concerning them which that theory endorses. This is a significant new piece of evidence supporting Sluga's view. The only question which might be raised about it is that since this semi-popular piece does not deploy the full-blown apparatus of sense and reference, it may be wondered whether the views there expressed were confronted by Frege with that apparatus, or whether the essay might not be seen as merely the latest of his early works. But to take such a line would be to concede a lot, and future claims that the context principle was discarded will have to confront this argument of Sluga's in detail.

Next Sluga offers a novel reading of the essay on the distinction between sense and reference which denies that, as has often been claimed, that distinction as there presented applies primarily to singular terms and their relations to the objects which are their referents, and hence commits Frege to an assimilation of sentences to terms which is incompatible with the context principle. The strategy here is, in effect, to deny that *'Bedeutung'* as Frege uses it *ever* has the relational sense which indicates correlation with an object. Relying on the Tugendhat essay mentioned above in connection with Bell, Sluga understands *'Bedeutung'* as a nonrelational semantic potential defined paradigmatically for sentences, in virtue of their role in inference. The introduction of this notion in the context of the consideration of identities involving singular terms is seen as a rhetorical device of presentational significance only. In the final theory subsentential expressions are taken to inherit indirect, inferential significances in virtue of their substitutional behavior in sentences, which alone are directly inferentially and hence semantically significant. Thus *'Bedeutung'* is paradigmatically a sentential notion.

To this analysis is conjoined an account of *'Sinn'* as a cognitive notion, as what matters for knowledge. But again, the units of knowledge are judgments, and subsentential expressions can become relevant only insofar as they can be put together to form sentences which can express judgments. So sense also should be seen as primarily a sentential notion, which applies to subsentential expressions only in a derivative way. This line of thought concerning senses is then combined with that concern-

ing reference in a subtle and sensitive account of the puzzling relations between the Lotzean rendering of identity locutions offered in the
Begriffsschrift and its successor in "Über Sinn und Bedeutung" ("ÜSB").

The previous discussion of Bell's interpretation suggests that these
readings leave something to be desired. Sluga does not acknowledge the
existence of any passage or considerations indicating that Frege does
have a relational notion of reference in play. Yet such passages and considerations do exist, and merely elaborating the nonrelational version of
Frege's concept, as Sluga does, does not obviate the necessity of investigating the relations between the two notions and the possibilities for
reconciling them. Similarly, Sluga pushes his discussion of the notion of
sense no farther than the discrimination of the cognitive role played by
that concept. He has nothing to say about the semantic notion of sense,
or accordingly about how senses are to be understood as determining
references, even nonrelational references. On these points Sluga's analytic net does not have as fine a mesh as Bell's. As a result, his ingenious
interpretation of sense and reference will require further filling in before
its eventual promise can be assessed.

The overall interpretation which results from all of these arguments,
however, is challenging and powerful. The primary objections to the
persistence of the context principle are that Frege nowhere explicitly endorses that principle after the 1884 *Grundlagen* formulation, and that
the principle is incompatible with two central doctrines of the 1891–92
essays, namely, the semantic assimilation of sentences to terms and the
account of concepts as functions from objects to truth values. Sluga
claims that his readings of the "Inertia" essay and of "ÜSB" meet these
objections. He does not say in detail how the doctrine about functions is
to be reconciled with the context principle, but does argue that the "Inertia" essay justifies us in attributing *Bedeutung* to any expression which
makes an appropriate contribution to the possession of truth values
by sentences containing it. Thus function-expressions may be assigned
(nonrelational) reference on this account. Using intersubstitution equivalence classes to move from Tugendhat's nonrelational sentential semantic significances to those of subsentential expressions does indeed justify
such an attribution. But in the "Inertia" essay, Frege seems to be using
'concept' in the ordinary sense rather than his technical one, that is, to
refer to the *senses* of predicate expressions rather than their references.
This being the case, it is not clear how the envisaged reconciliation of

the context principle with the view of concepts as functions from objects to truth values is to be achieved.

Besides the evidence of the essay on inertia, Sluga offers two further reasons to deny that the later Frege is silent on the topic of the context principle. First, he mentions in several places the posthumously published "Notes for Ludwig Darmstaedter" (of 1919) as showing that Frege continued to endorse the principle. He does not say what passages he has in mind, but he presumably intends the following: "What is distinctive about my conception of logic is that I begin by giving pride of place to the content of the word 'true,' and then immediately go on to introduce a thought as that to which the question 'Is it true?' is in principle applicable. So I do not begin with concepts and put them together to form a thought or judgement; I come by the parts of a thought by analyzing the thought."[46] Such a passage does show that sentences play a special explanatory role for the late Frege, but that much is not in question. At most such claims would show that a version of the context principle held for *senses*, confirming Sluga's claim that the cognitive origins of the concept of sense require that priority be given to sentences. No version of the context principle for referential significances follows from these claims. Unfortunately, Sluga never says what exactly he takes the context principle to be, whether a doctrine about senses, references, or both. Frege's original formulation, of course, preceded his making this distinction. So perhaps the best conclusion is that Sluga takes the principle to persist as applying to senses, that is, that it is only in the context of a thought that a term or other subsentential expression expresses a sense. This seems to be something Frege indeed did not surrender. Such a reading has the additional advantage that the doctrine that concepts are functions from the references of singular terms to truth values is not incompatible with it.

The final argument fares less well. It is claimed that Frege's late treatment of real numbers shows that his practice is still in accord with the context principle.[47] Here the point seems to be that the real numbers are given contextual definitions. Such an argument would be relevant to a context principle applying to reference rather than senses, since Frege does not pretend to specify the senses of numerical expressions in his formal definitions. But the definition of real numbers he offers is of just the same form as the *Grundgesetze* definition of natural numbers. If this style of definition does exhibit commitment to a form of the context principle, that case should be argued for the more central and important case of natural numbers. It is not clear how such an argument would go.

III. Frege's Argument

One of the themes around which Sluga usefully arranges his presentation of Frege's development is that of the pursuit of the definition of purely logical objects. The reason offered for the somewhat misleading order of presentation pursued in "ÜSB," which seems to give pride of place to singular terms rather than sentences, is that the road from the *Grundlagen* account of numbers to that of the *Grundgesetze* needed to pass through a more thorough understanding of identity claims. Sluga is quite clear that for Frege, beginning with the *Grundlagen,* the only concept we have of an *object* is as that which determines the semantic significance of a singular term. For an expression to play the semantic role of a singular term is for it to make a certain contribution to the inferential potential of sentences containing it, a contribution which is constituted by the appropriate (truth-preserving) substitutions which can be made for that expression. The substitution inference potential of a singular term is in turn codified in the endorsed identity claims involving that term. That what we mean by 'object' is according to Frege exhausted by our conception of that the recognition of which is expressed in identity claims in virtue of their licensing of intersubstitution is one genuinely transcendental element in his thought about which Dummett, Sluga, and Bell agree.

In the *Grundlagen,* Frege argued that according to this criterion, number-words are singular terms, so that if statements about them are ever objectively true or false, they must be so in virtue of properties of the objects which are identified and individuated in assertions of numerical identities. The logicist thesis that the truths of mathematics are derivable from the truths of logic by logical means alone accordingly entails that numbers are purely logical objects, in the sense that the identities which express the recognition and individuation of these objects are themselves logical truths. Sluga's ingenious suggestion is that Frege's concern in "ÜSB" with the nature of *synthetic* or potentially knowledge-extending identities specifying ordinary objects should be understood as a stage in the working out of his mature account of analytic (logically true) identities required for the adequate specification of the logical objects treated in the *Grundgesetze*. The specific interpretive use to which Sluga puts this general insight is hard to warrant, however.

For he claims that the difference between these two sorts of identities resides in the fact that the identities by which logical objects are identified and individuated express coincidence not just of reference but also of sense.[48] It is not clear what reasons there are to accept this reading, nor what interpretive advantages would accrue from doing so. For Frege explicitly affirms on a number of occasions that the two expressions '2^2' and '$2 + 2$' express different senses. And he seems committed to this view by structural principles of his approach, in particular by the compositionality principle as it applies to senses. Different function-expressions appear in these two complex designations, and the senses of components are parts of the senses of complexes containing them. Nor does the fact that such identities are to be logically true entail that they express identities of sense rather than merely of reference. Identity of sense would of course be sufficient for identity of reference. But we are often told that logic need be concerned only with truth and reference, and Frege's view seems to be that it can be logically true that two different senses determine the same reference.

This mistake aside, Sluga's tracing of the development of Frege's attempts to define abstract objects of the sort instantiated by logical objects is a valuable contribution, and raises issues of the first importance for our understanding of the constraints on interpretations of Frege's technical concepts. The story begins with the second definition of number which Frege tries out in the *Grundlagen* (*GL*). It states that two concepts have the same number associated with them if and only if the objects those concepts are true of can be correlated one-to-one.[49] He rejects such a definition as inadequate to specify numbers as objects, on the grounds that it will not determine whether, for example, Julius Caesar or England is identical to any number. Such a definition settles the truth values of identities (and hence the appropriateness of substitutions) only for terms which are the values for some argument expression of the function-expression "the number of the concept . . ." This procedure would be legitimate only if we had independently defined the concept (function from terms to truth values) <u>number</u> signified by this function-expression. But it is not possible simultaneously to specify that function and the objects for which it yields the value True. If objects had been specified by this definition, then there would be a fact of the matter as to whether Julius Caesar was one of them. But the definition does not settle this issue either way. On the basis of this objection, Frege motivates his third and final definition of numbers, considered below.

Sluga traces through the later works Frege's efforts to clarify the specification of numbers in such a way that it will not be subject to this objection, culminating in the *Grundgesetze (GG)* account of courses of values. Given the centrality to Frege's project of producing an adequate definition of number, this progress is of interest for its own sake. But the task of responding to the objection to the second *GL* definition of number is made especially urgent for interpreters of Frege by a consideration which Sluga does not mention. For the specifications of the abstract objects in terms of which Frege's semantic analysis proceeds (e.g., sense, reference, thought, truth value) are of the same objectionable form as the second *GL* definition of number. Nothing we are ever told about the senses of singular terms or sentences, for instance, settles the question of whether Julius Caesar can be such a sense. Though this may seem like a question of no interest, some interesting questions do take this form. For in interpreting the notion of sense, one is concerned *both* with subdividing the explanatory functional role played by the concept (as exhibited in the discussion of Bell) *and* with the possibility of identifying senses with things otherwise described—for example, the uses of expressions, sets of possible worlds, mental representations. Frege himself addresses such issues when he denies that the senses of sentences are to be identified with ideas in people's minds. How is the identity he wishes to deny given a sense?

All that is given is a criterion determining when the senses associated with two expressions are the same (namely, if they are intersubstitutable without change of cognitive value—*Erkenntniswerte*). If something is not specified as the sense associated with an expression (compare: number associated with a concept), its identity or nonidentity with anything which has been so given is entirely undetermined. Frege's procedure for introducing his technical concepts such as sense is invariably to attempt to specify *simultaneously* a realm of abstract semantic interpretants *and* a function which assigns a member of this realm to each expression.

We are, for instance, to associate truth values with sentences. But we are told only that the truth value associated with p is the same as the truth value associated with q just in case for no occurrence of p (either as a freestanding sentence or as a component in a more complex sentence) can a good inference be turned into a bad one by substituting q for that occurrence of p (reading the principle that good inferences never take true premises into conclusions that are not true as defining truth values in terms of the goodness of inferences). Even conjoining such a specification with the stipulation that the truth value associated with the sentence '2 + 2 = 4' is to be called "the True" does not settle the question of whether Julius Caesar is that truth value. He had better not be, for if the logicist program of *GG* is to be successful, truth values must be definable as purely logical objects. The current question is how the identity which is denied here is given a sense so that something could count as justifying that denial. The functions which associate the various kinds of semantic significances with expressions are always of the form: $f(x) = f(y)$ iff $R(x, y)$, where x and y range over expressions, and R is some relation defined in terms of the inferential potentials of those expressions. These are exactly the kind of definition Frege found wanting in *GL*.

Seeing how Frege believes he can overcome the objectionable indeterminateness of concepts such as that determined by the second *GL* definition of number is thus a matter of considerable importance for the appraisal of his success in specifying his own technical concepts, as well as for the narrower project of introducing numbers as logical objects. The third and final definition of number which Frege offers in *GL* is: "The Number which belongs to the concept F is the extension of the concept 'equal *(Gleichzahlig)* to the concept F.'"[50] The number three is thus identified with the extension of the concept, for example, "can be correlated one-to-one with the dimensions of Newtonian space." This definition does not have the form Frege had objected to. It, however, essentially involves a new concept, extension, which has not previously appeared in *GL*, nor indeed anywhere else in Frege's writings. In a footnote to the definition Frege says simply, "I assume that it is known what the extension of a concept is." Sluga points out that this definitionally unsatisfactory situation is not remedied in the remainder of the book. The result is scarcely up to the standards of definition to which Frege held others and himself. The project of *GL* could not be counted a success until and unless it could be supplemented with an account of the extensions of concepts.

Six years later, in "Funktion und Begriff," Frege offers such an account. The general notion of a function is explicated, and concepts are defined as functions from objects to truth values. The extension of a concept is defined as the "course of values" (*Wertheverlauf*) of that function. This is the first appearance of the concept of a course of values. Since extensions are reduced to them, the residual definitional burden bequeathed by *GL* is put off onto this new concept. What Frege tells us here is just that the course of values associated with function *F* is the same as the course of values associated with function *G* just in case for every argument the value assigned to that argument by *F* is the same as the value assigned to it by *G*. The trouble with such a stipulation, as Sluga says, is that it has exactly the objectionably indeterminate form of the second *GL* definition of number which it is invoked to correct. Frege wants to associate with each function a new kind of object, a course of values. This domain of objects and the function which assigns one to each function are introduced simultaneously. The result is that it has not been determined whether Julius Caesar is the course of values of any function. A given course of values has been individuated only with respect to other objects specified as the courses of values associated with various functions. In sum, the courses of values in terms of which the extensions of concepts are defined suffer from exactly the defect of definition which extensions of concepts were introduced to rectify or avoid.

In the *Grundgesetze*, when courses of values are introduced, this difficulty is explicitly acknowledged and described in the same terms used to raise the original objection in *GL* (though without reference to the earlier work). Frege introduces the same principle for determining when the courses of values of two functions are identical, and then points out that such a principle cannot be taken to determine any objects until criteria of identity and individuation have been supplied with respect to objects which are *not* given as courses of values. He proposes to supplement his definition so as to satisfy this demand. His proposal is that for each object not given as a course of values it be *stipulated* to be identical to an *arbitrary* course of values, subject only to the condition that distinct objects be identified with distinct courses of values.

Frege expresses the function which assigns to each function an object which is its course of values by means of an abstraction operator binding a Greek variable. The course of value of a function *F* is written as $\text{'}\delta(F\delta)$. Axiom V of the *Grundgesetze* tells us that:

(a) $\text{'}\delta(F\delta) = \text{'}\alpha\,(G\alpha)$ iff $(\forall x)\,[Fx <=> Gx]$.

Frege recognizes that this principle alone does not suffice to determine the identity of objects which are courses of values. To show this, he points out that if X is a function which yields distinct values if and only if it is applied to distinct arguments (what we may call an "individuation-preserving" function), then:

(a') $X('\delta(F\delta)) = X('\alpha\,(G\,\alpha))$ iff $(\forall x)\,[Fx <=> Gx]$

without its having been settled, for instance, whether

(a'') $X('\delta(F\delta)) = '\alpha\,(G\,\alpha)$

for any F and G (including the case in which $F = G$). The by now familiar point is that (a) determines only the truth values of *homogeneous* identities, those both terms of which are of the form $'\delta(F\delta)$. And (a') determines only the truth values of identities which are homogeneous in that both terms have the form $X('\delta(F\delta))$. But (a'') asks about *heterogeneous* identities, whose terms are of different forms. Another identity which is heterogeneous and whose truth value is accordingly not settled by principle (a) is Julius Caesar $= '\delta(F\delta)$.

To fix up this indeterminateness, which would result from taking Axiom V alone as the definition of courses of values, Frege proposes to supplement it by stipulating the truth values of the heterogeneous identities. Actually, he is required to specify the inferential behavior of course of value expressions in all contexts in which they can appear. In Frege's terminology such contexts are functions, so this requirement is equivalent to the demand that it be determined for every single-argument function-expression what value is designated by the substitution of any course of values expression in its argument place. Doing so will then determine all of the properties of the objects designated by expression of the form $'\delta(F\delta)$, for those properties just are concepts, that is, functions whose values are truth values. Among those properties are individuative properties, the facts corresponding to identity contexts involving course of values expressions. Thus the *Grundlagen* requirement that to introduce a new set of objects one must settle all identities involving them is in the *Grundgesetze* motivated by the omnicontextual condition. (It is worth noticing, as Sluga points out, that there is an endorsement of a strong context principle in Frege's claim that what it is to have introduced expressions of the form $'\delta(F\delta)$ as the names of definite objects is for the truth values of all sentential contexts in which those expressions can be substituted to have been settled.) In fact, in the spare environment of *GG* it turns out that it is not only necessary to settle the truth values of all identities involving course of value expressions in order to satisfy the omnicontextual requirement, but sufficient as well.

Indeed, in the system of the *Grundgesetze* at the time courses of values are introduced, the only objects already defined are the two truth values, and so the only heterogeneous identities Frege explicitly addresses are those involving a course of values and a truth value. But he must justify the *general* procedure of stipulating truth values for heterogeneous identities, and not just his application of it. For if he does not, then the *GG* definition of number will still be open to the objection to the second *GL* account of number (that it has not been settled whether Julius Caesar is one) which drove him to define the extensions of concepts and hence courses of values to begin with. Indeed, the concept logical object will not have been defined if it has not been settled whether Julius Caesar is one. Further, as we have seen, Frege's own definitions of his technical terms in general suffice only to determine the truth values of homogeneous identities, for example, identities of two truth values, or two senses, or two references, but not the heterogeneous identities which would be required to make the claim that Julius Caesar = the *Bedeutung* of the expression 'Julius Caesar', or that a certain linguistic role *is* the sense of some expression.

In particular, Frege's substitutional-inferential methodology determines only the nonrelational sense of '*Bedeutung*', according to which expressions are sorted into substitutional equivalence classes as having the same *Bedeutung*. For Frege to add to this determination of homogeneous identities (both of whose terms are of the form "the Bedeutung of the expression *t*") the relational sense of reference in which these *Bedeutungen* are *identified* with objects suitably related to all and only the members of the nonrelational substitutional equivalence class of expressions is precisely to stipulate the truth values of the *hetero*geneous identities. The question of whether such a procedure can be justified on Frege's own terms is thus exactly the question of whether the two notions of *Bedeutung* can be made into "two aspects of *one* notion," as Dummett claims and Frege is committed to, or whether they are simply conflated without warrant, as Bell claims. Following Sluga's development of Frege's attempted definition of terms which refer to logical objects thus leads to the argument which must justify the identification of the things playing the two explanatory roles which Bell has shown must be distinguished under the heading *Bedeutung*.

In section 10 of *GG*, Frege offers his justification of the procedure of stipulating the heterogeneous identities, in an argument which Gregory Currie has called "brilliantly imaginative."[51] The argument is a difficult one, and we shall have to examine it with some care. What is to be shown is that it is legitimate to stipulate (a) above, determining the homogeneous identities involving courses of values, together with the following stipulation for heterogeneous identities:

(b) $'\tau(L\tau) = t_1$ and $'\sigma(M\sigma) = t_2$

where $t_1 \neq t_2$ and $(\exists x)(Lx \neq Mx)$. L and M are to be arbitrary functions, and t_1 and t_2 are terms which are not of the form $'\alpha\ (F\alpha)$. For the purposes of the *GG* argument, the terms in question are "the True" and "the False." In the context of Sluga's point that Frege's defense of his own view against his objection to the second attempted definition of number in *GL* must be traced through the account of extension to the account of courses of values, it will be worth keeping in mind that for this purpose the argument must apply equally to the case in which t_1 is "Julius Caesar" and t_2 is "England." To emphasize this requirement, the exposition of Frege's argument which follows will use those values for t_1 and t_2 rather than the truth values which Frege employed. In any case, the point is that distinct objects which are *not* given as courses of values are stipulated to be identical to the courses of values of a like number of arbitrary distinct functions. The task is to show that such a stipulation is legitimate.

The strategy of the argument is to *construct* a domain of objects of which (a) and (b) can be *proven* to hold. To start, suppose it has been stipulated that:

(c) $\sim\eta(F\eta) = \sim\gamma(G\gamma)$ iff $(\forall x)\ [Fx <=> Gx]$,

that is, we stipulate the homogeneous identities for terms of the form $\sim\eta(F\eta)$, where the function which associates objects so denominated with functions F is unknown except that principle (c) holds. As was pointed out above by means of (a′) and (a″), the fact that both (a) and (c) hold does not in any way settle the heterogeneous identities one of whose terms is a course of values and the other of which is of the form $\sim\eta(F\eta)$. The next step is to use the arbitrary distinct functions L and M of (b) to construct an individuation-preserving function X as above. The function X is defined by five clauses:

(1) $X(\text{Julius Caesar}) = \sim\eta(L\eta)$

(2) $X(\sim\eta(L\eta)) = \text{Julius Caesar}$

(3) $X(\text{England}) = \sim\gamma(M\gamma)$

(4) $X(\sim\gamma(M\gamma)) = \text{England}$

(5)   For all other y, $X(y) = y$.

The function X is constant except when it is applied to either the two objects which are not specified as the result of applying $\sim$-abstraction to some function (Julius Caesar and England, or the True and the False) or to the result of applying $\sim$-abstraction to the arbitrarily chosen functions L and M. In these special cases, the function X simply permutes the distinguished values.

X is constructed to be individuation preserving, so that a correlation is preserved between distinctness of its arguments and distinctness of its values. It follows then that:

(d) $X(\sim\eta(F\eta)) = X(\sim\gamma(G\gamma))$ iff $(\forall x)[Fx <=> Gx]$.

In these terms we could now *define* the course of values notation (which has not previously appeared in this argument) by agreeing to let:

(e) $'\alpha(F\alpha) =_{\mathrm{df}} X(\sim\eta(F\eta))$ for all functions F.

Given the definition (e) and the truth of (d), principle (a) for courses of values follows immediately. The truth of (d), as we have seen, follows from (c), together with clauses (1)–(5) defining the function X. But clauses (2) and (4) of that definition, together with (e), entail principle (b) concerning courses of values (with the substitution of Julius Caesar for t_1 and England for t_2). Thus, given only the homogeneous identities in (c), we have constructed courses of values in such a way that their homogeneous identities in (a) can be shown to hold *and* in such a way that heterogeneous identities can be *proven* for two of them, since $'\alpha(L\alpha) = $ Julius Caesar $(= X(\sim\eta(L\eta)))$ and $'\delta(M\delta) = $ England $(= X(\sim\gamma(M\gamma)))$. The legitimacy of stipulating heterogeneous identities in the context of a principle determining homogeneous ones has been shown by reducing

the questionable stipulation to the composition of two obviously acceptable forms of stipulation: the specification of the values which the function X is to take for various arguments—in particular in clauses (2) and
(4), and the introduction of the expression "'$a(Fa)$'" (previously without
a use) as a notational abbreviation of "$X(\sim\eta(F\eta))$."

   This imaginative argument is Frege's ultimate response defending his
account of number and of logical objects generally against the objections he had raised but not answered in the *Grundlagen*. Seen in that
context, the argument is fallacious. The problem concerns the extremal
clause (5) of the definition of the individuation-preserving function X. If
that clause is expanded to make explicit what is contained in the condition "for all other y," it becomes:

(5') $(\forall y)[(y \neq$ Julius Caesar & $y \neq \sim\eta(L\eta)$ & $y \neq$ England
         & $y \neq \sim\gamma(M\gamma)) => X(y) = y]$.

It may then be asked whether it is appropriate at this point in the argument to make use of a condition such as $y \neq \sim\gamma(M\gamma)$. If the term substituted for y is also represented as the product of applying $\sim$-abstraction
to some function, then clause (c) will settle the truth value of the resulting identity. For it settles just such homogeneous identities. But what of
the case in which the identity is *heterogeneous?* All that has been fixed
concerning $\sim$-abstraction is principle (c), which says nothing about
such identities. Indeed, the whole strategy of the argument depends on
starting from a specification of purely homogeneous identities with one
sort of abstractor ($\sim$) and using the function X to construct an abstractor (') for which the heterogeneous identities are specified. Nothing
which has been said, or, given the strategy just indicated, *could* be said,
settles a truth value for heterogeneous identities such as

(f)   Julius Caesar $= \sim\gamma(M\gamma)$

and

(g)   England $= \sim\eta(L\eta)$.

For all that principle (c) concerning $\sim$-abstraction and the distinctness
of the functions L and M settle, (f) could be true and (g) false. Given the
truth of (f), substituting in clause (4) would yield that $X($Julius Caesar$)$
$=$ England, and so by clause (1) that England $= \sim\eta(L\eta)$, that is, that

(g) is true. So the definition of X presupposes valuations for heterogeneous identities which it is in no way entitled to.

Matters are just as bad if we consider some other object, say, the direction of the Earth's axis (also discussed in GL). It has nowhere been determined whether it is identical to $\sim\eta(L\eta)$ and so falls under clause (2), or identical to $\sim\gamma(M\gamma)$ and so falls under clause (4), or to neither and hence falls under clause (5). The definition of X, in terms of which it is to be shown acceptable to stipulate heterogeneous identities for $\sim$-abstraction, is well formed only if the heterogeneous identities involving $\sim$-abstraction have already been settled. They have not been settled. Further, to add to the argument the assumption that truth values for such heterogeneous identities involving expressions of the form $\sim\delta(F\delta)$ *have* been settled is to assume exactly what the argument as a whole is supposed to show, namely, that such matters are open for stipulation in the first place (so long as suitable care is taken to match distinct objects with the result of abstracting distinct functions). If more is supposed about $\sim$-abstraction than principle (c) fixing homogeneous identities, the question will be begged. And without some supposition about heterogeneous identities, the argument does not go through.

The intent of the offending extremal clause is to deal with all objects which can be represented by expressions of the form $\sim\delta(F\delta)$, where $F \neq L$ and $F \neq M$. Distinct objects not so representable are each to be dealt with by a pair of clauses, letting the function X permute them with the result of abstracting from corresponding arbitrarily chosen distinct functions. There is nothing in general wrong with such a definitional strategy. It may not be used in the context of this argument, however. The distinction between the cases which are to be dealt with by paired specific stipulations and those which remain to be dealt with by the extremal stipulation cannot be made precise without begging the question. For that distinction corresponds to the distinction between heterogeneous identities and homogeneous ones, in the sense of stipulations for objects not representable by expressions of the form $\sim\delta(F\delta)$ and those which are so representable. This distinction is not one which a principle like (c) specifying the purely homogeneous identities permits us to make, and we are entitled to presuppose no more than such a principle. Put otherwise, the form of definition essentially requires that there be a pair of specific clauses dealing with *every* object whose individuation with respect to the results of applying $\sim$-abstraction to functions has not been settled by principle (c). But this class of objects cannot be described or specified in the terms permitted for the definition if it is to play its appointed role in the larger argument.

The only way in which this situation might be remedied would be if there were some property available which could be independently appealed to in order to distinguish the two kinds of cases. Thus if to (c) were added:

(c') $\qquad (\forall y)[P(y) <=> (\exists F)(y = \sim\delta(F\delta))]$

then the extremal clause in the definition of X could be amended to

(5″) $\qquad (\forall y)[(P(y)\ \&\ y \neq \sim\eta(L\eta)\ \&\ y \neq \sim\gamma(M\gamma)) <=> X(y) = y]$

In the context of (c'), (5″) will have the desired effect of applying only to objects which can be designated by expressions of the form $\sim\delta(F\delta)$, where $F \neq L$ and $F \neq M$. More important, (c') would ensure that the identities in (5″) are homogeneous with respect to $\sim$-abstraction, and hence have had their truth values settled by (c). It was the failure to ensure the homogeneity that was responsible for the inadequacy of the original definition of X.

The trouble with this way out is that no such independently specifiable property is available. Already in the *Grundlagen*, Frege had pointed out that the account of when the numbers associated with two concepts were identical (settling identities homogeneous with respect to the form: the number of the concept F) could be defended against his objection if the concept . . . is a number were available. For then the truth values of the heterogeneous identities (such as those involving Julius Caesar) could be settled by specifying that for any t, *if* t is not a number, *then* it is not identical to the number of any concept. But the problem the desired definition was to solve was precisely that of specifying the concept . . . is a number, as the current task is to specify the concept . . . is a course of values. It would be circular to use for the property **P . . . is an x such that there is an F such that x = $\sim\delta(F\delta)$**. For that would precisely presuppose that the heterogeneous identities have somehow already been settled, rather than independently settling them. Nor could some property such as . . . **is not in the causal order** be used, for there are other logical objects (such as the True and the False) whose individuation with respect to objects specified by $\sim$-abstraction has not been determined. Nor in any case would such a property be available to a logicist.

Frege's argument does not work, then, and it cannot be made to work. If the *Grundgesetze* is meant to offer an account of number which will meet the demands set by the *Grundlagen,* then it is a failure by Frege's own standards. Further, this failure is not a matter of the inconsistency of the later system. Although Axiom V is the culprit in both cases, it is different features of that principle which are found objectionable in the two cases. The current complaint is that settling the truth values of the homogeneous identities alone, as that principle does, is definitionally too weak to meet the requirements imposed by the discussion of *GL.* Those demand the justification of the stipulative extension of the definition to heterogeneous identities. That it leads to inconsistency, however, shows that that axiom is inferentially too strong. Putting aside the question of inconsistency which makes the claim counterfactual, even if the account of courses of values in *GG* were technically adequate, it would not be philosophically adequate as a specification of its objects and concepts. For it has not settled whether Julius Caesar is the number three, nor shown that stipulating an answer in the case of logical objects such as the truth values is a legitimate procedure. Nor can this be shown with the materials at hand.

I take it that this definitional inadequacy has not been remarked on for two connected reasons. In the purely technical context of the *Grundgesetze,* the stipulation of the two heterogeneous identities concerning the truth values and arbitrary distinct courses of values is in fact perfectly acceptable. Further, provided that it is stipulated that neither of the truth values is identical to the result of applying ∼-abstraction to any function, Frege's argument shows that his procedure is in order. It is only in the larger philosophical context provided by Sluga's historical tracing of the stages in Frege's development of an answer to his own objections to the second attempted definition of number in *GL,* from the invocation of the extension of a concept in the third and final *GL* definition, via the reduction of concepts to a special kind of function and of extensions to courses of values in "Funktion und Begriff," to the final attempt to define courses of values adequately in the early sections of the *Grundgesetze* that it can be seen that satisfying the purely technical constraints will not suffice to render the definition of courses of values (and hence of logical objects generally) adequate by the philosophical standards Frege has insisted upon.

But the result is significant not just for the appraisal of the success in its own terms of Frege's account of the logical objects which were his explicit subject matter in *GG*. For as we have seen, the technical philosophical concepts Frege developed to use in that discussion, such as reference, and sense, and truth value, are all given the same form of definition as courses of values are, which individuates them only homogeneously. Thus, "we cannot say *what* the sense of an expression is. The closest we may approach to this is to say that the sense of a given expression E_1 *is the same as the sense of another expression, E_2*."[52] It follows that so far as *interpretation* (rather than further development) of Frege's concept of sense is concerned, one can *only* subdivide the explanatory roles played by his concept, but cannot identify anything as playing those roles. Thus it is legitimate and valuable to distinguish the cognitive role from the semantic role played by senses, or sense as content from sense as character, or input and output senses as Bell does. But to entertain hypotheses about whether thoughts are mental pictures (as Frege did by denying this) or sets of possible worlds, or denizens of some extracausal realm is to consider claims which have been given no sense by Frege's purely homogeneous specification of the entities in question. Truth values are similarly immune from heterogeneous identification, from identification in any other form than as the truth value associated with some expression.

Probably most important is the case of singular term reference. Here Frege tried explicitly to supplement the purely homogeneous sorting into semantic equivalence classes of the reference associated with various expressions (the nonrelational sense of '*Bedeutung*') with the stipulation of heterogeneous identities involving the references of expressions and ordinary objects. In accord with his inferential/substitutional methodology, these stipulations are grounded in the intersubstitutability for all terms *t* of the term itself and the expression 'the *Bedeutung* of *t*'. Bell has shown how much of Frege's conceptual scheme depends on the assumption that such heterogeneous identities are determined (and hence a relational sense of reference applies) for other parts of speech, given only the determination of the homogeneous identities (settling a nonrelational sense of reference) which is all that is available for expressions of these other categories. Pursuing further a line of thought Sluga initiated has shown that this assumption is indeed unwarranted, and that even Frege's attempted stipulation of coincidence of relational and nonrelational senses of 'reference' in the case of singular terms has not been justified by Frege's own standards. Thus extending Sluga's argument permits better understanding of the philosophical status of Frege's technical concepts in general, and in particular of the two sides of the concept of <u>reference</u> which Bell, following Dummett, has so usefully distinguished.

9

The Significance of Complex Numbers
for Frege's Philosophy of Mathematics

I. Logicism and Platonism

The topic announced by my title may seem perverse, since Frege never developed an account of complex numbers. Even his treatment of the reals is incomplete, and we have only recently begun to get a reasonable understanding of how it works.[1] Presumably for that reason, the secondary literature simply does not discuss how complex numbers might fit into Frege's project.[2] As I will show, we can be quite confident from what little he does say that Frege intended his logicist program to extend to complex numbers. What we do not know is how he might have gone about it. I will try to show that *however* he approached this task, he was bound to fail. This fact has profound implications, not just for his approach to arithmetic but for his whole understanding of mathematics—and indeed, for his understanding of what is required to secure reference to particular *objects* generally.

Frege is famous for his *logicism*. This is a doctrine not about mathematics generally, but only about one part of it: arithmetic, the science that studies *numbers*. Logicism is the thesis that arithmetic can be reduced to purely logical principles, by the application of logical principles alone. But Frege endorsed a very special form of logicism, what Dummett calls *platonistic* logicism. This is the thesis that numbers are purely logical *objects*. To call something a "logical object" in Frege's sense is to say that it is an object whose existence and uniqueness can be proven, and reference to which can be secured, by the application of purely logical principles.[3]

The mere reducibility of arithmetic discourse to logical discourse need not involve the further commitment to the existence of logical *ob-*

jects. The general logicist program might instead be pursued along the lines of *Principia Mathematica,* where arithmetic discourse is analyzed in terms of second- and third-order logical properties and relations. Frege, of course, also appeals to such higher-order properties and relations. But he insists in addition that numerical expressions are singular terms, and that those that occur essentially in true arithmetic statements refer to objects of a special kind. Endorsing the reducibility thesis of logicism notoriously entails shifting the boundary Kant established between the analytic and the synthetic, so as to include arithmetic in the former category. It is less often noticed that endorsing the analysis of numbers as logical objects that is distinctive of the specifically platonistic version of logicism similarly entails shifting the boundary Kant established between general and transcendental logic. For transcendental logic in Kant's sense investigates the relationship our representations have to the objects they represent. Formal logic, Kant thought, must be silent on such aspects of content. Platonistic logicism about numbers maintains on the contrary that, at least for arithmetic discourse, purely formal logic can deliver the whole of content, including reference to objects. In his *Grundlagen der Arithmetik,* Frege is pursuing the same project of transcendental logic that Kant pursues in his first *Kritik,* albeit exclusively for a kind of non-empirical discourse.

It is precisely the platonism that distinguishes Frege's variety of logicism that I will claim cannot be made to work for the case of complex numbers. Usually when questions are raised about Frege's logicism, the focus is on the claim that numbers are *logical* objects. But I will ignore those troubles and focus on the claim that they are logical *objects.* The difficulty is that structural symmetries of the field of complex numbers collide with requirements on singular referentiality that are built deep into Frege's semantics. That collision raises fundamental questions about Frege's conception of objects—and so about commitments that are at least as central as his logicism. After all, Frege eventually gave up his logicist project, in the face of Russell's paradox, while he never gave up either his platonism or the conception of objects that turns out to cause the difficulties to be identified here.

II. Singular Terms and Complex Numbers

Frege introduces what has been called the "linguistic turn" in analytic philosophy when in the *Grundlagen* he adopts the broadly Kantian strategy of treating the question of whether numbers are objects as just another way of asking whether we are entitled to introduce singular terms to pick them out. Although Frege's avowed topic is a very special class of terms and objects, namely numerical ones, it turns out that this narrow class is particularly well suited to form the basis of a more general investigation of the notions of singular term and object. For one thing, natural numbers are essentially what we use to count, and objects in general are essentially countables. So Frege's account of counting numbers depends on his discussion of the ordinary, nonmathematical, sortal concepts that individuate objects. For another, one evidently cannot hope to understand the semantic relation between singular terms and the objects they pick out simply by invoking causal relations between them (relations of empirical intuition, in Frege's neo-Kantian vocabulary) if the objects in question are, for instance, abstract objects. Since there are no causal (or intuitive) relations in the vicinity, one must think more generally about what it is for a term to pick out a particular object.[4]

Singular terms are essentially expressions that can correctly appear flanking an identity sign.[5] The significance of asserting such an identity is to license intersubstitution of the expressions flanking it, *salva veritate*.[6] If we understood how to use one paradigmatic kind of singular term, those principles would tell us how to extend that understanding to the rest. Frege takes *definite descriptions,* in which "a concept is used to define an object," as his paradigm:

> We speak of "*the* number 1," where the definite article serves to class it as an object.[7]

> The definite article purports to refer to a definite object.[8]

The question of when we are entitled to use an expression as a singular term—as "purporting to refer to a definite object," and in case the claim it occurs in is true, as succeeding in doing so—then reduces to the question of when we are justified in using the definite article.[9] The conditions Frege endorses are straightforward and familiar:

> If, however, we wished to use this concept for defining an object falling under it [by a definite description], it would, of course, be necessary first to show two distinct things:
>   1. that some object falls under the concept;
>   2. that only one object falls under it.
> Now since the first of these propositions, not to mention the second, is

false, it follows that the expression "the largest proper fraction" is senseless.[10]

Securing reference to particular objects (being entitled to use singular terms) requires showing *existence* and *uniqueness*. (This requirement is not special to definite descriptions, as Frege's discussion of criteria of identity and the need to settle the truth of recognition judgments shows. It is just that the definite article makes explicit the obligations that are always at least implicitly involved in the use of singular terms.)

In the context of these thoughts, Frege himself explicitly raises the issue of how we can be entitled to use singular terms to pick out complex numbers:

> It is not immaterial to the cogency of our proof whether "$a + bi$" has a sense or is nothing more than printer's ink. It will not get us anywhere simply to require that it have a sense, or to say that it is to have the sense of the sum of a and bi, when we have not previously defined what "sum" means in this case and *when we have given no justification for the use of the definite article.*[11]

> Nothing prevents us from using the concept "square root of -1"; but we are not entitled to put the definite article in front of it without more ado and take the expression "the square root of -1" as having a sense.[12]

What more is required? To show the existence and uniqueness of the referents of such expressions. Usually in discussions of Frege's logicism, questions are raised about what is required to satisfy the *existence* condition. In what follows, I ignore any difficulties there might be on that score and focus instead on the at least equally profound difficulties that arise in this case in connection with the *uniqueness* condition.

> *How are complex numbers to be given to us* then . . . ? If we turn for assistance to intuition, we import something foreign into arithmetic; but if we only define the concept of such a number by giving its characteristics, if we simply require the number to have certain properties, then there is no guarantee that anything falls under the concept and answers to our requirements, and yet it is precisely on this that proofs must be based.[13]

This is our question. The sense of "given to us" is not to begin with an *epistemic* one but a *semantic* one. The question is how we can be entitled to use singular terms to pick out complex numbers—how we can stick our labels on *them,* catch them in our semantic nets so that we can talk and think about them at all, even falsely.

III. The Argument

Here is my claim: In the case of complex numbers, one cannot satisfy the uniqueness condition for the referents of number terms (and so cannot be entitled to use such terms) because of the existence of a certain kind of symmetry (duality) in the complex plane. Frege's *semantic* requirements on singular term usage collide with basic *mathematical* properties of the complex plane. This can be demonstrated in three increasingly rigorous and general ways.

1. *Rough-and-ready* (quick and dirty): Moving from the reals to the complex numbers requires introducing the imaginary basis i. It is introduced by some definition equivalent to: i is *the* square root of -1. But one of the main points of introducing complex numbers is to see to it that polynomials have *enough* roots—which requires that *all* real numbers, negative as well as positive, have *two* square roots. In particular, once i has been properly introduced, we discover that $-i$ is *also* a square root of -1. So we can ask: *Which* square root of -1 is i? There is no way at all, based on our use of the real numbers, to pick out one or the other of these complex roots *uniquely,* so as to stick the label "i" onto it, and not its conjugate.

Now if we ask a mathematician, "*Which* square root of -1 is i?" she will say, "It doesn't matter: pick one." And from a *mathematical* point of view this is exactly right. But from the *semantic* point of view we have a right to ask how this trick is done. How is it that I *can* "pick one" if I cannot tell them apart? What must I do in order to be *picking* one—and picking *one?* For we really *cannot* tell them apart—and as the results below show, not just because of some lamentable incapacity of ours. As a medieval philosopher might have said, they are merely *numerically* distinct. Before we proceed, it is worth saying more precisely what the denial that the uniqueness condition on singular reference can be satisfied for complex numbers actually comes to.

2. *More carefully:* The extension of the reals to the complex numbers permits the construction of a particular kind of *automorphism* (indeed, it is an *involution,* a principle of duality—but our argument will not ap-

peal to the cyclic properties that distinguish this special class of auto-morphisms), that is, a function that:

is 1 − 1 and onto, with domain and range both being the complex numbers;

is a homomorphism with respect to (that is, that respects the struc-tures of) the operations that define the complex plane, namely, ad-dition and multiplication;

has a fixed basis, that is, is an identity mapping on the reals.

Such an automorphism (homomorphism taking the complexes into themselves)—call it a "fixed-basis automorphism"—is:

(i) a *trivial* (identity) mapping for the base domain of the definition (the reals), and

(ii) a *nontrivial* mapping for the extended domain (the rest of the com-plex plane).

The existence of such a fixed-basis automorphism would show that the extended domain cannot be *uniquely* defined in terms of the basis domain—in this case, that the reals (together with the operations of complex addition and multiplication on pairs of them) do not suffice *uniquely* to identify or define particular complex numbers.

Here is such a mapping, taking each complex number into its *complex conjugate:*

$$f(x + yi) = x − yi$$

If r is real, $f(r) = r$; so the basis is fixed.

Clearly the mapping is 1 − 1 and onto.

The complex plane is an algebraic *field,* which can be represented by a set of pairs of real numbers, together with operations of addition and multiplication.

So to show that f is a homomorphism, it must be shown that:

(a) $f[(a+bi) + (c+di)] = f(a+bi) + f(c+di)$ and

(b) $f[(a+bi) * (c+di)] = f(a+bi) * f(c+di)$.

To see (a): By the definition of $+$,

$$(a+bi) + (c+di) = (a+c) + (b+d)i.$$

So by the definition of f,

$$f[(a+bi) + (c+di)] = f[(a+c) + (b+d)i] =$$
$$f(a+bi) = a\text{-}bi, \text{ and } f(c+di) = c\text{-}di.$$
$$(a-bi) + (c-di) = (a+c) + (-b-d)i = (a+c)-(b+d)i.$$

To see (b): By the definition of $*$,

$$(a+bi) * (c+di) = (ac\text{-}bd) + (ad+bc)i.$$
$$f[(ac-bd) + (ad+bc)i] = (ac-bd)-(ad+bc)i.$$
$$f(a+bi) * f(c+di) = (a-bi) * (c-di) =$$
$$(ac-(-b)(-d)) + (-ad-bc) = (ac-bd)-(ad+bc)i.$$

So f is a fixed basis automorphism with respect to $+$, $*$, which extends $\Re$ to C.

3. Using a bit of (well-known) *algebraic power* to establish the same result with greater generality:

Definition: Let E be an algebraic extension of a field F. Two elements, $\alpha, \beta \varepsilon E$ are *conjugate over F* if $\mathrm{irr}(\alpha, F) = \mathrm{irr}(\beta, F)$, that is, if α, β are zeros of the same irreducible polynomial over F.

Theorem: The *Conjugate Isomorphism Theorem* says: Let F be a field, and let α, β be algebraic over F with $\deg(\alpha, F) = n$. The map $\Psi_{\alpha\beta}$: $F(\alpha) \rightarrow F(\beta)$ defined by

$$\Psi_{\alpha\beta}(c_0 + c_1 \alpha + \ldots + c_{n-1} \alpha^{n-1}) = c_0 + c_1 \beta + \ldots + c_{n-1} \beta^{n-1}$$

for $c_i \varepsilon F$ is an isomorphism of $F(\alpha)$ onto $F(\beta)$ if and only if α, β are conjugate over F.

Fact: The *complex conjugates* appealed to in defining the fixed-basis automorphism f in the argument above are *conjugate over* $\Re$ in the sense of the previous definition and theorem. For if $a, b \varepsilon \Re$ and $b \neq 0$, the complex conjugate numbers $a + bi$ and $a - bi$ are both zeros of $x^2 - 2ax + a^2 + b^2$, which is irreducible in $\Re[x]$.

The upshot of these results is that systematically swapping each complex number for its complex conjugate leaves intact all the properties of the real numbers, all the properties of the complex numbers, and all the relations between the two sorts of numbers. It follows that those properties and relations do not provide the resources to describe or otherwise pick out complex numbers uniquely, so as to stick labels on them. So it is *in principle* impossible to satisfy Frege's own criteria for being entitled to use complex-number designators as singular terms—that is, terms that purport to refer to definite objects. Frege is *mathematically* precluded from being entitled *by his own semantic lights* to treat complex numbers as *objects* of any kind, logical or not. Platonistic logicism is false of complex numbers. Indeed, given Frege's strictures on reference to particular objects, *any* and *every* kind of platonism is false about them. (At the end of this chapter I suggest one way those strictures might be relaxed so as to permit a form of platonism in the light of these observations.)

These are the central conclusions I want to draw. The results can be sharpened by considering various responses that might be made on Frege's behalf. But first it is worth being clear about how the problem I am raising differs from other criticisms standardly made of Frege's logicist program.

IV. Other Problems

Here are some potential problems with Frege's logicism that should *not* be confused with the one identified here. First, the problem does not have to do with whether the logicist's reduction base is really *logical*. This is the objection that arithmetic is not really being given a logical foundation, because one branch of mathematics is just being reduced to another: set theory. (For to perform the reduction in question, logic must be strengthened so as to have expressive power equivalent to a relatively fancy set theory.) One of the main occupations of modern mathematics is proving representation and embedding theorems that relate one branch of mathematics to another. One gains great insights into the structures of various domains this way, but it is quite difficult to pick out a privileged subset of such enterprises that deserve to be called "foundational."

Second, the problem pointed out here does not have to do with the definition of extensions—Frege's "courses of values." All the logical objects of the *Grundgesetze* are courses of values, and various difficulties have been perceived in Frege's way of introducing these objects as correlated with functions. Of course, one feature of Axiom V of the *Grundgesetze* (where courses of values are defined) that has seemed to some at least a minor blemish is that it leads to the inconsistency of Frege's system—as Russell pointed out. This is indeed a problem, but it has nothing to do with *our* problem. Although it is a somewhat unusual counterfactual, there is a clear sense in which we can say that the issue of how a platonistic logicist might satisfy the uniqueness condition so as to be entitled to introduce singular terms as picking out complex numbers would arise even if Frege's logic *were* consistent.

Again, the method of abstraction by which logical objects are introduced has been objected to on the grounds that it suffers from the "Julius Caesar problem" that Frege himself diagnosed in the *Grundlagen*.[14] As he puts it there, if we introduce *directions* by stipulating that the directions of two lines are identical just in case the lines are parallel, we have failed to specify whether, for instance, Julius Caesar is the direction of any line. The worry considered here does not have this shape, however; the question is not whether the logical objects that are complex numbers can be identified with anything not so specified, but rather in what sense two objects specified as complex numbers can be told apart in the case where they are related as complex conjugates of each other.

Nor is the problem whether or in what sense Frege can be successful in demonstrating the *existence* of complex numbers as logical objects. The issue concerns the uniqueness condition on entitlement to use singular terms, not the existence condition. Indeed, the concern here should be distinguished from two other sorts of objections to Frege's procedure that can be forwarded under the heading of uniqueness. In "What Numbers Could Not Be,"[15] Paul Benacerraf argues that there can be no sufficient reason to identify numbers with one set-theoretic object rather than another—for instance, no reason to identify 0,1,2,3 . . . with, for example:

$$\emptyset, \{\emptyset\}, \{\{\emptyset\}\}, \{\{\{\emptyset\}\}\} \ldots$$

rather than with

$$\emptyset, \{\emptyset\}, \{\emptyset,\{\emptyset\}\}, \{\emptyset,\{\emptyset\},\{\emptyset,\{\emptyset\}\}\} \ldots [16]$$

This is indeed a uniqueness problem, but it concerns the uniqueness of an identification of the complex numbers with things apparently of *another* kind, logical or purely set-theoretic objects specified in a different vocabulary. Our problem arises within complex-number talk itself.

Finally, the uniqueness problem for complex numbers identified here should be distinguished from the uniqueness problem that arises from the methodology of piecemeal extensions of definitions of number in the *Grundgesetze* (a methodology that Frege elsewhere rails against). Natural numbers, for instance, are initially defined as in the *Grundlagen*. But then rational numbers are defined as ordered pairs of integers. Since the natural numbers *are* (also) rational numbers, this raises a problem: What is the relation between, say, the rational number <2,4> and the natural number 2? Will the true natural number please stand up? This uniqueness problem ramifies when the reals are defined (or would if Frege had finished doing so), since both natural numbers and rational numbers are also real numbers. Frege does not say how he would resolve this problem.

V. Possible Responses

With the problem of how one might satisfy the uniqueness requirement on the introduction of singular terms for the case of designations of complex numbers identified and distinguished from other problems in the vicinity, we can turn to possible responses on Frege's behalf. In this section we consider four ultimately inadequate responses. In the following section we consider a more promising one.

One response one might entertain is "So much the worse for the complex plane!" Or, to paraphrase Frege when he was confronted with the Russell paradox: "(Complex) arithmetic totters!" That is, we might take ourselves to have identified a hitherto unknown surd at the basis of complex analysis. Even though this branch of mathematics seemed to have been going along swimmingly, it turns out on further reflection, we might conclude, to have been based on a mistake, or at least an oversight. But this would be a ridiculous response. The complex plane is as well studied and well behaved a mathematical object as there is. Even when confronted with the inconsistency of the only logic in terms of which he could see how to understand the natural numbers, Frege never seriously considered that the problem might be with *arithmetic* rather than with his account of it. And if principles of semantic theory collide with well-established mathematical practice, it seems clear that we should look to the former to find the fault. So, confronted with the difficulty we have identified, Frege never *would* have taken this line, and we *should* not take it.

A second response might be exegetical: perhaps Frege did not intend his logicist thesis to extend to complex numbers. After all, he only ever actually got as far as taking on the reals. Or, to vary the response, even if he was at one time a logicist about complex numbers, perhaps that is something he changed his mind about. Neither of these suggestions can be sustained, however. I have already cited some of Frege's remarks about complex numbers in the 1884 *Grundlagen*. Here is another passage that makes it clear that, at least at that point, Frege intended his logicism to encompass complex numbers:

> What is commonly called the geometrical representation of complex numbers has at least this advantage . . . that in it 1 and *i* do not appear as wholly unconnected and different in kind: the segment taken to represent *i* stands in a regular relation to the segment which represents 1 . . . A complex number, on this interpretation, shows how the segment taken as its representation is reached, starting from a given segment (the unit segment), by means of operations of multiplication, division, and rotation. [For simplicity I neglect incommensurables here.] However, even this account seems to make every theorem whose proof has to be based on the existence of a complex number dependent on geometrical intuition and so synthetic.[17]

Perhaps Frege gave up this view, then? In the second sentence of the introduction to the *Grundgesetze* of 1893, Frege says:

> It will be seen that negative, fractional, irrational, and complex numbers have still been left out of the account, as have addition, multiplication, and so on. Even the propositions concerning [natural] numbers are still not present with the completeness originally planned . . . External circumstances have caused me to reserve this, as well as the treatment of other numbers and of arithmetical operations, for a later installment whose appearance will depend upon the reception accorded this first volume.

A few years after the publication of the second volume of the *Grundgesetze*, Frege writes to Giuseppe Peano:

> Now as far as the arithmetical signs for addition, multiplication, etc. are concerned, I believe we shall have to take the domain of common complex numbers as our basis; for after including these complex numbers we reach the natural end of the domain of numbers.[18]

And as we know, even when, at the end of his life, Frege gave up his logicist program to turn to geometry as the foundation of arithmetic, his plan was to identify first the complex numbers, and the rest only as special cases of these.

Since this exegetical response will not work, one might decide to ignore what Frege *actually* intended, and insist instead that what he *ought* to have maintained is that, appearances to the contrary notwithstanding, complex numbers are not really numbers. That is, they belong on the *intuitive*, rather than the *logical*, side, of Frege's neo-Kantian partition of mathematics into geometry (which calls upon pure intuition for access to its objects), and arithmetic (which depends only on pure logic for access to its objects). After all, as Frege reminds us in the passage about the geometrical interpretation of complex numbers quoted above, multiplication by the imaginary basis i and its complex conjugate $-i$ correspond to counterclockwise and clockwise rotations, respectively. According to this proposed friendly amendment, Frege's Platonist logicism is not threatened by the impossibility of satisfying the uniqueness condition for introducing terms referring to complex numbers. For that result shows only that the boundaries to which that thesis applies must be contracted to exclude the offending case.

There are two difficulties with this response. First, uniquely specifying one of the directions of rotation (so as to get the label "i" to stick to *it*) requires more than pure geometrical intuition; it requires actual empirical intuition of the sort exercised in the use of public demonstratives. Second, if it *were* possible to pick one of the directions of rotation out uniquely in pure intuition, Frege is committed to taking the distinction that would thereby be introduced not to be an objective one—and so not one on which a branch of mathematics could be based.

For the first point: That multiplication by i or $-i$ corresponds geometrically to a rotation of $\pi/2$ radians is not conventional. But which *direction* each corresponds to is entirely conventional; if we drew the axes with the positive y axis below the x axis, i would correspond to clockwise instead of counterclockwise rotation. The question then is what is required to specify one of these directions uniquely, so as to be able to set up a definite convention. This problem is the same problem (in a mathematically strong sense, which we can cash out in terms of rotations) as asking, in a world that contains only the two hands Kant talks about in his *Prolegomena*, how we could pick out, say, the *left* one—for that is the one that, when seen from the palm side, requires *clockwise* rotation to move the thumb through the position of the forefinger to the position of the little finger. In a possible world containing only these two hands, we are faced with a symmetry—a duality defined by an involution—exactly parallel to that which we confronted in the case of the complex numbers. In fact it is exactly the *same* symmetry. Manifesting it geometrically does not significantly alter the predicament. If the world in question also contained a properly functioning clock, we could pick out the left hand as the one whose thumb-to-forefinger-to-little-finger rotation went *that* way—the same way *that* clock hand moves. But demonstrative appeal to such a clock takes us outside the hands, and outside geometry.

Inside the hands, we might think to appeal to biology. Because the four bonds of the carbon atom point to the vertices of a tetrahedron, organic molecules can come in left- and right-handed versions: enantiomers. Two molecules alike in all their physical and ordinary chemical properties might differ in that, treating a long chain of carbons as the "wrist," rotation of the terminal carbon that moved from an OH group through an NH_2 group to a single H is clockwise in the one and counterclockwise in the other. The sugars in our body are all right-handed in this sense (dextrose, not levose, which is indigestible by our other right-handed components). So we might think to appeal these "internal clockfaces" in the molecules making up the hands—appealing to biology rather than to geometry. But there is nothing biologically impossible about enantiomeric Doppelgänger, and for all Kant or we have said, the hands in question could be such. To pick out the left hand, it would have to be settled how the rotations defined by *their* sugars relate to *our* clocks. And biology won't settle *that*.

Similarly, we cannot break the symmetry of chirality, of handedness, by appeal to physics. The right-hand screw rule is fundamental in electromagnetic theory: If current flows through a wire in the direction pointed to by the thumb, the induced magnetic field spirals around the wire in the direction the fingers curl on a right hand: counterclockwise. But this fact does not give us a nondemonstrative way to specify counterclockwise rotation. For antimatter exhibits complementary chiral behavior. There is nothing physically impossible about antimatter hands, and for all Kant or we have said, the hands in question could be such. To pick out the left hand, it would have to be settled how the rotations defined by *their* charged particles relate to *our* clocks. And physics will not settle that.

So the geometrical interpretation in terms of directions of rotation will not allow us to specify uniquely *which* square root of -1 i is to be identified with, because we can only uniquely specify one direction of rotation by comparison with a fixed reference rotation, and geometry does not supply that—indeed, neither do descriptive (= nondemonstrative) biology, chemistry, or physics. This observation puts us in a position to appreciate the second point above. Even if pure geometrical intuition *did* permit us each to indicate, as it were internally, a reference direction of rotation ("By *i* I will mean *that* [demonstrative in pure inner intuition] direction of rotation"), nothing could settle that you and I picked the *same* direction, and so referred to the *same* complex number by our use of *i*. For the symmetry ensures that nothing we could *say* or *prove* would ever distinguish our uses. Frege considers a parallel case in the *Grundlagen:*

> What is objective . . . is what is subject to laws, what can be conceived and judged, what is expressible in words. What is purely intuitable [*das rein Anschauliche*] is not communicable. To make this clear, let us suppose two rational beings such that projective properties and relations are all they can intuit—the lying of three points on a line, of four points on a plane, and so on; and let what the one intuits as a plane appear to the other as a point, and vice versa, so that what for the one is the line joining two points for the other is the line of intersection of two planes, and so on, with the one intuition always dual to the other. In these circumstances they could understand one another quite well and would never realize the difference between their intuitions, since in projective geometry every proposition has its dual counterpart; any disagreements over points of aesthetic appreciation would not be conclusive evidence. Over all geometrical theorems they would be in complete agreement, only: interpreting the words differently in their respective intuitions. With the word 'point', for example, one would connect one intuition, and the other another. We can therefore still say that this word has for them an objective meaning, provided only that by this meaning we do not understand any of the peculiarities of their respective intuitions.[19]

Of course, in our case the "peculiarities of their respective intuitions" include just which complex number they indicate by '*i*'. So relinquishing logicism for the complex numbers in favor of the geometrical interpretation will not suffice to make a safe place for complex numbers in Frege's philosophy of mathematics.

As a fourth possible response, then, one might suggest that Frege give up his partition of mathematics into arithmetic and geometry: the bits where expression and demonstration can proceed by purely logical means and the bits where pure intuition is also required. In fact, Frege never seems to have considered relinquishing this neo-Kantian demarcation. As already remarked, even when he finally despaired of founding arithmetic on logic, he turned to geometry. But in fact there is no succor available for him through such a move in any case. For the problem lies not in the conception of logic or of geometry, but in the incapacity of his semantic requirements on singular terms to accommodate certain kinds of global symmetries. But structural symmetries of the sort rehearsed in detail for the complex numbers—symmetries that preclude demonstrations of uniqueness of the sort Frege demands to secure reference to objects—are ubiquitous in modern mathematics. Here are two examples chosen almost at random:

(a) The multiplicative group U_3 of the three solutions to $x^3 = 1$, namely,

$$\{1, -1/2 + (\sqrt{3}/2)*i, -1/2 - (\sqrt{3}/2)*i\}.$$

This is a concrete instance of the abstract group whose table is:

*	e	a	b
e	e	a	b
a	a	b	e
b	b	e	a

This has a permuting automorphism Ψ defined by: $\Psi(e) = e$, $\Psi(a) = b$, $\Psi(b) = a$. Similar results obtain for the abstract groups instantiated by the rest of the U_n.

(b) Klein's Viergruppe, V (which has nothing to do with complex numbers), has group table:

*	e	a	b	c
e	e	a	b	c
a	a	e	c	b
b	b	c	e	a
c	c	b	a	e

V has a permuting automorphism Ψ defined by:

$$\Psi(e) = e, \Psi(a) = c, \Psi(b) = b, \Psi(c) = a.$$

I have chosen examples from abstract group theory in part because Frege was certainly familiar with it. The definitive nineteenth-century German work on abstract algebra, Heinrich Weber's *Lehrbuch der Algebra,* was published in two volumes, the first appearing before Frege published the first volume of his *Grundgesetze,* the second well before the publication of Frege's second volume, at a time when Frege was still an active member of a mathematics department. Although Frege seems never to have used the word '*Gruppe*', in the second volume of the *Grundgesetze* he in fact proved an important theorem in group theory—one that would elude more conventional algebraists for more than fifteen years.[20]

VI. Categorically and Hypothetically Specifiable Objects

So complex numbers are just the tip of the iceberg. Large, important stretches of mathematics exhibit symmetries that preclude the satisfaction of Frege's uniqueness requirement on the introduction of singular terms. Is there any way to relax that requirement while remaining true to his motivations in introducing it? Here is a candidate. Frege's uniqueness requirement can be decomposed into two components, which we might designate *distinguishability* and *isolability.* Elements of a domain are distinguishable in case they are *hypothetically specifiable,* that is, specifiable (uniquely) *relative* to some other elements of the same domain, or *assuming* the others have already been picked out. Elements of a domain are isolable in case they are *categorically specifiable,* that is, can be specified uniquely by the distinctive role they play within the domain, or in terms of their distinctive relation to what is *outside* the domain, to what can be specified *antecedently* to the domain in question. Both of these notions can be defined substitutionally. Here are three examples: Suppose a geometer says, "Consider a scalene triangle. Label its sides 'A,' 'B,' and 'C.'" Now if someone asks, "*Which* side is to be labeled 'A'?" answers are readily available, for instance: "The one that subtends the largest angle." The case would be different if the geometer had said instead, "Consider an equilateral triangle. Label its sides 'A,' 'B,' and 'C.'" Now if someone asks "*Which* side is to be labelled 'A'?" there need be no answers available. In both cases the three sides are *distinguishable.* That is, it has been settled that the three sides are *different* from one another. For if, say, "A" and "B" labeled the *same* line segment, there would be no triangle to discuss. So "A" could not be substituted for "B" indiscriminately, while preserving truth. And assuming that references have been fixed for "A" and "B," we can say, "'C' is the *other* side of the triangle," even in the equilateral case. But the symmetries involved in the equilateral case preclude our doing there what we can easily do in the scalene case, namely, *isolate* what the labels pick out: *categorically* specify which sides are in question.

Next, consider extending the field of the natural numbers (with addition and multiplication) to the integers. Now consider the mapping on the extension field defined by $f(n) = -n$. We could say that this mapping mapped each integer onto its *sign conjugate* (or complement). Such sign conjugates are clearly *distinguishable* from one another, for we cannot substitute "$-n$" for "n" in the second place of $n * n = n^2$, *salva veritate*, since $n*(-n) = -n^2$. Nonetheless, f is a homomorphism with respect to addition. Are the elements of the extension field nonetheless categorically specifiable? Yes. For f is *not* a homomorphism with respect to multiplication. There is an underlying asymmetry between the positive and negative integers with respect to multiplication: multiplying two positive numbers always results in a positive number, while multiplying their negative conjugates results in the same, positive number. So the positive numbers can be not only *distinguished* from the negatives (as above), but also *categorically specified* as the numbers whose sign is not changed by multiplying them by themselves.

Contrast the *complex conjugates*, which are distinguishable but *not* isolable—hypothetically but not categorically specifiable. The first notion can be defined substitutionally by looking at *local* or *piecemeal* substitutions:

$$a + bi \neq a-bi,$$

since the former cannot be substituted for the latter, *salva veritate*, in:

$$(a + bi)*(a-bi) = a^2 + b^2, \text{ while}$$
$$(a + bi)*(a + bi) = a^2-b^2 + 2abi.$$

In this sense, the complex conjugates are *distinguishable* from one another. This means each element is *hypothetically specifiable*: specifiable *if* some other elements are.

The second demands the absence of *global* automorphisms (substitutional permutations). And that we have seen is *not* the case for the complex numbers.

Here is a third example. The group V above admits the automorphism Ψ. So its elements are not antecedently categorically specifiable (isolable). They are distinguishable, however, for if we substitute c for a in e * a = a, we get e * a = c, which is not true. Thus a and c cannot be *identified* with one another. They are *different* elements. It is just that we cannot in advance of labeling them say which is which, since the automorphism shows that they *play the same global role* in the group.

By contrast: The (nonabelian) Dihedral Group D4 of symmetries of the square consists of the following eight permutations (with the four vertices of the square labeled 1–4), together with the operation * (corresponding to composition) defined by the table below:

$$\rho_0 = (1,2,3,4) \rightarrow (1,2,3,4) \qquad \mu_1 = (1,2,3,4) \rightarrow (2,1,4,3)$$
$$\rho_1 = (1,2,3,4) \rightarrow (2,3,4,1) \qquad \mu_2 = (1,2,3,4) \rightarrow (4,3,2,1)$$
$$\rho_2 = (1,2,3,4) \rightarrow (3,4,1,2) \qquad \delta_1 = (1,2,3,4) \rightarrow (3,2,1,4)$$
$$\rho_3 = (1,2,3,4) \rightarrow (4,1,2,3) \qquad \delta_2 = (1,2,3,4) \rightarrow (1,4,3,2)$$

(So ρ_i are *rotations*, μ_i are *mirror images*, δ_i are *diagonal flips*.)

*	ρ_0	ρ_1	ρ_2	ρ_3	μ_1	μ_2	δ_1	δ_2
ρ_0	ρ_0	ρ_1	ρ_2	ρ_3	μ_1	μ_2	δ_1	δ_2
ρ_1	ρ_1	ρ_2	ρ_3	ρ_0	δ_1	δ_2	μ_2	μ_1
ρ_2	ρ_2	ρ_3	ρ_0	ρ_1	μ_2	μ_1	δ_2	δ_1
ρ_3	ρ_3	ρ_0	ρ_1	ρ_2	δ_2	δ_1	μ_1	μ_2
μ_1	μ_1	δ_2	μ_2	δ_1	ρ_0	ρ_2	ρ_3	ρ_1
μ_2	μ_2	δ_1	μ_1	δ_2	ρ_2	ρ_0	ρ_1	ρ_3
δ_1	δ_1	μ_1	δ_2	μ_2	ρ_1	ρ_3	ρ_0	ρ_2
δ_2	δ_2	μ_2	δ_1	μ_1	ρ_3	ρ_1	ρ_2	ρ_0

This group does not have a global automorphism: each element plays a unique role, and so not only is distinguishable from the others but is categorically specifiable (isolable) as well. Yet we want to be entitled to label the elements of the abstract group V, no less than those of D_4. We want to be able to say, "Call one of the elements that behaves this way [specification of its role with respect to e and b], 'a' and the other 'c.' It doesn't matter which is which."

Frege in fact recognizes this distinction. He appeals to it in distinguishing arithmetic from geometry:

One geometrical point, considered by itself, cannot be distinguished in any way from any other; the same applies to lines and planes. Only when several points, or lines, or planes, are included together in a single intuition, do we distinguish them . . . But with numbers it is different; each number has its own peculiarities.[21]

That is, the natural numbers are *antecedently categorically specifiable (isolable),* while geometrical objects are not (though they must still be distinguishable).

Here, then, is a suggestion. We could relax Frege's uniqueness requirement on entitlement to introduce singular terms by insisting on *distinguishability* but not on *isolability*—requiring the *hypothetical* specifiability of referents but not their *categorical* specifiability. The rationale would be that this seems in fact to be what we insist on in the case of mathematical structures that exhibit the sorts of symmetry we have considered. In the context of the *Grundlagen* project where it is introduced, uniqueness mattered originally because it was necessary for countability—where once existence has been settled, the issue of one or two or more is of the essence. But *distinguishability,* by *local* substitutions that do *not* preserve truth, is sufficient for countability. For this purpose we do not *also* have to insist, as Frege does, on *categorical specifiability,* which requires the absence of certain kinds of *global* truth-preserving substitutions or permutations. Since the latter requirement would oblige us to condemn vast stretches of otherwise unimpeachable mathematical language as unintelligible or ill formed, it seems prudent to refrain from insisting on it.

There are two ways in which such a relaxation of half of Frege's uniqueness condition might be understood—confrontational or accommodating. One would construe the move as reflecting disagreement about the proper characterization of a common category of expressions: singular terms. The other would take the suggestion as recommending recognition of a second, related category of expressions: (say) schmingular terms. According to the first sort of line, Frege was just wrong in thinking that categorical specifiability is a necessary condition for introducing well-behaved singular terms. According to the second, he was quite right about one kind of singular term, what we might call "specifying" terms, and wrong only in not acknowledging the existence of another kind, what we might call "merely distinguishing" terms.

The accommodating reading is surely more attractive. The confrontational stance seems to require commitment to a substantive and (so) potentially controversial *semantic axiom of choice* that stipulates that one can label arbitrary distinguishable objects.[22] One would then naturally want to inquire into the warrant for such a postulate. Going down this road seems needlessly to multiply the possibilities for metaphysical puzzlement. Frege's practice in the *Grundlagen* would seem to show that what matters for him is that we understand the proper use of the expressions we introduce: what commitments their use entails, and how we can become entitled to those commitments. We can be entitled to use merely distinguishing terms, for instance, the labels on the sides of a hypothetical equilateral triangle, provided we are careful never to make any inferences that depend on the categorical specifiability of what is labeled—that is, that our use of the labels respects the global homomorphisms that precluded such specifiability. This is a substantive obligation that goes beyond those involved in the use of (categorically) specifying terms, so it makes sense to distinguish the two categories of singular terms. But there is nothing mysterious about the rules governing either sort. If Frege thought there was something conceptually or semantically incoherent about merely distinguishing terms, then he was wrong—as the serviceability and indispensability of the language of complex analysis (not to mention abstract algebra) shows.

VII. Conclusion

So here are some of the conclusions I think we can draw to articulate the significance of complex numbers for Frege's philosophy of mathematics. First, structural symmetries of the field of complex numbers entail that Frege's *Platonistic* or *objectivist* version of logicism cannot be made to work in his own terms for this area because of a collision with requirements on singular referentiality built deeply into his semantics. Second, as a consequence, Frege's partition of mathematics into:

  (a) the study of *logical* objects, and
  (b) the study of the deliverances of pure (geometrical) *intuition*

cannot be sustained in his terms. For once we have seen how things are with the complex plane, it becomes obvious that vast stretches of modern mathematics, including most of abstract algebra, will not fit into Frege's botanization. For the sorts of global symmetries they share with the complex plane preclude Frege from allowing them in the first category, and they are not plausibly assimilated to the second. More constructively, however, I have suggested that we can make sense of reference to mathematical objects in the face of such symmetries if we are willing to relax Frege's requirements on entitlement to use singular terms, by insisting on *distinguishability* (hypothetical specifiability), but not on *categorical specifiability*.[23] Thus, looking hard at how complex numbers fit into Frege's theorizing in the philosophy of mathematics promises to teach us important lessons about the semantics of singular terms. This suggests a final general lesson: the philosophy of mathematics must pay attention to the details of the actual structures it addresses. Semanticists, metaphysicians, and ontologists interested in mathematics cannot safely confine themselves, as so many have done, to looking only at the natural numbers.

10

Heidegger's Categories in *Sein und Zeit*

In Division One of *Being and Time (Sein und Zeit)*, Heidegger presents a novel categorization of what there is, and an original account of the project of ontology, and consequently of the nature and genesis of those ontological categories. He officially recognizes two categories of Being: *Zuhandensein* (readiness-to-hand) and *Vorhandensein* (presence-at-hand). *Vorhanden* things are roughly the objective, person-independent, causally interacting subjects of natural scientific inquiry. *Zuhanden* things are those which a neo-Kantian would describe as having been imbued with human values and significances. In addition to these categories, there is human Being, or *Dasein*, in whose structure the origins of the two thing-ish categories are to be found. This chapter concerns itself with three of Heidegger's conceptual innovations: his conceiving of ontology in terms of self-adjudicating anthropological categories, as summed up in the slogan that "fundamental ontology is the regional ontology of Dasein"; his corresponding antitraditional assertion of the ontological priority of the domain of the *Zuhandensein* to that of the *Vorhandensein*, which latter is seen as rooted in or precipitated out of that more basic (Heidegger says "primordial") world of human significances; and the non-Cartesian account of awareness and classificatory consciousness as social and practical.

Section I presents an interpretation of Heidegger's notion of fundamental ontology and its relation to the "vulgar" ontology practiced by previous philosophers. Section II introduces *Zuhandensein*—the world of equipment, each element of which is experienced *as* having some practically constituted role or significance. Section III offers a reading of

Mit-Dasein, the social mode of Being which institutes the world of equipment. Finally, section IV discusses the move from a world of equipment, about which there are no facts over and above how things are *taken* to be by all the bits of Dasein involved, to a realm of things which have properties not exhausted by their possible roles in Dasein's practical dealings.[1]

I. Fundamental Ontology

The most striking thing about Heidegger's account of categories is his distinction between "vulgar" ontology and "fundamental" ontology, and the coordinate claim that fundamental ontology is the regional ontology of Dasein (the kind of Being we have). Vulgar ontology is the cataloguing of the furniture of the universe. Fundamental ontology is said to be deeper and more difficult than the vulgar variety, requiring the investigation of the significance of ontological categorization. For vulgar ontology, in its most careful versions, whether we consider Leibniz, Hegel, Frege, or Quine, a specification of such general kinds takes the form of a specification of *criteria of identity* and *individuation* for entities of those kinds. As an ontologist in this tradition, Descartes inaugurated the modern era with a bold reincarnation of a Platonic idea. things are to be distinguished according to criteria of identity and individuation couched in terms of *epistemic* privilege. In particular, he invented a new kind of thing, according to the scheme: an event or object is *mental* (or subjective) just in case it is whatever it is taken to be by some individual.[2] The rest of the (nondivine) universe he relegated to the physical or objective realm. These were things which are what they are regardless of how any individual takes them to be.[3] The contribution of the nineteenth century to this scheme was Hegel's notion (see section III) of a third category of *social* entities. What is at issue here is the domain of social *appropriateness* in which, as in etiquette, social practice is the highest court of appeal. Thus a group or community can be thought of as having the same sort of criterial dominion or authority over, and hence privileged access to, social things that individuals have over subjective things.

Before describing how Heidegger develops this idea into a detailed model of social practice and significance in *Being and Time,* let's consider some consequences which adding such an ontological category to the

Cartesian two-sorted ontology can have. In particular, we can ask the question of fundamental ontology: What is the ontological status of the distinction of entities into three kinds (subjective, social, and objective) based on the source of criterial authority for them? In particular, is the division of things into subjective, social, and objective a subjective distinction (as Berkeley would have it), a social distinction, or an objective one?[4] The conceptual status of such a question is unusual enough to warrant the citation of a few more familiar examples which exhibit the same structure.

First, consider the distinction between differences of *quality* and differences of *quantity*. Is this difference, we may ask, a qualitative or a quantitative one? Engels notoriously takes himself to have transformed the philosophical tradition by suggesting the latter response in place of the former. Whatever merit that suggestion may have, the issue it seeks to respond to seems to be perfectly intelligible.

Another example can be observed in the medieval notions of *distinctio rationis* and *distinctio realis*. The distinction between form and matter is only a distinction of reason, for we can never have one without the other. Only by, for example, rationally considering the relations a bronze cube stands in to a bronze sphere and a marble cube can we "separate" its being bronze from its being a cube. Between a piece of bronze and a piece of marble, however, there exists a real distinction, for these can be nonmetaphorically separated without reliance on rational abstraction by comparison. But now we must ask, as did the scholastics, whether the distinction between rational and real distinctions is itself a rational or a real distinction. Although issues of great moment for the debate about the ontological and epistemological status of universals turn on the answer to this question, our concern is with the structure of the question rather than with the plausibility of various answers to it.

A final example should make clear the phenomenon being pointed out. The U.S. Constitution gives the three broad branches of the federal government distinct responsibilities and jurisdictions. As part of the relations of authority and responsibility which exist between the branches (the "checks and balances" which regulate their interaction), the judiciary is given the authority and responsibility to interpret the proper region of authority and responsibility of *each* branch, itself included. In matters of constitutional import, we may say, the judiciary is given the authority to draw the boundaries between its own authority and that of the executive and legislative branches.

It is not easy to describe the structure which these examples share. In each case a family of concepts pertaining to identity and individuation is examined, and the root of the identity and individuation of those concepts is found to reside in one of them. (In the last example, instead of a concept with an extension including various things, we have a social institution with a jurisdiction including various things.) In each case the question can be raised whether one of those concepts (institutions) is *self-adjudicating* in the sense that it applies to the sort of identity and individuation which distinguishes it from the other concepts or institutions in that family. To raise this second-order sort of question about a scheme of ontological categories is to engage in fundamental ontology. And Heidegger's claim that fundamental ontology is the regional ontology of Dasein is the claim that Dasein-in-the-world-of-the-ready-to-hand is ontologically self-adjudicating in this sense. Not only is the distinction between the ontological categories of the ready-to-hand and the present-at-hand intelligible only in terms of the sort of Being that Dasein has, but also the difference between Dasein's sort of Being and readiness-to- and presentness-at-hand must itself be understood in terms of Dasein. It is this central feature of his early work which led the later Heidegger to dismiss *Being and Time* as "merely anthropological."

The ontological primacy of the social can be justified by appeal to a more specific thesis, pragmatism concerning *authority*. This is the claim that all matters of authority or privilege, in particular *epistemic* authority, are matters of social practice, and not objective matters of fact.[5] The pragmatist about authority will take the criterial distinctions between ontological categories to be social in nature, for those categories are distinguished precisely by the locus of criterial authority over them. The category of the social must then be seen as self-adjudicating, and hence as ontologically basic, so the broader claim of the ontological priority of social categories follows from the narrower doctrine concerning the social nature of authority. In what follows it will be argued that Heidegger develops precisely this line of thought in Division One of *Being and Time*.

II. *Zuhandenheit* and Practice

According to Heidegger, Dasein finds itself always amidst an already existing world of equipment, consisting of significant things each of which is experienced *as* something. The readiness-to-hand of a piece of equipment consists in its having a certain significance. This significance in turn consists in its appropriateness for various practical roles and its inappropriateness for others.

> But the 'indicating' of the sign and the 'hammering' of the hammer are not properties [*Eigenschaften*] of entities . . . Anything ready-to-hand is, at worst, appropriate [*geeignet*] for some purposes and inappropriate for others. (*BT* 114)

Properties, by contrast, are what characterize the present-at-hand independently of human practical ends—what would be taken to be true of objects before human beings "attach significances" to them on the neo-Kantian picture Heidegger wishes to invert. Heidegger's problem in the first part of *Being and Time* is to explain how such a category of objective Being could be constructed or abstracted out of the primitive system of appropriatenesses and significances which makes up the world in which we always already find ourselves.

How are we to understand this category of the ready-to-hand? To inhabit a *world* is to *take* each thing in that world *as* something. A piece of equipment is something experienced *as* something. Several points about this 'as' structure must be appreciated in order to understand the ready-to-hand as the kind of Being or significance a thing exhibits by being taken *as* something. First, the something$_1$s which are taken as something$_2$s must be understood as themselves things which are ready-to-hand as ways of taking still other pieces of equipment. "In interpreting we do not, so to speak, throw a 'signification' over some naked thing which is present-at-hand, we do not stick a value on it."[6] The something$_1$s which are given with respect to one set of takings must themselves have been socially constituted. Second, it must be understood how thoroughly non-Cartesian and unsubjective is Heidegger's notion of the classificatory activity in virtue of which things show themselves *as* something$_2$s. The world of the ready-to-hand is what we can be aware of, *as* we are or would be aware of it. For Heidegger, as for others, there is no awareness or experience without classification. But the "awareness" which is the appropriation of some bit of equipment *as* having a certain significance is a public behavioral matter of how the thing is treated or responded to, not a mental act. For Heidegger, the confused notion of the subjective arises when the category of the present-at-hand has been achieved, as that coordinate mental realm which must be invoked when one mistakenly takes the present-at-hand as ontologically primary and looks for something to *add* to it to explain the everyday world of the ready-to-hand. If this antisubjectivism is overlooked, the use of the notion of classification to bridge the gap between Heidegger's 'as'-structure and traditional notions of consciousness will be misleading. Finally, it must be noted that modeling understanding on taking-as is a device for interpreting the text, not a rendering of its terminology. Officially, discussions of 'as-structure' are restricted to the level of interpretation (which develops out of understanding), where something is noticed *as* a hammer not when it is hammered with (as the model of understanding would have it), but only when it is discarded as inappropriate for, or searched for as required by some practical project. The broader usage has an exegetical point, however, and the specific differences between understanding and interpretation can be accommodated within it, as we shall see. The positive account of treating or taking *as* has three features. First, takings are public performances which accord with social practices. Second, such performances are individuated as and by *responses*. Third, the responsive dispositions which constitute the social practices are related to one another so as to satisfy a strong systematicity condition. We examine these points below.

Where do the sorts or kinds or characters which are the something$_2$s according to which something$_1$s are classified come from? Any concrete object or event is similar to any other in an infinite number of respects, and dissimilar to it in an infinite number of others. For a respect of similarity is just a shared possible partial description, and these can be gerrymandered as we like. The practical discrimination of objects and performances into those appropriate for or according to some practice and those not is precisely the recognition of *some* of these infinitely numerous, abstractly generable respects of similarity as having a special privilege over the rest. Heidegger should be interpreted in accord with the pragmatist thesis about authority, as taking this privilege to consist in its social recognition, that is, as a matter of how some community does or would respond to things. Something$_2$s are response-types, and classifying something$_1$ as a particular something$_2$ is simply responding to it with a performance of that type. Equipment is originally introduced in section 15 as consisting of *pragmata*, "that which one has to do with in one's concernful dealings." The ready-to-hand is generically characterized by serviceability *(Dienlichkeit)*:

Serviceability . . . is not an appropriateness of some entity; it is rather the condition (so far as Being is in question) which makes it possible for the character of such an entity to be defined by its appropriatenesses. (*BT*, 115; *SZ* 83)

"Serviceability" is thus the potential which objects have to be caught up in the practices which institute specific respects of appropriateness. For something₁ to be so caught up is for it to be *involved:*

The Being of an entity within the world is its involvement [*Bewandtnis*]. (*BT* 116; *SZ* 84)

Such involvement in turn comprises a system of references or assignments:

To say that the Being of the ready-to-hand has the structure of reference or assignment [*Verweisung*] means that it has in itself the character of *having been assigned or referred.* (*BT* 115; *SZ* 84)

The appropriatenesses which are the significance of a particular entity exist in virtue of such reference or assignment. Referring or assigning is instituting relations among equipment (pen, ink, paper, etc.) and clearly is something that is *done,* though we must not assume for that reason that it is something any one of us can do, or even that it is something the whole community can do (except in a derivative sense), rather than something done by the community's practices as constitutive of those practices.[7] These assignments exist in virtue of the responsive dispositions which are appropriate in a community.

A further doctrine is that

an entity is discovered when it is assigned or referred to something, and referred as that entity which it is. (*BT* 115; *SZ* 84)

Discovering an entity is taking it *as* something (the non-Cartesian notion of awareness as behavioral classification). Referring or assigning is to be understood not only as instituting the social appropriatenesses which are the significances of objects and performances, but also as making possible the appropriation of such significances by those who discover objects in terms of them. 'Appropriation' (*Zueignung)* is Heidegger's nonsubjective epistemic activity. To discover something ready-to-hand, to appropriate it, is to take it *as* something, to respond to it in a certain way. In one of his rare examples, after telling us that signs can be taken as paradigmatic of equipment in general, Heidegger says that

> the kind of behaving (Being) which corresponds to the sign [a turn-signal arrow] is either to "give way" or stand still with respect to the car with the arrow. (*BT*, 110; *SZ* 79)

Here it is precisely how it is appropriate to respond to the turn signal in a context that makes it the bit of equipment it is. To take it *as* such a signal (discover it as such) is just to respond to it with the appropriate behavior.

The systematicity requirement may be put broadly by the claim that

> taken strictly, there "is" no such thing as *an* equipment. To the Being of any equipment there always belongs a totality of equipment, in which it can be the equipment that it is. (*BT* 97; *SZ* 68)

Anything ready-to-hand is so only in virtue of the role it plays in a "referential totality of significance or involvements."

> As the Being of something ready-to-hand, an involvement is itself discovered only on the basis of the prior discovery of a totality of involvements. (*BT*, 118; *SZ* 85)

In terms of what relations are such roles to be understood, and how must they fit together to form the appropriate kind of totality? Heidegger gives his answer in section 18, "Involvement and Significance—the Worldhood of the World." Although the account offered there deploys an unfamiliar set of technical terms, its basic characteristics may be straightforwardly set out. The bearers of the social significances making up readiness-to-hand are of two kinds: objects and performances. Objects and performances are what can be constitutively judged to be (in the sense of being responded to as) appropriate or not according to the social practices which are the medium of social significance. Heidegger calls those practices "in-order-to's" (*das Umzu*). Fastening one board to another by driving a nail would be an example. An object can be caught up in such a practice either by being used in the practice, or by being produced in that practice. In the former case, Heidegger calls the object (for example, a hammer or a nail, used in the different senses of 'employed' and 'consumed', respectively) the "with-which" (*das Womit*) of the practice, and in the latter case he calls the object which is produced the "towards-which" (*das Wozu*). The assignments of objects are the relations between them instituted by relations between the practices in which they are involved in these two ways. The role of an object (its involvement) is determined by those practices in which it is appropriately used, and those practices in which it can appropriately be produced.

Particular performances are called "in-whiches" (*das Wobei*). A social practice may be thought of as a class of possible performances, that is, as a performance *type*. Such an in-order-to consists, namely, of just those performances which are or would be (taken to be) appropriate according to it. For something to be (ready-to-hand as) a hammer is for it to be appropriate to respond to it with a performance of the hammering type, that is, to hammer with it. It is performances of using and producing objects which make up the social practices in virtue of which those objects acquire their involvements and significances. Social object types are then instituted by social practical types of the performances in which they are appropriately used or produced. In the world of the ready-to-hand, in which things are whatever they are (or would be) responded to *as*, then, the individuation of objects (by their roles as with- and toward-whiches) is determined by the individuation of social practices. Object types are instituted by performance types. So where do the appropriateness equivalence classes of performances, which are the social practices, come from?

As with objects, performance tokens exhibit infinite numbers of objective respects of similarity and dissimilarity. The privilege which one type or co-appropriateness class of performances exhibits as a practice can only have its source in its social recognition, that is, in how the type-privileged (co-typical) performance tokens would be treated or taken, or more generally responded to by the community in question. The performances comprised by a social practice are of the same type in that there is some other responsive performance type (something$_2$) such that each of the tokens of the instituted performance type (something$_1$) is, according to the community whose recognitions are constitutive in this domain, appropriately responded to by some performance belonging to the instituting type. A performance is recognized as being of the type by being responded to as such. For instance, what makes a certain class of performances all instances of the type *constructings of tribally appropriate dwelling huts* is that each of those possible performances would be appropriately responded to by a performance of the type *tribe members treating the produced object as a dwelling,* that is, *being prepared to dwell in it under suitable circumstances.* Whenever what is produced by one practice is used by another, the using practice plays the role of responsive recognition performance type (RRPT) with respect to the producing practice. The role of a social performance type in a "totality of involvements" is specified by saying what performance type is its RRPT. and what performance type it is an RRPT for.

The requirement of systematicity or of the autonomy of significance may then be stated in two parts. First, with respect to objects, every object type appropriately produced by one social practice must be appropriately usable in or by some other practice. The converse need not hold, for Heidegger says several times that *natural* objects are ready-to-hand as objects usable in human practice, but not requiring to be produced by it.[8] Second, with respect to performances, every performance type which is an RRPT for some performance type must have some other performance type as its own RRPT. Again the converse need not hold, since we can respond to natural events. To specify the role of an object in such a system is to specify those practices with respect to which it functions as toward-which, and those with respect to which it functions as with-which. To specify the role of a performance (in-which) is to specify the practice, that is, the performance type to which it belongs. And to specify such an in-order-to is to specify its RRPT and what it functions as an RRPT of. Doing so determines all of the assignment relations and involvements which hold between socially significant objects as such, as well as the instituting responsive relations defining social performance types. The non-Cartesian epistemic notion of appropriation of significance or discovery of the ready-to-hand is also given a natural social-behavioral reading on this account. For to grasp the involvement of an object is to achieve practical mastery of its various assignments. And such mastery consists simply in being able to act (use, produce, and respond) appropriately according to the practices which institute those involvements. To respond to an object or performance which is appropriate according to a practice *as* appropriate according to that practice, that is, to respond appropriately to it, is to discover it as what it is, as ready-to-hand for what it is ready-to-hand for. Such practical capacities can be described without invoking anything subjective on the part of the practitioners. The inhabitant of a Heideggerean world is aware of it as composed of significant equipment, caught up in various social practices, and classified by the involvements those practices institute. But this awareness is practical, social, and behavioral, consisting entirely in the exhibition of differential responsive dispositions according appropriately with those of the community.

The account suggested of the nature of the referential totality of significance within which we encounter the ready-to-hand explains the concept of the worldhood of the world in at least one straightforward sense. For the remarks above can be expressed in a first-order quantificational language. Such a language would need two different sorts of individual constants, to stand for object types and performance types, and three different predicates (corresponding to the three sorts of "assignment or reference" distinguished above): $U(o, p)$, interpreted as saying that object o is used in practice p, $P(p, o)$, interpreted as saying that object o is produced by practice p, and $R(p, p')$, interpreted as saying that p' is the RRPT of p. It is easy to see that the two halves of the systematicity condition can be expressed as quantificational sentences in such a language. It is equally easy to see how the model theory for such a language might go. Theories in the specified language that include the sentences codifying the systematicity conditions would be interpreted by model structures which consisted of domains of object and performance types (represented as sets of tokens) and relations between them of using, producing, and responding. A Heideggerean world is such a structure satisfying in the usual sense a first-order theory of the sort described which contains the systematicity conditions.[9] At the end of section 18, Heidegger summarizes the structure he discerns:

> The 'for-the-sake-of-which' signifies an 'in-order-to'; this in turn a 'to-wards-this'; the latter, an 'in-which' of letting something be involved; and that in turn the 'with-which'. These relationships are bound up with one another as a primordial totality; they are what they are *as* signifying . . . The relational totality of this signifying we call 'significance'. (*BT* 120; *SZ* 87)

This passage emphasizes the systematic structure of social significance and retraces the relations of use and response described above. It mentions the further technical expression 'for-the-sake-of-which' (*das Worumwillen*) which marks the point of contact of the categorial structure with the existential concerns of Division Two and so cannot be discussed here. A practical 'in-order-to' gives a point to performances of some type by providing a use for the 'toward-this' (a particular 'toward-which') produced by such performances. Those performances are 'in-which's individuated as types by their overall role or involvement in use of 'with-which's as means or production of 'toward-which's, as those 'toward-which's are individuated by their involvement not only in being produced by performances of a certain kind from raw materials of a certain kind, but also by their involvement in a further practice (an 'in-order-to' whose performances are themselves 'in-which's) which makes use of them. The communities whose responsive recognitive practices generate these structures of social significance will be considered next.

III. *Mitdasein*

Significance is a structure of Dasein's kind of Being:

> We have interpreted worldhood as that referential totality which constitutes significance. In Being-familiar with this significance and previously understanding it, Dasein lets what is ready-to-hand be encountered as discovered in its involvement. In Dasein's Being, the context of references or assignments which significance implies is tied up with Dasein's own-most Being. (*BT* 160; *SZ* 123)

Nothing like a full account of Dasein's kind of Being can be essayed here; that is the topic of the whole of *Being and Time*. Nevertheless, something must be said about the constitution of the community in whose dispositions (for appropriate responsive recognitions or takings) significance originates. Happily, the features of Dasein's kind of Being which must be understood if the precipitation of the present-at-hand out of the ready-to-hand is to be intelligible can be explained with the materials already available.

The first point, of course, is that Dasein's Being is *social* in nature:

> So far as Dasein *is* at all, it has Being-with-one-another as its kind of Being. (*BT* 163; *SZ* 125)

> Not only is Being toward Others an autonomous, irreducible relationship, as Being-with, it is one which, with Dasein's Being, already is. (*BT* 162; *SZ* 125)
> Dasein in itself is essentially Being-with (*BT* 156; *SZ* 120)

Next, Dasein's sociality is essential to the practical activity which constitutes worldly significance:

> Dasein-with remains existentially constitutive for Being-in-the-world. (*BT* 157; *SZ* 121; compare also *BT* 163; *SZ* 125)

Third, it is only in the context of such Dasein-with that individuals can be spoken of:

> In Being with and towards Others, there is thus a relationship of Being [*Seinsverhaltnis*] from Dasein to Dasein. But it might be said that this relationship is already constitutive for one's own Dasein. (*BT* 162; *SZ* 124)

> In terms of the 'they' [*das Man*] and as the 'they', I am given proximally to myself. (*BT* 167; *SZ* 129)

These doctrines can be understood according to the Hegelian model of the synthesis of social substance by mutual recognition. To belong to a community, according to this model, is to be recognized as so belonging by all those one recognizes as so belonging. Hegel's idea was that community-constitutive recognition is transitive de jure—that one must recognize those who are recognized by those one recognizes. The reflexive self-recognition that makes one a Hegelian individual will then follow if one can establish de facto symmetry, that is, achieve recognition by those one recognizes. To be entitled to recognize or regard oneself as an excellent chess player, one must be entitled to be regarded as such by those one so regards.

Of course, for an account along these lines to be helpful in interpreting Heidegger, recognition must not be taken to be a mental act, but as with awareness and classification must be given a social-behavioral reading in terms of communal responsive dispositions. What sort of response (RRPT) is taking or recognizing someone *as* one of us, a member of *our* community? Clues are to be found in two passages:

> In that with which we concern ourselves environmentally, the Others are encountered as what they are; they *are* what they do. (*BT* 163; *SZ* 126)

What is it that other community members as such do? They take objects and performances *as* ready-to-hand with respect to various practices *by* using them and responding to them in various ways. How does such behavior constitute the practitioners as other members of one's own community?

> By 'Others' we do not mean everyone else but me—those against whom the 'I' stands out. They are rather those from whom for the most part one does *not* distinguish oneself—those among whom one is too. (*BT* 154; *SZ* 118)

Not everyone is a communal Other, but only those one recognizes or responds to as such. To respond to them as such is not to distinguish them from oneself. But in what regard? The previous passage said that the Others are what they do, so it is their doings which one does not distinguish from one's own. And this is to say that one treats their *responses* and dispositions as one's own. What they take to be appropriate performances and usings and producings of equipment, one also takes as such. To give one's own responses no special status or priority in this way is to treat the kinds they institute as social. It is to take the authority over appropriateness boundaries to reside in the community, which is constituted by that very recognition.[10]

The suggestion is that my recognizing someone as a co-community member is responding to him in a certain way. That way is for me to respond to his responses as having the same authority to institute kinds and appropriateness equivalence classes that my own responses have. In particular, my recognitions of others *and myself* as members of the community have no special authority. My recognitions of myself as community member count only if they are taken to count by those I take to be community members. Their so taking my recognitions is in turn simply a matter of their recognizing me, that is, treating my responses as equally authoritative as theirs in determining appropriatenesses. The community, *Mitdasein,* then differs from the ready-to-hand in that its members are constituted not only by being *recognized* or responded to in a certain way, but also by their *recognizings* and responses as *recognizers*.

Being-together-with in the sense of forming a recognitive community is accordingly the existential basis of the consilience of practice which constitutes the category of the ready-to-hand and hence, as we shall see, the category of the present-at-hand as well. The distinction between the existential and the categorial terminologically marks that between *recognizers* and the merely *recognizeds* which do not have the kind of Being of one of us. The practical agreement of recognizing one another's recognizings can be called 'communication' "in a sense which is onto-logically broad":

> 'Communication' in which one makes an assertion—giving informa-tion, for instance—is a special case of the communication which is grasped in principle existentially. In this more general kind of commu-nicating the Articulation of Being-with one another understandingly is constituted. Through it a co-state-of-mind [*Mitbefindlichkeit*] gets 'shared', and so does the understanding of Being-with. (*BT* 205; *SZ* 162)

In the next section we investigate the genesis of the category of the pres-ent-at-hand out of the sort of understanding which consists in shared recognitive practice permitting communication about a world of equip-ment each bit of which is whatever it is recognized-by-us as.

IV. *Vorhandenheit* and Assertion

The claim to be developed in this section is that the category of the pres-ent-at-hand consists of ready-to-hand things which are appropriately re-sponded to by a certain kind of performance, *qua* things that can *only* be appropriately responded to by such a performance. That categorically constitutive kind of responsive recognition performance type is *asser-tion*. Since Heidegger holds that "assertion is derived from interpreta-tion, and is a special case of it,"[11] the story must begin with the notion of interpretation *(Auslegung)*.

Interpretation is a coordinate notion to that understanding which consists in the practical mastery of a totality of significations or assign-ments required if one is to live in a world at all. For "we never perceive equipment that is ready-to-hand without already understanding and in-terpreting it."[12] Four features of interpretation must be recognized. First, interpreting characterizes practical activity.

> Interpretation is carried out primordially not in a theoretical statement but in an action of circumspectful concern . . . [e.g.] laying aside the unsuitable tool. (*BT* 200; *SZ* 157)

Second, interpreting involves making something one's own. Interpreta-tion is described as "the working-out and appropriation of an under-standing."[13]

In understanding there lurks the possibility of interpretation—that is of *appropriating* what is understood. (*BT* 203; *SZ* 161. See also *BT* 191; *SZ* 150)

Taking something as something was the form of the act of understanding, that discovery of a bit of equipment which also disclosed a totality of equipmental involvments. What is it practically to appropriate such an understanding?

The answer is offered by a pair of passages, worth citing at length, which for the third point introduce the crucial *conditional* structure of interpretation, out of which the possibility of inference and hence assertion develops:

> Circumspection operates in the involvement-relationships of the context of equipment which is ready-to-hand. What is essential is that one should have a primary understanding of the totality of involvements . . . In one's current using and manipulating, the concernful circumspection . . . *brings* the ready-to-hand closer to Dasein, and does so by *interpreting* what has been sighted. The specific way of bringing the object of concern closer we call *deliberating* [*Überlegung*]. The schema particular to this is the 'if . . . then . . .'; if this or that, for instance, is to be produced, put to use, or averted, then some ways, means, circumstances or opportunities will be needed. (*BT* 410; *SZ* 359)

Interpretation classifies according to personal ends or projects, and hence appropriates. What new element is indicated by the invocation of the 'if . . . then . . .' as what is in this way brought closer to oneself?

> But if deliberation is to be able to operate in the scheme of the 'if . . . then . . .', concern must already have 'surveyed' a context of involvements and have an understanding of it. That which is considered with an 'if' must already be understood *as something or other* . . . The schema 'something-as-something' has already been sketched out beforehand in the structure of one's pre-predicative understanding. (*BT* 411; *SZ* 359)

Understanding appropriates equipment. It is exercised in taking something as something, for example, as a hammer. Interpretation at the level of deliberation adds to this use and appropriation of equipment the use and appropriation of equipmental *understanding* of particular involvements. One can not only take something as a hammer, but also take a hammer as one of the tools required for a certain practical project. What is appropriated is then the conditional serviceabilities of things. One uses and produces conditional understandings or the significance of particular something$_1$s as something$_2$s.

The fourth point is that this non-Cartesian cognitive notion of intepretation as the personal practical appropriation of a conditional appropriateness or equipmental involvement brings us closer to the notion of linguistic assertion:

> In the significance itself, with which Dasein is always familiar, there lurks the ontological condition which makes it possible for Dasein, as something which understands and interprets, to disclose such things as 'significations'; upon these, in turn, is founded the Being of words and of language. (*BT* 121; *SZ* 87)

'Significations' are the conditional appropriatenesses into which the totality of significations can be "dissolved or broken up."[14] What makes the transition to language possible is that one can come to respond differentially to (and hence disclose practically) not just things and performances but the significations which are their conditional dependencies. Deliberation develops toward asserting when what is surveyed from the point of view of a practical end is a field of 'if . . . then . . . 's', each of which may then itself be used or laid aside, just as with first-order equipment. Deliberation accomplishes a special kind of abstraction, requiring responsive recognition of the serviceabilities of equipment, rather than merely of the equipment itself.

The key to the precipitation of the present-at-hand out of the ready-to-hand lies in assertion:

> The levelling of the primordial 'as' of circumspective interpretation [the "existential-hermeneutical 'as'"] to the 'as' with which presence-at-hand is given a definite character [the "apophantical 'as'"] is the specialty of assertion. Only so does it obtain the possibility of exhibiting something in such a way that we just look at it. (*BT* 201; *SZ* 158)

The articulation leading to the discovery of the present-at-hand begins in the 'if . . . then . . .' of interpretation of the ready-to-hand. What matters is "what is awaited"[15] in the 'then . . .' part. In the basic case of interpreting something merely ready-to-hand, what is 'awaited' is the usability or producibility of some actual or envisaged object or performance— that is, the projection of a practical possibility. In presence-at-hand, the primary consequence of an 'if (something as something) . . .' is the appropriability of some *claim* or assertion. The difference between responding to something as present-at-hand and as merely ready-to-hand is that things which are present-at-hand are appropriately responded to as such only by producing a particular kind of performance, namely, assertions. The 'then' is still something ready-to-hand when we thematize (i.e., respond to something as present-at-hand), but it is an assertion, a very special kind of equipment.

The question is then:

> By what existential-ontological modification does assertion arise from circumspective interpretation? (*BT* 200; *SZ* 157)

The answer in brief is that assertions are equipment appropriately used for *inference*. Assertion is the topic of section 33, which offers three 'significations' of assertion. The central one of these is that "assertion means communication."

> As something-communicated, that which has been put forward in the assertion is something that Others can 'share' with the person making the assertion . . . That which is put forward in the assertion is something which can be passed along in further retelling. (*BT* 197; *SZ* 155)

> What is expressed becomes, as it were, something ready-to-hand within-the-world which can be taken up and spoken again. (*BT* 266; *SZ* 224)

Asserting thus has the significance of issuing a reassertion license to other community members. The assertion is produced as something usable by others.

The other two features by which assertion is introduced are "pointing out" some subject of assertion, and "giving it a definite character" by predicating something of it. What is shared, in other words, is the taking of something as something. Where before taking something as something (pointing it out and characterizing it) was something one could only *do,* now it becomes something one can *say.* What was implicit in performance now becomes an explicitly producible and usable bit of equipment, which one can appropriate and make available for others to appropriate. The pointing-out of a subject is socially transitive across authorized reassertions, and so guarantees communication in the sense of securing a common topic:

> Even when Dasein speaks over again what someone else has said, it comes into a Being-towards the very entities which have been discussed. (BT 266; SZ 224)

Such social preservation of a common subject matter is a necessary condition for the possibility of agreement and disagreement of assertion, as opposed to mere change of topic.

Predication, as explicitly communicable characterization, further extends the authorizing dimension of asserting. For predicates come in inferential families: *if* what is pointed out is appropriately characterizable by one speaker as red, *then* it is appropriately characterizable by another as colored. The practical conditional appropriatenesses of assertion which make up such families of predicates guarantee that an asserting licenses more than just reassertion, licensing others to draw conclusions beyond what was originally claimed. As members of inferential families, the predicates used to characterize objects in assertions codify the conditional significations responded to as such already in deliberation. It is in virtue of the socially appropriate inferential consequences of an asserting that it conveys information, authorizing a specific set of performances (including other assertions) which would have been inappropriate without such authorization. The taking of something$_1$ as something$_2$ of pre-predicative understanding becomes explicitly usable and sharable once linguistic terms are available as equipment for publicly pointing out something$_1$s, and predicates codifying as inferential significances the conditional serviceabilities discerned by deliberative interpretation are available as equipment expressing explicitly the involvements implicit in the something$_2$s things were taken as.

Understanding asserting as authorizing reassertion and inference specifies the appropriate *use* to which assertions, as bits of equipment, may appropriately be put. The recognitive responsive performance type of any asserting type will be the set of assertions which it may appropriately be seen as licensing, namely, those which follow from it according to the inferential practices of the community. But this is only half the story. What about the appropriate circumstances of ready-to-hand equipment? Corresponding to the dimension of authority governing the use of assertions as equipment-for-inference is a dimension of responsibility governing their production. For in producing an assertion one does not simply authorize others to use it inferentially; one also undertakes the responsibility to justify one's claim:

> Assertion communicates entities in the 'how' of their uncoveredness. If, however, these entities are to be appropriated explicitly with respect to their uncoveredness, this amounts to saying that the assertion is to be *demonstrated* as one that uncovers. The assertion expressed is something ready-to-hand. (*BT* 267; *SZ* 224, emphasis added)

As ready-to-hand, assertings are subject to social appropriatenesses of production as well as use. These concern when one is entitled to commit oneself to the claim, or in Heidegger's terminology, 'appropriate' it, so that the inference and reassertion license is in force:

> It is therefore essential that Dasein should explicitly appropriate what has already been uncovered, defend it against semblance and disguise, and assure itself of its uncoveredness again and again. (*BT* 265; *SZ* 222)

The responsibility to justify or defend one's claims undertaken as a matter of course in their appropriate production is essential to the special sort of communication which emerges with assertion. For even when Dasein speaks over again what someone else has said, though it comes into relation to the things pointed out and uncovered, "it has been exempted from having to uncover them again, primordially, and it holds that it has thus been exempted."[16] That is, he who relies on the authority of a previous speaker in reassertion is absolved of the responsibility to justify his claim which he would otherwise have undertaken by his performance of producing that assertion. His reliance on the authority of the first assertor just is his acquisition of the right to defer justificatory responsibility for his own assertion to the original speaker. The response which socially constitutes taking someone to have appropriately made an assertion (fulfilled or be able to fulfill his justificatory responsibility) is to treat his assertion as genuinely authoritative as licensing others, that is, to recognize as appropriate any deferrals of justificatory responsibility for that claim and its consequences to the original assertor by those relying on that authority. It is in this way that the dimensions of responsibility and authority, of appropriate production and use, are related so as to constitute assertions as equipment-for-communicating.[17]

This sketch of Heidegger's notion of assertion puts us in a position to understand the category of the present-at-hand. The crucial point to understand here is that the move from equipment ready-to-hand, fraught with socially instituted significances, to objective things present-at-hand, is one not of decontextualization but of recontextualization. Asserting and the practices of giving and asking for reasons which make it possible are themselves a special sort of practical activity. Responding to something by making an assertion about it is treating it *as* present-at-hand. Presence-at-hand is constituted by special appropriatenesses of response:

> In characterizing the change-over from manipulating and using and so forth which are circumspective in a 'practical' way, to 'theoretical' exploration, it would be easy to suggest that merely looking at entities is something which emerges when concern *holds back* from any kind of manipulation . . . But this is by no means the way in which the 'theoretical' attitude of science is reached. On the contrary, the tarrying which is discontinued when one manipulates can take on the character of a more precise kind of circumspection. (*BT* 409; *SZ* 357–358)

Claims, equipment for asserting, represent "more precise" interpretive responses because in them the significations which are merely implicit in ordinary equipment become explicit or "thematized," accessible to claims and inferences and hence to demands for justification. Treating something as present-at-hand is not ignoring its social significance but attending to a special sort of significance it can have, namely, significance for the correctness of assertions about it. Corresponding to a new social mode of response, asserting, there is a new kind of Being, presence-at-hand, constitutively uncovered by that response:

> Thematizing objectifies. It does not first 'posit' the entities, but frees them so that one can interrogate them and determine their character 'objectively'. Being which objectifies and which is alongside the present-at-hand within-the-world is characterized by a *distinctive kind of making-present*. (*BT* 414; *SZ* 363)

The present-at-hand may thus be defined as what is ready-to-hand as a with-which for the practice of assertion, that is, as what is responded to as such only by making a claim about it. We have seen what kind of a performance assertings are. What is the relation between what is responded to as ready-to-hand for assertion and what is pointed out as present-at-hand in the assertion? Heidegger explains this in terms of a transformation:

> The entity which is held in our fore-having—for instance the hammer—is proximally ready-to-hand as equipment. If this entity becomes the 'object' of an assertion, then as soon as we begin this assertion, there is already a change-over in the fore-having. Something *ready-to-hand with which* we have to do or perform something turns into something *'about which'* the assertion that points it out is made. Our foresight is aimed at something present-at-hand in what is ready-to-hand . . . Within this discovery of presence-at-hand, which is at the same time a covering-up of readiness-to-hand, something present-at-hand which we encounter is given a definite character in its Being-present-at-hand-in-such-and-such-a-manner. Only now are we given access to *properties* or the like . . . This leveling of the primordial 'as' of circumspective interpretation to the 'as' with which presence-at-hand is given a definite character is the specialty of assertion. Only so does it obtain the possibility of exhibiting something in such a way that we just look at it. (*BT* 200; *SZ* 158)

The present-at-hand is first discovered *in* something already ready-to-hand, which we are related to by being practically involved with it. It is then possible to adopt a special stance, shifting from the original practical context to that of assertion. The referentiality of the relation to the original piece of equipment is inherited by assertions about the object discovered in it. Dealing with the object in such a context, where practical significance is restricted to significance for inference, is attributing properties to something present-at-hand pointed out in the assertions about it.

One question remains: In what sense does responding to something by making an assertion about it count as treating it as having objective properties? What sort of independence of the social appropriatenesses of use and production constitutive of the ready-to-hand is attributed to the present-at-hand when we understand its defining recognitive responsive performance type to be asserting? Equipment as such is always equipment serviceable for the pursuit of some practical end. Significance flows from the practically orienting projects to the 'with-which's and 'to-

ward-which's whose involvements are their roles in instrumental practices. The objectivity of the present-at-hand consists in the indifference
of the appropriatenesses of assertion to the practical ends motivating
assertors. Taking something as a hammer is taking it as appropriate for
hammering. When the property of heaviness is discerned in the present-
at-hand object which was ready-to-hand as a hammer, a claim is made
whose appropriateness is not a matter of serviceability for or obstruction
of any particular practical ends or projects. The justifiability and hence
appropriateness of such a claim is not a matter of answering to some
practical need.

The autonomy of justification and inference with respect to the pursuit of practical projects is the source of the autonomy of the properties
of the present-at-hand with respect to the appropriatenesses of practice.
It is this autonomy that is invoked when it is said that the truth of assertions answers to the things pointed out in assertion. Authority is a social
matter, and in the game of asserting and giving and asking for reasons,
authority over the appropriateness of claims has been socially with-
drawn from the sphere of usefulness for practical ends.

The claim that the objectivity of the present-at-hand consists in its
insulation by assertion from Dasein's practical activity can be given a
strong or a weak reading, and it is important to distinguish these. On the
strong reading, the present-at-hand would be entirely irrelevant to practical concerns. On this account, the only appropriate response to something present-at-hand is an assertion, the only use which can be made of
assertion is inference, and inference is restricted to *theoretical* inference,
that is, inference whose conclusion is another assertion. Assertions are
seen as irrelevant to practice, as mere representations of an independent
reality indifferent to practical projects. This practical indifference is then
inherited by the present-at-hand, since it can only be the subject of such
assertions. This idea is present in Heidegger. It is not presence-at-hand,
however, but what he calls the doctrine of *pure* presence-at-hand (or,
sometimes, 'Reality'):

> ['Reality'] in its traditional signification stands for Being in the sense of
> pure presence-at-hand of Things . . . [But] *all* the modes of Being of
> entities within-the-world are founded ontologically upon the world-
> hood of the world and accordingly the phenomenon of Being-in-the-
> world. From this arises the insight that among the modes of Being of

entities within-the-world, Reality has no priority, and that Reality is a kind of Being which cannot even characterize anything like the world or Dasein in a way which is ontologically appropriate. (*BT* 211; *SZ* 254)

Presence-at-hand corresponds to a weaker reading of the insulation assertional practices provide between the objects present-at-hand and practical projects. For although it is correct to see assertions as the only appropriate responses to the present-at-hand as such, and although the only use that can appropriately be made of assertions is inference, it is simply a mistake to think of all inference as theoretical inference. There is also practical inference, whose premises are assertions and whose conclusion is a practical performance which is not an assertion but, in virtue of its genesis as the result of such deliberation, an action. Assertions about the present-at-hand can be practically relevant. We can use information about the merely present-at-hand properties of things, such as the heaviness of the hammer. Without the possibility of language exits through non-assertional performance, theoretical or intralinguistic inference would lose much or all of its point.[18]

If it is then incorrect to see the present-at-hand as completely irrelevant to practical pursuits, as in pure presence-at-hand, what *is* meant by its objectivity? Just this. The *only* way in which the present-at-hand can affect Dasein's projects is by being the subject of an assertion which ultimately plays some role in practical inference. It is not that the present-at-hand is irrelevant to non-assertional practice; it is that its relevance is *indirect*. Assertions are the only interface between the present-at-hand and the rest of our practice. The mistake of the doctrine of pure presence is to see no interface at all.[19] The genuine difference between the present-at-hand (which can be thought of in an extended sense as ready-to-hand for the practices of assertion and inference) and what is ready-to-hand is that one can make practical use only of assertions about the present-at-hand, never of what is present-at-hand itself. Its assertional proxies are serviceable equipment, but the present-at-hand itself is not. Only as represented in assertions can the present-at-hand partake of the equipmental totality of significance which is the world within which Dasein lives and moves and has its Being. Discovery of the present-at-hand is an authentic possibility of Dasein's Being, instantiated by all human communities ever discovered. Pure presence-at-hand is a philosophers' misunderstanding of the significance of the category of presence-at-hand, and a Bad Idea.

The categorial nature of the present-at-hand, no less than that of the ready-to-hand (or for that matter the existential nature of Dasein itself as *Mitdasein*) is constituted by its being appropriately responded to in a certain way, in this case by assertions. In this fact resides Heidegger's ontological pragmatism, and the self-adjudicating nature of *Mitdasein*-in-the-world. Heidegger sees social behavior as generating both the category of equipment ready-to-hand within a world, and the category of objectively present-at-hand things responded to as independent of the practical concerns of any community. In virtue of the social genesis of criterial authority (the self-adjudication of the social, given pragmatism about authority), fundamental ontology (the study of the origin and nature of the fundamental categories of things) is the study of the nature of social Being—social practices and practitioners. Only because Dasein as socially constituted and constituting masters communal practices classifying things according to kinds which are whatever they are taken to be

> can Dasein also understand and conceptualize such characteristics of Being as independence, the 'in-itself', and Reality in general. Only because of this are 'independent' entities, as encountered within-the-world, accessible to circumspection. (*BT* 251; *SZ* 207)

We have been concerned with three conceptual innovations presented in *Being and Time*. One of these is Heidegger's hierarchy of non-Cartesian cognitive notions. At its base is understanding—the disclosure of a totality of social significance and the discovery within it of individual pieces of equipment by mastery of communal responsive practices. At the next level is deliberative interpretation by appropriation of the conditional significances implicit in the understanding of the ready-to-hand. Finally there is the discursive appropriation of the present-at-hand through assertion of sentences which in virtue of their social inference potentials explicitly thematize the significations one becomes aware of in interpretation. Second, we have seen how the category of presence-at-hand arises within and yet is distinct from the more fundamental category of readiness-to-hand. Third, in terms of the first two points it is clear that the ready-to-hand is first among equals among the categories because of the self-adjudicating nature of the social (*Mitdasein* in a world which is a totality of practical significance). Understanding in this way the basic ontological structure of Heidegger's account in Division One is the necessary preparation for understanding both his account of the individuation of Dasein and the institution of temporality by the personal appropriation of projects in Division Two, and his profound reading of that tradition of philosophy which has left us in such a mistaken position that "in general our understanding of Being is such that every entity is understood in the first instance as present-at-hand."[20]

11

Dasein, the Being That Thematizes

I. Background

Does the structure of Heidegger's account commit him to understanding Dasein as involving language in principle? I argue here that he is committed to the claim that the sort of linguistic assertional practice he calls "thematizing" is an essential feature of Dasein, and so that nothing could be Dasein unless it treats some things as occurrent (present-at-hand). To see why this would be an interesting and important result, it is necessary to rehearse some of the basic features that make Heidegger's approach distinctive and original. *Being and Time* can be understood as propounding a normative pragmatism. The explanatory strategy invoked by this expression comprises two distinct commitments. The first regards the relation between the normative and the factual realms; the second regards the relation between norms taking the explicit form of rules and norms taking the implicit form of proprieties of practice.

In each case the question is one of conceptual and explanatory priority. The philosophical tradition treats the factual as the basic form of the real and seeks to explain the normative by *adding* something, which might generically be called values. What is objectively real has a cloak of subjective values or significances thrown over it by its relation to human interests or desires.[1] By contrast, Heidegger treats as primitive a certain kind of social normative articulation and seeks to define the factual as a special case picked out by *subtracting* something, namely, certain kinds of relations to human projects. Again, the philosophical tradition treats norms as canonically codified in the form of explicit *rules* which determine what is correct by *saying* or describing what is correct. Each propriety of *practice*, the grasp of which consists in knowing *how* to do something correctly, is conceived as underwritten by a *principle*, the grasp of which consists in knowing *that* a particular sort of performance is correct. By contrast, Heidegger treats as primitive a certain kind of norm that is *implicit* in practice and seeks to define *explicit* rules, principles, and claims in terms of the practical proprieties of using them.

Heidegger sets out these commitments in the form of an account of the relations among three fundamental ontological categories, or more officially, regions of Being within which different sorts of entities are disclosed: Dasein, *Zuhandensein,* and *Vorhandensein.* Dasein is the kind of Being we ourselves have.[2] Although the task of the whole book is to lay out the basic makeup (*Grundverfassung*) of Dasein, two features may be singled out by way of introduction. First, Dasein is an essentially *social* sort of being. Heidegger's term for our sociality is *Mitsein,* or being-with.[3] Second, an essential structure of Dasein is that it always already finds itself in a *world.*[4] To say this is to say that the ontological categories of Dasein and *Zuhandensein* (availability) are internally related.[5] For apart from others whose way of being is also that of Dasein, the world consists of what is *zuhanden,* that is, ready-to-hand, or available. The available comprises what Heidegger calls equipment (*Zeug*)— things that are used or dealt with in social practices and so are thick with practical proprieties or significances that determine how it is appropriate to treat them. To call something available is to treat it as something that can be used correctly or incorrectly, according to proprieties implicit in practices instituted and pursued by Dasein. Hammers are a paradigm of a kind of entity that exhibits this sort of being: they are properly used in the practice of driving nails, although it is possible to use them as ballast or weapons.[6] The practical norms determining the correct way of using bits of equipment typically relate them to other bits of equipment—hammers to nails, nails to boards, tires to cars, cars to roads, and so on. The world is a holistic totality of such practical normative equipmental involvements.[7]

Vorhandensein (occurrence, presence-at-hand) is the realm of objective facts. It consists of objects that are merely present and of their matter-of-factual, nonnormative properties. Treating things as *vorhanden* is taking them to be what they are, independently of any proprieties of practice instituted by Dasein's activities. Thus occurrence is Heidegger's way of talking about what the philosophical tradition talked about under the heading of Reality. What is occurrent differs from what is available in that it is not made to be what it is by being caught up in normative social practices, which situate it with respect to Dasein's projects.[8]

In *Being and Time*, Heidegger's primary complaint against the tradition is that it gives ontological and explanatory pride of place to this category—attempting to understand and explain Dasein, the proprieties Dasein institutes by its social practices, and the equipmental roles defined by those practices in terms of what is merely occurrent.[9] This approach, he thinks, is wrongheaded and doomed to failure. The thought underlying this claim is that if norm-laden practices are taken for granted, it is possible to explain what it is to treat things as matters of fact, while if one starts with matters of fact, norms of all sorts will be unintelligible—construable only in terms of essentially subjective responses to facts.[10] What matters for the present story is how Heidegger pursues the direction of explanation that he endorses, rather than how he thinks the reverse direction can be seen to be defective.

As was already remarked, Heidegger is clear that there is no equipment without Dasein, and no Dasein without equipment. Dasein and *Zuhandensein* mutually presuppose each other as substructures of being-in-the-world. *Vorhandensein,* by contrast, is a derivative category, to be understood and explained in terms of the other two.[11] How is the occurrent derived from the other two sorts of being? This is a long story, for which only the barest sketch can be provided here. In outline, it goes like this: Some of the equipment that is available in the environing totality of equipmental involvements practically disclosed in the world is specifically *linguistic* equipment. In particular, one sort of equipment is *sentences,* used in practice to make *assertions* or claims. Heidegger calls using sentences as one does in the paradigm case of assertion *thematizing.*[12] The basic understanding of such sentences consists in being able to distinguish in practice between correct and incorrect uses, as with any sort of equipment. The proprieties of practice characteristic of sentence use in thematizing are of three fundamental sorts on Heidegger's account: noninferential uses in making perceptual reports, inferential uses (as premises and conclusions), and interpersonal communicative uses. Grasping the significance of the claims made by sentences consists in practical mastery of these kinds of proprieties of use. This is the practical knowing *how* in terms of which the capacity to thematize explicitly, knowing *that* something is the case, is to be explained.[13]

Ordinarily, Heidegger thinks, a thing is first disclosed to Dasein as available in terms of the practical proprieties governing what it would be correct to do with it. Even unfamiliar things first come into our world as equipment we do not know what to do with.[14] Responding to something as merely occurrent requires a certain sort of holding back from practical involvement.[15] Instead of treating the thing as available for various sorts of practical uses, one treats it as appropriately responded to *only* by making assertions about it.[16] This is a theoretical rather than a practical response, the difference being marked out by the fact that the assertional or judgmental responses are themselves available or serviceable[17] for formulating the upshot of perception, using as fodder for inferences, or for communicating to others. The assertions with which it is appropriate to respond to something perceptible do not depend on the particular practical projects that animate the activities of the assertor (though the practical inferences in which one goes on to use those assertions as premises may well so depend). The holding-back that underlies treating something as merely occurrent, the "just looking" at it, consists in mediating one's practical responses by a level of assertion, the practical proprieties of which swing free of particular practical projects. This is why "occurrence . . . is the specialty of assertion" (*BT* 201; *SZ* 158).[18] It is in this way that know-how, practical mastery of which constitutes specifically linguistic competence, distances objects and states of affairs from the projects of Dasein by responding to them (for instance, perceptually). Knowing-that is founded on knowing-how.

A special case of the thematizing use of sentences is to state *rules*. With respect to this pragmatic commitment to the explanatory priority of norms implicit in practice over those explicit in rules, Heidegger belongs in a box with the later Wittgenstein. For in the *Investigations,* Wittgenstein argues that explicit rules cannot be the only form taken by norms, on the basis of the regress that is revealed when it is noticed that following a rule is itself something that can be done correctly or incorrectly. Calling a rule that governs the application of another rule an "interpretation," Wittgenstein argues that "there must be some way of following a rule that does not consist in an interpretation, but in following or going against it in practice."[19] The possibility of making norms explicit in the form of rules, which determine what is correct and incorrect by *saying* what does and does not qualify, depends on an underlying possibility of discriminating norms implicit in the practice of *doing* things correctly and incorrectly and responding to such performances nonlinguistically *as* correct and incorrect. Without such practical abilities, rules could not be applied. It cannot be interpretation (in this sense) all the way down.[20]

These, then, are the two components of Heidegger's normative pragmatism: first, understanding the factual in terms of the normative (via the norms governing the use of assertions, which are the only appropriate response to the occurrent as such); and second, understanding government by norms explicit in the form of propositionally statable rules in terms of government by norms implicit in the form of skillful practical discriminations of appropriate and inappropriate performances (in particular, applications to individual unrepeatable cases of the repeatable sentences that express general rules). The first is understanding *Vorhandensein* in terms of *Zuhandensein,* and the second is understanding *Zuhandensein* as in the first instance a matter of social practice rather than individual propositionally contentful cognition or intellectual achievement ("thematizing"). It is natural to understand these priority claims in terms of a "layer cake" model, according to which there could be Dasein and *Zuhandensein* without *Vorhandensein,* which arises from them only if Dasein adopts certain optional practices and practical attitudes, involving the use of certain sorts of sophisticated equipment, namely, sentences used to make claims and state rules. This is an understanding according to which the claim that "assertion is derived from interpretation and understanding" (*BT* 203; *SZ* 160) invokes derivation in a sense implying the *autonomy* of the underlying layer of "circumspective" (that is, practical) acknowledgments of proprieties in dealing with equipment. The level of assertions, and so of adopting the practical attitude of treating things as occurrent, looks like an optional superstructure, which might be erected on top of human existence (Dasein) and the being of equipment (*Zuhandensein*), but which equally well might not be found along with them.[21] In answering the fundamental question *"By what existential-ontological modifications does assertion arise from circumspective interpretation?"* (*BT* 200; *SZ* 157), Heidegger apparently says nothing that would indicate that, given the sort of being from which they are derived, assertion and presentness *must* arise. It would seem possible, and in the spirit of the enterprise, to suppose that one could coherently take some community to consist of entities with Dasein's kind of being, instituting by their practices a world of *zuhanden* equipment, while not supposing that they can talk, and do so while denying that they treat anything as *vorhanden.* On this reading, Heidegger portrays an autonomous, preconceptual, prepropositional, prelinguistic level of intentionality—namely, practical, skill-laden, norm-governed directedness toward equipment treated as available. As being-in-the-world, Dasein can already be discerned at this level. It may or may not be the case for any particular community of existing entities, entities whose way of being is that of Dasein, that on this practical base a theoretical superstructure of conceptual, propositional, linguistic, or in Heidegger's terminology thematic intentionality is erected.

Those interpreters of *Being and Time* who take it to be a pragmatist work in something like the dual sense delineated above, most prominently Dreyfus, Haugeland, and Okrent, typically understand the priority Heidegger accords to practical over propositional intentionality according to this "layer cake" model.[22] It is the thesis of this essay that application of this model of the priority doctrine is a mistake. Heidegger is committed to the claim that there is no Dasein (and hence no *Zuhandensein*) without language, without thematizing, without treating things as *vorhanden*. As the passage quoted in the title indicates, Dasein is the being (entity) that thematizes. Another way of putting this claim is to say that the capacity to treat things as extant or occurrent is an *Existentiale,* a permanent and constitutive possibility of Dasein. This is not to say that there cannot be norms implicit in social practices without norms explicit in the form of rules, which determine what is correct by saying or describing what is correct and, hence, without linguistic practices including assertion. It is to say that such a prelinguistic community would not count as Dasein. An instructive case in point is Haugeland's rich and original rendering of the norms implicit in the practices that institute equipment. He explains these norms in terms of social constellations of dispositions that qualify as "conformist." He asks us to imagine under this heading creatures who not only conform their behavior to that of other community members in the sense of imitating one another, and so tend to act alike (normally in the sense of typically) in similar circumstances, but also sanction one another's performances, positively and negatively reinforcing responses to stimuli so as to make it more likely that future behavior will conform to the emergent standards.

The clusters that coalesce can be called "norms" (and not just groups or types) precisely because they are generated and maintained by censoriousness; the censure attendant on deviation automatically gives the standards (the extant clusters) a de facto normative force (Haugeland, "Heidegger," 16).

It is in terms of norms implicit in social practice in this sense that he explains the proprieties constitutive of equipment and the constitution of the norm-governed community as the anyone (*das Man*), the conforming individual creatures. Dasein is then identified with this community and any normative structures instituted by it (Haugeland, "Heidegger," 19). My thesis is that although such an account is no doubt of crucial importance in understanding how Heidegger approaches intentionality,[23] it cannot be correct as an account of what Dasein and *Zuhandensein* consist in. For this account can be told about pre- or nonlinguistic creatures, as exemplifying an autonomous level of functioning on which the capacity for linguistic practice is causally and conceptually parasitic. And, it will be argued, Heidegger is committed to the claim that anything that does not have language and does not make assertions (and therefore does not treat things as *vorhanden*) cannot qualify as Dasein, and so cannot institute proprieties that qualify as a world of *Zuhandensein*.[24]

Why not say that one can give a separable account of an autonomous level of practice that, for instance, Dasein's being-in-a-world of equipment consists in, hoping later to add those features required to explain other characteristics of Dasein, for instance, its Being being an issue for it, or care, which need not be exhibited at the base level? Such an approach is precluded on basic methodological grounds. Heidegger claims that in his discussion of Dasein he is doing not just anthropology but fundamental ontology. Part of the cash value of this claim must be that he is not merely offering us a set of descriptions, in however rich a vocabulary, which all just happen to be true of us. Rather, his characterizations form a tightly interlocked set of features, no one of which could be exhibited without all the others. When he tells us that Dasein is being-in-the-world, Dasein is its disclosedness, and that Dasein is the entity whose Being is an issue for it,[25] for instance, part of the specifically *onto-logical* force of these claims, what raises them above the merely ontic force of anthropological observations or generalizations, is their internal relation. In effect the commitment being undertaken is that anything that is correctly specified as worlded must therefore also be identified with its disclosedness, and must count as having its Being as an issue for it, that nothing whose Being is an issue for it could fail to be worlded or to be its disclosedness, and so on. The *Existentiale* of Dasein come as a package. Thus to claim that entities could exhibit some of these ways of being without others is to claim that there is no such thing as Dasein, that Heidegger has gotten it wrong. It is by that same token to cast doubt on one's interpretation of what is required to count as, for example, worlded, or structured by care, relative to an alternate reading that does not permit these characteristics of Dasein's basic constitution to fall apart from one another. If, I argue here, it can be shown that assertional language is an essential structure of the basic constitution of Dasein, then it will follow that, for Heidegger, nothing can be worlded, and so treat things as equipment available unless it can also treat things as objectively occurrent.

II. Direct Arguments for Dasein's Having *Sprache*

The basic argument to be presented can be put schematically in four steps:

1. There can be no Dasein without *Rede* (discourse).
2. There can be no *Rede* without *Gerede* (idle talk).
3. There can be no *Gerede* without *Sprache* (language).
4. There can be no *Sprache* without *Aussage* (assertion).

This argument will then be situated within a larger frame, which argues more generally that

5. There can be no Dasein without *Verfallen* (falling).

Verfallen exhibits three characteristic substructures, *Gerede*, *Neugier* (curiosity), and *Zweideutigkeit* (ambiguity). *Gerede* is dealt with in the first argument.

To complete the framing argument, it is argued that

6. There can be no *Neugier* without *Aussage*.
7. There can be no *Zweideutigkeit* without *Aussage*.

The conclusion is that

8. There can be no Dasein without *Aussage*.

And so:

9. There can be no Dasein that cannot treat things as *vorhanden*.

Each of these steps requires explanation and justification.

Assuming for the moment that such justifications can be given, the architectonic commitments attributed by these premises will require rejection of the "layer cake" model of the conceptual priority of the way of being of the available over that of the occurrent, in view of the untenability of the picture of an autonomous stratum of practice in which entities already count as having Dasein's characteristic being and as operating amidst a world of equipment but are not yet taken to be able to talk. The priority thesis must then be understood to address the order of explanation—one cannot understand *Vorhandensein* unless one first understands *Zuhandensein*. The reason for this explanatory priority is that indicated above: to treat something as merely occurrent is to treat it as only appropriately responded to by making the sorts of judgments about it that are expressed by assertions (including the judgments that are the output of perception).[26] But such assertions are a kind of equipment, something available, whose use must be understood as governed by proprieties implicit in practice—paradigmatically intrapersonal inference and interpersonal communication. By contrast, the proprieties of practice that institute prelinguistic equipment can be understood in advance of any understanding of specifically linguistic equipment. This can be true even though, as will be argued, unless such prelinguistic proprieties of practice are accompanied by linguistic ones, they will not count as instituting a world, and the instituting entities will not count as having the sort of being characteristic of Dasein.

III. No Dasein without *Rede*

Dasein, we are told, is its disclosedness (*BT* 171; *SZ* 133).[27] "Disclosedness" is Heidegger's term for, roughly, Dasein's ontological access to any entity's sort of Being. (His term for merely ontic access to entities, as opposed to their Being, is "discovery.") The first thing we are told about the structure of disclosedness is that "the fundamental *existentialia* which constitute the being of the 'there' [Dasein], the disclosedness of being-in-the-world, are situatedness [*Befindlichkeit*] and understanding [*Verstehen*]" (*BT* 203; *SZ* 160). '*Existentiale*' is a term Heidegger uses for structures of Dasein's being without which it would not qualify as Dasein. The list of *existentialia* associated with Dasein's disclosedness is given in different forms in different places (more will be said about the other forms later). Almost immediately, though, we are told, with emphasis, that "discourse [*Rede*] is equiprimordial [*existenzial gleich-*

ursprünglich] with situatedness and understanding" (*BT* 203; *SZ* 161). To say this is to say that one cannot have *Befindlichkeit* or *Verstehen* without *Rede*. Since the former are *existentialia*, so is the latter.[28] Thus there is no Dasein without *Rede*.

This much is not in any way a controversial claim. But if it is not controversial that *Rede* is part of the basic constitution of Dasein, then can it not immediately be concluded that language is? After all, '*Rede*' is the ordinary German word for discourse, for telling, for articulating in language. This conclusion is not immediate, however, for Heidegger uses '*Rede*' as a technical term, which at least includes, and is often taken to be limited to, various kinds of prelinguistic articulation. Haugeland, for instance, offers the following definition:

> Telling (Rede) is the articulation of significance or intelligibility, both in the sense of separating or carving up, and in the sense of expressing in words. The carving up is . . . an essential public or shared way of distinguishing determinate entities in determinate regards. ("Dasein's Disclosedness," 64)

Thus *Rede* is the articulation by which a shared world of equipment is instituted by social practice. The gloss, Haugeland suggests, on this is that the basic notion is that of telling, in the sense of distinguishing in practice those performances that are appropriate or in accord with implicit norms from those that are not: "The ur-phenomenon of telling is telling whether behavior does or does not accord with the common norms—in effect telling right from wrong" ("Dasein's Disclosedness," 65). One important consequence of this pragmatic reading of '*Rede*', as he goes on to point out, is that "such telling would indeed be the originary articulation of significance, and would, at the same time, be fundamental to the possibility of correctness—for example of assertions." This is an important benefit of the pragmatic interpretation, because Heidegger emphasizes (invoking his sense of "interpretation" as "circumspective," practical, prelinguistic know-how), "Discourse is the articulation of intelligibility. Therefore it underlies both interpretation and assertion" (*BT* 204; *SZ* 161), and "we have seen that assertion is derived from interpretation, and is an extreme case of it . . . *The existential-ontological foundation of language is discourse or talk* [*Rede*]" (*BT* 203; *SZ* 160–161). Here again, then, we see expressions of the priority thesis concerning the grounding of linguistic practice in prelinguistic know-how, which it is tempting to interpret as commitments to the possibility of an autonomous level of practical circumspective interpretation by Dasein of equipment making up a world of *Zuhandensein*.

Again, the claim to be defended here by contrast is that although such an autonomous level of practice is no doubt possible—talking does not develop ex nihilo—it would not be proper to describe it in Heidegger's terminology as characterized by Dasein, being-in-the-world, *Zuhandensein*, or, the presently relevant point, as articulated by *Rede*. Heidegger says that "the way in which discourse [*Rede*] gets expressed is language [*Sprache*]" (*BT* 204; *SZ* 161). This is compatible with the view that *Rede* comes in two forms, an implicit form in which it consists in practically discriminating the proprieties that institute a world and an optional, derivative form in which those proprieties can be explicitly expressed and discussed. The question is whether it is optional that the articulation that is *Rede* be expressed. The claim that it *must* be explicitly expressed can be understood in either a local or a global sense. In the local sense, the claim would be that no particular practical articulation or discrimination of proprieties could count as discursive (*redend*) unless *it* was expressed explicitly, that is, in language. In the global sense, the claim would be that no practical articulation or discrimination of proprieties could count as discursive unless *some* such articulations or discriminations are expressed explicitly in language. The stronger local claim would seem to be incompatible with any version of the priority thesis. It is clear that not all "articulation of intelligibility according to significations" (the definition of *Rede*) takes the form of explicit assertions.[29] In any case, it is the weaker, global claim that is to be defended here. Heidegger does seem to say that it is not optional that *Rede* be expressed in this global sense:

> Because discourse [*Rede*] is constitutive for the being of the there (that is, for situatedness and understanding), while "Dasein" means Being-in-the-world, Dasein as discursive Being-in has already expressed itself. Dasein has language. Man shows himself as the entity which talks. This does not signify that the possibility of vocal utterance is peculiar to him, but that he is the entity which is such as to discover the world and Dasein itself. (*BT* 208; *SZ* 165)

Recall the previous argument to the effect that Heidegger should be telling us not about characteristics that Dasein just happens to have, ontic features of some interesting entities, but only about definitive, internally related ontological characteristics. Since it is not optional that Dasein be discursive being-in, it is not optional that it express itself, and so it is not optional that it have language.

Another direct argument is available for the conclusion that there is no *Rede* without *Sprache*. This has to do with the role of explicit expressions of the articulations comprising *Rede* in *communication,*[30] the role of such communication in being-with, and the role of being-with in being-in-the-world. The claim is that all of these are necessary features of Dasein. Here is the central passage:

> Discoursing or talking is the way in which we articulate "significantly" the intelligibility of Being-in-the-world. Being-with belongs to Being-in-the-world, which in every case maintains itself in some definite way of concernful Being-with-one-another. Such Being-with-one-another is discursive [*redend*] as assenting or refusing [*zu- und absagen*], as demanding, or warning, as pronouncing [*Aussprache*], consulting [*Rücksprache*], or interceding [*Fürsprache*], as "making assertions," and as talking in the way of "giving a talk" [*Redenhalten*]. (*BT* 204; *SZ* 161)

Every member of this list of paradigmatic ways in which being-with is articulated discursively is explicitly and essentially linguistic. Since being-with is not an optional feature of Dasein, but rather a fundamental characteristic of its *Grundverfassung*, and since *Rede* likewise has this status, the exclusively linguistic character of this botanization of modes of discursive being-with certainly suggests, though it falls short of demonstrating, that there can be no *Rede,* and therefore no Dasein, without *Sprache*.

IV. *Rede* and *Gerede*

The strongest argument, however, for the conclusion that there is no *Rede* (and therefore no Dasein) without *Sprache* is not a direct argument relying on passages such as these, but an indirect one. This proceeds in two steps: There is no *Rede* without *Gerede* (idle talk), and no *Gerede* without *Sprache*. These points will be addressed sequentially. *Gerede* is a special form of *Rede*: "Discourse, which belongs to the essential state of Dasein's Being and has a share in constituting Dasein's disclosedness, has the possibility of becoming idle talk" (*BT* 213; *SZ* 169). The first question is whether it is optional that this possibility be realized. Could entities qualify as articulating practical significances in the form of *Rede* if they never articulate them in the form of *Gerede*? Again it is important to distinguish two ways in which this question can be understood. It is clear that not every articulation according to significations takes the form of *Gerede*. Thus the stronger, local form of the claim that there is no *Rede* without *Gerede* does not hold—not every bit of *Rede* is a bit of *Gerede*. Nonetheless, it will be claimed that the weaker, global form of the dependence claim does hold—unless some articulations take the form of *Gerede*, none count as *Rede*—and so the creatures in question, although they might by their social practices institute norms that they implicitly acknowledge as governing their performances, would not count as Dasein.

What sort of modification of *Rede* is *Gerede*? The first point is that *Gerede* is just the *everyday (alltäglich)* form of *Rede*. "The expression 'idle talk' [*Gerede*] is not to be used here in a 'disparaging' signification . . . it signifies a positive phenomenon which constitutes the kind of Being of everyday Dasein's understanding and interpreting" (*BT* 211; *SZ* 167).[31] The initial question thus becomes whether it is optional that *Rede* sometimes appears in its everyday form. Heidegger says of *Gerede*:

> This everyday way in which things have been interpreted is one into which Dasein has grown in the first instance, with never a possibility of extrication. In it, out of it, and against it, all genuine understanding, interpreting, and communicating, all rediscovering and appropriating anew, are performed. (*BT* 213; *SZ* 169)

Thus *Gerede*, the everyday form of *Rede*, forms the background for the other forms. It is not an optional species but a fundamental one. The reason for this privileged status is that "idle talk is the kind of Being that belongs to Being-with-one-another itself" (*BT* 221; *SZ* 177). Being-with, of course, is itself not optional. It is a fundamental characteristic of Dasein's *Grundverfassung*.

These passages make it clear that there is no *Rede* (and therefore no Dasein) without its everyday form, *Gerede*. In order to see, however, that *Gerede* is an essentially *linguistic* phenomenon, it is necessary to look more closely at what idle talk is, as the everyday form in which significances are articulated. Its essence is, as the word suggests, *gossip*. Here is the central passage to be unpacked:

What is said-in-the-talk [*das Geredete*] as such, spreads in wider circles and takes on an authoritative character. Things are so because one says so. Idle talk is constituted by just such gossiping and passing the word along—a process by which its initial lack of grounds to stand on [*Bodenständigkeit*] becomes aggravated to complete groundlessness [*Bodenlosigkeit*]. (*BT* 212; *SZ* 168)

Gerede is fundamentally a structure of authority, a way in which justificatory grounds can be treated in practice. (This is one of many places where it can seem that Heidegger is sinning against his own precept that *Gerede* is not to be taken in a disparaging sense. This impression ought to be alleviated by the realization that, although Heidegger is far from recommending this structure of authority, he thinks that it provides the pervasive background against which alone it is possible to understand the possibility of more authentic justificatory structures.) *Gerede* consists in the thoughtless passing on of what is said-in-the-talk, *das Geredete*. Understanding what this means requires reverting to the fundamental structure of *Rede:*

The items constitutive for discourse are: what the discourse is about (what is talked about) [*das Worüber der Rede (das Beredete)*]; what is said-in-the-talk, as such [*das Geredete als solches*]; the communication [*die Mitteilung*]; and the making-known [*die Bekundung*]. (*BT* 206; *SZ* 162)

Only the first two of these, what is talked about and what is said-in-the-talk, *das Beredete* and *das Geredete,* matter here. The other two can be understood in terms of them, since communication is the passing along of *das Geredete,* and the making-known is the establishment of a relation to *das Beredete* by such passing along. What is said-in-the-talk and what is talked about are the two essential elements in the existence of specifically *linguistic* contents, two aspects of a distinctive kind of equipment, equipment employed in order to communicate and make-known.

Thus these elements have all been introduced before we ever hear about idle talk. What-is-said-in-the-talk is introduced, without use of that particular term, when we first hear about assertion, as the essence of the role assertion plays in communication:

As something communicated, that which has been put forward in the assertion is something that Others can "share" with the person making the assertion, even though the entity which he has pointed out and to which he has given a definite character is not close enough for them to grasp and see it. That which is put forward in the assertion is something which can be passed along in "further retelling." There is a widening of the range of that mutual sharing which sees.[32] (*BT* 197; *SZ* 155)

Again before we are introduced to *Gerede,* we hear about the other structural element and its relation to the first:

> Talking is talk about something [*Reden ist Rede über*]. What the discourse is about is a structural item that it necessarily possesses; for discourse helps to constitute the disclosedness of Being-in-the-world, and in its own structure it is modeled upon this basic state of Dasein. In any talk or discourse, there is something said-in-the-talk as such [*ein Geredetes als solches*] whenever one wishes, asks, or expresses oneself about something. In this "something said," discourse communicates. (*BT* 205; *SZ* 162)

It is possible to understand *Gerede* in terms of these two structural elements, *das Geredete* and *das Beredete. Gerede* is discourse that pays attention only to *das Geredete,* to what is said-in-the-talk, but not to what the talk is about:

> What is said-in-the-talk [*Geredeten*] gets understood; but what the talk is about is understood only approximately and superficially. We have the same thing in view, because it is in the same averageness that we have a common understanding of what is said. (*BT* 212; *SZ* 168)

It will emerge that for linguistic equipment genuinely to be in play, both structural elements of saying must in fact be present. Without them no genuine contents are instituted by the practice of using them to communicate, and so no knowledge or information is actually shared by passing them around. What is distinctive of *Gerede* is not that *das Beredete,* what is talked about, is absent, but rather that its crucial contribution to the authority structure distinctive of talking is not acknowledged by those who are nonetheless dependent on that structure.

To understand exactly what implicit presuppositions of linguistic practice *Gerede* fails to acknowledge, it is helpful to apply a model of the structure of authority that is distinctive of specifically linguistic equipment.[33] Declarative sentences, which are equipment for asserting, are governed by two different dimensions of authority, one corresponding to their use in *communication,* the other to their use in *inference.* These correspond to two different ways in which one can become entitled to the sort of propositionally articulated commitment that is expressed by an assertion. By the first mechanism, commitments can become shared, spreading from one individual to another, as the speaker who expresses an assertion communicates to and possibly infects an audience. In this way, entitlement to make a claim can be inherited by the consumer of an assertion from its producer. In such inheritance of entitlement by communication, the content of the commitment is preserved intact and merely transferred. This, however, is not the only way in which an individual can become entitled to a claim. It is also possible to justify a commitment inferentially by exhibiting it as a consequence of further premises to which one is committed and entitled. The particular content determines what follows from commitment to that content, and what that content follows from, what it justifies and what justifies it. That it is caught up in such inferences both as premise and as conclusion is what makes it a specifically *propositional* (or assertible) content at all. That it exhibits the particular inferential grounds and consequences that it does makes it the particular determinate content that it is—settling, for instance, what information it conveys, the significance that undertaking a commitment with that content would have for what else one is committed and entitled to. The first, or communicational, mechanism is interpersonal, intracontent inheritance of entitlement to a propositional commitment. The second, or inferential, mechanism is intrapersonal, intercontent inheritance of entitlement to a propositional commitment (since the contents of premises and conclusions will differ in any inference that is nontrivial in the sense of being available to do justificatory work). The functions performed by both mechanisms are essential to the use of sentences as equipment for expressing propositional commitments in the form of assertions. Without the articulation provided by proprieties governing the practice of inferring, including inferences from the commitments that agents find themselves with perceptually, sentences would not express determinate propositional contents at all. Without acknowledgment in practice of the propriety of inheriting entitlement to claims from the assertions of others, there would be no communication of information, and assertion would be socially idle, instituting no sort of equipment at all.

With this conceptual apparatus, it is possible to characterize straightforwardly the practical attitude Heidegger calls *Gerede*. *Gerede* consists in acknowledging only the communicative structure of authority and not the inferential. "What-is-said-in-the-talk" is passed along, but never grounded in "what-is-talked-about"—it does not have to answer to any justificatory demands beyond a communicational provenance. Those repeating a claim they overhear do not take personal responsibility for it, merely deferring to what "they" (*das Man*) say:

> The fact that something has been said groundlessly, and then gets passed along in further retelling, amounts to perverting the act of disclosing [*Erschliessen*] into an act of closing off [*Verschliessen*]. For what is said is always understood proximally as "saying" something— that is, an uncovering something. Thus, by its very nature, idle talk is a closing-off, since to go back to the ground of what is talked about is something which it leaves undone. (*BT* 213; *SZ* 169)

Thus the function of what is talked about, *das Beredete*, is to *ground* the *authority* of the contents that are communicated. Taking a claim back to its ground is justifying it in some way *other* than by appeal to what others say. It is taking responsibility for it oneself, justifying it by appeal to other claims, including but not limited to perceptually acquired ones, that the individual also takes responsibility for. *Gerede* is a practical stance that ignores such grounding in *das Beredete*, and cleaves only to *das Geredete*, ignoring grounding in favor of just passing things along. The trouble is that entitlement can be inherited from, and responsibility deferred to, another only if the other individual is entitled or can fulfill the justificatory responsibility implicit in making a claim. If everyone adopts the attitude of *Gerede*, and defers responsibility without accepting it, then all of the titles supposedly passed around by communicating are defective and empty. That is, in the words quoted above:

> What is said-in-the-talk [*das Geredete*] as such, spreads in wider circles and takes on an authoritative character. Things are so because one says so. Idle talk is constituted by just such gossiping and passing the word along—a process by which its initial lack of grounds to stand on [*Bodenständigkeit*] becomes aggravated to complete groundlessness [*Bodenlosigkeit*]. (*BT* 212; *SZ* 168)

Gerede is the everyday, inauthentic version of *Rede* precisely because of the failure to take personal responsibility that is its essence. To come into an authentic practical relation to one's commitments is to take on responsibility for justifying them, rather than deferring it or evading it by appeal to what everyone *(das Man)* says. One always already finds oneself "falling," that is, equipped with and constituted by a set of commitments one just finds oneself with, without in general being able to justify them by grounding them in what they are about. This is why the practice of *Gerede* is the background out of which every authentic claiming and justifying must arise and from which it must distinguish itself.[34] To undertake responsibility oneself is to acknowledge in practice a basic ontological feature of Dasein—that it comes in what Haugeland calls "units of accountability," or "primitive loci of accountability *(je meines)*": "Heidegger places this structure, which he calls 'in-each-case-mineness' *(Jemeinigkeit)*, among Dasein's most fundamental characteristics" (Haugeland, "Heidegger," 21, 24).[35] *Gerede* precisely refuses to assign accountability for the propriety of a claim to any particular individual, deferring demands for justification instead to the general practice, appealing to "what one says" or "what is said." In fact, however, the public social practice of communicating and the undertaking of individual responsibility presuppose and complement each other. Unless both were always already in play, no genuinely contentful claims (or equipment for asserting and informing) would be instituted at all. *Gerede* exclusively acknowledges the contribution of the public communicative dimension while ignoring that of *Jemeinigkeit* (here the individual undertaking of justificatory responsibility). One thing lost when the dual structure of authority characteristic of claiming is collapsed by *Gerede* into a single dimension is *experience* (in something like Hegel's sense), in which claims and concepts are winnowed and groomed as the commitments one undertakes responsibility for oneself (including those one finds oneself with perceptually, and their inferential consequences) are confronted by those one would be entitled to pick up from the assertions of others. It is the interplay of these two dimensions of authority that makes it possible for what it is correct to say to exhibit a kind of independence both from what I happen to be committed to and from what others happen to be saying. This is answering to the way the objects are, and, in this sense, being about objects. This *objectivity* is what Heidegger talks about as assertions representing things as occurrent, as factual and constraining in a different way from the social proprieties of practice that institute equipment, by settling a common way in which one uses (that is, ought to use) a hammer.[36]

It should be clear at this point that *Gerede* is a thoroughly *linguistic* phenomenon, indeed a specifically *assertional* one. The concept of gos-

sip cannot be made sense of in prelinguistic terms. The distinction between communication and inference as two structures of authority—
passing along what is said-in-the-talk *(das Geredete)*, and taking individual responsibility for grounding what is said in what the talk is about
(das Beredete)—defines equipment for making and communicating
propositionally contentful *claims*. Indeed, the specific practical failure to
comprehend this dual structure of authority that Heidegger identifies
with *Gerede* (focusing on *das Geredete* to the exclusion of *das Beredete*)
amounts to misunderstanding the distinctly linguistic assertional equipment employed in expressing and communicating a discursive articulation of implicit significances by assimilating it to ordinary equipment
such as hammers. The proprieties concerning the latter are exhausted by
how one uses a hammer—there is only "what one does with hammers,"
in the sense of how it is appropriate for anyone to use a hammer. The
public proprieties one picks up from others are all there is to such
nonlinguistic equipment; if one uses hammers as others do, then one
uses them correctly. *Gerede* fails to appreciate how the dual structure of
authority governing the use of equipment for making assertions differs
from the unidimensional structure governing the use of prelinguistic
equipment. Thus *Gerede* is a linguistic phenomenon involving the use of
assertions. Since it has already been argued that there is no *Rede* without
Gerede (in the global rather than the local sense), and no Dasein without
Rede, it follows that to take something as exhibiting the kind of being
Heidegger calls Dasein is to take it to be a linguistic entity, one that can
make assertions, and so one that can treat things as occurrent.

V. Falling: *Gerede, Neugier, Zweideutigkeit*

This argument concerning the linguistic and assertional nature of
Gerede, the matrix of everydayness out of which the expression of other
forms of the articulation of intelligibility must arise, can be confirmed
and extended by considering it in the larger framework in which the discussion of *Gerede* occurs. Recorded at the close of the sections of Division One that are being discussed, Heidegger offers the following summary:

> Our theme has been the ontological constitution of the disclosedness
> which essentially belongs to Dasein. The Being of that disclosedness is

constituted by situatedness [*Befindlichkeit*], understanding [*Verstehen*], and discourse [*Rede*]. Its everyday kind of being is characterized by idle talk [*Gerede*], curiosity [*Neugier*], and ambiguity [*Zweideutigkeit*]. These show us the movement of falling [*Verfallen*].[37] (*BT* 224, translation revised; *SZ* 180)

Falling is the everyday form of disclosedness, and the relation between *Gerede* and *Rede* is simply a special case of the relation between falling and disclosedness. As we saw that, in the particular case, there is no *Rede* without *Gerede* (in the global rather than the local sense), so, in the general case, there is no disclosedness without falling. "Being-in-the-world is always fallen" (*BT* 225; *SZ* 181). As we saw that in the particular case, *Gerede* is a thoroughly linguistic phenomenon—depending on the use of sentences as equipment for communication by assertion—so is it in the general case for the other forms of everyday disclosedness: curiosity and ambiguity.

Consider first curiosity, which translates *Neugier,* literally "greed for what is new." It is associated with a "tendency just to perceive" (*BT* 216; *SZ* 172) and is introduced as the everyday form of understanding (just as *Gerede* is the everyday form of *Rede):*

> In our analysis of understanding [*Verstehen*] and of the disclosedness of the "there" in general, we have . . . designated the disclosedness of being-in as Dasein's clearing, in which it first becomes possible to have something like sight. Our conception of "sight" has been gained by looking at the basic kind of disclosure which is characteristic of Dasein—namely, understanding. The basic state of sight shows itself in a peculiar tendency-of-Being which belongs to everydayness—the tendency towards "seeing." We designate this tendency by the term "curiosity" [*Neugier*], which characteristically is not confined to seeing, but expresses the tendency towards a peculiar way of letting the world be encountered by us in perception. (*BT* 214; *SZ* 170)

Three features of perception are of interest here. First, merely perceiving involves bracketing one's practical interests and concerns with proprieties of action. Second, this bracketing is accomplished by making claims—the output of perception for Heidegger is an assertion. As has been pointed out, assertions are available as equipment for inference, both practical and theoretical. That is, one responds appropriately to assertions as such by drawing conclusions from them, using them to justify either nonsentential performances or further assertions. But their appropriateness as responses to an observable situation are not hostage to any particular practical project. Third, responding to things perceptually, by making noninferential reports (which are themselves then available for further inferences), is treating them as occurrent. We find all three themes combined in an earlier passage dealing with perception:

> In this kind of "dwelling" as a holding-oneself-back from any manipulation or utilization, the perception of the occurrent is consummated. Perception is consummated when one addresses oneself to something as something and discusses it as such. What is thus perceived and made determinate can be expressed in propositions, and can be retained and preserved as what has thus been asserted. (*BT* 89; *SZ* 62)

Adopting the attitude of perceiving can be done authentically, when the ultimate concern is with understanding, or it can be inauthentic, a form of falling, as curiosity, when the assertions it results in are employed only in a kind of inferential play. (In the discussion of ambiguity below, this sort of inferential play will be called "surmising" [*ahnen*]).

> When curiosity has become free, however, it concerns itself with seeing, not in order to understand what is seen . . . but just in order to see it. It seeks novelty only in order to leap from it anew to another novelty. It concerns itself with a kind of knowing, but just in order to have known. (*BT* 216–217; *SZ* 172)

It should be clear that curiosity, no less than *Gerede,* is, for Heidegger, a phenomenon that presupposes language, specifically assertional language, and so the capacity to treat things as occurrent. As a form of falling, it amounts to an inauthentic way of treating things as occurrent. It contrasts with science, which is an authentic way of understanding things as merely present.[38] Each of these depends on the possibility of responding to things by making claims about them.

The third form of fallen disclosedness, ambiguity, is equally a linguistic affair. By this term Heidegger refers to a way of talking about things that both evades any genuine search for understanding and separates itself in principle from the possibility of action. Ambiguity is a kind of *speaking,* which substitutes for actual understanding:

> When, in our everyday being-with-one-another, we encounter the sort of thing which is accessible to everyone, and about which anyone

can say anything, it soon becomes impossible to decide what is disclosed in a genuine understanding, and what is not. This ambiguity [*Zweideutigkeit*] extends not only to the world, but just as much to Being-with-one-another as such, and even to Dasein's Being towards itself. Everything looks as if it were genuinely understood, genuinely taken hold of, genuinely spoken, though at bottom it is not. (*BT* 217; *SZ* 173)

Falling into social practices embodying ambiguity involves holding back from action in a stronger sense than merely making assertions does. Indeed, the practices instituting ambiguity demand that one refuse to commit oneself to assertions. For these can be used as premises for inferences, including the practical inferences whose conclusions are actions and commitments to act. Instead, one merely *entertains* claim contents, employing them only in *surmises:*

Even supposing that what "they" have surmised and scented out should someday be actually translated into deeds, ambiguity has already taken care that interest in what has been realized will promptly die away. Indeed, this interest persists, in a kind of curiosity and idle talk, only so long as there is a possibility of a non-committal just-surmising-with-someone-else. When confronted with the carrying-through of what "they" have surmised together, idle talk readily establishes that "they" "could have done that too." In the end, idle talk is even indignant that what it has surmised and constantly demanded now actually happens. In that case, indeed, the opportunity to keep on surmising has been snatched away. In the ambiguity of the way things have been publicly interpreted, talking about things ahead of the game and making surmises about them curiously, gets passed off as what is really happening, while taking action and carrying something through get stamped as something merely subsequent and unimportant. (*BT* 218; *SZ* 174)

The cash value of this is that the claim contents are employed only in *hypothetical* reasoning—reasoning of the "what if" sort. Formally this means that they appear not as propositions with assertional force, to which the speaker is undertaking a commitment, but only as embedded as the unasserted antecedents of asserted conditionals. The claim contents that appear thus embedded, however, acquire their contents from their assertional use. In particular, one must be able to make actual inferences using an assertion as a premise in order to be able to use a conditional in which that same content appears unasserted. For the conditional merely makes explicit, in the form of a claim, what is implicit in the actual performing of an inference. The possibility of merely surmising is thus a sophisticated, latecoming possibility, one that is built on and depends on the capacity to take responsibility for ordinary assertions, which are available, as mere surmises are not, for employment in practical inferences leading to action. The practical mistake underlying falling as ambiguity consists in treating this parasitic form of discourse as if it were autonomous, a game one could play though one played no other.

Thus all of *Gerede, Neugier,* and *Zweideutigkeit* are for Heidegger essentially linguistic phenomena—further, ones that depend on the capacity to make assertions, and so to treat things as occurrent. These are the essential substructures of *Verfallen,* which is an *existentiale* of Dasein. Specifically, they are the fallen forms of Dasein's disclosedness, and Dasein is its disclosedness. Thus there is no Dasein which does not fall into these practices, and hence no Dasein that cannot and does not make assertions and treat things as occurrent.

The widespread interpretive impression to the contrary among readers of *Being and Time* is the result of misunderstanding three sorts of passages. The first sort asserts the ontological priority of *Zuhandensein* over *Vorhandensein.* These passages are to be understood in terms of explanatory priority—that assertion is to be understood as a kind of equipment (assertions are something available[39] (BT 267; SZ 224)), while equipment is not to be understood in terms of matter-of-factual presence plus something. This does not entail that it is coherent to describe a situation in which Dasein has the capacity to treat things as *zuhanden* and not to treat things as *vorhanden.* The second sort of passage insists that there can be cases of circumspective understanding, and even interpretation, which do not take the form of assertion, or it makes the same sort of claim of priority for interpretation over assertion.[40] Here it is necessary to keep in mind the distinction between local independence—it must be admitted that not all cases of interpretation are cases of assertion—and the global claim that the *capacity* to interpret could exist without being accompanied by the *capacity* to assert. These passages do not support the stronger, global claim, which is the one being denied here. Also, it is not denied that creatures that do not qualify as Dasein, because they do not have *Rede, Gerede,* and so on, might nonetheless have practices that institute something a lot like equipment and do something a lot like interpreting according to it. It is claimed that such creatures would not qualify as Dasein, and so, given the package deal that Heidegger's ontological claims involve, that what they institute cannot qualify as *Zuhandensein*, and what they are doing is not strictly interpreting. Finally, there are passages that point out that there is more to talking than asserting—that not all *Sprache* is *Aussage*, because there is also wishing, commanding, and so on.[41] Again, however, these passages do not speak against the global claim that one could not have the capacity to do these things unless one also had the capacity to assert, though of course not all instances of exercising the one capacity are instances of exercising the other.

The conclusion, then, is that when Heidegger talks about Dasein, he is talking about a kind of being that essentially involves the capacity to use language. More particularly, it essentially involves the capacity to use assertional language, that is, to make claims whose correctness as claims does not depend on the particular projects of those who make them. Thus it essentially involves the capacity to treat things as occurrent. Heidegger is indeed a normative pragmatist in the sense of the two theses stated at the opening of this chapter. But the sort of entity about which he is such a pragmatist is, as the passage quoted in the title puts it, "Dasein, the being (entity) that thematizes."

12

The Centrality of Sellars's
Two-Ply Account of Observation to the
Arguments of "Empiricism
and the Philosophy of Mind"

"Empiricism and the Philosophy of Mind" is one of the great works of twentieth-century philosophy. It is rich, deep, and revolutionary in its consequences. It cannot, however, be ranked among the most *perspicuous* of philosophical writings. Although it is fairly easy to discern its general tenor and tendency, the convoluted and digressive order of exposition pursued in the essay has obscured for many readers the exact outlines of such a fundamental concept as _givenness_—with the result that few could at the end of their reading accurately trace its boundaries and say what all its species have in common, being obliged instead to content themselves with being able to recognize some of its exemplary instances. Again, I think that partly for this reason, readers of "EPM" seldom realize just how radical is its critique of empiricism—just how much of traditional empiricist ways of thinking must be rejected if Sellars's arguments are accepted. And if the full extent of the work's conclusions is hard to appreciate, all the more difficult is it to follow its argumentative path through all its turnings. In what follows my aim is to lay out one basic idea of Sellars's, which I see as underlying three of the most important arguments he deploys along the way to his conclusions. My concern here will be not in how those arguments contribute to his overall enterprise, but rather in how they are rooted in a common thought. Sellars does not make this basic idea as explicit as one would like, and does not stop along the way to observe how each of the three individual arguments depends on it. But if I am right, we will understand the essay better by being able to identify and individuate this thread in the tapestry.

The master idea I want to start with is Sellars's understanding of observational capacities: the ability to make noninferential reports of, or to form perceptual judgments concerning, perceptible facts. My claim is that he treats them as the product of two distinguishable sorts of abilities: the capacity reliably to discriminate behaviorally between different sorts of stimuli, and the capacity to take up a position in the game of giving and asking for reasons. The three central strategic moves in the essay that I seek to understand in terms of that two-factor approach to observation are, first, the way he dissolves a particular cartesian temptation by offering a novel account of the expressive function of 'looks' talk; second, his rationalist account of the acquisition of empirical concepts; and third, his account of how theoretical concepts can come to have observational uses.

I. Sellars's Two-Ply Account of Observation

If we strip empiricism down to its core, we might identify it with the insight that knowledge of the empirical world depends essentially on the capacity of knowing organisms to respond differentially to distinct environing stimuli. I call this claim *basic,* or "stripped down" empiricism; it could equally well be called the *trivial* thesis of empiricism.[1] Surely no rationalist or idealist has ever denied *this* claim. While differential responsiveness is obviously a necessary condition for empirical knowledge, it is clearly nothing like a sufficient condition. A chunk of iron responds differentially to stimuli, for instance, by rusting in some environments and not in others. To that extent, it can be construed as *classifying* its environments, taking or treating them as being of one of two kinds. In the same way, as Hegel says, an animal takes something as food by "falling to without further ado and eating it up."[2] But this sort of classificatory taking something *as* something should not yet be classed as a *cognitive* matter, on pain of losing sight of the fundamental ways in which genuine observationally acquired knowledge differs from what is exhibited by merely irritable devices such as thermostats and land mines.

A parrot could be trained to respond to the visible presence of red things by uttering the noise "That's red." We might suppose that it is disposed to produce this performance under just the same circumstances in which a genuine observer and reporter of red things is disposed to produce a physically similar performance. There is an important respect in which the parrot and the observer are alike. We could call what they share a *reliable differential responsive disposition* (which I will sometimes shorten to "RDRD"). RDRDs are the first element in Sellars's two-ply account of observational knowledge. At least in the basic case, they are characterizable in a naturalistic, physicalistic vocabulary.[3] The concept of an RDRD is meant to capture the capacity we genuine knowers share with artifacts and merely sentient creatures such as parrots that the basic thesis of empiricism insists is a necessary condition of empirical knowledge.

The second element of Sellars's two-ply account of observational knowledge is meant to distinguish possessors of genuine observational belief and knowledge from merely reliable differential responders. What is the crucial difference between the red-discriminating parrot and the genuine observer of red things? It is the difference between *sentience* and *sapience*. For Sellars's purposes in "EPM," the difference between merely differentially responding artifacts and genuinely sentient organisms does not make an essential cognitive or epistemological difference. *All* we need pay attention to in them is their exercising of reliable differential responsive dispositions. But he is very concerned with what distinguishes both of these sorts of things from genuine observers. His thought is that the difference that makes a difference is that candidates for observational knowledge do not just have reliable dispositions to respond differentially to stimuli by *making noises,* but have reliable dispositions to respond differentially to those stimuli by *applying concepts.* The genuine observer responds to visible red things by coming to believe, claiming, or reporting *that* there is something red. Sapient awareness differs from awareness in the sense of mere differential responsiveness (the sort exhibited by any organism or device that can, for instance, be said in the full sense to be capable of avoiding obstacles) in that the sapient being responsively classifies the stimuli as falling under concepts, as being of some conceptually articulated kind.

It is obvious that everything turns on how one goes on to understand concept application or the conceptual articulation of responses. For Sellars, it is a linguistic affair: grasping a concept is mastering the use of a word. Then we must ask what makes something a use of a word, in the sense relevant to the application of concepts. Sellars's answer is that for the response reliably differentially elicited by the visible pres-

ence of a perceptible state of affairs to count as the application of a concept, for it to be properly characterized as a reporting or coming to believe *that* such-and-such is the case, is for it to be the making of a certain
kind of move or the taking up of a certain kind of position in a game of
giving and asking for reasons. It must be committing oneself to a content that can both serve as and stand in need of *reasons,* that is, that can
play the role both of premise and of conclusion in *inferences.* The observer's response is conceptually contentful just insofar as it occupies a
node in a web of inferential relations.

What the parrot lacks is a *conceptual understanding* of its response.
That is why it is just making noise. Its response means nothing to the
parrot—though it may mean something to us, who *can* make inferences
from it, in the way we do from changes in the states of measuring instruments. The parrot does not treat red as entailing colored, as entailed by
scarlet, as incompatible with green, and so on. And because it does not,
uttering the noise "red" is not, for the parrot, the adopting of a stance
that can serve as a reason committing or entitling it to adopt other
stances, and potentially in need of reasons that might be supplied by still
further such stances. By contrast, the observer's utterance of "That's red"
is making a move, adopting a position, in a game of giving and asking for
reasons. And the observer's grasp of the conceptual content expressed by
her utterance consists in her practical mastery of its significance in that
game: her knowing (in the sense of being able practically to discriminate, a kind of knowing *how*) what follows from her claim and what it
follows from, what would be evidence for it and what is incompatible
with it.

Although Sellars does not carefully distinguish them, two different
strands can be discerned within this second element of his account. First
is the idea that for performances (whether noninferentially elicited responses or not) to count as *claims,* and so as expressions of *beliefs* or
judgments, as candidates for *knowledge,* they must be in what he calls
"the dimension of endorsement."[4] This is to say that they must have a
certain sort of pragmatic significance or force: they must express the endorsement of some content by the candidate knower. They must be the
adoption of a certain kind of normative stance: the undertaking of a
commitment. Second, that the commitment is a *cognitive* commitment,
the endorsement of a *conceptual content,* is to be understood in terms of
its *inferential* articulation, its place in the "space of reasons," its being a

move in the "game of giving and asking for reasons."[5] This is to say at least that in making a claim one commits oneself to its suitability as a premise from which conclusions can be drawn, a commitment whose entitlement is always at least potentially liable to demands for vindication by the exhibition of other claims that can serve as reasons for it.

This two-factor account of perceptual judgments (claims to observational knowledge) is a version of a broadly kantian strategy: insisting on the collaboration of capacities characterizable in terms of receptivity and spontaneity. It is a pragmatic version, since it is couched in terms of know-*how:* practical abilities to respond differentially to nonlinguistic stimuli, and to distinguish in practice what inferentially follows from or serves as a reason for what. The residual empiricism of the approach consists in its insistence on the need for the exercise of some of our conceptual capacities to be the exercise of RDRDs. Its residual rationalism consists in its insistence that the responses in question have cognitive significance, count as applications of concepts, only in virtue of their role in reasoning. What otherwise would appear as language-entry moves, without language-language moves, are blind. What otherwise would appear as language-language moves, without language-entry moves, are empty. (I say "what otherwise would appear" as moves because such blind or empty moves do not for Sellars qualify as moves in a *language* game at all.)[6]

It follows from this two-pronged approach that we must be careful in characterizing perceptual judgments or reports of observations as 'noninferential'. They are noninferential in the sense that the particular acts or tokenings are noninferentially *elicited.* They are not the products of a process of inference, arising rather by the exercise of reliable capacities to noninferentially respond differentially to various sorts of perceptible states of affairs by applying concepts. But *no* beliefs, judgments, reports, or claims—in general, no applications of concepts—are noninferential in the sense that their content can be understood apart from their role in reasoning as potential premises and conclusions of inferences. Any response that does not at least potentially have an inferential significance—which cannot, for instance serve as a premise in reasoning to further conclusions—is cognitively idle: a wheel on which nothing else turns.

This rationalist claim has radical consequences. It means that there can be no language consisting only of noninferential reports, no system of concepts whose *only* use is in making perceptual judgments. Non-inferential reports do not form an autonomous stratum of language—a game one could play though one played no other. For that they are *reports* or *claims,* expressions of *beliefs* or *judgments,* that they are applications of *concepts* at all, consists in their availability to serve as premises and conclusions of inferences. And this is so no matter what the subject matter of the reports might be—even if what is reported, that of which one is noninferentially aware, is one's own current mental state. Awareness that reaches beyond mere differential responsiveness—that is, awareness in the sense that bears on *cognition*—is an essentially inferentially articulated affair.

So observational concepts, ones that have (at least some) noninferential circumstances of appropriate application, can be thought of as *inference laden.* It does not follow, by the way, that they are for Sellars for that reason also *theory laden.* For, as will appear below, Sellars understands theoretical concepts as those that have only inferential circumstances of appropriate application—so that noncompound claims in which they occur essentially are those that one can become entitled to only as the result of an inference. His rationalist rendering of the notion of conceptual contentfulness in terms of role in reasoning commits Sellars only to the claim that for any concept to have noninferential uses, it must have inferential ones as well. He is prepared to countenance the possibility of an autonomous language game in which every concept has noninferential as well as inferential uses. Such a language game would be devoid of theoretical terms.

II. 'Looks' Talk and Sellars's Diagnosis of the Cartesian Hypostatization of Appearances

One of the central arguments of "EPM" applies this two-legged understanding of the use of observational concepts to the traditional understanding of claims about how things *look* as reports of *appearances.* The question he addresses can be variously put. In one form it is the question of whether looks-red come before is-red conceptually (and so in the order of explanation). Put in a form more congenial and comprehensible to a pragmatist—that is, in a form that concerns our abilities to *do* something—this becomes the question of whether the latter can be defined in terms of the former in such a way that one could learn how to use the defining concept (<u>looking-φ</u>) first, and only afterwards, by means of the definition, learn how to use the defined concept (<u>is-φ</u>). Since Sellars understands grasp of a concept in terms of mastery of the use of a word, this then becomes a question about the relation between practices of using 'looks-φ' talk and the practices of using 'is-φ' talk. This is a relatively clear way of asking about an issue that goes to the heart of the cartesian project of defining the ontological realm of the mental in terms of the epistemic privileged access in the sense of incorrigibility of mental occurrences.

Descartes was struck by the fact that the appearance/reality distinction seems not to apply to appearances. While I may be mistaken about whether something *is* red (or whether the tower, in the distance, *is* square), I cannot in the same way be mistaken about whether it *looks* red to me now.[7] While I may legitimately be challenged by a doubter, "Perhaps the item is not *really* red; perhaps it only *seems* red," there is no room for the further doubt "Perhaps the item does not even *seem* red; perhaps it only *seems* to seem red." If it seems to seem red, then it really does seem red. The *looks, seems,* or *appears* operators collapse if we try to iterate them. A contrast between appearance and reality is marked by the distinction between <u>looks-φ</u> and φ for ordinary (<u>reality-indicating</u>) predicates 'φ'. But no corresponding contrast is marked by the distinction between <u>looks-to-look-φ</u> and <u>looks-φ</u>. Appearances are reified by Descartes as things that really are just however they appear. He inferred that we do not know them mediately, by means of representings that introduce the possibility of *mis*representing (a distinction between how they really are and how they merely appear, i.e., are represented as being). Rather, we know them *immediately*—simply by having them. Thus appearings—thought of as a realm of entities *reported* on by noninferentially elicited claims about how things *look* (for the visual case), or more generally *seem,* or *appear*—show up as having the ideal qualifications for epistemologically secure foundations of knowledge: we cannot make mistakes about them. Just *having* an appearance ("being appeared-to φ-ly," in one of the variations Sellars discusses) counts as *knowing* something: not that something is φ, to be sure, but at least that something *looks-, seems-,* or *appears-φ*. The possibility accordingly arises of reconstructing our knowledge by starting out only with knowledge of this sort—knowledge of how things look, seem, or appear—and building up in some way to our knowledge (if any) of how things really are (outside the realm of appearance).

This project requires that concepts of the form looks-ϕ be intelligible in principle in advance of grasping the corresponding concepts ϕ (or is-ϕ). Sellars argues that Descartes got things backwards. 'Looks' talk does not form an autonomous stratum of the language—it is not a language game one could play though one played no other. One must already be able to use 'is-ϕ' talk in order to master 'looks-ϕ' talk, which turns out to be parasitic on it. In this precise practical sense, is-ϕ is *conceptually* (Sellars often says "logically") *prior to* looks-ϕ.

His argument takes the form of an account of how 'looks' talk can arise piggybacked on 'is' talk. In "EPM" Sellars does not try to support the strong modal claim that the various practices *must* be related in this way. He thinks that his alternative account of the relation between these idioms is so persuasive that we will no longer be tempted by the cartesian picture. It is an interesting question, which I will not pursue here, whether his story can be turned into a more compelling argument for the stronger claim he wants to make. What he offers us is the parable of John in the tie shop.

At the first stage, John has mastered the noninferential use of terms such as 'green' and 'blue'. So he can, typically, reliably respond to green things by applying the concept green, to blue things by applying the concept blue, and so on. To say that his responsive dispositions are reliable is to say that he usually turns out to be right—so the inference from his being disposed to call something 'green' or 'blue' to its being green or blue is a generally good (though not infallible) one.

At the next stage, electric lights are installed in the shop, and John discovers that they make him prey to certain sorts of systematic errors. Often, when under the electric lights inside his shop he observes something to be green, it turns out in fact—when he and others examine it outside in daylight—to be blue. Here it is obviously important that John have access to some ways of entitling himself to the claim that something is blue, besides the term he is initially disposed to apply to it. This can include his dispositions to respond to it outside the shop, together with his beliefs about the circumstances in which ties do and do not change color, the assessments of others, and the fact that the proper use of color terms was originally keyed to daylight assessments. At this point, John becomes cautious. When viewing under the nonstandard conditions of electric lighting, he does not indulge his otherwise reliable disposition to respond to some visible ties by calling them green. Instead he says something like, "I'm disposed to call this green, and if I didn't know that under these circumstances I'm not a reliable discriminator of green things, I would give in to that temptation and call it green."

At the final stage, John learns under these circumstance to substitute the expression "It *looks* green" for this long expression of temptation withstood. Using the expression "looks-ϕ" is doing two things. First, it is evincing the same usually reliable differential responsive disposition that in other circumstances results in the claim that something *is*. But second, it is *withholding* the endorsement of the claim that something is green. In other words, it is doing something that agrees with an ordinary noninferential report of green things on the first component of Sellars's two-ply account of observation reports—sharing an RDRD—but disagrees with it on the second component, withholding endorsement instead of undertaking the commitment.

The idea is that where collateral beliefs indicate that systematic error is likely, the subject learns not to make the report 'x is ϕ', to which his previously inculcated responsive dispositions incline him, but to make a new kind of claim: 'x *looks* (or seems) ϕ'. The cartesian temptation is to take this as a new kind of report. This report then is naturally thought of as reporting a minimal, noninferentially ascertainable, foundationally basic item, an appearing, about which each subject is incorrigible. Sellars's claim is that it is a mistake to treat these as reports at all—since they *evince* a disposition to call something ϕ but do not do so. They do not even *report* the presence of the disposition—that is, they are not ways of *saying* that one has that disposition.

This analysis of what one is doing in using 'looks' explains the incorrigibility of 'looks' talk. One can be wrong about whether something *is* green because the claim one endorses, the commitment one undertakes, may turn out to be incorrect. For instance, its inferential consequences may be incompatible with other facts one is or comes to be in a position to know independently. But in saying that something *looks* green, one is not endorsing a claim but *withholding* endorsement from one. Such a reporter is merely evincing a disposition to do something that for other reasons (e.g., suspicion that the circumstances of observation lead to systematic error) he is unwilling to do—namely, endorse a claim. Such a reporter cannot be wrong, because he has held back from making a commitment. This is why the *looks, seems,* and *appears* operators do not iterate. Their function is to express the withholding of endorsement from the sentence that appears within the scope of the operator. There is no sensible contrast between 'looks-to-look ϕ' and 'looks-ϕ', of the sort there is between 'looks-ϕ' and 'is-ϕ', because the first 'looks' has already withheld endorsement from the only content in the vicinity to which one might be committed (to something's being ϕ). There is no further withholding work for the second 'looks' to do. There is nothing left to take back. Since asserting 'X looks ϕ' is not undertaking a propositionally contentful commitment—but only expressing an overrideable disposition to do so—there is no issue as to whether or not that commitment (which one?) is correct.

Sellars accordingly explains the incorrigibility of appearance claims, which had so impressed Descartes. He does so in terms of the practices of using words, which are what grasp of the relevant appearance concepts must amount to, according to his methodological linguistic pragmatism. But once we have seen the source and nature of this incorrigibility—in down-to-earth, practical, resolutely nonmetaphysical terms—we see also why it is precisely unsuited to use as an epistemological foundation for the rest of our (risky, corrigible) empirical knowledge. For, first, the incorrigibility of claims about how things merely *look* simply reflects their emptiness: the fact that they are not really claims at all. And second, the same story shows us that 'looks' talk is not an autonomous language game—one that could be played though one played no other. It is entirely parasitic on the practice of making risky empirical reports of how things actually are. Thus Descartes seized on a genuine phenomenon—the incorrigibility of claims about appearances, reflecting the non-iterability of operators like *looks, seems,* and *appears*—but misunderstood its nature, and so mistakenly thought it available to play an epistemologically foundational role for which it is in no way suited.

III. Two Confirmations of the Analysis of 'Looks' Talk in Terms of the Two-Ply Account of Observation

Sellars finds that the analysis of 'looks' talk in terms of the two-pronged account of perceptual judgments is confirmed by its capacity to explain

features of appearance talk that are mysterious on the contrasting cartesian approach.

(i) The apple over there is red.
(ii) The apple over there looks red.
(iii) It looks as though there were a red apple over there.

Utterances of these sentences can express the same responsive disposition to report the presence of a red apple, but they endorse (take responsibility for the inferential consequences of) different parts of that claim.
Sentence (i) endorses both the existence of the apple, and its quality of
redness. Sentence (ii) endorses only the existence of the apple. The
'looks' locution explicitly cancels the qualitative commitment or endorsement. Sentence (iii) explicitly cancels both the existential and the
qualitative endorsements. Thus, if someone claims that there is in fact
no apple over there, he is asserting something incompatible with (i) and
(ii) but not with (iii). If he denies that there is anything red over there,
he asserts something incompatible with (i) but not with (ii) or (iii).
Sellars's account of the practice of using 'looks', in terms of the withholding of endorsement when one suspects systematic error in one's
responsive dispositions, can account for the difference in scope of endorsement that (i)–(iii) exhibit. But how could that difference be accounted for by an approach that understands 'looks' talk as reporting a
distinctive kind of particular, about which we are incorrigible?

Sellars finds a further confirmation of his account of 'looks' talk—and
so of the two-factor account of observational capacities that animates
it—in its capacity to explain the possibility of reporting a merely *generic*
(more accurately, merely determinable) look. Thus it is possible for an
apple to look red without its looking any specific shade of red (crimson,
scarlet, etc.). It is possible for a plane figure to look many-sided without
there being some particular number of sides (say, 119) which it looks to
have. But if 'looks' statements are to be understood as reports of the presence before the eye of the mind of a particular which is ϕ, how can this
possibility be understood? Particulars are completely determinate. A
horse has a particular number of hairs, though, as Sellars points out, it
can *look* to have merely 'a lot' of them. It is a particular shade of brown
(or several shades), even though it may look only darkly colored. So
how are such generic, merely determinable looks possible? Sellars's account is in terms of scope of endorsement. One says that the plane figure

looks 'many-sided' instead of '119-sided' just in case the disposition one is evincing and resisting is a willingness only to endorse (be held responsible for justifying) the more general claim. Particulars, even if they are sense contents, cannot be colored without being some determinate color and shade. How, then, can the sense datum theorist—who wants to say that when something *looks* φ to S, something in S *is* φ—account for the fact that something can look colored without looking to be any particular color, or look red without looking to be any particular shade of red? So Sellars's account of 'looks' talk in terms of endorsement can account for two aspects of that kind of discourse that no theory that invokes a given can explain: the scope distinctions between qualitative and existential lookings, and the possibility of merely generic or determinable lookings.

IV. A Rationalist Account of the Acquisition of Empirical Concepts

It is characteristic of empiricism as Sellars understands (and rejects) it that it countenances a notion of awareness or experience meeting two conditions. First, it goes beyond mere differential responsiveness in having some sort of cognitive *content*—that is, content of the sort that under favorable circumstances amounts to knowledge. This is the idea of a notion of awareness or experience *of* a red triangle in one's visual field that can at the same time be (or be one's evidence for) knowledge *that* there is a red triangle in one's visual field. Second, this sort of awareness is *preconceptual*: the capacity to be aware in this sense or have experiences of this sort is prior to and independent of the possession of or capacity to apply concepts. The idea of a kind of awareness with these two features is what Sellars calls the "Myth of the Given."

Whatever difficulties there may be with such a conception—most notably the incoherences Sellars rehearses in the opening sections of "EPM"—it does provide the basis for a story about concept acquisition. Concepts are understood as acquired by a process of *abstraction*, whose raw materials are provided by exercises of the primitive capacity for immediate, preconceptual awareness.[8] One may—and Sellars does—raise questions about whether it is possible to elaborate this story in a coherent fashion. But one ought also to ask the corresponding question to the empricists' rationalist opponents. Rationalists like Sellars claim that *all* awareness is a conceptual affair. Being aware of something, in any sense that goes beyond mere responsiveness in its potential cognitive significance—paradigmatically in its capacity to serve as *evidence*—is bringing it under a concept. Sense experience cannot be the basis for the acquisition of concepts, since it presupposes the capacity to apply concepts. So how *do* knowers acquire concepts? At this point in the dialectic, classical rationalists such as Leibniz threw up their hands and invoked innate ideas—denying that at least the most basic and general concepts *were* acquired at all. Sellars owes either a defense of innatism or an alternative account of concept acquisition.

Sellars rejects innatism. Grasp of a concept is mastery of the use of a word, so concepts are acquired in the process of learning a language. But if we do not acquire the concept green by noticing green things, since we must already have the concept in order to notice green things as such (by applying the concept to them), how is it possible for us to learn the use of the word 'green', and hence acquire the concept? We each start by learning the corresponding RDRDs: being trained to respond to visibly green things by uttering what is still for the novice just the *noise* "green." This much the parrot can share. Besides these language-entry moves, the language learner must also master the inferential moves in the vicinity of 'green': that the move to 'colored' is OK, and the move to 'red' is not, and so on. Training in these basic language-language moves consists in acquiring more RDRDs, only now the stimuli, as well as the responses, are utterances.

If a two-year-old wobbles into the living room and utters the sentence "The house is on fire," we will not generally take him to have claimed or expressed the belief that the house is on fire. He does not know what he is saying—in the sense that he does not yet know what he would be committing himself to by that claim, or what would be evidence for it or against it. If a five-year-old child utters the same sentence, though, we may well take the utterance to have the significance of a claim, the expression of a belief. We take it to be the adoption of a stance in the dimension of endorsement, to be the undertaking of a commitment, by *holding* the child responsible for her claim: asking for her evidence, asking her what she thinks we should do about it, and so on. For it is now presumed that she can tell what she is committing herself to, and what would entitle her to that commitment, and so knows what she is saying, what claim she is endorsing, what belief she is expressing. When the child masters enough of the inferential moves in the vicinity of a responsively elicited utterance of "That is red," she is taken to have endorsed a claim, and so to have applied a concept.

On the inferential account of distinctively conceptual articulation, grasping a concept requires mastering the inferential connections between the appropriate use of some words and the appropriate use of others. So on this account there is no such thing as grasping just one concept: grasping *any* concept requires grasping *many* concepts. Light dawns slowly over the whole.

light dawns

How good must one be at discriminating the appropriate antecedents and consequents of using a word in order to count as grasping the concept it expresses? Sellars does not explicitly address this question in "EPM," but I think his view is that whether or not one's utterance has the significance of endorsing a claim, and so of applying a concept, is a question of how it is treated by the other members of the linguistic community. The normative status of committing oneself—taking up a position in the dimension of endorsement—is a social status. One must be good enough at anticipating and fulfilling one's responsibilities in order to be *held* responsible, and so for one's remarks to be accorded authority, in the sense of being treated as providing suitable premises for inferences by others. How much is enough is not a metaphysical matter of recognizing the crossing of some antecedently specifiable boundary, but a social matter of deciding when to recognize a performance as authoritative and hold the performer responsible. It is a question that belongs in a box with when writing one's name at the bottom of a piece of paper counts as committing oneself to pay the bank a certain sum of money every month for thirty years. Some seventeen-year-olds may actually understand what they would be committing themselves to better than some twenty-two-year-olds. But the community is not therefore making a metaphysical mistake in treating the latter but not the former as able genuinely to commit themselves.

Sellars's account of concept acquisition starts with reliable differential responsive dispositions to respond to environing stimuli by uttering sentences. What is then required is that one's utterance come to have the significance of making a move in the game of giving and asking for reasons. That requires two elements: the practical inferential know-how required to find one's way about in the inferential network connecting different sentences, and the social acknowledgment of that know-how as sufficient for one's performances to have the significance in the linguistic community of commitments to or endorsements of the inferentially articulated claims expressed by those sentences. This story is structured and motivated by Sellars's two-pronged account of observation reports, as noninferentially elicited endorsements of inferentially articulated claims.

V. Giving Theoretical Concepts an Observational Use

As a final example of the work Sellars calls on his two-pronged analysis of observational capacities to do in "Empiricism and the Philosophy of Mind," we might consider his account of how theoretical concepts can acquire an observational use. His reason for addressing the issue is that he wants to make intelligible the idea that some sorts of paradigmatic mental occurrences—thoughts and sense impressions—might first become available to us purely theoretically, and only later come to be observable by us. For showing that such a development in our capacities *is* intelligible provides a means of confounding the cartesian idea of immediate (that is, noninferential) observability as *essential* to the very idea of mental occurrences. But my concern here is with the general point, rather than this particular application of it.

The first point to realize is that, as I mentioned above, according to Sellars's view, the distinction between theoretical objects and observable objects is *methodological* rather than *ontological*. That is, theoretical and observable objects are not different kinds of thing. They differ only in how we come to know about them. Theoretical objects are ones of which we can only have *inferential* knowledge, while observable objects can also be known noninferentially. Theoretical concepts are ones we can only be entitled to apply as the conclusions of inferences, while concepts of observables also have noninferential uses. But the line between things to which we have only inferential cognitive access and things to which we also have noninferential cognitive access can shift with time, for instance, as new instruments are developed. Thus when first postulated to explain perturbations in the orbit of Neptune, Pluto was a purely theoretical object; the only claims we could make about it were the conclusions of inferences. But the development of more powerful telescopes eventually made it accessible to observation, and so a subject of noninferential reports. Pluto did not then undergo an ontological change. All that changed was its relation to us.[9]

It might be objected to this view that when the issue of the ontological status of theoretical entities is raised, they are not considered merely as objects in principle like any others save that they happen at the moment to be beyond our powers of observation. They are thought of as *unobservable* in a much stronger sense: permanently and in principle inaccessible to observation. But Sellars denies that anything is unobservable in this sense. To be observable is just to be noninferentially reportable. Noninferential reportability requires only that there are circumstances in which reporters can apply the concepts in question (the dimension of inferentially articulated endorsement) by exercising reliable differential dispositions to respond to the objects in question (the causal dimension), and know that they are doing so. In this sense, physicists with the right training can *noninferentially* report the presence of mu mesons in cloud chambers. In this sense of 'observation', nothing real is in principle beyond the reach of observation. (Indeed, in Sellars's sense, one who mastered reliable differential responsive dispositions noninferentially to apply *normative* vocabulary would be directly observing normative facts. It is in this sense that we might be said to be able to *hear,* not just the noises someone else makes, but their *words,* and indeed, *what they are saying*—their *meanings.*) It is an empirical question what circumstances we can come reliably to respond to differentially. The development of each new sort of measuring instrument potentially expands the realm of the here-and-now observable.

Once one sees that observation is not based on some primitive sort of preconceptual awareness, the fact that some observation reports are riskier than others and that when challenged we sometimes retreat to safer ones from which the originals can be inferred will not tempt one to think that the original reports were in fact the products of inference from those basic or minimal observations. The physicist, if challenged to back up his report of a mu meson, may indeed justify his claim by citing the distinctively hooked vapor trail in the cloud chamber. This is something else observable, from which the presence of the mu meson can, in the right circumstances, be inferred. But to say that is not to say that the original report was the product of an inference after all. It was the exercise of a reliable differential responsive disposition keyed to a whole chain of reliably covarying events, which includes mu mesons, hooked vapor trails, and retinal images. What makes it a report of mu mesons, and not of hooked vapor trails or retinal images, is the inferential role of the concept the physicist noninferentially applies. (It is a consequence of something's being a mu meson, for instance, that it is *much* smaller than a finger, which does *not* follow from something's being a hooked vapor trail.) If <u>mu meson</u> is the concept the physicist applies noninferentially, then if he is sufficiently reliable, when correct, that is what he *sees*. His retreat, when a question is raised, to a report of a hooked vapor trail, whose presence provides good inferential reason for the original, noninferentially elicited claim, is a retreat to a report that is safer in the sense that he is a *more* reliable reporter of hooked vapor trails than of mu mesons, and that it takes less training to be able reliably to report vapor trails of a certain shape, so that is a skill shared more widely. But the fact that an inferential justification can be offered, and that the demand for one may be in order, no more undermines the status of the original report as noninferentially elicited (as genuinely an observation) than does the corresponding fact that I may under various circumstances be obliged to back up my report of something as red by invoking my reliability as a reporter of red things in these circumstances—from which, together with my disposition to call it red, the claim originally endorsed noninferentially may be inferred.

Thus one can start with grasp of a concept that consists entirely in mastery of its use as a premise and conclusion in inferences—that is, as a purely theoretical concept—and by the addition of suitable RDRDs come to be able to use them observationally, perhaps in observations whose standard conditions include not only such items as good light (as in the tie shop case) but also the presence of various sorts of instruments. This argument once again appeals to and depends on Sellars's understanding of observational capacities as the product of reliable noninferential responsive dispositions and mastery of inferential norms.

VI. Conclusion: On the Relation between the Two Components

Sellars's primary explanatory target in "Empiricism and the Philosophy of Mind" is our knowledge of the current contents of our own minds. He wants to rethink our understanding of the way in which we experience or are aware of what we are thinking and how things perceptually seem to us. The point I have been trying to make is that the master idea that guides his argument is a particular way of thinking, not about our knowledge of the contents of our own minds, but about our observational knowledge of ordinary empirical states of affairs. It is because he understands perceptual awareness of a red apple in front of one as he does that Sellars rejects a host of traditional ways of thinking about awareness of having a sense impression of a red apple or the thought that there is a red apple in front of one.

I have claimed that Sellars understands the sort of perceptual awareness of external objects that is expressed in observation reports as the product of exercising two different sorts of capacities: the capacity reliably to respond differentially to stimuli (which we share both with merely sentient creatures such as parrots and with merely irritable devices such as thermostats and land mines) and the capacity to take up positions and make moves in a game of giving and asking for reasons. I have rehearsed the way I see some of the major arguments and conceptual moves in the essay as rooted in this two-ply conception: the account of the use of 'looks' talk that underlies the incorrigibility of sincere contemporaneous first-person reports of how things perceptually seem to one, including the treatment of scoped and generic 'looks' claims, Sellars's approach to the issue of concept acquisition, which caused so much trouble for traditional rationalists, and his rendering of the distinction between theoretical and observational concepts.

I would like to close with some observations and questions about the relations between the two kinds of ability whose cooperation Sellars sees as required for observation. The two sorts of capacities define dimensions of perceptual awareness that are in a certain sense orthogonal. We saw in the discussion of concept acquisition the broad outlines of a story about how one might move from possession of mere RDRDs to the capacity to apply observational concepts. And we saw in the discussion of theoretical and observational concepts how one might move from the purely inferential capacity to apply a concept, by the addition of suitable RDRDs, to mastery of a fully observational concept. That is, we saw in the case of particular observational concepts how one could have either of the two components without the other, and then move to having both.

But this shows only *local* independence of the two components: that one can have the RDRD of an observational concept without having the concept, and one can have a concept without having the RDRD needed to be able to apply it observationally. The corresponding global independence claim is not true. Purely theoretical concepts do not form an *autonomous* language game, a game one could play though one played no other. For one must be able to respond conceptually to the utterances of others in order to be talking at all. So one could not play the game of giving and asking for reasons at all unless one could apply at least *some* concepts noninferentially in the making of observation reports. But this does not mean that there could not be an *insulated* region of purely theoretical concepts, say, those of pure mathematics—'insulated' in the sense that they had no inferential connection to anything inferentially connected to a concept that had an observational use. I do not say that any actual mathematics is like this, though it may be. Pure mathematics, I think, is in principle *applicable* to ordinary empirical objects, both those accessible through observation and those (now) accessible only inferentially. Applying an abstract mathematical structure to concrete objects is using the former to guide our inferences concerning the latter. But this relation ought not to be assimilated to that between theoretical objects and observable objects. It is not clearly incompatible with a kind of inferential insulation of the game of giving and asking for reasons concerning the mathematical structures. I think there are many interesting issues in the vicinity that are as yet not fully explored.[10]

It might seem that there could be no interesting question concerning the potential independence of RDRDs, corresponding to this question about the potential independence of the game of giving and asking for reasons. For it seems obvious that there can be reliable differential responsive dispositions without conceptual capacities. That is what mere sentients and artifacts have. But I think in fact there is a subtle question here, and I want to end by posing it. To begin with, what is obvious is at most that the RDRDs corresponding to *some* observational concepts can be exhibited by creatures who lack the corresponding concepts. And we might doubt even this. The story of John in the tie shop reminds us that our dispositions actually to call things red can be quite complex, and interact with our background beliefs—for instance, about what are standard conditions for observing red things, and what conditions we are in—in complex ways. Though this claim goes beyond what Sellars says, I think that learning about systematic sources of error can lead us to alter not just how we express our dispositions (substituting 'looks ϕ' for 'is

ϕ'), but eventually even those dispositions themselves. I think, though I cannot say that I am sure (a condition that itself ought to give some sorts of cartesians pause), that familiarity with the Müller-Lyer illusion has brought me to a state in which one of the lines no longer even *looks* to me to be longer than the other. The more theoretically laden our concept of standard conditions for some sort of observation are (think of the mu meson case, where those conditions involve the presence of a cloud chamber), the less likely it is that a creature who could deploy no concepts whatsoever could master the RDRDs of a sophisticated observer.

Besides creatures who lack concepts entirely (because they are not players in any game of giving and asking for reasons), we could ask about which RDRDs are in principle masterable by concept users who for some reason lack the specific concepts that for the genuine observer are keyed to the RDRDs in question. It might be, for all I know, that by suitable reinforcement I could be trained to sort potsherds into two piles, which I label with the nonsense terms 'ping' and 'pong', in such a way that I always and only put Toltec potsherds in the 'ping' pile and Aztec ones in the 'pong' pile. What would make my noises *nonsense* is that they do not engage inferentially with my use of any other expressions. And we might suppose that I do not have the concepts Toltec and Aztec. If told to substitute the labels 'Toltec' and 'Aztec' for 'ping' and 'pong', I would then be a kind of idiot savant with respect to the noninferential applicability of those concepts (which I would still not grasp). Perhaps there are no conceptual limits to such idiot savantry. But I find it hard to conceive of cases in which someone who lacks all the relevant concepts nonetheless can acquire the RDRDs necessary to serve as a measuring device (not, by hypothesis, a genuine reporter) of observable instances of the applicability of thick moral concepts such as courage, sensitivity, cruelty, justice, and so on. Of course, unless one endorses something like Sellars's account of what is required for something to be observable, it will seem that such properties are not suitable candidates for being observable by *anybody*, never mind by idiot savants. But for those of us who do accept his approach, this sort of question is one that must, I think, be taken seriously.

NOTES

Introduction

1. I tell this story in Chapter 8 of *Making It Explicit* (Cambridge, Mass.: Harvard University Press, 1994), and in simplified form in chap. 5 of *Articulating Reasons* (Cambridge, Mass.: Harvard University Press, 2000).
2. I argue for these claims in chap. 6 of *Articulating Reasons*.
3. I say in further detail what it is for a practice to respect these sorts of relations in chap. 3 of *Making It Explicit*.
4. Discussed, respectively, in chaps. 3 and 4 of *Making It Explicit*.
5. This picture is motivated and elaborated in chap. 2 of *Making It Explicit* and chap. 1 of *Articulating Reasons*.
6. I discuss this way of thinking about practical reasoning in chap. 2 of *Articulating Reasons*.
7. In Chapter 7 an analogy is invoked at this point between Quine's critique of Carnap and Hegel's critique of Kant.
8. Indeed, Hegel published only two books in his lifetime. (The rest of his twenty-plus-volume oeuvre consists of lecture notes—a monument to what institutional demands can extract from a real thinker.) One of those books, the *Phenomenology*, is a systematically presented history. The other, the *Logic*, is a historically presented system.
9. Wordsworth said that the child is the father of the man. But his *Prelude* was more than just his account of how he started out and developed on his way to being who and getting where he is at the time of writing it. It is the greatest achievement of his maturity. That account of the roots of his self, his sensibility, and his work *is* his achieved self, sensibility, and work.

1. Contexts

1. I am indebted to my friend and former colleague John Haugeland for this way of telling the story. See chap. 1 of his *Artificial Intelligence: The Very Idea* (Cambridge, Mass.: MIT Press, 1985).

2. This story is told in Chapter 4, "Adequacy and the Individuation of Ideas in Spinoza's *Ethics.*"

3. This story is told in Chapter 5, "Leibniz and Degrees of Perception."

4. This story is told in Chapter 7, "Some Pragmatist Themes in Hegel's Idealism."

5. I discuss this sort of change in connection with Sellars's resolution of the rationalists' difficulties in my Study Guide to his classic *Empiricism and the Philosophy of Mind* (Cambridge, Mass.: Harvard University Press, 1997).

2. Texts

1. Searle would say 'intrinsic' intentionality, and Haugeland would call it 'original' intentionality, intending in each case a contrast with the intentionality exhibited by linguistic expressions. See John R. Searle, *Intentionality: An Essay in the Philosophy of Mind* (Cambridge: Cambridge University Press, 1983); John Haugeland, *Having Thought* (Cambridge, Mass.: Harvard University Press, 1998).

2. Fred I. Dretske, *Knowledge and the Flow of Information* (Cambridge, Mass.: MIT Press, 1981).

3. See, for instance, Donald Davidson, "The Second Person," *Midwest Studies in Philosophy* 17 (1992): 255–267.

4. I have slightly rearranged this passage from Chapter 4.

5. Leibniz says generally, "One thing expresses another . . . when there is a constant and regulated relation between what can be said of the one and of the other."

6. For the purposes of this summary discussion, I am suppressing the significant differences of detail between the somewhat parallel stories concerning perceptions and ideas. The essay itself is somewhat more careful.

7. John Searle, *Intentionality* (Cambridge: Cambridge University Press, 1983), p. 2.

8. This is not to say that Hegel has nothing to say about the relation between conceptual content and representational purport. But that story, as I understand it, should be told *after* the two stories presented here (even though Hegel presents it already in his introduction to the *Phenomenology*).

9. A pregnant remark of Haugeland's, characterizing Heidegger's view. See John Haugeland, "Heidegger on Being a Person," *Noûs* (March 1982): 15–26.

10. Leibniz had: "Ideas, when reason cannot judge of their *compatibility or connection*, are confused."

11. G. W. F. Hegel, *Science of Logic,* trans. A. V. Miller (Oxford: Oxford University Press, 1969), pp. 554–555.

12. Gottlob Frege, *Begriffsschrift,* hereafter Frege, *BGS,* sec. 3 (emphasis added).

13. This way of specifying the explanatory target to which semantic theories, including referential ones, are directed is picked up by Frege's student Carnap, who in the *Logical Syntax of Language* defines the content of a sentence as the class of non-valid sentences which are its consequences (i.e., can be inferred from it). Sellars in turn picks up the idea from him.

14. From "Boole's Logical Calculus and the Concept-Script," ed. Hans Hermes, Friedrich Kambartel, and Friedrich Kaulbach, in *Gottlob Frege: Posthumous Writings,* trans. P. Lond and R. White (Chicago: University of Chicago Press, 1981), pp. 12–13.

15. Ibid., p. 16.

16. By deploying a number of such inferentially expressive devices (including negation, which makes incompatibilities explicit), along the lines of Part Three of the *Begriffsschrift,* Frege is able (in his long essay on Boole) to offer his version of the definition of continuity of a function—one that articulates its conceptual content so well that a number of substantial mathematical results (for instance, the uniform convergence theorem) can be derived from it by purely quantificational inferences.

17. In fact, any (nontrivial) way the truth values of all *Begriffsschrift* conditionals over a certain vocabulary are fixed settles the truth values of all of the nonlogical sentences from which they are constructed. See my essay "A Semantic Paradox of Material Implication," *Notre Dame Journal of Formal Logic* 22, no. 2 (April 1981): 129–132.

18. It is controversial whether the converse is even intelligible. For definite descriptions, such as "the current ambassador to the Court of St. James," it seems one can hold the mode of presentation fixed while associating it with different objects with respect to different indices (times, say, or possible worlds). But for proper names and demonstratives, this is much more questionable.

19. Gottlob Frege, *Grundlagen der Arithmetik,* trans. J. L. Austin (Evanston, Ill.: Northwestern University Press, 1967), §62 hereafter Frege, *GL.*

20. By 'object' here is meant 'individual' or 'particular' (not that any of these is an individuating sortal)—a category that includes, rather than contrasting with, events and processes, for instance.

21. W. V. O. Quine, *Word and Object* (Cambridge, Mass.: MIT Press, 1960), p. 96; see also p. 90.

22. I discuss this substitutional approach at greater length in sections 1–3 of

chap. 6 of *Making It Explicit* (Cambridge, Mass.: Harvard University Press, 1994).

23. Frege, *GL*, §65.

24. This thought entails the existence of something called "abstract objects," a distinctive kind of object, rather than a distinctive mode of access to objects, only in the presence of further substantial and controversial commitments. I do not think there is any reason to believe that Frege countenanced such an object kind.

25. I tell this story in "What Are Singular Terms, and Why Are There Any?" chap. 3 of *Articulating Reasons* (Cambridge, Mass.: Harvard University Press, 2000), and at greater length in chap. 6 of *Making It Explicit*.

26. There is an interesting compare-and-contrast story to be told relating this difference to that discussed in "What Are Singular Terms, and Why Are There Any?" in *Articulating Reasons*.

27. The question for them is not about their *Eigenschaften*, but only about what is *geeignet* for them, Heidegger says (in a passage quoted in section I of Chapter 10).

28. The first Heidegger chapter has this to say about the Hegelian recognitive structure of communities: "The community, *Mitdasein*, differs from the ready-to-hand in that its members are constituted not only by being *recognized* or responded to in a certain way, but also by their *recognizings* and responses as *recognizers*."

29. Cf. Geach in "Ascriptivism," and "Assertion," both reprinted in P. T. Geach, *Logic Matters* (Berkeley: University of California Press, 1972). It is for this reason that Frege does not permit us to make inferences from false premises. What we should do instead is assert conditionals that have false antecedents.

30. The community, *Mitdasein*, differs from the ready-to-hand in that its members are constituted not only by being *recognized* or responded to in a certain way, but also by their *recognizings* and responses as *recognizers*. I argue in Chapter 10 that Heidegger adapts Hegel's model of social substance as synthesized by reciprocal recognition (as discussed in Chapter 7 on Hegel). Here one might usefully compare Descartes's division of things into representings (making up minds) and what can only be represented (the physical), and Leibniz's subsequent denial—of great significance for subsequent idealism—of genuine reality to anything that is not itself a representing.

31. Both were written in response to invitations from Bert Dreyfus and David Hoy to talk about Heidegger at some of the legendary NEH Summer Institutes they organized. Without their impetus, I would never have worked through this material.

32. It is one that I have discussed elsewhere in terms of the *institution* of normative statuses and, in the case where the consequential and inheritance proprieties governing those states have the right structure, the *conferral* of content.

3. Pretexts

1. Roughly placed by the botanization I sketch in "Pragmatik und Pragmatismus," in *Die Renaissance des Pragmatismus,* ed. Michael Sandbothe (Velbrück Wissenschaft, 2000), pp. 29–58, forthcoming as "Pragmatics and Pragmatisms" in a book edited by James Conant and Urszula Zeglen, *Hilary Putnam: Pragmatism and Realism* (London: Routledge, 2002).
2. G. E. M. Anscombe, *Intention* (Ithaca, N.Y.: Cornell University Press, 1957; rpt. Cambridge, Mass.: Harvard University Press, 2001).
3. Whether and how the account I go on to offer of the conceptual hermeneutics of discursive commitments should then be taken to reflect on the case of empirical knowledge and practical agency is a question I will not pursue here.
4. This is the line I pursue in chap. 8 of *Making It Explicit* (Cambridge, Mass.: Harvard University Press, 1994). At the end of the story, talk of 'meaning' and 'content' gives way to talk about the practical capacity of navigating between different doxastic-inferential contexts of collateral commitments.
5. I have talked about how I understand the task of philosophy in "Reason, Expression, and the Philosophic Enterprise," in *What Is Philosophy?*, ed. Clyde Ragland and Sarah L. Heidt (New Haven: Yale University Press, 2001): 74–95.
6. Chap. 4 of *Articulating Reasons* (Cambridge, Mass.: Harvard University Press, 2000) explains how *substitution* inferences then permit the extension of the notion of conceptual content to essentially subsentential expressions, paradigmatically singular terms and predicates.
7. This emphasis is in part a consequence of the non-monotonicity of material inference: the fact that just because p by itself gives good reason for q, it does *not* follow that for arbitrary r, $p\&r$ gives good reason for q. This issue is discussed in chap. 2 of *Articulating Reasons*.
8. In philosophical works written by the now dead, paradigmatic demonstrative and indexical phenomena recede to a bare minimum. Nonetheless, cognoscenti will see both the analogies and the disanalogies between Kaplan's dual relativity of the content of some such expressions to context of utterance and context of evaluation and the inferential perspectives made explicit by *de dicto* and *de re* specifications of conceptual content as indicated in the text.

9. As well one might be. I read it as an expression of (a) conceptual realism, the doctrine that objective reality is conceptually structured by relations of material incompatibility (and so material consequence, including modally robust, counterfactual-supporting lawful connections); (b) objective idealism, the reciprocal sense dependence of conceptions of objective relations and conceptions of subjective processes of resolving incompatible commitments; and (c) the conceptual idealism that moves beyond objective idealism by seeing the whole sense dependence structure as itself a *process* modeled on the processes of subjectivity. Thereon hangs a tale. Like Kant, Hegel claimed that conceptual realism is intelligible only within a more encompassing idealism.

10. Michael Forster, *Hegel's Idea of a Phenomenology of Spirit* (Chicago: University of Chicago Press, 1998), is good on this issue.

11. Chap. 8 of *Making It Explicit* discusses how the interpersonal capacity to pick up another's tokening anaphorically—for the potential ascriber to be able to respond to S's claim "A bunch of bloodthirsty fanatics occupied the village" by "They are gallant freedom fighters"—is incorporated into and expressed by the intrasentential ascription–structural anaphoric connection between the antecedent "gallant freedom fighters" and "they" in "S believes of a bunch of gallant freedom fighters that they occupied the village."

12. Assuming one has settled on a suitable set of basic sortals that would allow one to count "objects."

4. Adequacy and the Individuation of Ideas in Spinoza's *Ethics*

I thank Margaret Wilson, Arthur Szathmary, and Bruce Kuklick for their comments on earlier versions of this chapter.

1. Daisy Radnor, "Spinoza's Theory of Ideas," *Philosophical Review* (July 1971): 338–359.

2. *Eth.* ii, Def. 4. All citations are from Benedict de Spinoza, *Ethica Ordine Geometrico Demonstrata*, trans. R. H. M. Elwes (New York: Philosophical Library, 1960), except as otherwise noted.

3. *Eth.* ii, 28, Dem.

4. *Eth.* ii, 7, Scholium.

5. In the first half of Radnor's article (see note 1), she chronicles the difficulties various commentators have been led to by attempting to carry this project through.

6. *Eth.* ii, 17, Scholium to Corollary.

7. Radnor, "Spinoza's Theory of Ideas."

8. Actually, Radnor's arguments require only the weaker condition that the thing represented by an idea be *deducible* from the object of the idea.

9. *Eth.* ii, 38.

10. See discussion after the fourth axiom after Prop. 13; also Axioms 1 and 2.

11. Lemma 3 after Prop. 13.

12. Axiom 2 after Prop. 13.

13. Def. after Axiom 2 after *Eth.* ii, 13 (from the William White–Amelia Stirling translation [London: T. Fisher Unwin, 1894]); cf. Lemma 7.

14. Lemmas 4–7 after the second axiom after *Eth.* ii, 13.

15. Scholium to Lemma 7 after *Eth.* ii, 13.

16. Epistle 64. This and all subsequent references to Spinoza's corespondence are to the Abraham Wolf translation, as included in *Spinoza Selections,* ed. John Wild (New York: Scribners, 1930), pp. 401–479.

17. Talk of momentum here may not be quite right, since it is not clear what Spinoza's view on the *directions* of motions is, but this does not affect our discussion.

18. *Eth.* ii, 13, Postulate 5.

19. *Eth.* ii, 38.

20. Spinoza argues at *Eth.* ii, 37, that none of these "notiones communes" can constitute the essence of any particular thing, since his definition of essence requires that such an essence be inconceivable apart from the thing of which it is the essence. Thus such an essence could not be common to all things.

21. Cf. *Eth.* i, 21–23; Epistle 64.

22. *Eth.* ii, 40, Scholium.

23. Ibid.

24. Axiom 2 after Lemma 3 after *Eth.* ii, 13.

25. *Eth.* i, Def. 5.

26. Definition of 'infinite modes', *Eth.* i, 23, Epistle 64; *Eth.* i, Axiom 4; *Eth.* ii, 37–38.

27. *Eth.* iii, 6 and 7.

28. *Eth.* ii, 9.

29. *Eth.* i, 34.

30. *Eth.* iii, 4.

31. *Eth.* i, 34; *Eth.* i, 36, Dem.

32. *Eth.* i, 18.

33. *Eth.* ii, 40, Scholium.

34. Epistle 83; *Eth.* ii, 40, Scholium.

35. *Eth.* v, 4; *Eth.* v, 4, Scholium; *Eth.* v, 31, Dem.

36. Epistle 64.

37. If we view the causal commerce of the modes of extension *sub specie aeternitatis,* it will appear as a net, rather than as a chain, of individuals with particular states of motion-and-rest. The appearance of time is simply a confused idea owing to one's identification with his own body as a standpoint. In our scheme this means that a direction is induced into the infinite net by following the career of a few individuals (the bodily parts) through all their changes of motion until the dissolution of the whole they constitute, and thereby picking out a chain such that the mind associated with that body may order things according to the order in which they (arbitrarily, from the divine point of view) impinge on the privileged dimension of the chain. This ordering may not represent the causal relations which actually obtain. It is, I think, clear how a systematically confused ordering of events could be constructed by taking a one-dimensional ordering abstracted out of a two-or-more-dimensional matrix and projecting all the events onto that ordering. Spinoza might even take a hint like this from Galileo's treatment of time as a geometrical dimension, seeing causal events in four-space under the aspect of eternity. Spinoza's doctrine of temporality as confusion owing to limited perspective would in that case foreshadow the relativistic notion of local times. But all of this interpretation follows only if we allow some sort of directedness among the causal relations of states of individuals which are nodes of the initial net. This notion is consistent with his paradigm case of logical relations in the parallel attribute of thought. For deductive relations are asymmetric (directed) but do not form a total ordering. On this view, then, time is a confused perception because I choose to order my experience according to the order in which things affect me, rather than according to the much more complex order which obtains in nature.

38. Spinoza uses the notion of a proximate cause (the last cause in a chain before the effect in question) in several places, e.g., at *Eth.* ii, 3, Dem.

39. *Eth.* i, Axiom 3: if there is no effect in the mind in question, then the motion in the parts of the body which are the objects of the ideas of the mind in question is not being communicated, and that body and mind are destroyed.

40. E.g., *Eth.* ii, 41.

41. Spinoza's discussion is at *Eth.* ii, 18, Scholium. Ultimately, of course, all relations of ideas are universal logical relations. If we restrict our attention to those which take place within a single finite individual, however, an idiosyncratic abstraction from the universal relations may be made by the boundary of that individual. This arbitrary limitation of viewpoint is the source of confused ideas, and hence of error and evil.

42. *Eth.* ii, 18.

43. *Eth.* ii, 38, 39.
44. These claims are puzzling in terms of our actual experience, for we are surely not in general aware of such ideas. Spinoza may well have no idea corresponding to mental contents of which we are unaware. Yet it seems to me that he has the resources for such a doctrine in the contrast between ideas as enduring individuals and ideas as "states of understanding" of such individuals, and the different ways these two categories behave in the mind. I shall not try to develop such an account here, however.
45. *Eth.* iii, 9, Scholium.
46. *Eth.* ii, 49.
47. *Eth.* ii, Def. 3.
48. *Eth.* iii, Def. 2.
49. *Eth.* iv, 4.
50. *Eth.* iii, 3.
51. I have corrected Elwes's erroneous translation of *Eth.* ii, Def. 7; Spinoza's comment to this definition is also relevant.
52. *Eth.* ii, 32.
53. Radnor never takes up the issue of *idea ideae.*
54. *Eth.* iii, 9.
55. *Eth.* ii, 21, Scholium.
56. Only two attributes could be involved, according to Epistle 66.
57. See Epistles 63–66, 70, 72.
58. Thus any idea in a mind which follows logically from the previous idea in that mind is itself conceived adequately by that mind. This, I assert, is the basis for Spinoza's claim at *Eth.* ii, 40, that any idea which logically follows from an adequate idea is itself adequate. If we do not read this proposition in this way, it is inconsistent with the interpretation of adequacy I have presented (since nothing can be known of what the idea following the adequate idea is taken by the mind to represent until we see the ideas of which it is the proximate cause).

5. Leibniz and Degrees of Perception

I thank Nicholas Rescher and Margaret Wilson for many useful conversations about Leibniz's thought.
1. *Die philosophischen Schriften von G. W. Leibniz,* ed. C. I. Gerhardt, 7 vols. (Berlin, 1875–1890), 2:121, 311; 3:69, 574; 6:598, 608; 7:317, 529, hereafter Leibniz, *G.*
2. I ignore here appetitions, which, while also modifications of the attribute of perception, as differentials of perceivings (their tendencies to give rise to one another) are in a double sense *derivative* modifications.

3. See John Earman, "Perceptions and Relations in the Monadology," *Studia Leibnitiana* 9, no. 2 (1977): 212–230.

4. This characterization does not shortchange the individuality of monads, for that individuality is expressed by an individual concept or law, which is just a representing from which all the representings "belonging" to a monad can be inferred.

5. Leibniz, *G*, 2:112, a letter to Arnauld. See also Mark Kulstad, "Leibniz' Concept of Expression," *Studia Leibnitiana* 9, no. 2 (1977): 55–76.

6. "Discourse on Metaphysics," in Leibniz, *G*, 4:422–463. Translations herein are from sec. 9 of *G. W. Leibniz: Philosophical Papers and Letters*, trans. L. E. Loemker, 2nd ed., 2 vols. (Dordrecht: D. Reidel, 1969), hereafter Leibniz, *D*, cited by section numbers. "Monadology," in Leibniz, *G*, 6:607–623. Translations are from sec. 62 in Loemker, hereafter Leibniz, *M*, cited by section numbers.

7. Leibniz, *M*, 60.

8. Leibniz, *D*, 15.

9. Leibniz, *D*, 15.

10. Leibniz, *M*, 49.

11. Montgomery Furth, "Monadology," *Philosophical Review* 76 (1967), reprinted in *Leibniz: A Collection of Critical Essays*, ed. H. G. Frankfurt (New York: Doubleday Anchor, 1972), p. 129.

12. Leibniz, *M*, 61.

13. "Principles of Nature and Grace," in Leibniz, *G*, 6:598–606; sec. 13 in Loemker, hereafter Leibniz, "PNG," cited by section numbers.

14. G. W. Leibniz, *New Essays Concerning Human Understanding*. trans. A. G. Langley, 3rd ed. (LaSalle, Ill.: Open Court, 1949), sec. 2, 19, p. 166, hereafter Leibniz, *NE*, cited by section and page numbers. I have emended the translation herein where necessary.

15. Leibniz, *G*, 7:529.

16. Leibniz, *M*, 24, 25.

17. See passage in Leibniz, *G*.

18. Leibniz, *M*, 62.

19. Leibniz, *D*, 33.

20. E.g., in Leibniz, *NE*.

21. Leibniz, *NE*, 2, 21, p. 178.

22. Leibniz, *D*, 16.

23. Frederick Copleston, *A History of Philosophy*, 8 vols. (New York: Doubleday Anchor, 1963), 4:318ff.

24. Leibniz, *G*, 4:422–426.

25. Leibniz, *D*, 27.

26. Leibniz, *G*, 4:422.

27. Leibniz, *D*, 24.

28. Leibniz, *G*, 7:319.

29. For instance, see Robert McRae, *Leibniz: Perception, Apperception, and Thought* (Toronto: University of Toronto Press, 1976), chap. 5, certainly the fullest and most thoughtful treatment of these general issues we have. McRae is particularly helpful on the relations between sensibility and understanding.

30. Leibniz, *NE*, 2, 23, p. 227; see also 2, 29, p. 274.

31. Leibniz, *NE*, 2, 29, p. 274.

32. Leibniz, *NE*, 4, p. 446.

33. Leibniz, *NE*, 2, 1, p. 109.

34. Leibniz, *D*, 35.

35. Leibniz, *NE*, 2, 31, pp. 278–279.

36. Leibniz, *NE*, 2, 29, p. 267; *D*, 24; *G*, 4:423–424.

37. Leibniz, *NE*, intro., p. 45. See also 1, 1, p. 45; 1, 2, p. 111; 4, 2, p. 410; 4, 10, p. 499.

38. Leibniz, *D*, 27.

39. Leibniz, *NE*, 2, 1, p. 111.

40. Leibniz, *NE*, 2, 13, p. 152.

41. Leibniz, *D*, 8.

42. Leibniz, *D*, 8. On the logic of such accidents, see Leibniz *G*, 7:236–247.

43. Leibniz, *G*, 7:263.

44. Leibniz, *D*, 6.

45. *Opuscules et fragments inédits de Leibniz,* ed. Louis Couturat (Paris, 1903), p. 15.

46. Leibniz, *M*, 12, 13.

47. Leibniz, *D*, 16.

48. We cannot just compare numbers of accidents, since each perception may express an infinite number of them.

49. Leibniz, *D*, 7. See Leibniz, *D*, 15, for talk of "more perfect expression of phenomena."

50. Martha Kneale, "Leibniz and Spinoza on Activity," in Frankfurt, *Leibniz,* pp. 215–237, hereafter Kneale, "LSA."

51. Leibniz, "PNG," 4, 13. Leibniz, *NE*, intro., p. 51; 2, 9, p. 142; 2, 19, p. 166; 2, 21, pp. 178, 201, 219–220. See also Leibniz, *G*, 3:574; 4:522, 562–565; 6:500–501.

52. Kneale, "LSA."

53. Leibniz, *M*, 52.

54. Leibniz, *NE*, 4, 5, p. 448.

55. Leibniz, "PNG," 4.

56. Leibniz, *NE*, preface.

57. Leibniz, *NE*, intro., pp. 45, 47; 2, 19, p. 165; 2, 22, p. 222; 2, 27, pp. 248, 250. Leibniz, "PNG," 4; Leibniz, *M*, 19.

58. On perceptions producing others, see Leibniz, *G*, 2:372; 4:523–524, 563–565; Leibniz, *NE*, intro., p. 49; 2, 1, p. 116; 2, 21, p. 211; 2, 33, pp. 283–284.

59. See Leibniz, *NE*, 2, 21, p. 201.

60. Leibniz, *G*, 4:426. See also Leibniz, *NE*, preface, p. 50; 2, 1, p. 118; 2, 9, p. 136.

61. Leibniz, *NE*, 2, 23, p. 228.

62. Leibniz, *D*, 14. See also Hide Ishiguro's response to Furth on this point, in "Leibniz' Theory of the Ideality of Relations," in Frankfurt, *Leibniz*, pp. 191–213, esp. 210–213.

63. Leibniz, *NE*, 1, 3, p. 102.

64. Leibniz, *NE*, 2, 1, p. 113; 2, 13, p. 150; 2, 21, p. 187; 2, 23, p. 228; Leibniz, *G*, 4:557–559.

65. Leibniz, *NE*, 2, 17, p. 160; 4, 16, p. 552; Leibniz, *G*, 4:555–556; Couturat, *Opuscules*, p. 523.

66. Leibniz, *NE*, 4, 6, p. 459.

67. So called at Leibniz, *NE*, 2, 19, p. 165.

68. Leibniz, *NE*, 2, 3, p. 120.

69. Leibniz, *NE*, 2, 29, p. 267.

70. Leibniz, *NE*, 2, 29, p. 267.

71. See Leibniz, *NE*, preface, pp. 44–45.

72. Leibniz, *NE*, 3, 4, p. 340.

73. Leibniz, *NE*, 3, 10, p. 384.

74. Leibniz, *NE*, 3, 17, p. 570.

75. Leibniz, *NE*, 2, 21, p. 178.

76. See Leibniz, *NE*, 2, 21, p. 201.

6. Holism and Idealism in Hegel's *Phenomenology*

I am grateful to John McDowell for helping me to separate out distinct threads in this argument and to see just how to characterize the view I am attempting to reconstruct and attribute to Hegel.

1. By way of warning, if not preparation, for those who may not have read the fuller discussion of this issue in Chapter 3, I should say that it is a *de re* reading of the relevant portions of the text, not a *de dicto* one. As I use and develop these notions in *Making It Explicit*, these are two styles in which one can specify the contents of the very same claims. By "content" I understand broadly inferential role. Grasping a content is, to a first approximation, knowing what follows from it, what is incompatible with it, and what

would be evidence for it. But now an issue arises concerning the source of the auxiliary hypotheses one conjoins with it in order to extract those inferential consequences. Presenting the content in the *de dicto* way requires restricting oneself to appeal only to other collateral commitments specified in terms in which one takes it the one to whom one attributes the claim in question would also acknowledge commitment. Presenting the content in the *de re* way relaxes this restriction, and permits the employment of auxiliary hypotheses the interpreter takes to be *true,* whether or not the target of the ascription knows or believes them. At several crucial junctures in my story, I will help myself to moves that Hegel does *not* explicitly make, but that *I* endorse as correct and important insights, in characterizing the thought that Hegel is expressing. (As an alternative model of this procedure, one might think of domain extension in mathematics. Often an important pattern involving one domain of objects—say, the distribution of roots of polynomial equations with coefficients in the real numbers—becomes apparent only when one considers them as a subset of a wider domain, for instance, the complex numbers. Only the perspective of the extended structure lets us see what is already true of the more restricted one.) In the present case, I signal explicitly when I am importing something into the Hegelian story to make the underlying rationale I discern more visible.

2. All citations from the *Phenomenology* are paragraph numbers from A. V. Miller's 1969 Oxford University Press translation, hereafter cited as M. Cf. M 114, quoted below (note 4).

3. He can then reject the merely formal principle in the sense that he does not take it to be an adequate expression of the crucial relation of *determinate negation.*

4. M 114.

5. M 120.

6. As can universality, though that is another story. See G. W. F. Hegel, *Science of Logic,* trans. A. V. Miller (Atlantic Highlands, N.J.: Humanities Press International, 1990), hereafter, *SL:* "Universality is a *form* assumed by the difference, and the determinateness is the *content*" (*SL,* p. 608).

7. Note that I will try to sketch only one part of this story. An account of how representational relations can be understood in terms of relations among graspable senses, of how the concept of <u>noumena</u> arises out of relations among *phenomena,* is a story for another occasion.

8. But the thought is, of course, pervasive in Hegel's writings. Thus, for instance, "Immediacy in general proceeds only from mediation, and must therefore pass over into mediation. Or, in other words, the determinateness of the content contained in the definition, because it is determinate-

ness, is not merely an immediate, but is mediated by its opposite; consequently definition can apprehend its subject matter only through the opposite determination and must therefore pass into *division*" (*SL*, p. 800).

9. M 113.
10. See my discussion of this point in Chapter 10.
11. See §42Z of the *Encyclopedia*. Worse, Hegel insists that we cannot help ourselves to the category <u>object</u> in defining properties, since the categories <u>object</u> and <u>property</u> themselves stand in a symmetric holistic relation, each in principle intelligible only in terms of the other.
12. M 141.
13. M 163.
14. M 161.
15. M 161.
16. M 161.
17. M 168.
18. M 161.
19. M 162.
20. M 111.
21. M 164.
22. M 134.
23. Gilbert Harman, "Logic and Reasoning," *Synthèse* 60 (1984): 107–128.
24. To begin with, grounded ones.
25. This fact is sometimes obscured for those reading the *Phenomenology* in English translation, since "syllogism," unlike *Schluß*, does not have a naturally associated verb form. In the *Science of Logic*, Hegel often explicitly uses the phrase "Verlauf der Schlüsse."
26. As Hegel says at Encyclopedia §555, "The subjective consciousness of the absolute spirit is essentially and intrinsically a process."
27. This relation should be understood as symmetrical and reciprocal: one also does not understand the idea of purportedly representational commitments, and so <u>incompatibility</u>$_{subj}$, unless one also understands the idea of a determinate world whose determinateness means that it can be other than as it is represented. This is an idea articulated by relations of <u>incompatibility</u>$_{obj}$.
28. This might be called "coarse" reference dependence, which claims only that if one property is instantiated somewhere in a world, the other is instantiated in that same world. "Fine" reference dependence would then claim that if some object instantiates the one property, *that same object* instantiates the other. <u>Teacher</u> and <u>student</u> are (given some straightforward stipulations) related in the first way, while <u>square</u> and <u>rectangle</u> are related in the second.

29. Since hammers are meant to be used to do many things besides driving nails, the relationship would not be reciprocal in this case.

30. I am not sure whether Heidegger was confused on this point in the first division of *Being and Time,* but certainly some of the commentators on the "equipmental involvements" that structure *Zuhandensein* have failed clearly to distinguish the two claims I am calling "sense dependence" and "reference dependence."

31. Though both of these structures are eventually *aufgehoben* in favor of something even more holistic, the 'infinite' holistic incompatibility relational structure of the end of "Consciousness," and situated, embodied communities, by the end of "Reason."

32. I have defended the first two explicitly in *Making It Explicit,* and also there set out some of the raw materials that would need to be assembled to back up the third, Sellarsian claim.

33. Of course, those who are sufficiently impressed by Sellars's analysis of the relation between **looks-red** and **is-red,** in "Empiricism and the Philosophy of Mind," will not be much tempted by such an account. But a more sophisticated analysis of secondary quality concepts is available to them. I discuss one in a forthcoming essay, "Non-inferential Knowledge, Perceptual Experience, and Secondary Qualities: Placing McDowell's Empiricism."

34. M 157–160.

35. Doing this need not be assuming that the notion of immediate difference is autonomously intelligible. There will always be some actual content to the difference: the sign designs exhibit incompatible shapes, for instance. But we can abstract from that content and employ in our reasoning only some of its consequences: the mere difference of the signs. As Hegel says in the *Encyclopedia* "Logic" (§115): "Abstraction is . . . the transformation of something inherently concrete into this form of elementary simplicity. And this may be done in two ways. Either we may neglect a part of the multiple features which are found in the concrete thing (by what is called analysis) and select only one of them; or, neglecting their variety, we may concentrate the multiple character into one."

36. The sanction might be being (counted as being) *obliged* to *do* something that one would not otherwise be obliged to do—for instance, to alter the conditions under which one is disposed to produce tokenings of other signs in the domain in systematically (systematizably) constrained ways. In this example, the relations are generically socially instituted normative relations of relative practical incompatibility of act kinds. But this is *just* an example (though not chosen at random).

37. Abstraction in the usual sense requires an equivalence relation on the un-

derlying domain, while the variety considered here relies on a *nonreflexive, nontransitive* relation. (Indeed, it need not even be considered as symmetric, though Hegel seems to treat determinate negation as symmetric.)

38. "Traversing" is Miller's translation of *durchlaufen*—literally, running or walking through. See, for instance, M 47, where Hegel says that the topic of philosophy is "existence within its own Notion. It is, and this whole movement constitutes what is positive *the process which begets and traverses its own moments* [in it] and its truth" (emphasis added).

39. M 237.

40. M 111.

41. "Force is the unconditioned universal which is equally in its own self what it is *for another;* or which contains the difference in its own self—for difference is nothing else than being-*for-another*" (M 136). "Being for another" is Hegel's way of talking about *relations*—in the case that matters, relations of strong exclusion.

42. Hegel sometimes—I think, less happily—talks about the situation in which one posits, say, properties now as immediate and again as mediated, as one in which the same *content* (a determinate property) shows up in two different *forms.*

43. "In the consummation of the syllogism . . . where objective universality is no less posited as totality of the form determinations, the distinction of mediating and mediated has disappeared. That which is mediated is itself an essential moment of what mediates it, and each moment appears as the totality of what is mediated" (*SL*, p. 703).

44. M 53.

45. Here, as often, he talks about this movement as something that *happens,* rather than something we *do.* But that is just a way of emphasizing that all we are doing in moving this way is bringing out into the explicit light of day what is implicit in each conception we entertain. The path of the movement required to understand them is accordingly determined by the holistic, relational nature of the conceptual contents we are grasping.

46. M 789 (emphasis added).

47. Particularly noticeable by its absence in this sketch is an account of how the subject's engaging in the process of revising the commitments it finds itself with in response to their material incompatibilities underwrites understanding them as presenting (representing, being about, answering for their correctness to) a world articulated by objective relations of material incompatibility. Hegel begins to tell such a story in the "Introduction" to the *Phenomenology.* It is an account of how the representational dimension of concept use emerges from the process of rectifying one's commitments, about how concern with *reference* emerges from concern with *sense* and the sorts of sense dependence considered here. I tell that story elsewhere.

48. Another strand is what I call "conceptual" idealism. I understand *absolute* idealism as roughly the product of objective and conceptual idealism. Conceptual idealism is the sort discussed in Chapter 7, "Some Pragmatist Themes in Hegel's Idealism," under the slogan "The structure and unity of the concept is the same as the structure and unity of the self-conscious self." From the point of view of the present discussion, it is what one gets by applying the strengthened Harman point one more time, and construing subjective processes and objective relations not as standing to each other as elements in a relational structure but as aspects of a process. This is construing how things stand between objective relations and subjective processes, as modeled on the processes of subjects, rather than the relations of objects. It is within *this* process that the "for others" of the second stage comes to encompass relations between the objective and the subjective. But that is another story.

7. Some Pragmatist Themes in Hegel's Idealism

1. Kant usually says "rules" but he means something that, though statable, can be implicit, not just what is already explicitly stated.

2. To be able to do that is to be *free*. To be free is accordingly to be able to bind oneself by the norms that are concepts. The *only* thing that Kantian agents can *do*, in the strict sense of *do* that involves the exercise of freedom, is apply concepts—whether theoretically in judgment or practically in action. Activity that consists in the application of concepts is *rational* activity. So we are free exactly insofar as we are rational.

3. "Judgment in general is the faculty of thinking the particular as contained under the universal. If the universal (the rule, the principle, the law) be given, the judgment which subsumes the particular under it . . . is *determinate* [*bestimmend*]. But if only the particular be given for which the universal has to be found, the judgment is merely *reflective*." Immanuel Kant, *Critique of Judgment* (1790), trans. I. H. Bernard (New York: Macmillan, 1951), intro., sect. 4, para 1.

4. Given Kant's other commitments, neither term can be applied without qualification, which fact sets up the problematic of the third Critique.

5. Only the "ultimate" subjects, since the role of the pure concepts in making them possible is the proximate subject.

6. I will indicate briefly how Hegel sees immediacy as exercising an authority that constrains the application of concepts, and so how particulars are given a normatively significant voice that must negotiate with the reciprocal authority of mediating universals, all of it administered by those who attribute determinately contentful conceptual commitments.

7. It should be noticed in this connection that invoking the temporal *schema-*

tism of concepts is not a responsive answer to this challenge (quite apart from the obscurity of the details). For the schematism of the understanding at most explains how a concept could get a grip on (apply or not apply to) a particular intuition. But the question regarding determinateness is rather what it is for us to get a hold of one completely determinate universal rather than a closely related one that applies to almost but not quite all the same particulars.

8. Saul Kripke, *Wittgenstein on Rules and Private Language* (Cambridge, Mass.: Harvard University Press, 1982). Only "related to" because Kripke imports constraints on the problem that Hegel would not share. It is fair to ask what it is about how we have *actually* applied concepts in the past that determines how we *ought* to apply them in the future, what determines how we have *committed* ourselves to do so. For to ask that is to ask how the actual practice of *application* manages to *institute* one norm rather than another. But there is no legitimate standpoint from which one is entitled to restrict one's specification of that practice of application, as Kripke implicitly does, to what can be stated in a *nonnormative* vocabulary. Using an expression *correctly* or *incorrectly* is also something we *actually* do.

9. The origins of this way of thinking about Hegel's problems lie in Robert Pippin's pathbreaking work *Hegel's Idealism: The Satisfactions of Self-Consciousness* (Cambridge: Cambridge University Press, 1989).

10. Among the many nontrivial differences between them is that Carnap's is a *globally* two-phase picture, while Kant's is only *locally* two-phase. That is, nothing in Kant's account suggests the possibility of making *all* one's reflective judgments first, only then to begin making determinant judgments. The structural similarity consists only in the common commitment to there being two quite different sorts of things one is doing, in making meanings or concepts available, and then in employing them.

11. Notice that this is not yet to say anything about the vocabulary in which the use is to be specified by the theorist. In particular, focusing on *use* is not the same thing as focusing on *use specified in a nonnormative vocabulary.*

12. So one of Hegel's fundamental claims is that a suitable *dynamic* account of the relation between conceptual contents and experience, the institution of concepts and their application, can reconcile the rationalist insight and the empiricist insight (that the content of empirical concepts must be understood as deriving from experience), while rejecting both innateness and abstractionism. This *pragmatist* strategy looks to the *development* of concepts through their use in experience, that is, in the practices of judging and acting.

13. Recognizing that every concept actually applied in any empirical judgment

is only a more or less adequate expression of the implicit articulation of things entails acknowledging that no determinate judgment ought to be taken to be unqualifiedly true. (For Hegel it is different with the concepts of logic, whose distinctive expressive task it is to make explicit the process by which the system of determinate concepts and judgments—the Concept—progresses and develops.) So to take the judgment to be the unit of cognition (as Kant does, because it is the minimal unit of cognitive *responsibility*) is already to commit oneself to an unsustainable view of the nature of the determinateness of conceptual content.

14. G. W. F. Hegel, *Science of Logic* (1831), trans. A. V. Miller (New York: Humanities Press International, 1969), p. 584, hereafter *SL*.

15. *SL*, p. 585.

16. The phrase is from John Haugeland, "Heidegger on Being a Person," *Noûs* 16 (1982). Of course, the social institution is not unconstrained. As we will see, the history of previous applications of a concept, including those immediately elicited by the particulars to which they are applied, exercises a crucial authority over such an institution.

17. For Hegel, true general recognition is an equivalence relation: symmetric, reflexive, and transitive.

18. The discussion of the Law of the Heart in the *Phenomenology* is one place where this issue of the conditions of the possibility of determinately binding oneself is explored.

19. So it would be a mistake to assert a strict identity between the application and the institution of determinately contentful concepts: to say, for instance, that meaning is use. It is essential to see the identity that is genuinely involved (according to the pragmatist) as what Hegel calls a "speculative" identity—that is, one that essentially incorporates a difference.

20. Though to say it is "secured" by others is not to say that it is fully *determined* by them. As will emerge, the authority of particularity, asserted through immediate judgments, according to the other two recognitive dimensions (inferential and historical), constrains the community and constitutes an essential element of the content those judgments administer—the content of the norms that have reciprocal authority over them.

21. If X has some sort of authority over Y, then Y is insofar as such responsible to X. But Hegel's way of working through the Rousseau-Kant understanding of autonomy as the essence of normative bindingness (validity, *Gültigkeit*) requires that if X has some sort of authority over Y, then X also has some sort of responsibility toward Y—that is, Y has a reciprocal authority over X. This is a claim about the very nature of authority and responsibility: the nature of the normative as such. A commitment to the coherence of construing X as having authority over Y (dually: Y's responsi-

bility to X) that is not balanced by Y's reciprocal authority over X (dually, X's responsibility to Y) is an index of thinking that remains at the meta-conceptual level Hegel calls Understanding, failing to advance to the meta-conceptual level he calls Reason. It is failing to make the categorical conceptual move from *independence* to *freedom,* in the sense of *autonomy:* being bound by norms, but by exactly those one has bound *oneself* by.

Analyzing commitments and other normative statuses as products instituted by attitudes of both acknowledgment and attribution (and so two sorts of independence or authority, and two corresponding sorts of dependence or responsibility) is appealing to the idea of mutual recognition. But the recognition involved is *specific* rather than *general.* To recognize someone in the general sense is to take her to be a normative subject of commitments and responsibilities. One does that by attributing specific commitments and responsibilities. That is, recognition in general is an abstract notion. It is what is common to all instances of specific recognition. To be a self, one must have some actual, specific commitments and responsibilities. Recognition in general is just an abstract way of talking about what is common to all specific recognition. One cannot *merely* recognize someone. Recognizing someone is always attributing some specific commitments and responsibilities—though perhaps different ones in each case. This is why *actual* reciprocal recognition is required for me to *be* a self in the normative sense.

22. Talk of *negotiation* is bound to sound far too irenic a rendering for the sort of strife and confrontation of inconsistent demands Hegel depicts. But, though the issue cannot be pursued here, I think there are good reasons to treat the martial, uncompromising language Hegel is fond of as misleading on this point. Nothing is absolutely other, nor are any claims or concepts simply inconsistent for him. It is always material incompatibilities of content (rather than formal inconsistencies) whose mutual confrontation obliges an alteration of commitments.

23. This argumentative structure has not been obvious to Hegel's readers, and I think one reason is the order of exposition he adopts in the *Phenomenology.* For Hegel starts by introducing a notion of *general* recognition (in the "Self-Consciousness" section), that is, taking or treating someone as a normative subject of commitments and responsibilities in general. He asserts the essentially social character of recognition, and explores some consequences of not appreciating the essentially *reciprocal* structure that can alone make sense of normative statuses. But the content of the concept does not really emerge until later (in the section on "Reason"), when he discusses *specific* recognition—that is, the acknowledgment and attribution of the specific, *determinate* commitments and responsibilities involved

in the use of particular, determinately contentful *concepts,* in judgment and action. It is only looking back from this vantage point (at the end of the "Reason" section) that we can see recognition in general as an abstraction from specific recognition, as what all specific recognitive attitudes (the only ones that are actual) have in common. And it is at this level that the account of recognition as essentially social and reciprocal must be motivated. For this reason, the social dimension of recognition, with which I began my exposition, in the end shows itself not to be fully intelligible apart from the inferential and historical dimensions, since the determinately contentful conceptual commitments that are attributed by specific recognitive attitudes are not.

24. It is up to me both what concept I apply in judging or acting, and who has the authority to administer it. For a norm to be intelligible as *binding,* as having genuine normative *force,* though, the moment of independence (authority) exercised by the one on whom it is binding (in virtue of *his* acknowledgment of that normative status) must be understood as balanced by a moment of dependence on (responsibility to) those who attribute and assess it. And as we will see, this is not the only moment of normative dependence in play. Those who attribute and assess the commitment are obliged also to acknowledge the authority of prior applications (which includes the authority of immediacy) in their administration of the content those applications institute.

25. Readers of my book *Making It Explicit* are liable, at this point, to suspect me of simply reading my own views into Hegel, starting with a socially perspectival normative approach to pragmatics, and now moving on to an inferential approach to semantics. The similarity is not coincidental, but the order of influence runs in the other direction: I came to these thoughts from reading Hegel, and went on to develop them in my own way. I construe what I am doing now as trying to acknowledge the debt, rather than foisting my views on Hegel.

26. In the syllogism:

> Judgments are applications of concepts,
> Applications of concepts are inferentially articulated,
> therefore
> Judgments are inferentially articulated,

the concept application of concepts plays the role of the middle term, which mediates the inference from the applicability of the concept judgment to the applicability of the concept inferentially articulated. The mediating concept formulates the conclusion of the inference from "X is a judgment" to "X is the application of a concept" and the premise of the in-

ference from "X is the application of a concept" to "X is inferentially articulated."

27. The inferences in question are not (just) formally or logically good inferences, such as the syllogism, but also the *materially* correct inferences that
are implicit in their premises. These are inferences whose goodness depends on and articulates the *nonlogical content* of the concepts involved. In
the example above, that judgments (and actions) are applications of concepts, is an element essential to the contents of those particular concepts.
An example would be the inference from "Pittsburgh is to the west of New
York" to "New York is to the east of Pittsburgh." Given material, that
is, content-articulating, proprieties of inference, various sorts of formally
valid inferences can be understood as material proprieties that are robust
under corresponding kinds of substitution.

28. Another example might be the incompatibility involved in a Newtonian
mass accelerating in the absence of imposed forces.

29. One can derive relations of mediation from those of determinate negation—that is, relations of material *inference* from those of material *incompatibility.* For *p* incompatibility entails *q* just in case everything incompatible with *q* is incompatible with *p* (though perhaps not conversely). Thus,
being a dog entails being a mammal, because everything incompatible with
being a mammal is incompatible with being a dog. Hegel often talks as
though *negation* were the fundamental content-articulating notion.

30. It is ultimately in terms of them that we must understand the analogue of
recognitive relations for concepts: what plays the role for concepts that reciprocal recognition in the paradigmatic sense plays for individual self-
conscious selves, according to the idealist thesis. But we must remember
the pragmatist thesis as well. That thesis, common ground between Hegel
and Quine, says that *instituting* conceptual norms and *applying* them are
two sides of one coin, two aspects of one process. Doing the former is settling *meanings,* determining the boundaries distinguishing *correct* or *appropriate* application from applications that would be incorrect or inappropriate. Doing the latter is making judgments (and performing actions),
and assessing such performances—in practice *taking* particular applications to be correct or incorrect, *treating* them as appropriate or not. Thus
Quine insists that settling one's meanings is not a process separate from
settling one's beliefs. For Hegel, it is in making and assessing judgments
and actions—that is, in experience—that we determine the contents of the
conceptual norms that govern that process. The coordinate status of concepts and judgments is an essential feature of the monistic approach to
which these pragmatists are committed. So material inferential and incompatibility relations among concepts must be understood as features of the

process of adopting actual attitudes, actually applying those concepts: taking or treating some applications *as* appropriate by undertaking conceptually articulated commitments in the form of judgments (or actions), and by assessing the appropriateness of such commitments. It is this process that, according to the idealist, can usefully be construed as involving constitutive relations of mutual recognition.

31. Of course, even these are inferentially *articulated*: they are applications of concepts, and so essentially something that can serve as premises for inference. Their immediacy consists in their being *non*inferential *only* in the sense that commitment that is the judgment was not undertaken as the result of a process of inference. That this is the only sense in which judgments can be noninferential is one of the central lessons of the "Perception" section of the *Phenomenology*, and of Sellars's seminal essay "Empiricism and the Philosophy of Mind." See my discussion in Wilfrid Sellars, *Empiricism and the Philosophy of Mind*, with an introduction by Richard Rorty and a Study Guide by Robert Brandom (Cambridge, Mass.: Harvard University Press, 1997).

32. G. W. F. Hegel, *Phenomenology of Spirit* (1807), trans. A. V. Miller (Oxford: Oxford University Press, 1977), §109, p. 65.

33. For empirical concepts, at any rate, I do not think that Hegel is committed to there being in every case a unique answer that can be settled in advance to the question of how such conflicts ought to be resolved, which commitments should be modified or relinquished. Such a concrete conflict might be resolved, for instance, by judging that one cannot reliably noninferentially apply color terms if the objects in question are illuminated only by incandescent electric lights, or that the applicability of Q is entailed only by the applicability of $P\&S$, not of P by itself.

34. Talk of this process of experience as driven by the "restless negativity" of concepts is an appeal to the role played in it by the fact that makes our empirical concepts permanently subject to the possibility of revision: their potential to give rise to determinately incompatible judgments (immediate and mediate). And though the point cannot be pursued here, it is of the utmost significance that because concepts develop and become more determinate in this way, *immediacy, contingency,* and *particularity* are *incorporated* into the contents of those concepts. Suppose we have well-developed differential responsive dispositions leading us immediately to classify particulars as *sour* and as *red* or *blue*, and inferential commitments to the propriety of inferring the applicability of the universal *acid* from that of *sour,* and to acids turning litmus paper red. Then upon being confronted with something that tastes sour and turns litmus paper blue (which by our own lights again is incompatible with its being red), we are committed to

changing our commitments. Whether it is our noninferential differential responsive dispositions or our inferential commitments that we adjust, the world's immediacy has been incorporated into our concepts by this development. What is required by our concepts is denominated "necessary," so what is here incorporated is also intelligible as the *contingency* of the world. And it is the authority of particulars over our universals that is thereby exercised by the judgments we find ourselves with immediately.

35. Recognitive relations model the reciprocal dimensions of authority in play here at two levels. On the one hand, the Concept stands to its constituent, determinate empirical concepts, as community to individual self. On the other hand, the determinate empirical universal stands to the characterized individual as community to self. It is judgments that tie together the two limbs of this structure. In fact this one process of experience *is*—not just is modeled on—the process by which *self-conscious selves* are synthesized. Selves in the *normative* sense introduced by Kant are the loci of responsibility for sorting out incompatibilities. The transcendental unity of apperception is what is responsible *for* judgments, its obligation to sort out incompatibilities among applications of concepts being what makes them *its* judgments. So it is misleading to think of the mutual recognition synthesizing selves as available in principle in advance of understanding the inferentially articulated reciprocal authority of universals and particulars. For general recognition is an abstraction from specific recognition, which involves negotiating the potentially competing authority of particulars and universals. That requirement constrains and makes determinate the content those who attribute a commitment administer.

The responsibility you and I have to negotiate the claims of different authorities so as to eliminate incompatibilities between *your* empirical judgments and *mine,* while real, is in principle secondary to and derived from the responsibility each of us has to sort out incompatibilities among our *own* commitments. (Although I cannot pursue the matter here, in the "Perception" section of the *Phenomenology,* Hegel develops an account of *objects* [particulars]—what our judgments are responsible *to* on the side of particularity—as units of account for the responsibilities triggered by incompatibilities in a parallel fashion. To say that two colors are incompatible properties is to say that no *one particular* can exhibit both, not that two different objects cannot exhibit them severally. And it is in terms of just this fact that we are to draw boundaries around particulars. A corresponding dual condition applies to the individuation of properties or concepts.) The self-conscious individual self is the self who exerts specific recognitive authority and is subject to specific recognitive responsibility, the self who undertakes and attributes determinately contentful conceptual commitments by making judgments (including assessments of the judgments of others). We understand the structure and unity of such selves, and of their communities, in terms of reciprocal recognition. And it is in exactly the same terms that we understand the structure and unity of both the characterized individuals that are the topics of (the most basic form of) judgment, and the determinately contentful concepts or universals that are applied in making those judgments. This is Hegel's fundamental idealist thesis.

36. *SL*, p. 583.

37. *SL*, p. 583.

38. Only "includes" because it has other dimensions as well. For instance, the judge has the authority to sort the various respects of similarity and dissimilarity between the facts of the present case and the facts of the previously decided cases, treating some as more important than others for the issue of whether the legal concept in question should be applied to or withheld from the present facts. This makes some of the prior cases already classified as properly decided more, and others less, relevant to the decision in question. That in turn affects the authority of prior applications of inferentially related concepts.

39. Kant's two-phase account would correspond to an insistence that every tradition of common or case law be grounded in some prior statute. This is a kind of intellectualism, which insists that behind every norm implicit in a practice there must be a norm explicit in a rule. (Pragmatism is the converse of intellectualism in this sense, insisting that any sort of explicit, theoretical knowing *that* have as its background some sort of implicit practical knowing *how.*) The intellectualist thinks that only *if fully* and *finally* determinate norms have already been instituted has any distinction between their correct and incorrect application been made available for the next phase. Hegel, the pragmatist, denies that any concepts are fully and finally determinate in this sense, that is, independently of the actual course of the practice of applying them. For Hegel's purposes (and mine) the details (such as they are) of Kant's account of the institution or discovery of conceptual norms in judgments of reflection does not matter at all. *All* that is important is the two-phase structure he envisages.

40. Hegel thinks that because concepts acquire determinate content only as a result of their role in such a tradition of being applied, their contents can be presented or conveyed only by offering a rationally reconstructed trajectory by which they might have developed. This is what he does for his most basic logical concepts in both the *Phenomenology* and the *Science of Logic*. The proprieties that govern the use of the vocabulary Hegel uses to make explicit the workings of ordinary concepts are conveyed by explor-

ing various *misuses* and misunderstandings which, while capturing some of the eventual content, still lead to discordant and incompatible commitments. In taking the explanatory tack that I do in this chapter, I am implicitly disagreeing that this procedure is necessary. I think that the logical concepts are different from ordinary empirical concepts (Hegel's "determinate" concepts), since they get their content from their explicitating role. I think it is possible to bypass the rehearsal of a path of development of their content and directly present the contents those concepts are taken to have at the end of Hegel's two books. My strategy here has been to use the model of reciprocal recognition to do that.

41. Although the emphases are different in each of the great systematic works—more on the social and historical dimensions in the *Phenomenology,* more on the inferential in the *Science of Logic*—I think that the whole three-dimensional structure is present throughout. The big test for this reading will be the sense it can make of Hegel's radically new construal of the relation of reciprocal authority (and so responsibility) between subject and object (certainty and truth, what things are *for* consciousness and what they are *in* themselves, concept and being), which articulates the structure at once of consciousness (including the relation between spontaneity and receptivity, making and finding) and of the Idea. I think that we can learn a lot about this central relation by examining the interactions among the three dimensions of reciprocal authority that I have examined here. I hope to be able to tell this story on another occasion.

8. Frege's Technical Concepts

1. See Hans Hermes, Friedrich Kambartel, and Friedrich Kaulbach, eds., *Gottlob Frege: Posthumous Writings,* trans. Peter Long and Roger White (Chicago: University of Chicago Press, 1981).
2. Michael Dummett, *Frege: Philosophy of Language* (New York: Harper and Row, 1973), hereafter Dummett, *FPL.*
3. Michael Dummett, *The Interpretation of Frege's Philosophy* (Cambridge, Mass.: Harvard University Press, 1981), hereafter Dummett, *IFP.*
4. Dummett, *IFP,* pp. xii–xvi.
5. The most influential proponents of the view were Reinhardt Grossmann, "Frege's Ontology," *Philosophical Review* 70 (1961): 23–40; William Marshall, "Frege's Theory of Functions and Objects," *Philosophical Review* 62 (1953): 347–390; and William Marshall, "Sense and Reference: A Reply," in *Essays on Frege,* ed. E. D. Klemke (Urbana: University of Illinois Press, 1968), 298–320.

6. Peter Geach and Max Black, eds., *Philosophical Writings of Gottlob Frege* (Oxford: Blackwells, 1970), p. 65, hereafter Geach and Black, *PWGF.*

7. David Bell, *Frege's Theory of Judgement* (Oxford: Oxford University Press, 1979), hereafter Bell, *FTJ.*

8. As in the title of Dummett's book, *Frege: Philosophy of Language.*

9. Dummett, *IFP,* pp. 476–495.

10. In section 3 of *BGS,* reprinted in Geach and Black, *PWGF,* Frege says that the *begriffliche Inhalt* of two judgments is the same just in case "all inferences which can be drawn from the first judgement when combined with certain other ones can always also be drawn from the second when combined with the same other judgements."

11. Frege, *Posthumous Writings,* pp. 9–46.

12. For instance by Michael Resnik in "The Context Principle in Frege's Philosophy," *Philosophy and Phenomenological Research* 27 (1967): 356–365; and Michael Resnik, "Frege's Context Principle Revisited," in *Studien zu Frege,* ed. M. Schirn (Stuttgart: Frommann-Holzboog, 1967), 3:35–49. See also Ignacio Angelelli, *Studies on Gottlob Frege and Traditional Philosophy* (Dordrecht: D. Reidel, 1967).

13. Bell, *FTJ,* pp. 139–140.

14. I have my say in "Asserting," *Noûs* 17 (1983): 637–650.

15. Bell, *FTJ,* p. 42.

16. Dummett, *IFP,* pp. 478–479.

17. In Ernst Tugendhat, "The Meaning of 'Bedeutung' in Frege," *Analysis* 30 (1970): 177–189.

18. Dummett, *IFP,* p. 479.

19. I have argued that a purely intralinguistic anaphoric account of such facts can be offered by construing 'refers' and its cognates as complex pronoun-forming operators, in "Reference Explained Away," *Journal of Philosophy* 84 (1984): 769–792.

20. Saul Kripke in "Naming and Necessity," and Hilary Putnam in "The Meaning of Meaning," both in *Semantics of Natural Language,* ed. Gilbert Harman and Donald Davidson (Dordrecht: D. Reidel, 1972).

21. Most prominently John Perry, "Frege on Demonstratives," *Philosophical Review* 86 (1977): 474–497; David Kaplan, "The Logic of Demonstratives," in *Contemporary Perspectives on Philosophy of Language,* ed. Theodore Uehling, Howard Wettstein, and Peter French, Midwest Studies in Philosophy (Minneapolis: University of Minnesota Press, 1978); and David Kaplan, *Demonstratives,* 1980 John Locke Lectures (Oxford: Oxford University Press, 1984).

22. Bell, *FTJ,* p. 112.

23. Bell, *FTJ*, p. 115.

24. Bell, *FTJ*, p. 51.

25. Bell, *FTJ*, p. 64.

26. Bell, *FTJ*, p. 65.

27. First in Dummett, *FPL*, pp. 293–294, then at greater length as chap. 13 of Dummett, *IFP.* Citations here from p. 251 of the latter.

28. In Peter Geach, "Review of Dummett's *Frege: Philosophy of Language*," *Mind* 85 (1975): 436–449.

29. Dummett, *FPL*, pp. 251–252.

30. Frege, *Posthumous Writings*, p. 119. Bell's other quotations are from Bell, *FTJ*, p. 72.

31. Bell, *FTJ*, pp. 74–78.

32. See Hans Sluga, *Gottlob Frege* (London: Routledge and Kegan Paul, 1980), hereafter Sluga, *GF.*

33. Michael Dummett, "Frege, Gottlob," in *Encyclopedia of Philosophy*, ed. Paul Edwards (New York: Macmillan, 1967), 4:225, quoted in Sluga, *GF,* p. 8.

34. In Dummett's defense it should be said that in the final chapter of *FPL*, the main historical significance of Frege's work is taken to be precisely his anti-empiricist and anti-psychologist shifting of concern from the acquisition of concepts to what such mastery consists in—from how the cognitive trick is performed (e.g., by material beings of our sort) to what counts as performing it. The injudicious invocation of a dominant Hegelianism as the psychologistic culprit is explicitly made subsidiary to this central point.

35. Sluga, *GF,* p. 59.

36. Michael Dummett, in "Frege as Realist," *Inquiry* 19 (1976): 476–485.

37. M. Bierich, "Freges Lehre von dem Sinn und der Bedeutung der Urteile und Russells Kritik an dieser Lehre" (Diss., University of Hamburg, 1951).

38. Sluga, *GF,* pp. 53, 192.

39. Sluga, *GF,* pp. 59–60.

40. Sluga, *GF,* pp. 44–45 and 106.

41. Sluga, *GF,* p. 60.

42. Sluga, *GF,* p. 60.

43. Sluga, *GF,* p. 91.

44. Sluga, *GF,* p. 181.

45. Sluga, *GF,* p. 95.

46. Frege, *Posthumous Writings*, p. 253.

47. Sluga, *GF,* p. 134 and note 21 to chap. 4.

48. E.g., Sluga, *GF,* p. 156.

49. Sections 62, 63 of Gottlob Frege, *Grundlagen der Arithmetik,* trans. J. L.

Austin (Evanston, Ill.: Northwestern University Press, 1967), hereafter Frege, *GL.*

50. Section 68 of Frege, *GL.* Equality of concepts in the sense invoked here has been defined as obtaining iff the objects of which the concepts are true can be put into one-to-one correspondence.

51. Gregory Currie, *Frege: An Introduction to His Philosophy* (Totowa, N.J.: Barnes and Noble, 1982), p. 69.

52. Bell, *FTJ,* p. 55. He goes on to point out an analogy with the Fregean concept of concept reference: "Concept words refer, but we cannot stipulate *what* it is they refer to." But in this case the reasons are purely substitutional, since expressions like "the concept <u>horse</u>" will never be intersubstitutable with predicative function-expressions. This shows that all heterogeneous identities involving function-expressions on one side and singular terms on the other must be false.

9. The Significance of Complex Numbers for Frege's Philosophy of Mathematics

Special thanks to Ken Manders, Jim Conant, and Susan Sterrett. Originally presented at the meeting of the Aristotelian Society, held in the Senior Common Room, Birkbeck College, London, on Monday, May 13, 1996.

1. See Peter M. Simmons, "Frege's Theory of Real Numbers," and Michael Dummett, "Frege's Theory of Real Numbers," reprinted in *Frege's Philosophy of Mathematics*, ed. William Demopolous (Cambridge, Mass.: Harvard University Press, 1995), pp. 358–385 and 386–404.

2. Here is Dummett's whole discussion of the issue: "If Volume III [of the *Grundgesetze*] had contained only the conclusion of Part III, it would have been extremely short. Possibly Frege had in mind a Part IV, dealing with complex numbers. It may be thought that would have been pointless, *since it is easy to define the complex numbers in terms of the reals;* but Frege was much concerned with applications, and the applications of complex analysis are by no means immediately evident from the representation of complex numbers as ordered pairs of reals, or even from the geometrical interpretation, which in any case he would have disliked as involving the intrusion into arithmetic of something dependent on intuition." *Frege: Philosophy of Mathematics* (Cambridge, Mass.: Harvard University Press, 1991), p. 242 (emphasis added).

3. Logical objects are a special kind of object. This concept should not be confused with that of objects in a logical sense—that is, objects in general—which coincides for Frege with the notion of countables.

4. Cf. *Grundlagen der Arithmetik,* §62. See Gottlob Frege, *Foundations of*

Arithmetic, trans. J. L. Austin (Evanston, Ill.: Northwestern University Press, 1959), hereafter Frege, *GL.*

5. Frege, *GL,* §76.
6. Frege, *GL,* §§65, 107.
7. Frege, *GL,* §57.
8. Frege, *GL,* §74n.
9. Frege, *GL,* §102.
10. Frege, *GL,* §74n.
11. Frege, *GL,* §102 (emphasis added).
12. Frege, *GL,* §97.
13. Frege, *GL,* §104 (emphasis added).
14. In "Frege's Technical Concepts," in *Frege Synthesized: Essays on the Philosophical and Foundational Work of G. Frege,* ed. Lila Haaparanta and Jaakko Hintikka, Synthese Library (Dordrecht: D. Reidel, 1986), pp. 253–295, I diagnose philosophical problems of this sort with Frege's technical argument in §10 of the *Grundgesetze,* the argument in which Frege explicitly addresses the "Julius Caesar" issue. These are also problems that have nothing to do with the inconsistency of the logic that results.
15. Paul Benacerraf, "What Numbers Could Not Be," *Philosophical Review* 74 (1965): 47–73.
16. Of course, this objection does not directly address Frege's construction, which identifies the natural number *n* with the extension of the concept equinumerous with the concept [ ], and inserts in the brackets the specification of a concept logically guaranteed to apply to exactly *n* things—for instance, for 0 the concept not identical to itself.
17. Frege, *GL,* §103. Given the ruthless and heroic intellectual honesty of his response to Russell's paradox, it is clear that Frege would not talk this way if he realized the magnitude and character of the obstacles that stood in the way of extending his treatment to the complex numbers.
18. Gottlob Frege, *Philosophical and Mathematical Correspondence* (Oxford: Basil Blackwell, 1980), pp. 125–126.
19. Frege, *GL,* §26.
20. See Peter M. Neumann, S. A. Adelke, and Michael Dummett, "On a Question of Frege's about Right-ordered Groups," in Demopolous, *Frege's Philosophy of Mathematics,* pp. 405–421.
21. Frege, *GL,* §13.
22. Such a semantic axiom need not be construed as entailing the *mathematical* axiom of choice, which makes a difference only by permitting the choice of arbitrary elements from each of the elements of the power sets of arbitrary infinite sets.
23. This move is potentially an important piece of the puzzle about the sta-

tus of objects introduced by abstractive definitions (the second sort of *Grundlagen* definitions, for which the Julius Caesar problem arises), but that issue cannot be pursued here.

10. Heidegger's Categories in *Sein und Zeit*

1. The general orientation of this chapter owes much to John Haugeland, particularly to his account of transcendental constitution as and by social institution in "Heidegger on Being a Person," *Noûs* (March 1982): 15–26. I also thank my fellow staff members and the seminar participants at the Council for Philosophic Studies 1980 Summer Institute, "Phenomenology and Existentialism: Continental and Analytic Perspectives on Intentionality," for their responses to an earlier version of the ideas presented here. References are to page numbers in Martin Heidegger, *Being and Time*, trans. John Macquarrie and Edward Robinson (New York: Harper and Row, 1962), hereafter *BT;* and idem, *Sein und Zeit*, vol. 2 of Heidegger's *Gesamtausgabe* (Frankfurt am Main: Klostermann, 1976), hereafter *SZ*.

2. See Richard Rorty's "Incorrigibility as the Mark of the Mental," *Journal of Philosophy* 67, no. 12 (June 25, 1970): 399–424.

3. Of course, Descartes held other views about the substances to which these categories applied as well. He filled in the abstract ontological categorization of epistemic kinds with specifications, for example, of the objective realm as having its essence exhausted by geometric extension, and of the epistemic subject whose incorrigible "takings" define the mental as itself identical with the sum of mental things it is aware of. The current concern is with the ontological framework rather than with Descartes's theories about the entities it categorized.

4. In "Freedom and Constraint by Norms," *American Philosophical Quarterly* 16 (April 1977): 187–196, I investigate the sort of norm inherent in the appropriatenesses instituted by social practices. I take it to be significant that the social/objective distinction can be seen as the origin of the value/fact distinction, and that both naturalists, who want to reduce one category to the other, and non-naturalists, who do not, presumed that it was an *objective* distinction between facts and values which was at issue. I explore the consequences of treating the social/objective, and hence the value/fact, distinction as itself social rather than objective, that is, as a matter of how the community responds to various things, not how they are independently and in themselves.

5. As Richard Rorty has argued (*Philosophy and the Mirror of Nature* [Princeton: Princeton University Press, 1979]), on the plausibility of such a claim rest Sellars's and Quine's twin attacks on the two varieties of unjustified

justifiers ("privileged representations") which foundationalists, particularly positivistic ones, had relied on as the foundations of our inferential structures. Thus Quine dismantled the picture of *language* as a source of authority immune to social revision ("intrinsic credibility," "self evidence," etc.) for some sentences thought to be true-in-virtue-of-meaning, and Sellars performed the same service for the picture of the mind as a source of supposedly socially impervious privilege for "reports" of thoughts and sensations.

6. *BT,* 190; *SZ,* 150.
7. Cf. the "sich verweisenden Verstehen" of *BT,* 119.
8. See, e.g., *BT,* 100; *SZ,* 70.
9. Such a model must be used with caution, however. Heidegger is concerned that the structures so taken as worlds involve *concrete* relations of use, production, and response, rather than simply structurally analogous relations. He says: "The context of assignments or references, which, as significance, is constitutive for worldhood, can be taken formally in the sense of a system of Relations. But one must note that in such formalizations the phenomena get levelled off so much that their real phenomenal content may be lost . . . the phenomenal content of these 'relations' and 'relata'—the 'in-order-to,' the 'for-the-sake-of,' and the 'with-which' of an involvement—is such that they resist any sort of mathematical functionalization" (*BT,* 121–122; *SZ,* 88).
10. This view represents a normative version of the 'conformism' discussed by Haugeland ("Heidegger on Being a Person"), without what I take to be the ontologically irrelevant account of its ontic genesis which he offers.
11. *BT,* 203; *SZ,* 160.
12. *BT,* 190; *SZ,* 150.
13. *BT,* 275; *SZ,* 231.
14. *BT,* 204; *SZ,* 161.
15. *BT,* 411; *SZ,* 360.
16. *BT,* 266; *SZ,* 224, following the passage on speaking-over quoted earlier.
17. I have presented the details of an account of asserting along these lines in "Asserting," *Noûs* 17, no. 4 (November 1983): 637–650.
18. Here 'theoretical' inference refers to language-language moves, by contrast to 'practical' inference involving language-exit moves (in Sellars's sense). In a different sense, 'theoretical' claims are those which can be arrived at *only* inferentially, and not as noninferential reports. Discussion of the relevance to the understanding of presence-at-hand of claims which are theoretical in this sense is beyond the scope of this chapter.
19. The semantics of the points of view generated by such 'interfaces'—where

a set of claims can make a difference to practical deliberations only insofar as it makes a difference to some other set of claims which then affects the deliberations—is discussed in my "Points of View and Practical Reasoning," *Canadian Journal of Philosophy* 12 (June 1982): 20.

20. *BT,* 268; *SZ,* 225.

11. Dasein, the Being That Thematizes

This chapter is a discussion of Heidegger's "Thematisierende Seiende, das Dasein" (*BT,* 415; *SZ,* 364). References are to Martin Heidegger, *Being and Time (BT),* trans. John Macquarrie and Edward Robinson (New York: Harper and Row, 1962); and idem, *Sein und Zeit (SZ),* vol. 2 of Heidegger's *Gesamtausgabe* (Frankfurt am Main: Klostermann, 1976). Special thanks are due to John Haugeland for many conversations and much assistance with the topics discussed here, to Bill Blattner, to my fellow staff members, and to the participants at the NEH Summer Institute on Heidegger and Davidson during which the original version of this chapter was written, and to the NEH for supporting that form of Dasein.

1. Heidegger formulates his view by opposition to this: "In interpreting we do not, so to speak, throw a 'signification' over some naked thing which is present-at-hand, we do not stick a value on it" (*BT,* 191; *SZ,* 150). See also *BT,* 97; *SZ,* 68, and *BT,* 132; *SZ,* 99.
2. The section titled "The Theme of the Analytic of Dasein" states, "We are ourselves the entity to be analyzed" (*BT,* 67; *SZ,* 41).
3. "Dasein in itself is essentially Being-with" (*BT,* 156; *SZ,* 120). "So far as Dasein is at all, it has Being-with-one-another as its kind of Being" (*BT,* 163; *SZ,* 125).
4. "'Being-in' is thus the formal existential expression for the Being of Dasein, which has Being-in-the-world as its essential state" (*BT,* 80; *SZ,* 54). "'Dasein' means Being-in-the-world" (*BT,* 208; *SZ,* 165).
5. I use *category* here not in Heidegger's technical sense (for *Existenz* is not in that sense a category), but in the sense of "ontological category" that I detail in "Heidegger's Categories in *Being and Time,*" *Monist* 66 (1983): 387–409, reprinted in *Heidegger: A Critical Reader,* ed. Hubert L. Dreyfus and Harrison Hall (Oxford: Blackwell, 1992), pp. 45–64, and as Chapter 10 of this work.
6. "But the 'indicating' of the sign and the 'hammering' of the hammer are not properties of entities. Anything ready-to-hand is, at the worst, appropriate for some purposes and inappropriate for others" (*BT,* 114–115; *SZ,* 83). "Serviceability, too, however, as a constitutive state of equipment . . . is not

an appropriateness of some entity; it is rather the condition (so far as Being is in question) which makes it possible for the character of such an entity to be defined by its appropriatenesses" (*BT,* 115; *SZ,* 83).

7. "As the Being of something ready-to-hand, an involvement is itself discovered only on the basis of the prior discovery of a totality of involvements" (*BT,* 118; *SZ,* 85). "Being-in-the-world, according to our interpretation hitherto, amounts to a nonthematic circumspective absorption in references or assignments constitutive for the readiness-to-hand of a totality of equipment" (*BT,* 107; *SZ,* 67).

8. These projects are not to be understood as explicitly conceived and adopted. "Projecting" is an implicit practical attitude or orientation: "Projecting has nothing to do with comporting oneself towards a plan that has been thought out. The character of understanding as projection is such that the understanding does not grasp thematically that upon which it projects—that is to say, possibilities" (*BT,* 185; *SZ,* 145).

9. "In general our understanding of being is such that every entity is understood in the first instance as occurrent" (*BT,* 268, translation revised; *SZ,* 225).

10. I argue for this interpretation of Heidegger's project in Chapter 10.

11. ". . . the ontological meaning of cognition, which we have exhibited as a *founded* mode of being-in-the-world. To lay bare what is just occurrent and no more, cognition must first penetrate *beyond* what is available in our concern" (*BT,* 101, translation revised; *SZ,* 71).

12. E.g., (*BT,* 189; *SZ,* 149, and *BT,* 405; *SZ,* 354).

13. For details on how to read Heidegger this way, see Chapter 10.

14. "The question simply remains as to *how* entities are discovered in this previous encountering, whether as mere things which occur, or rather as equipment which has not yet been understood—as something available with which we have hitherto not known 'how to begin.' And here again, when the equipmental characters of the available are still circumspectly undiscovered, they are not to be Interpreted as bare Thinghood presented for an apprehension of what is just occurrent and no more" (*BT,* 112, translation revised; *SZ,* 81).

15. "If knowing is to be possible as a way of determining the nature of the occurrent by observing it, then there must be first a *deficiency* in our having-to-do-with the world concernfully. When concern holds back from any kind of producing, manipulating, and the like, it puts itself into what is now the sole remaining mode of Being-in, the mode of just tarrying alongside. This kind of being towards the world is one which lets us encounter entities within-the-world purely in the *way they look*" (*BT,* 88; *SZ,* 61). "Thematizing Objectifies. It does not first 'posit' the entities, but frees

them so that one can interrogate them and determine their character 'Objectively.' Being which Objectifies and which is alongside the occurrent within-the-world, is characterized by a *distinctive kind of making-present*. This making-present is distinguished from the Present of circumspection in that—above all—the kind of discovering which belongs to the science in question awaits solely the discoveredness of the occurrent. We shall not trace further how science has its source in authentic existence. It is enough for now if we understand that the thematizing of entities within-the-world presupposes Being-in-the-world as the basic state of Dasein" (*BT*, 414, translation revised; *SZ*, 363).

16. Thus one can thematize (make assertions about) what is not present-at-hand: "Even that which is ready-to-hand can be made a theme for scientific investigation. The ready-to-hand can become the 'Object' of a science without having to lose its character as equipment" (*BT*, 413; *SZ*, 361). Much of *Being and Time* does just that (cf. the title of section 28: "The task of a thematic analysis of Being-in").

17. "The assertion is something available" (*BT*, 267, translation revised; *SZ*, 224).

18. The whole passage reads: "This leveling of the primordial 'as' of circumspective interpretation to the 'as' with which presence-at-hand is given a definite character is the specialty of assertion. Only so does it obtain the possibility of exhibiting something in such a way that we just look at it." (See also *BT*, 89; *SZ*, 62, concerning the relation between perception and assertion, which is discussed later in connection with curiosity.)

19. Ludwig Wittgenstein, *Philosophical Investigations* (New York: Macmillan, 1953), p. 201.

20. I discuss this line of thought in more detail in the first chapter of *Making It Explicit* (Cambridge, Mass.: Harvard University Press, 1994).

21. In fact, I endorse priority of implicit practical norms over the capacity to make anything explicit in *Making It Explicit*. But I have come to believe that, tempting as it is to attribute this view to Heidegger, as I argue later, he is in fact committed to rejecting it.

22. See Hubert L. Dreyfus, *Being in the World: A Commentary on Heidegger's "Being and Time"* (Cambridge, Mass.: MIT Press, 1991); John Haugeland, "Heidegger on Being a Person," *Noûs* 16 (1982): 15–26, reprinted in *Heidegger: A Critical Reader*, ed. Hubert L. Dreyfus and Harrison Hall (Oxford: Blackwell, 1992), hereafter cited in text; and Mark Okrent, *Heidegger's Pragmatism* (Ithaca, N.Y.: Cornell University Press, 1988).

23. I take issue with the reduction of the normative to regularities of behavior and disposition (even to censure) in chap. 1 of *Making It Explicit*, and I would take issue with it also as a reading of Heidegger.

24. Haugeland does say, "In my pains to avoid any hidden presupposition of mentality or reason, I have spoken exclusively of dispositions, behavior, and know-how—making everything sound 'mindless' and inarticulate. But of course it isn't. Among Dasein's many institutions are those of language" (Haugeland, "Heidegger," p. 23). The question is thus one of the status of this institution. We have also been told that among Dasein's institutions are chemistry, philately, Christmas, and Cincinnati (p. 19). For all Haugeland says here, language could be as optional and late-coming in Dasein's development as these are. It is this possibility that the present reading attempts to close off.

25. E.g., see *BT*, 208; *SZ*, 165, *BT*, 171; *SZ*, 133, and *BT*, 182; *SZ*, 143.

26. "In this kind of 'dwelling' as holding-oneself-back from any manipulation or utilization, the perception of the occurrent is consummated. Perception is consummated when one *addresses* oneself to something as something and discusses it as such. What is thus perceived and made determinate can be expressed in propositions, and can be retained and preserved as what has thus been asserted" (*BT*, 89, translation revised; *SZ*, 62).

27. The best discussion of this doctrine is John Haugeland, "Dasein's Disclosedness," *Southern Journal of Philosophy* 28 (1989): 51–73.

28. At *BT*, 209; *SZ*, 165, we hear about "the basic *a priori* structure of discourse as an *existentiale*."

29. About the special sort of equipment that consists of actual signs, Heidegger uses *Zeichen*. We are told explicitly that not all *Rede* has propositional form: "We must inquire into the basic forms in which it is possible to articulate anything understandable, and to do so in accordance with significations; and this articulation must not be confined to entities within-the-world which we cognize by considering them theoretically and which we express in sentences" (*BT*, 209; *SZ*, 165). This specific wording of the definition of *Rede* cited earlier is significant, however. "According to significations" is *bedeutungsmässige*, and the word that Kant uses to talk about norms explicit in the form of rules is *regelmässige*. Heidegger may be picking up on this usage and thereby emphasizing the second thesis of his normative pragmatism, that norms implicit in practice must be presupposed in explaining those explicit in rules.

30. "Discourse which expresses itself is communication [*Mitteilung*]" (*BT*, 211; *SZ*, 168). We see again that it is not optional that *Rede* be expressed (in the global, not the local sense), for communication is not an optional structure of Dasein. Thus: "For the most part [*zumeist*], discourse [*Rede*] is expressed by being spoken out, and has always been so expressed; it is language [*Sprache*]" (*BT*, 211; *SZ*, 167). These passages cannot yet be taken to be decisive, however, because they are balanced by others such as:

"'Communication' in which one makes assertions—giving information, for instance—is a special case of that communication which is grasped in principle existentially" (*BT,* 205; *SZ,* 162). Heidegger is not contradicting himself here, because there is more to language than assertion: not all *Sprache* is *Aussage.* It will be argued, however, that there is no *Sprache* without *Aussage* (in the global sense that the capacity to talk at all requires the capacity to make assertions).

31. Talk of interpreting (a form of understanding) is talk of *Rede,* for *Rede* underlies all these forms of intelligibility: "Discourse is the articulation of intelligibility. Therefore it underlies both interpretation and assertion" (*BT,* 203–204; *SZ,* 161).

32. Notice that communicating by asserting is the sharing of seeing, that is, of treating things as occurrent.

33. The case that this general model is found in *Being and Time* is argued in detail in Chapter 10. Only the barest sketch of this argument can be presented here. I undertake, rather than attribute to Heidegger, commitment to a recognizable, similar model in the first four chapters of *Making It Explicit.*

34. As in the passage quoted from *BT,* 213; *SZ,* 169.

35. Heidegger introduces the idea in the first two sentences of the body of Part One of *Being and Time,* "We Are Ourselves the Entities to Be Analysed: The Being of any such entity is in *each case* mine [*je meines*]" (*BT,* 67; *SZ,* 42). He says just a bit further along, "Because Dasein has in *each case mineness* [*Jemeinigkeit*], one must always use a *personal* pronoun when one addresses it: 'I am,' 'you are'" (*BT,* 68; *SZ,* 42). (I am not sure how well chemistry, Christmas, and philately score on this criterion for being cases of Dasein.)

36. These few remarks cannot pretend to be more than an indication of the region within which we should look for an account of objectivity. I discuss the issue in Chapter 10 and in much greater detail in chap. 8 of *Making It Explicit.*

37. Also: "Idle talk, curiosity, and ambiguity characterize the way in which, in an everyday manner, Dasein is its 'there'—the disclosedness of Being-in-the-world. In these, and in the way they are interconnected in their being, there is revealed a basic kind of Being which belongs to everydayness [*Alltäglichkeit*]; we call this the *'falling'* [*Verfallen*] of Dasein. This term does not express any negative evaluation" (*BT,* 219–220; *SZ,* 175).

38. "The kind of discovering which belongs to the science in question awaits solely the discoveredness of the occurrent. This awaiting of discoveredness has its existentiell basis in a *resoluteness* by which Dasein projects itself towards its potentiality-for-Being in the 'truth.' This projection is possible

because Being-in-the-truth makes up a definite way in which Dasein may exist. We shall not trace further how science has its source in authentic existence" (*BT,* 414, translation revised; *SZ,* 369).

39. This view of Heidegger's treatment of assertion is not common currency. I argué for it in Chapter 10.

40. E.g., *BT,* 189–190; *SZ,* 149, *BT,* 195; *SZ,* 154, *BT,* 201; *SZ,* 158, *BT,* 203; *SZ,* 160–161, and *BT,* 266; *SZ,* 223.

41. E.g., *BT,* 205; *SZ,* 162, *BT,* 204; *SZ,* 161, and *BT,* 209; *SZ,* 165–166.

12. The Centrality of Sellars's Two-Ply Account of Observation to the Arguments of "Empiricism and the Philosophy of Mind"

1. I would call it "minimal empiricism," except that John McDowell, in the introduction to the paperback edition of *Mind and World* (Cambridge, Mass.: Harvard University Press, 1996), has adopted that term for a *much* more committal thesis.

2. *Phenomenology,* para. 109, in the numeration of A. V. Miller's translation (Oxford: Oxford University Press, 1979).

3. They would not be so characterizable in cases where the response is specified in, say, normative or semantic vocabulary—for instance, as *correctly* using the word 'red', or as applying the *concept* red.

4. Sellars's discussion begins at "EPM" 16. All references are to section numbers of Sellars's *Empiricism and the Philosophy of Mind,* reprinted with an introduction by Richard Rorty and a Study Guide by Robert Brandom (Cambridge, Mass.: Harvard University Press, 1997).

5. See, for instance, "EPM" 36.

6. The idiom of "language-language" moves and "language-entry" moves is drawn from Wilfrid Sellars, "Some Reflections on Language Games," in *Science, Perception, and Reality* (London: Routledge, Kegan Paul, 1963): 321–358.

7. I might be mistaken about whether **red** is what it looks, that is, whether the property expressed by the word 'red' is the one it looks to have. But that, the thought goes, is another matter. I cannot be mistaken that it looks that way, like *that,* where this latter phrase is understood as having a noncomparative use. It **looks-red,** a distinctive phenomenal property, which we may inconveniently only happen to be able to pick out by its association with a word for a real-world property.

8. It is tempting to think that on this line concepts are related to the contents of preconceptual experiences as universals to particulars. But as Sellars points out, the empiricists in fact took as primitive the capacity to be aware already of *repeatables,* such as redness and squareness. This might suggest

that the relation is better understood as one of genus to species. But **scarlet** is not strictly a *species* of the genus **red**, since there need be no way to specify the relevant differentiae without mentioning the species. (Compare the relation between the phenomenal property of redness and that of being colored.) So the relation between immediately experienceable contents and the concepts under which they are classified is better understood as that of *determinate* repeatable to *determinables* under which it falls.

9. Notice that this realism about theoretical entities does not entail scientific realism in the sense that privileges science over other sorts of cognitive activity, although Sellars usually discusses the two sorts of claims together.

10. See, for instance, John McDowell's discussion in "Brandom on Inference and Representation," *Philosophy and Phenomenological Research*, 57, no. 1 (March 1997): 157–161, and my reply at 189–193; and a paper by John MacFarlane titled "McDowell's Kantianism," forthcoming in a volume devoted to McDowell's work.

CREDITS

Chapter 4, "Adequacy and the Individuation of Ideas in Spinoza's Ethics," from *Journal of the History of Philosophy* 14, no. 2 (April 1976): 147–162.

Chapter 5, "Leibniz and Degrees of Perception," from *Journal of the History of Philosophy* 19, no. 4 (October 1981): 447–479.

Chapter 7, "Some Pragmatist Themes in Hegel's Idealism," from *European Journal of Philosophy,* August 1999, 164–189.

Chapter 8, "Frege's Technical Concepts," from *Frege Synthesized: Essays on the Philosophical and Foundational Work of G. Frege,* ed. Lila Haaparanta and Jaakko Hintikka, Synthese Library (Dordrecht: D. Reidel, 1986), pp. 253–295.

Chapter 9, "The Significance of Complex Numbers for Frege's Philosophy of Mathematics," *Proceedings of the Aristotelian Society* 94 (Winter 1996): 293–315; reprinted by courtesy of the Editor of the Aristotelian Society: © 1996.

Chapter 10, "Heidegger's Categories in *Sein und Zeit,*" from *Monist* 66, no. 3 (July 1983): 387–409.

Chapter 11, "Dasein, the Being That Thematizes," from *Epoché* 5, nos. 1 and 2 (1997; published fall 1999): 1–40.

Chapter 12, "The Centrality of Sellars's Two-Ply Account of Observation to the Arguments of 'Empiricism and the Philosophy of Mind,'" appeared in a shorter version in German in *Deutsche Zeitschrift für Philosophie* Berlin 48 (2000): 599–613.

INDEX

I would like to thank Kevin Scharp for invaluable assistance in preparing this index.

411

concept(s) *(continued)*
364–367, 374n9, 378n4, 383n33,
385nn48,2,5, 385n7, 386nn8,11,12,
387nn16,19, 388nn22,23, 389nn24,26,
390nn27,30, 391n34, 392n35, 393nn38–
40, 394n41, 396n34, 397nn50,52,
406nn3,8; acquisition of, 30–31, 85, 86,
359–361, 365 (*see also* innateness); application of, 13–15, 30–31, 39, 46, 47, 48,
49, 52–54, 56–57, 84–85, 87, 88, 89, 92,
109, 213–215, 219–222, 224–226, 229–
231, 234, 350, 352–353, 359–361, 363–
364, 366–367, 385nn2,6, 386nn7,11,
387nn16,19, 389n24, 390nn26,27,
391nn30,31, 392n35, 393nn38,39,
393n40; determinateness of, 55–57, 213–
214, 216, 224–225, 227, 229, 386n7,
387nn13,19, 389n23, 392n35,
393nn39,40, 394n40; empirical, 52, 56,
85, 211–214, 216, 225, 349, 359, 386n11,
391nn33,34, 392n35, 394n40. *See also*
awareness; content; discursive; explicit;
inference; intentionality; rationalism; rationality; reason; semantics; universal
conceptual, 77, 85–86, 89, 105–106, 115–
116, 181, 185, 330, 352. *See also* inference; rationalism
conclusion(s), 3–4, 9, 48, 60, 63, 75, 79, 94,
192, 223–224, 343, 345, 351–353, 364
conditional, 9–10, 50, 59–61, 79, 192, 313,
315, 345–346, 372n29. *See also* inference;
logic
conjugate isomorphism theorem, 283
consciousness, 14–15, 40–42, 96, 140, 146–
147, 153, 182, 188–191, 202, 207, 303,
382n26, 394n41. *See also* apperception;
awareness; explicit; Hegel: "Consciousness"; Hegel: *Phenomenology;* 'I'; self; self-
consciousness
consequence(s), 6, 49, 60, 100, 102–103,
108, 181, 374n9, 381n1. *See also* inference
constitution, 16, 54–55, 81, 90, 217, 231,
309, 310, 311, 317, 318, 329, 331–338,
340–342, 372n28, 400n9, 401n6, 402n7
constraint, 29, 31, 50, 54–55, 92, 94, 104,
105, 215–216, 225, 230–234, 341, 385n6,
387n16. *See also* authority; autonomy;
bindingness; norm; responsibility
content(s), 3, 5–7, 9–11, 15–16, 28–29, 31–

32, 37, 43–46, 49–51, 54–61, 64, 66, 71,
74–75, 77, 79, 84–85, 87, 91–92, 94–95,
98, 100–104, 106–112, 158–159, 164–
166, 169–171, 174–176, 178, 181, 184,
191, 201–203, 205–208, 210, 215–216,
219–223, 221–222, 225, 230–234, 238,
245, 253, 255, 259, 261, 278, 337–338,
340–342, 345–346, 351–352, 357, 359,
364, 371n13, 373nn4,8, 380n1, 381n6,
384n42, 385n6, 387n20, 389n23, 390n27,
391n34, 392n35, 393n40, 394n40, 406n8,
407n8; conceptual, 4, 6, 28, 46, 52, 53, 55,
57–61, 74, 79, 84–85, 92, 94–97, 99, 101–
102, 104–110, 111, 114–115, 117–118,
183, 186–187, 215, 221, 225, 351, 370n8,
371n16, 373n6, 384n45, 386n12, 387n13;
conferral of, 37, 44, 52–53, 58, 231,
373n32; *de dicto* specification of, 94, 96–
99, 101, 105–106, 109, 116, 117, 373n8;
de re specification of, 99–102, 105–107,
109, 117, 373n8; determinateness of, 47,
48, 52–53, 99, 178, 182–184, 191–192,
201–202, 205, 207, 220–223, 225, 339,
381n8; perspectival character of, 104, 106,
117; propositional, 6, 61, 197, 339, 342,
357; representational, 35, 81–82, 164–165.
See also concept; explicit; inference;
intentionality; semantics
contentfulness, 12, 50, 183, 111, 186, 204,
223, 353
context(s), 16, 28, 33, 54, 78–79, 83, 89, 95–
111, 114, 116–117, 122–123, 134, 246–
249, 267–268, 373nn4,8; principle, 239–
240, 248, 257–261, 267. *See also* background; content; hermeneutics; interpretation; text
Copernicus, 24
corpora simplicissima, 124–125. *See also* extension; Spinoza
correctness, 4, 6, 10, 13–14, 16, 21–23, 27,
46–47, 53, 58–59, 61–62, 70, 76–77, 82,
92, 104, 106, 193–194, 212, 214–215,
219–222, 230, 253, 255, 318, 325–327,
329, 333, 341–342, 347, 356, 364,
384n47, 386n8, 390nn27,30, 393n39,
406n3. *See also* commitment; entitlement;
norm; proprieties
counterfactual reasoning, 35, 198, 199, 207.
See also conditional; modality; necessity